WILDFLOWERS

of the

SANTA

MONICA

MOUNTAINS

COVER PICTURES

FRONT COVER

A field of California Poppy and Parry's Phacelia in Encinal Canyon about one mile north of Charmlee Park. Picture was taken on 26 March 1979 by James P. Kenney.

BACK COVER

Milt McAuley hiking through riparian woodland in Santa Ynez Canyon.
Picture taken on 4 August 1980 by Maxine McAuley.

ILLUSTRATIONS

Illustrations are line drawings or photocopies of actual plants. All by Milt McAuley, except for 5 line drawings. These 5 are from a public domain USDA Forest Service publication *"Forest Trees of the Pacific Slope"* issued October 1, 1908 — which of incidental interest to me is that it was one of my texts when attending The School of Forestry, Oregon State College.

WILDFLOWERS

OF THE

SANTA MONICA

MOUNTAINS

by
Milt McAuley

photography by
James P. Kenney

ISBN 0-942568-27-3

Library of Congress Card Number 84-73487

Canyon Publishing Company
8561 Eatough Avenue
Canoga Park, CA 91304

Acknowledgements

My thanks go to Dr. Paul Meyers for his guidance, encourage-ment, and willingness to share his sound botanical knowledge. His precisely taught courses of botany and dynamic field trips are inspirations.

Jim Kenney whose outstanding photographs speak for them-selves, has enthusiastically and wholeheartedly contributed his energy and talent to this book. I am much indebted.

My thanks to Tim Thomas for writing the section on "Plant Geography," his photographs of unusual plants, and his on the spot advice and plant identification.

Bill McAuley, our son, spent endless hours compiling the index so that we can all find our way through the book by cross-referenc-ing technical names, common names, and pictures. We could not have accomplished this task without his dedicated computer expertise.

Pat Maylard-Romolo, our daughter, devoted many many hours of editing and proof reading during the final preparation of the book. We can't begin to expess our gratitude for this diligent, loving task.

Finally my deepest gratitude to my wife Maxine for a sustained faith in the project, and her endless hours of typesetting and devotion to all of the tasks required to publish the book.

Photography Credits

All photographs were taken by **James P. Kenney,** with the following exceptions.

MILT McAULEY   Plates, 3, 8, 55, 61, 64, 67, 71, 86, 89, 103, 119,
125, 168, 193, 208, 223, 229, 248, 261, 268, 283, 289, 296,
297, 302, 318, 326, 327, 336, 371, 374, 384, 385, 390, 395,
410, 412, 413, 425, 452, 453, 464, 467, 470, 471, 472, 473,
474, 477, 479, 480

LINDA HARDIE-SCOTT: Plates 62, 97, 281, 313, 331, 356

TIM THOMAS: Plates 82, 200, 226, 387, 488

GARY RICHARDSON: Plates 185, 231. 325

WARD DENNIS: Plates 185, 231, 325

JOHN KENNEY: Plate 2

ROB CREER: Plate 149

JOHN ADAMS: Plate 277

Table of Contents

An asterisk * placed before the common name of a plant, beginning on page 161 and continuing through page 543, indicates an introduced plant.

Preface to the
Second Edition

When the first edition of this book came out in 1985 I thought "never again." But here we are ten years later compiling information that can never be complete and I am sure will be improved on by others in the future. Along the way hundreds of people have taken time to write, call and show me their favorite fields of flowers. I thank each of you for your help and inspiration. Writing this book has been emotionally rewarding by itself but your acceptance has been the greatest reward of all.

Now for some thoughts about the book:

Wildflowers of the Santa Monica Mountains is written for non-professionals. For most of the people I know, to discover a plant and put a name to it is worthwhile. This book should help the process. Readers want clear, neat, and simple language when dealing with an unknown subject. Botany doesn't always lend itself to this idea and most of us can't understand many of the terms often used to describe a plant. A working botanist doesn't have time to go into a detailed verbalization of plant parts when describing some feature. The botanist uses a language that is precise. As an example, the word "utricle" conjures a picture in the botanist's mind. Most of us must look it up to find that usually a "utricle" is a dry indehiscent fruit from a compound pistil in which a single seed is loosely enclosed by the ovary wall. (At this point one might need to know what is meant by "indehiscent.") My point is that this book will sacrifice exact preciseness so that we don't get lost in a language we don't understand. The trained botanists among us will need to cope with less sophistication, so the rest of us may better understand.

Many readers also want to use common names, not technical. This book uses both and they are cross-referenced in the index. We will talk more about this in the introduction but for now thanks for your interest in the wildflowers of these mountains.

Introduction

The Santa Monica Mountain area is a great wildflower garden in southern California. Bordered on the north by the San Fernando and Conejo Valleys and the Oxnard Plain and on the west and south by the Pacific Ocean and Los Angeles, this east-west range is 46 miles in length and about 10 miles wide. This is the area with which the book is concerned. We floristically describe the canyons, slopes, ridges, and marshes. We can see many of the flowers from the road; for others, we need to get out and walk mountain trails, and some we will find only by climbing over rocks or scrambling through chaparral.

The term "wildflower," for purposes of this book, is not strictly applied — I have included sections on trees, shrubs, ferns, and others. All flowering plants except grasses that are known to live in the Santa Monica Mountains are described. This list is comprehensive now, but occasionally a plant is discovered that was not previously known here, so the list can grow.

ABOUT THE PHOTOGRAPHY

The photographic work in this book is an attempt to combine botanical accuracy with aesthetic excellence. All of the photographs were taken in the Santa Monica Mountains, with each plant pictured in its natural habitat. Jim Kenney's color organization of the photographs can be useful to both beginning flower enthusiasts and by cross-referencing, to more advanced botanists as well. Most of the 100-plus plant families in this mountain range are represented. Pictures of some plants of limited importance or of similar appearance to close relatives have been omitted, but all species are described in the text.

Emphasis is placed on native plants but not to the exclusion of introduced plants that have become important. Those plants that are dominant in their plant community are emphasized. As an example, all 9 species in the *Rhamnaceae* family are pictured — we see acres of their spring blooms in the chaparral. The choice of photographs may indicate a preference for the spectacular, but identifying characteristics are not neglected. Jim Kenney took most of these pictures.

Additional photographic credits are listed on page 6.

HOW TO USE THIS BOOK

Find a photograph that resembles the flower, leaf, or berry you want to identify. The flower photographs are categorized by color, and by leafing through the section should disclose a representative look-alike. Each picture has a caption with the common name and a page number. Turn to that page for a description of the plant. Plant descriptions of the same family are near each other.

The code sequence is white, yellow, orange and red, rose to pink, purple to blue, brown and maroon, greenish, leaves, fruit, trees, ferns, grasses, fungi.

The plant descriptions are listed alphabetically by family, genus and species.

The plant index lists both common and botanical names. It will direct you to one or more photographs when available and to a detailed description.

INTRODUCED PLANTS

The honor of being first to introduce non-native plants to California is usually given to the Spanish under Father Junipero Serra who founded the first European settlement in May 1769 at San Diego. Possible introduction could have occurred as early as 1542 with the arrival of Juan Rodriquez Cabrillo along the California coast. It has been calculated that 10% of the ultimate number of introduced plants were brought in by the Spaniards during a 56 year period of occupation, and another 15% during the Mexican and American pioneer development. Most of the alien species arrived after homesteading began. Introduced plants are more often found in disturbed areas, such as along the roads and where human encroachment is obvious. A plant new in the environment is considered introduced when it continues to reproduce and prosper without human interference. * indicates an introduced plant.

SCIENTIFIC AND COMMON NAMES

Scientific names of plants have two parts: the first part usually of Greek origin is a noun defining the genus; the second part, usually of Latin origin, is an adjective defining the species. Because technical names are often long and hard to pronounce, we also use common names. Common names often have ancient origins, sometimes describing a plant feature or use, sometimes honoring a person, or an odor as with the "Maple-sugar plant." One problem with the use of common names, however,is that no rules govern their use. For example, Pitcher sage found in Upper Zuma Canyon is not the same Pitcher sage found in Triunfo Pass. They look nowhere near alike. Also, about 8 different plants are called popcorn flower, but this isn't all bad because they look somewhat alike. Many people refer to all 9 *Gnaphaliums* as "Pearly Everlasting" when, in fact, as most books tell us, Pearly Everlasting does not even grow in the Santa Monica Mountains. In this book, plants are indexed and cross-referenced by both common and scientific names.

The scientific names used in this book are in accord with *The Jepson Manual, Higher Plants of California, 1993*. We believe this nomenclature to be an up-to-date status. Historically, several authorities have been leaders in bringing information on California plants together under single publications. Parts of Willis Linn Jepson's *A Flora of California* appeared in print in 1909. The work progressed periodically throughout his life. After his death in 1946 his students continued his work — Volume 4, Part 2 was published in 1979. In 1925 Jepson completed his *Manual of the Flowering Plants of California*. This publication was the principal authority of all the plants growing wild in California until 1959 when Leroy Abrams' *Illustrated Flora of the Pacific States* was published. Philip A. Munz's *A California Flora* was also published in 1959, later to be supplemented by Munz. The plant nomenclature of the Munz book has been in general use since its publications and presently is being updated by the Jepson Manual.

The common names used in this book have been selected by noting the principal California botanical manuals and considering local usage. I found it difficult because local usage is influenced by the wide geographic background of the people who now live in the Santa Monica Mountain area. This diversity is reflected in the use of different common names for the same plant and also in different plants being called by the same name. Most of us like to use descriptive common names and it just might be that part of the charm is in the informality of their use. If the common name in use makes no sense to you — just use the technical name.

THE EFFECT OF FIRE ON THE VEGETATION OF THE SANTA MONICA MOUNTAINS

Roaring flames, smoke billowing over the city, sirens wailing, and the aftermath of thousands of acres of blackened hillsides looks like complete devastation. No so — it is merely one incident in the healthy life cycle of the chaparral.

11

Fire has been a routine event in the Santa Monica Mountains for thousands of years. Estimates have been made that fire has covered the area 500 times in the 11,500 years since the last ice age. Plants subjected to this severe process are either adapted to fire, or they no longer exist in the area. Research shows that certain plants have adapted to fire and learned to live with it so well that it has become an essential to life.

How do fires begin? Human causes such as accidents, carelessness and arson are major factors today; obvious natural causes such as lightning were a greater factor in pre-historic times. Lightning from thunderstorms started fires that must have raged for weeks, eventually reaching lower coastal ranges before arriving at the ultimate firebreak, the Pacific Ocean. Regardless of the cause, when the temperature is high, the humidity low, and the winds are strong, the stage is set for a major fire. These conditions typically occur in the fall, when the shrubs are dehydrated, the dead grasses are tall, and the underlying debris is tinder-dry.

Almost all plant communities respond to fire. The chaparral community is the dominant vegetation element in the Santa Monica Mountains and may be more responsive to fire than the others. Within a few days after fires, most chaparral shrubs will sprout from the root-crown. The root system furnishes stored food and water for immediate growth at a time when the soil is dry and competition from other plants is absent. The root system has an established position so the plant is already in a favorable place for its growth, and the new growth rapidly outstrips seedling growth. A vigorous cover will suppress other growth by taking moisture, nutrients, and shade. Many sprouting chaparral plants can quickly produce toxic substances to prevent competing growth.

The winter and spring following a chaparral fire is a time of rebirth and regeneration. Seeds of annuals and perennials have lain dormant for decades, and bulbs have marked time waiting for the moment. The winter rains produce dramatic new growth and immediate erosion control. Masses of plants that have been missing for years burst upon the scene and complement the sprouting of the larger shrubs. Every hillside, each canyon and all the ridges are freed of the overburden of senile mature chaparral and suddenly the new growth has space, light, food and water. The first season after fire is truly one of nature's wonders. Phacelias, Penstemons, Mariposa lilies, and dozens more species flood the area. Some annuals such as the Fire Poppy, will bloom only after a fire. It is the heat generated that renders some seeds permeable to moisture.

In the absence of shrubs and their toxic inhibitors, waves of bloom begin in February and often last until July with stands of Scarlet Larkspur on the higher slopes contrasting with the stately Humboldt Lilies in the canyons.

Along with the flowers about twenty species of pioneer shrubs, such as buckwheat and sage, germinate and flourish for years after a fire but become less important to the Chaparral community as it matures. Eventually the growth of plants in Chaparral stagnates, a few species become dominant and only a fire will start the cycle again.

Prominent fire-following annual plants include the following: Large-flowered Phacelia, Parry's Phacelia, Caterpillar Phacelia, California Poppy, Fire Poppy, White Pincushion, Yellow Pincushion, Foothill Lupine, Coulter's Lupine, Stinging Lupine.

The fire of late 1993 burned upper Hondo Canyon. Chaparral slopes having no recent appearance of Bush poppy were covered with thousands of seedling plants during the spring of 1994. These Bush poppies grew to heights of 4 or 5 feet but no blooms until the spring of 1995. What a transformation! The Bush poppies have stabilized the slopes and may dominate for several years until other chaparral plants take over. The poppies will drop millions of seeds which will lie dormant until the next fire — maybe 40 years from now.

The following genera of shrubs and trees, most of which are found in chaparral, are root-crown sprouting: *Adenostoma, Cercocarpus, Comarostaphylis, Garrya, Heteromeles, Lonicera, Malosma, Marah, Pickeringia, Prunus, Quercus,* and *Rhamnus.* One species of *Arctostaphylos* crown sprouts, the other does not; three Ceanothus crown Sprout, three do not.

PLANT COMMUNITIES

Plant communities in the Santa Monica Mountains are identified by and consist of a number of different plant combinations, each combination being identifiable as a distinct community. My intent is to describe each major community, primarily through listing the indicator plants found in a regional element of vegetation, for the presence of certain plants determines the plant community. We recognize in advance that many plants are found in several different communities and that the dividing lines are not always distinct. Pockets of a community may be located within another community. Each of the communities could be subdivided into more precise

13

elements, but for the purposes of this flower guide the habitats are deemed adequate and are used as a part of the plant descriptions.

The communities are (1) Coastal Strand, (2) Coastal Salt Marsh, (3) Freshwater Marsh, (4) Coastal Sage Scrub, (5) Southern Oak Woodland, (6) Chaparral, (7) Riparian Woodland, (8) Grassland, (9) Cactus Scrub, (10) Cliffside, (11) Vernal Moist Habitat.

1.   Coastal Strand

Coastal Strand includes a narrow interrupted belt along the ocean from Santa Monica to Point Mugu. It includes the beaches, sand dunes, and stabilized soil to the foot of the cliffs and mountains, much of which has been altered or totally destroyed by development. The Pacific Coast Highway travels through this area.

Characteristic Plants:

Abronia sp	Sand Verbena
Ambrosia chamissonis	Silver-beachweed
Anemopsis californica	Yerba Mansa
Atriplex leucophilla	Saltbush
Cakile maritima	Sea Rocket
Calystegia soldanella	Beach Morning Glory
Camissonia cheiranthifolia	Beach Primrose
Capobrotus	Ice Plant
Dudleya caespitosa	Dudleya
Mesembryanthemum sp	Ice Plant

2.   Coastal Salt Marsh

A saltwater marsh is a wet area in the tidal zone of the ocean, usually a protected lagoon. All plants that live in this habitat have adaptations which allow them to exist in standing salt water at least part of the time. Hollow passages from leaves to roots allow air movement, salt concentration in the roots reverses the osmotic flow so the plants can absorb water, and glands on leaves and stems excrete salt. Mugu Lagoon and Malibu Lagoon are significant examples of saltwater marshes.

Characteristic plants:

Atriplex semibaccata	Salt Bush
Batis maritima	Saltwort
Cuscuta salina	Dodder
Distichlis spicata	Salt grass
Frankenia salina	Alkali Heath
Jaumea carnosa	Jaumeae
Limonium californicum	Marsh Rosemary
Salicornia sp	Pickleweed
Suaeda calceoliformis	Sea-blite

Where fresh water drains into saltwater marshes, fluctuations of the two waters present a habitat in which a plant must be able to survive in either fresh or salt water concentrations. Some brackish marsh plants will be found upstream beyond the upland boundary of the marsh.

Characteristic plants of Brackish Marsh:

Alisma plantago-aquatica	Water-plantain
Aster subulatus	Aster
Cotula coronopifolia	Brass Buttons
Juncus sp	Juncus
Phragmites communis	Reed
Ruppia spiralis	Ditch-grass
Scirpus sp	Alkali Bulrush

3. Freshwater Marsh

A freshwater marsh is part of the mountains' drainage system and contains either standing or slowly moving water. Plant adaptations for water living include air tubes from leaves to roots, air pockets for bouyancy, and a concentration of photosynthesizing bodies near the upper leaf surface of floating plants. Century Lake, La Jolla Pond, and Nicholas Flat Pond have examples of freshwater marshes. This plant community also includes seepages. Seasonally moist pools will support some plants of Freshwater Marshes.

Characteristic plants in Freshwater Marsh:

Callitriche marginata	Water Starwort
Carex sp	Sedge
Juncus sp	Rush
Nuphar luteum	Pond-lily
Oenanthe sarmentosa	Water Parsley
Polygonum arenastrum	Common Knotweed
P. amphibium	Water Smartweed
P. punctatum	Water Smartweed
Potamogeton sp	Pondweed
Rorippa nasturtium-aquaticum	Water-cress
Scirpus sp	Bulrush
Typha sp	Cat-tail

4. Coastal Sage Scrub

Coastal Sage Scrub vegetation is found on the lower slopes and plateaus of the mountains, both ocean facing and inland. Compared with Chaparral it occupies drier sites and shrubs do not grow as closely together. The root zone is relatively shallow because the plant has adapted its growth period to the cool winter moisture and remains inactive during dry periods. Sage leaves contain terpenes, which account for the aroma on warm days. When leaves fall, the terpenes inhibit competing growth of other plants. Because many sage species seeds are wind-dispersed, they often reseed a burned Chaparral area, only to eventually give way to the Chaparral. Most woody sage species root-crown-sprout.

Characteristic plants in Coastal Sage Scrub:

Artemisia californica	Calif. Sagebrush
Encelia californica	Bush Sunflower
Eriogonum fasciculatum	Calif. Buckwheat
E. cinereum	Ashy-leaf Buckwheat
Hazardia squarrosus	Sawtooth Goldenbush
H. venetus	Coast Goldenbush
Opuntia sp	Prickly Pear Cactus
Malosma laurina	Laurel Sumac
Salvia apiana	White Sage

S. leucophylla	Purple Sage
S. mellifera	Black Sage
Trichostema lanatum	Woolly Blue-curls

5. Southern Oak Woodland

Southern Oak Woodland is dominated by Coast Live Oaks, groves of which are located on slopes and ridges throughout the mountains. An understory of smaller trees, shrubs and herbal vegetation is an important part of the woodland. Many Southern Oak Woodlands can be found in the Santa Monica Mountains. The picnic area at Trippet Ranch and the slope to the ridge offer an accessible and popular woodland. The Old Cabin Site in Upper Sycamore Canyon and many places dotted along the north slope of Boney Mountain are good examples of this community, as are the Woodlands at Tapia Park and the picnic area near the end of the south meadow in Malibu Creek State Park. The slopes near most streams support Southern Oak Woodlands, and in fact, many intermittent stream sites are Southern Oak Woodlands rather than Riparian Woodlands.

Characteristic plants of Southern Oak Woodland:

Dryopteris arguta	Coastal Woodfern
Heteromeles arbutifolia	Toyon
Juglans californica	Walnut
Quercus agrifolia	Coast live oak
Rhamnus californica	Coffeeberry
Rhus ovata	Sugar Bush
Solanum sp	Nightshade
Toxicodendron diversilobum	Poison Oak
Umbellularia californica	California Bay

6. Chaparral

California chaparral is a plant community composed mainly of evergreen shrubs that are adapted to fire and drought. The name "chaparral" comes from the Spanish "chaparro," which describes a thicket of scrub oaks. Chaparral grows in areas with poor, rocky soil, hot dry summers, and a limited rainfall (12-14 inches) most of which falls during the winter. The summer dry climate, termed Mediterranean climate, occurs only in 5 areas of the world: (1) The

Mediterranean, (2) The California Coast and Baja, (3) The central section of Chile, (4) South Africa, and (5) Southwest Australia. All of these areas have similar climatic conditions and contain similar plants that have small leathery leaves, are mostly evergreen, and have adapted to winter growth and dry summer survival. Chaparral forms an important community in the Santa Monica Mountains because it grows under most severe conditions and is unsurpassed in its ability to stabilize slopes and minimize erosion.

Most of the stands of Chaparral are at a higher elevation than Coastal Sage Scrub and often adjacent to it. The borders are distinct but irregular. Occasional patches of sage will be found in Chaparral and vice versa.

Most of the Chaparral shrubs have the ability to crown-sprout after the top is killed by fire or by physical removal. This capability gives them an advantage over other plants so that the Chaparral will prevail. Sprouting begins immediately by drawing on stored energy in the root and can occur before a rainfall allows seeds to sprout. Some chaparral plants protect themselves from other plants by putting chemical toxins into the soil so that seed germination and new growth is inhibited. Chamise does this by producing water-soluble (phenolic) compounds in the leaves during summer drought. Fog and rain drip carry the inhibitors to the soil under the plant so that other plants cannot grow. Manzanita has inhibitors in all parts of the plant, roots, bark, fruit, fallen litter, etc. so that a persistent layer of inhibitors surrounds the plant. Competition for light and moisture is intense, and only those plants that have survived the adaptive process remain as part of the Chaparral.

Characteristic plants of Chaparral:

Adenostoma fasciculatum	Chamise
A. sparsifolium	Red Shanks
Arctostophylos, 2 species	Manzanita
Ceanothus, 6 species	Ceanothus
Cercocarpus betuloides	Mountain Mahogany
Dendromecon rigida	Bush Poppy
Heteromeles arbutifolia	Toyon
Malosma laurina	Laurel Sumac
Prunus ilicifolia	Holly-leaved Cherry
Quercus dumosa	Scrub Oak
Rhamnus ssp crocea	Redberry
Rhus ovata	Sugarbush

7. Riparian Woodland

In the Santa Monica Mountains, a Riparian Woodland is usually flanked by Southern Oak Woodland but it is distinguished from it by its proximity to water. Riparian Woodland is the habitat along the shore of a stream or, in some situations, a pond. The continuous source of water needed by some of the species may not always be visible on the surface since underground water available at the root zone is also important. On occasion, a Riparian Woodland merges with Freshwater Marsh, as occurs when Malibu Creek enters Century Lake. The combination of plant species defines the habitat. Malibu Canyon, Topanga Canyon, Santa Ynez Canyon, Zuma Canyon, Cold Creek Canyon, Arroyo Sequit, Sycamore Canyon and others support Riparian Woodlands.

Characteristic plants of riparian Woodland:

Acer macrophyllum	Big-leaf Maple
Alnus rhombifolia	White Alder
Epipactus gigantea	Stream Orchid
Equisetum, 2 species	Horsetail
Juglans californica	Black Walnut
Mimulus cardinalis	Scarlet Monkeyflower
Platanus racemosa	Sycamore
Populus, 2 species	Cottonwood
Pteridium aquilinum	Bracken Fern
Quercus agrifolia	Coast Live Oak
Rubus ursinus	California Blackberry
Salix, 3 species	Willow
Toxicodendron diversilobum	Poison Oak
Umbellularia californica	California Bay
Veronica anagallis-aquatica	Veronica

8. Valley Grassland

Valley Grassland is located throughout the mountains in well-drained areas at all elevations. Most of the communities are small, a few acres or so, but one expanse of 600 acres is located in upper La Jolla Valley. Except for areas that were cultivated at one time or another, the location of today's grasslands are the same as they were before the arrival of the Spanish. Introduced species of grass and herbs, many of which are annual, have made permanent alterations to the composition of the grasslands. The native, perennial needlegrasses have been partially replaced by the more competitive introduced annuals. Overgrazing, summer drought (annuals can survive a drought as seeds), cultivation, and change in fire patterns all favor the introduced aliens. Recovery to the pristine state as it was 200 years ago is not likely to happen, so we may as well look at grassland as it exists today. La Jolla Valley has been set aside as a primitive area where substantial stands of Needlegrass (*Stipa pulchra, Stipa lepida*) are found. Grassland is not all grass and many native and introduced plants make up the community.

Characteristic plants of Valley Grassland:

Calochortus catalinae	Mariposa Lily
Hemizonia fasciculata	Tarweed
Sisyrinchium bellum	Blue-eyed Grass
Stipa lepida	Foothill Needlegrass
Stipa pulchra	Purple Needlegrass
Introduced species:	
Avena barbata	Slender Wild Oat
Avena fatua	Wild Oat
Brassica nigra	Black Mustard
Bromus rubens	Foxtail Brome-grass
Erodium sp.	Filaree
Hordeum leporinum	Wall Barley
Lolium multiflorum	Italian Rye-grass
Phalaris tuberosa	Harding Grass

Infrequent or small plant communities generally are not designated as distinct communities, but their existence deserves brief consideration.

9. Cactus Scrub.

Cactus Scrub is usually found on a south or west facing slope in Coastal Sage Scrub or Chaparral. Some of these communities are up to 200 feet in diameter and are pure stands of *Opuntia littoralis* or *Opuntia oricola*.

A Cactus Scrub community attracts an animal community to the mutual benefit of each. Rabbits and ground squirrels live in the protective cover of cactus where coyotes and birds of prey are discouraged from hunting. Rabbits will venture from protection to eat

20

vegetation outside the cactus cover. The resulting bare ground allows the slow expansion of the cactus community. And it only takes a resident snake or two and a patrolling owl to keep the rabbit population under control.

10. Cliffside

Cliffs and the rock debris at their base provide a harsh environment for most plants, but some plants would appear to thrive on seeming adversity. "Rupicolous plants" by definition live among or grow on rocks. We find them throughout the mountains in deep canyons, outcroppings, and cliffs caused by volcanic intrusions. Cliffs of Santa Monica Slate can be found in Rustic Canyon; passive cliffs and slopes of volcanic rock are accessible in upper Carlisle Canyon, and volcanic cliffs are found along Mendenhall Creek and Malibu Creek in Malibu Creek State Park, to name a few. The following plants may grow in other places occasionally, but usually are found in rock crevices or at the base of cliffs:

Cheilanthes covillei	Coville's Lip Fern
Dudleya lanceolata	Live Forever
Epilobium canum	California Fuchsia
Eriophyllum confertiflorum	Golden Yarrow
Galium angustifolium	Shrubby Bedstraw
Selaginella biglovii	Spike Moss
Stephanomeria cichoriacea	Tejon Milk-aster

Sometimes found on rock surfaces:

Brickellia californica	California Brickelbush
Corethrogyne filagnifolia	Woolly Aster
Cryptantha muricata	Popcorn Flower
Dudleya pulverulenta	Chalk Dudleya
Erigeron foliosus	
var. *stenophyllus*	Fleabane Aster
Mimulus aurantiacus	Bush Monkey Flower

11. Vernal Moist Habitat

Vernal moist habitats are rare in the Santa Monica Mountains but some do exist. They are formed when winter rains make a pond out of a low place. The dry summer reduces the size of the pond and eventually it becomes dry. Some plants tolerate fluctuations of water level, in fact, may require it. Plants that need submersion for germination and a low water level to flower and set seed have a competitive advantage over others in a vernal pool or mudflat habitat. Trees, shrubs, and stem succulents do not occur in these seasonally moist habitats.

Vernal moist habitats form along some of the streams in the Santa Monica Mountains. (Malibu Creek, Sycamore Creek) The plant community is important because it is the only habitat that will support some of the species that live there. The following plants are indicators of a vernal moist habitat:

Ammania coccinea	Long-leaved Ammania
Elatine californica	Waterwort
Gnaphalium palustre	Lowland Cudweed
Juncus bufonius	Toad Rush
Lythrum californicum	California Loosestrife
Psilocarpus tenellus	Woolly Heads
Sida hederacea	Alkali Mallow
Trifolium fucatum	Bull Clover
T. variegatum	White-tipped Clover

Structure of a flower

It is difficult to discuss plants and flowers without naming the parts, so a brief discussion appears to be in order. A typical bisexual flower has some sepals (usually green, but not always) as the outer layer. Collectively they form the calyx. Next is the corolla, composed of petals, and in some flowers the petals grow together, forming a tube or a bell. Next inward are the stamens, each consisting of a filament and the pollen producing anther. One or more pistils are at the flower's center, each with an ovary, style, and a terminal stigma that is rough and sticky so as to catch the pollen. Stamens and pistils are sometimes in separate flowers — sometimes even on separate plants.

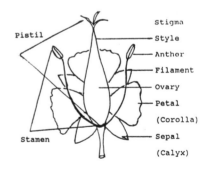

Glossary

Achene. A small, dry, hard, 1-seeded fruit. Typical of Asteraceae family.

Aestivate. To become dormant in summer.

Alien. An introduced species. Not native.

Alternate. (leaves) one side then the other. Not opposite.

Alternate. (stamens to petals) The members of the stamen whorl attached between members of petal whorl.

Androecium. The floral series between the corolla and gynoecium. The collective term for stamens of a flower (see flower.)

Annual. Living through one season only.

Anther. The pollen-bearing organ of flower. (see stamen)

Ascending. Curving upward in growth.

Awn. A stiff, bristle-like appendage.

Axil. The angle formed by a leaf with the stem to which it is attached.

Axillary. Situated in the axil of a leaf.

Basal. (leaves) Produced at ground level.

Beak. A prominent, firm, slender, elongation of a fruit.

PAPPUS

BEAK

OvulE

Biennial. Of 2 years duration.

Bifid. 2-parted.

Bilabiate. 2-lipped, as the corollas of mints and figworts

23

Bipinnate. Twice pinnately compound. (see pinnate)

Bisexual. (in flowers) Having both stamen and pistils.

Blade. The flat part of a leaf or petal. (see leaf)

Bloom. A whitish waxy or powdery covering.

Bract. A much-reduced leaf, usually subtending a flower.

Calyx. The outer whorl of perianth segments. Collective name for sepals. (see flower)

Companulate. Bell-shaped.

Capitate. In a dense, head-like cluster.

Carpel. The basic unit of a gynoecium (stigma, style, and ovary).

Catkin. A spike of inconspicuous and usually unisexual flowers.

Cauline. Borne on the stem.

Chaparral. A shrub area, mostly hardwood and evergreen, a dominant community of the Santa Monica Mountains.

Clasping. Partially surrounding a stem as the lower portion of some leaves.

Clawed. (petal) Having a narrow base or stalk.

Cleft. Deeply cut.

Compound leaf. A leaf blade divided into segments or leaflets.

Community. An interacting group.

Cordate. Heart-shaped.

Corolla. Collective name for the petals.

Corona. A crown or collar, often within the corolla.

Corymb. An arrangement of flowers that is flat topped or rounded; pedicels of different length.

Crenate. Rounded marginal teeth.

Cuneate. Wedge-shaped.

Cyme. A flower cluster usually opposite branched, with terminal blooming. first.

Deciduous. Falling off at the end of a growing season.

Decumbent. Flat on the ground with a raised tip.

Decurrent. Leaves whose bases continue down the stem beyond the point of attachment.

Dehiscent. Opening when ripe to discharge contents (anther or seed container)

Deltoid. Triangular in shape.

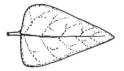

Dentate. Toothed.

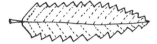

Dioecious. Plants that bear staminate flowers on one individual and pistillate flowers on another.

Disk-Flowers. The central regular or tubular flowers of the Asteraceae family.

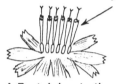

Dorsal. Pertaining to the part of an organ facing away from plant axis, as underside of a leaf.

Drupe. A fleshy one-seeded fruit, as a cherry or plum.

Elliptical. Ellipse in shape.

Endemic. A native plant restricted to a state area.

Entire. Smooth margined.

Evergreen. Remaining green during dormant season.

Exserted. Protruding.

Fascicle. Cluster.

25

Fertile. Having a seed or spore bearing organ.

Filament. The stalk that supports an anther. (see stamen)

Flower. The assemblage of reproductive structures.

Free. Separate, not united.

Frond. Fern leaf.

Fruit. Seed bearing part of plant.

Genus. First element of a scientific name. A taxonomic grouping that contains related species.

Glabrous. Without hairs.

Glaucous. Having a whitish bloom, or a blue-gray or sea-green color.

Gynoecium. Collective name for the carpels in a flower. (see pistil)

Habitat. The immediate area in which a plant lives.

Hastate. Arrowhead shape with basal lobes pointing outward.

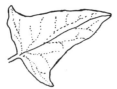

Head. A compact flower cluster.

Herb. A plant that dies back to ground level each year.

Herbaceous. Not woody.

Indehiscent. Not splitting open, as an achene or a walnut.

Indusium. A membrane formed from leaf tissue covering the sorus of ferns.

Inferior ovary. One in which perianth and androecium are inserted above the ovary.

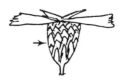

Involucre. A whorl of bracts (phyllaries) subtending a flower cluster, such as Asteraceae.

Labiate. Lipped, as of mint corolla.

Lake. A body of water without current that lacks vegetation at the immediate shoreline.

Lanceolate. Lance-shaped.

Leaf. The principal flattened lateral organ borne on a stem.

Leaflet. One of the elements of a compound leaf. Can be identified from a leaf by the absence of an axillary bud.

Linear. Long and narrow.

Littoral. The part of seashore covered by high tide and exposed at low tide.

Lobe. Rounded division of leaf or flower.

Marsh. An area dominated by herbs growing in saturated soil, but does not accumulate peat.

Merous. Referring to the number of parts of a structure. 4-merous flower will have 4 sepals, 4 petals and usually 4 stamens.

Midvein. The main or central vein of a leaf.

Monoecious. Having the stamens and pistils in separate flowers on the same plant.

Mucronate. Having a minute abrupt point at the apex.

Node. The area of a stem where a leaf or branch arises.

Ob. A prefix meaning "the reverse."

Oblanceolate. Inversely lanceolate with the widest part slightly above the middle and gradually tapering toward the base.

Obovate. Egg-shaped, with the narrow end at the base.

Opposite. (leaves) originating in pairs on the stem.

Opposite. (stamens to petals) members of stamen whorl attached directly in front of the petals.

Orbicular. Circular

Ovary. The part of the gynoe-cium which contains the seeds. (see pistil)

Ovate. Egg-shaped with wide end at the base.

Palmate. Having lobes, veins, or segments radiating from a single point.

Panicle. A repeatedly branched floral collection.

Pappus. The modified calyx of Asteraceae (bristles or awns) crowning the ovary or seeds of some species.

Pedicel. The stalk of a single flower.

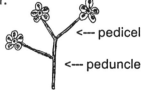

<--- pedicel

<--- peduncle

Peduncle. The stalk of a flower cluster.

Perennial. Living several seasons.

Perianth. Collective term for sepals and petals.

Petal. An inner perianth segment. (see flower)

Petaloid. Like a petal.

Petiole. Leaf stalk.

Phyllaries. Bracts of the involucre of a compositae.

Pinnate. With leaflets arranged on both sides of a common axis.

Pistil. The collective name for the stigma, style, and ovary. (see flower)

Pistillate. Having pistils but not stamens. A female flower.

Pond. A body of water without current that has vegetation extending from surrounding land into the water, without interruption of a beach.

Prostrate. Lying flat on the ground.

Pubescent. Hairy.

Raceme. An elongate, unbranched main stem along which single stalked flowers appear.

Ray-flowers. The strap-like, radially arranged flowers of Asteraceae. Each flower has the appearance of a petal.

Receptacle. The base of a flower or flowers.

Reflexed. Bent abruptly downward.

Refugium. A small area in which plants have survived after the surrounding area has become uninhabitable because of climate change.

Rhizome. A prostrate underground stem, rooting at the nodes.

Riparian. A streamside environment.

Rosette. A dense basal cluster of leaves arranged in circular fashion.

Saline. A water or soil environment containing soluble salts detrimental to most plants.

Salverform. A corolla with an elongate tube and an abruptly flared flat surface.

Samara. A winged fruit.

Seed. A ripened ovule.

Sepal. a segment of the calyx, the outer perianth segment. (see flower)

Serrate. Toothed with the points directed toward the apex.

Sessile. Lacking a stalk.

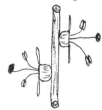

Shrub. A woody plant smaller than a tree, having many stems.

Simple. (leaf) With a single blade.

Simple. (stems) Not branched.

Sorus. A cluster of sporangia.

Spatulate. Flattened, spoon-shaped.

Species. A distinct kind of plant; the biological classification ranking immediately below the genus.

Spike. An elongate, un-branched main stem along which single sessile flowers appear.

Spinose. With a spine at the tip.

Sporangium. A spore case or sac.

Spur. A hollow projection of a sepal or petal.

Ssp. Subspecies.

Stamen. The pollen-producing organ of a flower. (see flower)

Staminate. Having stamens but not pistils. A male flower.

Stand. A homogeneous group of plants, the same species and age, living in an area.

Sterile. Not producing seed or spores.

Stigma. The pollen receiving part of the pistil. (see pistil)

Stipule. An appendage (usually in pairs at the base of the leaf stem.

Style. The slender upper part of a pistil. (see pistil)

Sub. Prefix — means almost.

Superior. Refers to the position of the ovary in a flower. The ovary is superior when it is attached only at its base and nowhere else.

Tendril. A slender, twining outgrowth of stems or leaves.

Tepal. A component of a perianth which is not distinctly a calyx or corolla; used when it is difficult to determine whether structure is sepal or petal.

Tree. A woody plant larger than a shrub and having one stem. Usually 9 feet or more high at maturity.

Trifoliate. Having 3 leaves, not to be confused with the following.

Trifoliolate. Having 3 leaflets per leaf.

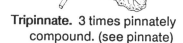

Tripinnate. 3 times pinnately compound. (see pinnate)

Ultimate leaf. The smallest leaflet in a compound leaf or a fern frond.

Umbel. A cluster of flowers in which pedicels radiate from a single point.

Unisexual. A flower or plant having either stamens or pistils, never both.

Ventral. On the side facing the stem.

Viscid. sticky.

Weed. any plant growing where man does not want it to grow.

Whorl. 3 or more leaves or other structures arranged in a circle about a stem or other common axis.

LEAF MARGINS

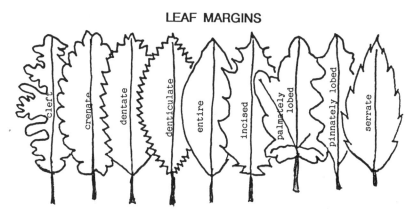

cleft crenate dentate denticulate entire incised palmately lobed pinnately lobed serrate

MILT McAULEY has had a life-long love of the outdoor life. Born near the base of Mt. Shasta, raised in the mountains of Oregon, he now lives in Canoga Park with his wife Maxine. He is author of seven hiking and wildflower books about the Santa Monica Mountains and frequently takes groups on walks. All of his books, including this one, are written so that the average person can better understand and enjoy an outdoor experience.

JAMES P. KENNEY has lived on the edge of the Santa Monica Mountains since 1965. His wildflower photography has appeared in local and national publications, and he has published articles on both native plants and chaparral fire ecology. His photography portrays our flora artistically but always with plant identification as a primary objective.

TIMOTHY THOMAS was born in Los Angeles and raised in the San Fernando Valley. He has served the Santa Monica Mountains with his work for the Nature Conservancy and with the National Park System in Resource Management. He now works for the U.S. Fish and Wildlife Service.

Milt McAuley

James P. Kenney

Timothy Thomas

33

4   Chaparral   Los Liones Canyon

5   Valley Grassland   La Jolla Valley

6   Cliffside   Santa Ynez Canyon

7   Saltwater Marsh   Mugu Lagoon

8   Southern Oak Woodland   Carlisle Canyon

9   Coastal Strand   Point Mugu

10   Chaparral
     (Interior View)

11   Coastal Sage Scrub
     Sycamaore Canyon

12 Freshwater Marsh - Nicholas Flat

13 Riparian Woodland-Santa Ynez Cyn

14   Fire   23 October 1978   Temescal Canyon

15   The Day After The Fire   24 October 1978

16   Spring Recovery

17   Mouse-eared Chickweed   p. 295

18   Dolores Campion   p. 298

19   Douglas Sandwart   p. 295

20   Many-nerved Catchfly   p. 298

21   Chickweed   p. 300

22   Windmill Pink   p. 297

38

23   Sugar Bush   p. 169

24   Laurel Sumac   p. 168

25   Elderberry   p. 293

26   Poison Oak   p. 171

27   White Nightshade   p. 530

28   Annual Bedstraw   p. 500

29   Narrow-leaved Bedstraw   p. 499

40

30   Sea-Cliff Buckwheat   p. 467

31   California Buckwheat   p. 466

32   Ashyleaf Buckwheat   p. 464

41

33   Virgin's Bower   p. 481

34   Western Virgin's Bower   p. 481

35   California Tea   p. 358

36   Yellow-throated Phacelia   p. 387   37   Mountain Phacelia   p. 391

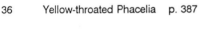

38   Branching Phacelia   p. 393   39   Caterpillar Phacelia   p. 388

| 40 | Caterpillar Phacelia | p. 388 |

| 41 | Eucrypta | p. 385 |

| 42 | White-flowered Filaree | p. 379 |

43   Coast Boykinia   p. 506   44   Woodland Star   p. 507

45   White Chaparral Currant   p. 382   46   California Saxifrage   p. 507

45

47   Hillside Gooseberry   p. 382

48   Miner's Lettuce   p. 476

49   Willow-Herb Clarkia   p. 434

50   Summer Holly   p. 331   51   Wild Cucumber   p. 324

52   Bigberry Manzanita   p. 330   53   Bleeding Heart   p. 447

55   Celery   p. 172

54   Poison Hemlock   p. 173

56   Wild Celery   p. 171   57   Woolly Lomatium   p. 175

48

58   Datura, Tolguacha   p. 527   59   Cream Cups   p. 449

60   Matilija Poppy   p. 450   61   Prickly Poppy   p. 446

62   Beach Morning Glory   p. 315

63   Morning Glory   p. 314

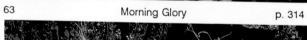

64   Dodder   p. 326

| 65 | Valley Lupine | p. 353 | 66 | White Sage | p. 402 |

| 67 | Rigid Hedge Nettle | p. 405 | 68 | White Hedge Nettle | p. 405 |

69   Horehound   p. 399   70   Pitcher Sage   p. 399

71   Spearmint   p. 400   72   White Sweet-clover   p. 356

73   Globe Gilia   p. 457 74   Flax-flowered Linanthus p. 459

75   Red-skinned Onion p. 408 76   Angel's Gilia   p. 456

78   California Blackberry   p. 497

77   Willow Herb   p. 438

79   Wedge-leaf Horkelia   80   Common Montia   p. 475

54

82   Southern Mountain Misery p. 493

81   White Everlasting   p. 220

83   Two-tone Everlasting   p. 218   84   California Everlasting   p. 219

85   California Filago   p. 218

86   Oak Mistletoe   p. 542

87   Cudweed   p. 221

88   Sycamore Mistletoe   p. 541

89   Toyon   p. 494   90   Cream Bush   p. 494

91   Chamise   p. 491   92   Red Shank   p. 492

93	Hoary-leaved Ceanothus	p. 486	94	White Thorn	p. 487
95	Big-pod Ceanothus	p. 488	96	Buck-Brush	p. 487

58

97   Squaw Spurge   p. 333

98   Turkey Mullein   p. 335

99   Rattlesnake Weed   p.174

100	Bird's Beak	p. 514	101	Chaparral Yucca	p. 415
102	White Snapdragon	p. 508	103	English Plantain	p. 452

104   Narrow-leaved Fringe-Pod   p. 282

105   Hoary Cress   p. 270

106   Tower Mustard   p. 266

107   Milkmaids   p. 269

109   Shepherd's Purse   p. 269

108   Sea Rocket   p. 269

110   Water Cress   p. 279   111   California Mustard   p. 274

113   California Chicory   p. 244

112   Cliff-Aster   p. 239

114   Mayweed   p. 193   115   Wand Chicory   p. 252

117   Slim Aster   p. 195

116   Yarrow   p. 187

118   Common Ice Plant   p. 163   119   Yerba Mansa   p. 505

120   Globe Lily   p. 411

121   Catalina Mariposa Lily   p. 411

122   Butterfly Mariposa Lily   p. 413

123   Soap Plant   p. 414   124   Star Lily   p. 416

125   Indian Milkweed   p. 182   126   Narrow-leaved Milkweed   p. 183

127   Large-flowered   p. 262
          Popcorn Flower

128   Popcorn Flower, Minute   p. 262

129   Popcorn Flower   p. 266

130   Hollyleaf Cherry   p. 496

131   Wild Heliotrope   p. 263

| 132 | Mule Fat | p. 197 | 133 | Plummer Baccharis | p. 197 |

| 134 | Coyote Brush | p. 196 | 135 | Horseweed | p. 208 |

136   California Brickellbush   p. 199

137   Nevins Brickellbush   p. 200

138   Little Horseweed   p. 208

139   Rock Rose   p. 313

69

140 Downy Monkey Flower p. 519	141 Yellow Monkey Flower p. 517

142 Creek Monkey Flower p. 519	143 Johnny-Jump-Up p. 540

145   Bermuda Buttercup   p. 444

144   Moth Mullein   p. 523

146   Oxalis   p. 443   147   Tree Tobacco   p. 528

149   Bladder Pod   p. 291

148   Bush Poppy   p. 446

150   Stick-leaf   p. 418   151   Golden-Currant   p. 381

153   Sun-cup   p. 430

152   Mustard Eve. Primrose   p. 431

154   Small Eve. Primrose   p. 432   155   Beach Eve. Primrose   p. 431

157   Dobie Pod   p. 283

156   Hooker's Evening   p. 440
Primrose

158   Yellow Water-weed   p. 439   159   Prickly Pear   p. 286

160   Mediterranean Mustard   p. 274   161   Coast Wallflower   p. 274

162   Winter Cress   p. 268   163   Jewel Flower   p. 270

164   Tansy Mustard   p. 271

165   Oriental Mustard   p. 281

166   Hedge Mustard   p. 280

167   London Rocket   p. 280

168   Black Mustard   p. 268

169   Chinese Caps   p. 335

170   Whispering Bells   p. 384

172   Gourd   p. 323

171   Santa Monica Mountains   p. 320
             Dudleya

173   Bur-clover   p. 355   174   Golden Stars   p. 410

| 175 | Sweet Fennel | p. 174 | 176 | Shiny Lomatium | p. 176 |
| 177 | Hog Fennel | p. 176 | 178 | Southern Tauschia | p. 179 |

180   Turkey Pea   p. 178

179   Pacific Sanicle   178

181   Chaparral Honeysuckle p. 292   182   Snake Root   p. 177

183   Silverweed   p. 495

184   Sticky Cinquefoil   p. 495

185   Yellow Mariposa Lily   p. 412

186   Yellow Mariposa Lily   p. 412

187   Meadow Rue (male)   p. 485

188   Small-flowered Fiddleneck p. 260

189   Common Fiddleneck   p. 261

191   French Broom   p. 340

190   Deerweed   p. 346

192   Deerweed   p. 346   193   Spanish Broom   p. 359

194   Silver Lotus   p. 342

195   Large-flowered Lotus   p. 343

196   Coastal Lotus   p. 345

198   Strigose Lotus   p. 346

197   Santa Barbara Locoweed   p. 340

199   So. California Locoweed   p. 339   200   Clustered Broomrape   p. 442

201   Marsh Jaumea   p. 233

202   Common Madia   p. 237

203   Tidy Tips   p. 236

204   Sticky Madia, Gumweed   p.238

206   Bristly Ox-tongue   p. 243

205   Prickly Sow-thistle   p. 250

207   Sow-thistle   p. 250   208   Dandelion   p. 253

87

| 209 | Prickly Lettuce | p. 234 | 210 | Mountain Dandelion | p. 189 |

| 211 | Annual Malacothrix | p. 239 | 212 | Hawkweed | p. 230 |

88

213   Slender Tarweed   p. 227

214   Santa Susana Tarweed   p. 227

215   Brassbuttons   p. 211

216   Common Sunflower   p. 226

217   Slender Sunflower   p. 226

218   Canyon Sunflower   p. 255

219   Telegraph Weed   p. 228

90

220   Giant Coreopsis   p. 210

221   Giant Coreopsis   p. 210

222   Annual Coreopsis   p. 209

223   Canyon Sunflower   p. 255

224   Bush Sunflower   p. 213

225   Gumplant   p. 223

226   Stonecrop   p. 322

227   Golden Yarrow   p. 217

228   Beggar Ticks   p. 199

229   Yellow Star-thistle   p. 201

230   Yellow Pincushion   p. 203   231   California Buttercup   p. 483

232   Lyon's Pentachaeta   p. 242   233   Western Goldenrod   p. 217

234   Coast Goldfields   p. 235   235   California Goldenrod   p. 249

| 236 | Sawtooth Goldenbush | p. 224 | 237 | Conejo Buckwheat | p. 465 |
| 238 | Palmer's Goldenbush | p. 215 | 239 | Coast Goldenbush | p. 232 |

95

240   Bush Seneco   p. 247

241   German Ivy   p. 247

242   Scale Broom   p. 236

243   Common Groundsel   p. 248

244   Brewer's Butterweed   p. 246

245　　　California Poppy　　　p. 448

246　　　Collarless　　　p. 447
California Poppy

247　　　Fire Poppy　　　p. 449

248　　　Wind Poppy　　　p. 450

249   Humboldt Lily   p. 415

250   Live-forever   p. 319

251   Blow Wives   p. 187

252   Pigmy Weed   p. 317

253   Western Wallflower   p. 273

254   Russian Thistle   p. 311

255   Scarlet Pimpernel   p. 479

256   Bush Monkey Flower   p. 516

257   Scarlet Monkey Flower   p. 518

258   Heart-leaved Penstemon   p. 515

259   Fuchsia-flowered Gooseberry   p. 384

260   Scarlet Bugler   p. 520   261   Scarlet Larkspur   p. 481

262   Hoary Fuchsia   p. 437   263   California Fuchsia   p. 436

264   Annual Paintbrush   p. 513   265   Indian Paintbrush   p. 512

266   Woolly Paintbrush   p. 512   267   Indian Warrior   p. 519

268   Chalk Live-forever   p. 321

269   Indian Pink   p. 297

270   California Milkweed   p. 182

271   Crimson Pitcher Sage   p. 403

272   Shooting Star   p. 479

273   Oyster Plant   p. 254

274   Lemonade Berry   p. 169

275   Chaparral Currant   p. 383

277   Bush Mallow   p. 420

276   Elegant Clarkia   p. 435

278   Speckled Clarkia   p. 433   279   Purple Clarkia   p. 435

280   Farewell-to-Spring   p. 433

281   Checker Bloom   p. 422

282   Bitter Root   p. 476

283   Purple Owl's-clover   p. 511   284   Hedge Nettle   p. 406

285   Purple Sage   p. 402   286   Henbit   p. 398

287   Wild Sweet Pea   p. 341

288   Braunton's Rattle-Weed   p. 337

289   Bush Lupine   p. 350

291   Spanish Clover   p. 345

290   Bush Lupine   p. 350

292   Bajada Lupine   p. 348   293   Broad-leaved Lupine   p. 350

294   Collar Lupine   p. 354   295   Stinging Lupine   p. 349

296   Spring Vetch   p. 364   297   Chaparral Pea   p. 357

| 298 | Sour Clover | p. 360 | 299 | Tomcat Clover | p. 363 |

| 300 | Snowberry | p. 293 | 301 | Milkwort | p. 462 |

303   Long-beaked Filaree   p. 377

302   Carolina Geranium   p. 380

304   Sand Cress   p. 475   305   Red-stem Filaree   p. 378

307   Ground-Pink   p. 458

306   Prickly Phlox   p. 458

308   Linanthus   p. 459   309   Wild Radish   p. 278

310   Rose Snapdragon   p. 509   311   Violet Snapdragon   p. 510

312   Chinese Houses   p. 513   313   Canchalagua   p. 377

314   White Pincushion   p. 203

315   Turkish Rugging   p. 463

316   Wild Rose   p. 496

317   Water Smartweed   p. 470   318   Water Smartweed   p. 468

319   Wand Buckwheat   p. 465   320   Meadow Rue (Female)   p. 485

322   Fleabane Aster   p. 216

321   Perezia   p. 188

323   Woolly Aster   p. 237

324   Tejon Milk-aster   p. 252

325   Red Thistle   p. 206
Cobwebby Thistle

326   Milk Thistle   p. 248

327   Bull Thistle   p. 207

328   California Thistle   p. 205

329   Wishbone Bush   p. 426   330   Pink Sand Verbena   p. 426

331   Peninsular Onion   p. 409   332   Salt-marsh Sand Spurry   p. 299

333   Red Maids   p. 474   334   Brewer's Red Maids   p. 473

336   Lilac Mariposa Lily   p. 413

335   Catalina Mariposa Lily   p. 411

337   Plummer's Mariposa Lily   p. 412   338   Plummer's Mariposa Lily   p. 412

| 339 | Hairy-leaved Ceanothus | 489 | 340 | Greenbark Ceanothus | p. 489 |

| 341 | Chicory | p. 205 | 342 | Yerba Santa | p. 385 |

343   Parry's Phacelia   p. 392   344   Sticky Phacelia   p. 394

345   Fern-leaf Phacelia   p. 389   346   Tansy-leaf Phacelia   p. 393

347   Fiesta Flower   p. 394

348   Large-flowered Phacelia   p. 390

349   Baby Blue-Eyes   p. 386

| 350 | Meadow Nemophila | p. 387 | 351 | Blue-eyed Grass | p. 396 |
| 352 | Large-flowered Phacelia | p. 390 | 353 | Parry's Phacelia | p. 392 |

354 Dove Lupine p. 347   355 Coulter's Lupine p. 352

356 Foothill Lupine p. 353   357 Winter Vetch p. 365

| 358 | Blue Larkspur | p. 483 | 359 | Blue Larkspur | p. 482 |

| 360 | Common Vervain | p. 539 | 361 | Purple Nightshade | p. 532 |

362	Downy Navarretia	p. 460	363	Persian Speedwell	p. 524
364	Stinky Gilia	p. 455	365	Speedwell	p. 523
366	Sapphire Wool Star	p. 456	367	Alfalfa	p. 356

368   Blue Dicks   p. 414

369   Wild Brodiaea   p. 410

370   Monardella   p. 401

| 371 | Leather Root | p. 341 | 372 | Blue Toadflax | p. 516 |

| 373 | Pennyroyal | p. 400 | 374 | Cardoon, Wild Artichoke | p. 212 |

376   Foothill Penstemon   p. 520

375   Notable Penstemon   p. 521

377   Twining Snapdragon   p. 509   378   Woolly Blue-Curls   p. 406

380   Chia   p. 402

379   Black Sage   p. 403

381   Skullcap   p. 404

382   Vinegar Weed   p. 407

384   California Peony   p. 445

383   Chocolate Lily   p. 415

385   Coast Figwort   p. 522   386   Stream Orchid   p. 440

387 Chaparral Broomrape p. 442

388 Broad-leaved Cattail p. 534

389 Curly Dock p. 471

390 Wild Rhubarb p. 472

133

391   California Sagebrush   p. 193   392   Wild Tarragon   p. 194

393   Mugwort   p. 194   394   California Chorizanthe   p. 468

396   Annual Stinging Nettle   p. 535

395   Stinging Nettle   p. 536

397   Mountain Mahogany   p. 493

398   Pineapple Weed   p. 204

399   Western Ragweed   p. 192

400   Silver Beach-bur   p. 191

401   Durango Root   p. 328

402   Coast Goosefoot   p. 308

404   Redberry   p. 490

403   Squaw Bush   p. 170

405   Coffeeberry   p. 490   406   Hollyleaf Redberry.   p. 491

408   Beach Saltbush   p. 303

407   California Plantain   p. 451

409   Quail Bush   p. 302   410   Common Plantain   p. 452

411   Grape   p. 542   412   California Barberry   p. 259

413   Coast Cholla   p. 286   414   Poison Oak   p. 171

415   Chalk Live-forever   p. 321   416   Lance-leaf Live-forever   p. 320

417   California Buckwheat   p. 466   418   Ashyleaf Buckwheat   p. 464

420   White Nightshade   p. 530

419   Wild Cucumber   p. 324

421   Purple Nightshade   p. 532   422   Datura, Tolguacha   p. 527

423   Elderberry   p. 293   424   Wild Rose   p. 496

425   Snowberry   p. 293   426   Chaparral Honeysuchle   p. 292

428   Coffeeberry   p. 490

427   Toyon   p. 494

429   Hollyleaf Redberry   p. 491   430   Hollyleaf Cherry   p. 496

431   Lemonade Berry   p. 169   432   Golden Currant   p. 381

433   Sugar Bush   p. 169   434   Chaparral Currant   p. 383

435   Australian Saltbush   p. 304   436   Fuchsia-flwr Gooseberry   p.384

438   Greenbark Ceanothus   p. 489

437   Eastwood Manzanita   p. 330

439   Big Pod Ceanothus   p. 448   440   Bigberry Manzanita   p. 330

441   Mountain Mahogany   p. 493

442   Silk-tassel Bush   p. 376

443   California Blackberry   p. 497

444   Castor-Bean   p. 336

446 Beggar Ticks p. 199

445 Shiny Peppergrass p. 276

447 Gourd p. 323 448 Lace Pod p. 282

449	Silver Puffs	p. 254
450	Brown Microseris	p. 251
451	Mountain Dandelion	p. 189
452	Blow Wives	p. 187

453   Virgin's Bower   p. 481   454   Spiny Clotbur   p. 256

455   Scrub Oak   p. 367

456   Coast Live Oak   p. 366

457   Valley Oak   p. 367

458   Coast Live Oak   p. 366

459   California Laurel, Bay   p. 407

460   Arroyo Willow   p. 504

461   California Black Walnut   p. 396   462   California Black Walnut   p. 396

464   Big Leaf Maple   p. 161

463   Western Sycamore   p. 453

465   Western Sycamore   p. 453   466   White Alder   p. 259

467   Fremont Cottonwood   p. 502

468   Valley Oak   p. 367

469   Scrub Oak   p. 367

470   Arizona Ash   p. 428

153

471   Venus Hair- Fern   p. 369   472   Bird's- Foot Fern   p. 373

473   Giant Chain-Fern   p. 375   474   Western Bracken Fern   p. 374

475   Goldback Fern   p. 373

476   Polypody   p. 374

477   California-Lace Fern   p. 370

478   Coffee Fern   p. 372

479   Coastal Wood-Fern   p.371

480   Smooth Scouring Rush   p. 329

481   Spike Moss   p. 524

482   Red Brome

483   Wild Oats

484   Golden Top

485   Fountain Grass

157

486   Giant Rye

487   Rabbitfoot Grass

488   Rough Sedge

489   Iris Leaved Rush

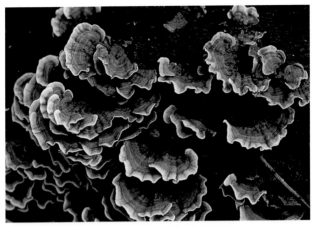

490   Shell Fungus

491   Earthstar

492   Fungus

159

493   Puffball

494   Witch's Butter

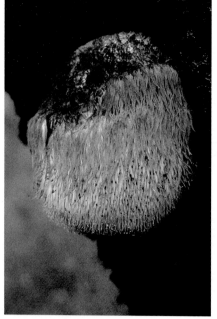

495   Heartwood Fungus

496   Stalked Puffball

ACERACEAE

MAPLE FAMILY

Maples are scarce in the Santa Monicas and are cherished when found. They prefer good moist soil but are usually found growing out of rock in the bottom of canyons because the environment out in the open doesn't afford the cool, damp, protected shelter that is essential. Their winged seeds (samaras) are in pairs. Acer is the only genus in the Santa Monicas, and it is represented by two species: Big Leaf Maple and Box Elder.

Acer macrophyllum   Plate 464   **BIG LEAF MAPLE**

DESCRIPTION: Broad-crowned, 100 feet tall (but usually less), a rare recluse found in a few deep, protected canyons where cool, flowing water reaches the root zone. About 2 dozen trees grow in Cold Creek Canyon; 6 mature trees and some seedlings grow in Blue Gorge; uncounted numbers stretch along Topanga Canyon Creek, and most of the north and east running streams in Malibu Creek State Park support maples. Perhaps the most well-known is the maple at the base of the waterfall in upper Sycamore Canyon.

FLOWERS: Drooping clusters of small, greenish flowers, each having 5 sepals. The single pistil, with a 2-celled ovary and 2 styles, ripens into double samaras. When leaves fall in October, the samaras remain on the branches. The main seed body is covered with stiff hairs.

LEAVES: Opposite, palmately divided into 5 fingers. About 10 inches in diameter. Leaves are green above and paler on the underside.

FLOWERING: April - May

Acer negundo ssp. californicum   ***BOX ELDER**

DESCRIPTION: A subspecies of the eastern Box Elder and smaller, usually 20 to 50 ft. high. The trunk is short; the crown is broad, rounded, and dense.

161

ACERACEAE

Found along streams in sandy or gravelly soil. (Sleeper Creek in Tapia Park)

FLOWERS: Male and female greenish flowers grow on separate trees.   Staminate (male) flowers occur in clusters of drooping, unbranched stems. Pistillate (female) flowers are on a drooping branched stem.   Seeds are a samara that remain on the tree most of the winter.

LEAVES: Pinnately compound, usually 3 leaflets with the terminal leaflet somewhat larger. 4 inches long.   Leaflets ovate, and coarsely toothed.

FLOWERING: March - April

AIZOACEAE

FIG-MARIGOLD FAMILY

Plants mainly of hot climates; this family has 130 genera and 2500 species. 6 species grow in the Santa Monicas, all introduced.

RECOGNITION CHARACTERISTICS: fleshy, low herbs, many stamens, often with petaloid sterile stamens. Petals numerous in genus *Mesembryanthemum*. Mostly coastal plants.

Aptenia cordifolia

*ICE PLANT

DESCRIPTION: Perennial herb, succulent, prostrate, 1 to 2 feet long. Found as an escape from cultivation.

FLOWERS: On 5/16 to 5/8 inch long stems. Sepals 5 unequal, 2 large and flat — the others awl shaped; petals many, purple, about 3/16 inch long; stamens many.

LEAVES: Opposite, ovate, flat, 3/8 to 1¼ inches long, on stems.

FLOWERING: April - May

162

AIZOACEAE

Carpobrotus chilensis   ***SEA FIG**

DESCRIPTION: Perennial herb, succulent, many trailing stems 3 feet long — more or less — forming mats. Found along the coast on sand dunes and bluffs. Common.

FLOWERS: Terminal, on a short stem or none, 1¼ to 2 inches across. Sepals 5, unequal, leaf-like; petals many, magenta; stamens many. Lightly fragrant.

LEAVES: Opposite, 3-sided, straight, 1½ to 3 inches long.

FLOWERING: April - September

Carpobrotus edulis   ***HOTTENTOT FIG**

DESCRIPTION: Perennial herb, succulent, many trailing stems 3 feet long — more or less — forming mats. Planted on banks and along highways throughout. Found as an escape along the coast. Common.

FLOWERS: Terminal on a short stem or none, 3 to 4 inches across. Sepals 5 unequal; petals many, yellow; stamens many.

LEAVES: Opposite, 3-sided, curved, some are saw-toothed, 2½ to 4 inches long.

FLOWERING: April - October

Mesembryanthemum crystallinum   Plate 118   ***COMMON ICE PLANT**

DESCRIPTION: Annual, succulent, prostrate, branching, 8 to 24 inches long. Entire plant is covered with transparent shining bumps. Found along the coast. (Point Mugu) Common.

FLOWERS: Axillary, solitary, on short thick stems or none. Sepals 5; petals many, thread-like, white or tinged rose, about 1/4 inch long; stamens many, short.

AIZOACEAE

LEAVES: Alternate, ovate or spatulate, wavy, 3/4 to 4 inches long.

FLOWERING: March - October

FIELD NOTE: The plant is known to add salt to the surrounding soil. This prevents many other species of plants from germinating and growing, thereby allowing less competition for its own regeneration.

Mesembryanthemum nodiflorum   ***SLENDER-LEAVED ICE PLANT**

DESCRIPTION: Annual, branching from the base, somewhat erect, 2 to 8 inches long, covered with tiny colorless bumps. Found along the coast. (Point Mugu; Malibu Lagoon)

FLOWERS: Axillary, solitary, on short thick stems or none. Sepals 5, 3/16 inch long; petals about the same length, white.

LEAVES: Alternate, linear, cylindrical, 3/8 to 3/4 inch long.

FLOWERING: April - November

Tetragonia tetragonioides   ***NEW ZEALAND SPINACH**

DESCRIPTION: Annual, succulent, trailing, 1 to 2 or more feet long, covered with glistening bumps. Found along the coast. Common.

FLOWERS: Axillary, solitary, on short stems, yellow-green. Sepals 5, spreading; petals none; stamens many.

LEAVES: Alternate, deltoid-ovate, smooth margined, sometimes wavy, 3/4 to 2 inches long.

FLOWERING: April - September

ALISMATACEAE

WATER PLANTAIN FAMILY

The water Plantain (or Arrowhead) family comprises 13 genera and 90 species of aquatic and marsh plants. 2 of these are found in the local mountains. Our flowers are bisexual, 3 sepals, 3 petals, 6 or 12 stamens, and many pistils. You may see both species at Rocky Oaks pond.

Alisma plantago-aquatica   WATER PLANTAIN

DESCRIPTION: Perennial herb, basal leaves only, erect leafless flower stems to 4 feet high. Common along the margins of ponds, streams, and marshy areas. (Triunfo Creek, Malibu Creek)

FLOWERS: On stems 2 to 4 feet tall, in a panicle of whorled branches, each branch bearing an umbel of flowers. 3 sepals, 3 white petals 1/4 inch long, 6 stamens, many pistils.

LEAVES: All basal, oblong to ovate sometimes narrower, the blade 6 inches long on 1 foot stems. Innermost pair of secondary leaf veins diverge from the mid-vein well above the base of the leaf.

FLOWERING: June - July

FIELD NOTE: Water Plantain reaches its southern coastal limits in disjunct Santa Monica Mountain populations.

Echinodoros berteroi   BURHEAD

DESCRIPTION: Annual, basal leaves only, several erect leafless flower stems to 1½ feet high. Found in wet places, often partially submerged in water. (Lake Eleanor, Lake Sherwood)

FLOWERS: Open umbels of white petalled flowers spaced along leafless stems, can be 1½ feet tall. 3 - 12 flowers on a plant. Heads to 3/8 inch in diameter. 3 sepals, petals, 1/4 to 3/8 inch long; 12 stamens and many pistils.

165

ALISMATACEAE

LEAVES: Basal leaves broadly ovate up to 6 inches long on long stems. Innermost pair of secondary leaf veins diverge from the mid-vein at the base of the leaf.

FLOWERING: July - September

AMARANTHACEAE

PIGWEED FAMILY

Of the 60 or more genera and 900 species of the Pigweed family, only the genus Amaranth and 5 species grow in the local mountains. They are coarse annual herbs, usually branched. Leaves are alternate, not divided or toothed, and have stems. The small, green to purplish flowers are subtended by 3 bracts and are in compact cymes or clusters. Male and female flowers are separate but on the same plant. 1-5 sepals, no petals; stamens are united by their filaments.

Amaranthus albus   *TUMBLEWEED

DESCRIPTION: Annual, erect, branching to form a bush 1 to 4 feet high. When dry this tumbleweed rolls about the countryside distributing seeds. Found in cultivated fields and disturbed areas. Common.

FLOWERS: In small clusters on axillary spikes. Bracts 3, awl-shaped. Sepals 3, much shorter than the bracts. All green. No petals; 3 stamens, united.

LEAVES: Alternate, elliptic to spatulate or obovate, 3/8 to 1½ inches long, on short stems.

FLOWERING: June - October

166

AMARANTHACEAE

Amaranthus blitoides   ***PROSTRATE PIGWEED**

DESCRIPTION: Annual, prostrate, branching, often purplish, without hairs. Branches 1½ feet long. Widely scattered and occasionally found in cultivated places.

FLOWERS: In dense axillary clusters only. 3 ovate-oblong bracts about as long as the sepals. 4-5 oblong sepals 1/8 inch long. Seeds round, dull, black, 1/16 inch in diameter.

LEAVES: Alternate, pale green, spatulate to obovate, crowded, up to 1 inch long.

FLOWERING: July - November

Amaranthus californicus   **CALIFORNIA AMARANTH**

DESCRIPTION: Annual, prostrate, branching, often reddish tinged, matted plant without hairs. Branches up to 7 feet long. Found in dried mud flats.

FLOWERS: In small axillary clusters only. 3 lanceolate bracts, 2-3 sepals with only 1 developed in pistillate flowers, no petals.

LEAVES: Alternate, crowded, pale green, obovate to oblong about 1/2 inch long.

FLOWERING: July - October

Amaranthus deflexus   ***LOW AMARANTH**

DESCRIPTION: Annual, prostrate or ascending, slender, much branched. Found in gardens, along streets and roads, and other disturbed areas.

FLOWERS: In lobed dense terminal spikes or panicles, 4 inches long. Bracts 1/16 inch long; sepals 2-3, green. No petals.

LEAVES: Alternate, rhombic-ovate to lanceolate, 1 inch long, on slender stems.

FLOWERING: May - November

AMARANTHACEAE

Amaranthus retroflexus   ***ROUGH PIGWEED**

DESCRIPTION: Annual, stout, erect, branched, downy plant 1 to 5 feet tall. Found in disturbed soil and as a weed in gardens.

FLOWERS: In dense terminal spikes and many short lateral spikes. Bracts 3, ovate, awl-shaped; sepals 5, about 1/2 the length of the bracts; petals none; stamens 5, united.

LEAVES: Alternate, ovate or oblong-ovate, 1¼ to 4 inches long on long stems.

FLOWERING: June - November

ANACARDIACEAE

SUMAC FAMILY

Shrubs and trees of importance in the plant communities of the local area. Alternate leaves. 5-merous flowers. The well-known Poison Oak and the introduced Peruvian Pepper belong to the same family as the Sugar Bush and Lemonade Berry.

Malosma laurina Plate 24   **LAUREL SUMAC**

DESCRIPTION: A 10 to 15 foot high shrub or tree, evergreen, aromatic, found on dry slopes in Chaparral and Coastal Sage Scrub.

FLOWERS: In terminal dense panicles, the framework of which remains on the tree long after the flowers are gone. Calyx 5-lobed, petals 5, white.

LEAVES: Alternate, oblong-lanceolate, 3 to 6 inches long, folded along the midrib. Leaf veins, stems and small twigs reddish.

FLOWERING: June - July

ANACARDIACEAE

Rhus integrifolia Plates 274, 431   **LEMONADE BERRY**

DESCRIPTION: An evergreen, bush-like tree to 10 feet tall. A short, stocky trunk and many wide-spreading limbs and twigs forming an open and irregular crown. Found in Coastal Sage Scrub and Chaparral communities facing the ocean. With few exceptions, not found on inland facing slopes.

FLOWERS: Small pinkish-white flowers in closely packed clusters. Calyx 5-cleft; 5 petals; 5 stamens. The seed matures in summer, is circular in outline, flattish, and densely covered with a fine, deep brown-red down. A thin, sticky, pulp covers the hard stone. This pulp has a lemonade flavor.

LEAVES: Alternate, simple, leathery, and borne singly along the twigs. Oval shaped, 2½ inches long, not pointed, and smooth on the top side, shiny. Leaves persist on the plant for 2 years.

FLOWERING: February - April

Rhus ovata Plates 23, 433   **SUGAR BUSH**

DESCRIPTION: A 10 to 15 foot tall shrub of Chaparral and Southern Oak Woodland plant communities. Not found close to the ocean.

FLOWERS: Pinkish-white in clusters at the ends of branches. Calyx, 5-cleft; 5 petals; 5 stamens. The red-brown seed is covered with a tart, sticky pulp. Flower buds begin to appear in December.

LEAVES: Alternate, 2½ inches long, thick, leathery, oval and pointed. Folded along the mid-vein, taco-like, shiny. Many, but not all, of the leaves are serrated. Plants growing in deep shade have larger leaves with less fold.

FLOWERING: January - May

ANACARDIACEAE

Rhus trilobata Plate 403   **SQUAW BUSH**

DESCRIPTION: Diffusely branching shrub to 3½ feet high, found in canyons and slopes of Coastal Sage Scrub and Southern Oak Woodland plant communities. Occasionally in openings of the chaparral.

FLOWERS: Spikes of yellowish-green flowers appear in the spring before the leaves are out. Calyx, 5-cleft; 5 petals, 5 stamens. The 1/4 inch fruit is sticky, fuzzy and red. (Poison oak has white berries.)

LEAVES: Compound, with 3 leaflets on very short stems. The terminal leaflet is deeply lobed.

FLOWERING: March - April

FIELD NOTE: *Trilobata* in Latin means, "three-lobed."

Schinus molle   ***PERUVIAN PEPPER**

DESCRIPTION: Cultivated evergreen tree, occasionally takes root in the mountains and has become established. Usually 20-30 feet high, has drooping branches.

FLOWERS: Male and female flowers on separate trees. Female flowers, yellowish-white in drooping clusters, give way to clusters of rose-colored berries in the fall. Male flowers: 5-parted calyx, 5 petals, 10 stamens.

LEAVES: Alternate, bright green, pinnately compound leaves about 12 inches long. Many narrow leaflets 1½ to 2 inches long.

FLOWERING: Spring

ANACARDIACEAE

Toxicodendron diversilobum   Plates 26, 414   **POISON OAK**
[Rhus diversiloba]

DESCRIPTION: Normally an erect shrub 4 to 8 feet tall, sometimes a vine, twining 15 or 20 feet along a tree trunk and, seldom, a tree-like shrub to 15 feet. Commonly found in moist, shaded areas and is widespread throughout the mountain range.

FLOWERS: The small, greenish-white flowers are borne in a drooping panicle. The 1/4 inch fruit is white. Calyx, 5-cleft; 5 petals; 5 stamens.

LEAVES: Alternate, 3 ovate lobed leaflets constitute each leaf. The 2 inch leaves are shiny green on top, turn red and drop in the fall.

FLOWERING: March - April

APIACEAE
CARROT FAMILY

300 genera and 3000 species are found worldwide, primarily in the temperate northern hemisphere. About 75 genera and 300 species are native to the United States. 15 genera and 22 species are found in the Santa Monica Mountains.

Our plants are annual and perennial herbs characterized by alternate leaves (except Bowlesia), usually compound; 5-merous flowers with a 2-loculed inferior ovary; always an umbel. The fruit is a schizocarp (splits into two 1-seeded closed segments) and is an important identifying feature.

Apiastrum angustifolium   Plate 56   **WILD CELERY**

DESCRIPTION: Annual, slender, 2 to 20 inches high, smooth, branching. Stem is not purple dotted. Found on hillsides and in dry sandy valleys. Common after fire.

171

APIACEAE

FLOWERS: In umbels on stems growing from leaf axils. Sepals obsolete; 5 petals, white; 5 stamens. Fruit is covered with minute conical bumps; the ribs are not conspicuous.

LEAVES: Alternate, finely dissected into filiform divisions. 3/4 to 2 inches long.

FLOWERING: March - April

Apium graveolens Plate 55   *CELERY

DESCRIPTION: Perennial herb, erect, branching, not purple dotted, 1½ to 5 feet high. Celery odor. Found in salt marshes and other wet places. Uncommon.

FLOWERS: In compound umbels on stems growing opposite leaf axils and terminal. Sepals obsolete; 5 petals, white, small; 5 stamens. Fruit 1/16 inch long, twice as long as wide, with several slightly raised ribs.

LEAVES: Alternate, pinnate. Basal leaves 4 to 24 inches long, with stems; upper leaves much smaller, shorter stems to almost no stems. Leaflets 5-9, 1 to 2-3/4 inches long, coarsely incised.

FLOWERING: May - July

Berula erecta   WATER PARSNIP

DESCRIPTION: Perennial herb, aquatic, erect, branched, 8 to 32 inches high. Found in marshy areas.

FLOWERS: In compound umbels on terminal stems or from leaf axils. Sepals, minute; 5 petals, white, minute; 5 stamens. Fruit flattened laterally, ribs inconspicuous.

LEAVES: Alternate, pinnate with leaflets; 5 to 9 pairs and a terminal. Leaflets oblong, saw-toothed or scalloped, 5/8 to 1-1/2 inches long.

FLOWERING: July - October

APIACEAE

Bowlesia incana   ***BOWLESIA**

DESCRIPTION: Annual, slender, forking in pairs, trailing, 4 to 20 inches long. Found on partially shaded slopes in Coastal Sage Scrub, and Oak Woodland.

FLOWERS: In umbels on short axillary stems, 1 to 6 flowers per plant. Sepals 5-lobed, prominent; 5 petals, white; 5 stamens. Fruit broadly ovoid, no ribs, 1/16 inch long.

LEAVES: Opposite, kidney shaped in outline, 3/16 to 1-1/4 inches wide, on long stems, 5 to 7 lobed, palmate.

FLOWERING: March - April

Ciclospermum leptophyllum   ***MARSH PARSLEY**

DESCRIPTION: Annual, some stems lying on the ground, and some erect, 4 to 24 inches high. Found near habitations as an escape.

FLOWERS: Minute flowers in compound umbels on terminal stems or on stems opposite the leaves. Sepals obsolete; 5 petals, white, minute; 5 stamens. Fruit ovoid, 1/16 to 1/8 inch long, prominent ribs, as wide as long.

LEAVES: Alternate, 3 or 4 times pinnately compound, 1-1/4 to 4 inches wide. Upper leaves smaller and on shorter stems. Leaf-divisions filiform or linear, 3/16 to 1-1/4 inches long.

FLOWERING: April - August

Conium maculatum   Plate 54   ***POISON HEMLOCK**

DESCRIPTION: Biennial herb, erect, branching above, not hairy, purple dotted stem, 1½ to 10 feet high. Found in colonies under partial shade. (Temescal Canyon, Musch Ranch, along Pacific Coast Highway near Point Mugu.) Common.

APIACEAE

FLOWERS: In compound umbels on terminal stems and from leaf axils. Hundreds of flowers on each plant. Sepals obsolete; 5 petals, white; 5 stamens. Fruit broadly ovoid, ribs prominent, 1/8 inch long.

LEAVES: Alternate, pinnate, compound, cleft into narrow segments. Lower leaves on stems, upper without stems. Leaf blades 6 to 12 inches long.

FLOWERING: April - July

Daucus pusillus Plate 99   RATTLESNAKE WEED

DESCRIPTION: Annual, erect with a few branches above, bristly, 1/2 to 2 feet high. Found on dry slopes in disturbed soil or after a fire. (Called *Yerba de Vibora* by the early Spanish-Californios because it was used as an antidote to rattlesnake bite.)

FLOWERS: In umbels on stems 4 to 16 inches long. Subtended by bracts; calyx teeth obsolete; 5 petals, white; 5 stamens. Fruit oblong, about 3/16 inch long with several rows of stiff bristles.

LEAVES: Alternate, pinnate, compound, 1-1/4 to 4 inches long on long stems.

FLOWERING: April - June

Foeniculum vulgare Plate 175   *SWEET FENNEL

DESCRIPTION: Perennial herb, erect, branching above, not hairy, 3 to 6 feet high. Odor of anise or licorice is distinctive. Found along roads, trails and streambeds. Common.

FLOWERS: In large compound umbels. Sepals obsolete; 5 petals, yellow; 5 stamens. Fruit, oblong, 1/8 inch long.

APIACEAE

LEAVES: Alternate, pinnate, compound, about 1 foot long. Ovate to deltoid in outline, divided into threadlike divisions up to 1½ inches long. Leaf stems attach to the main stem in a sheath, clasping.

FLOWERING: May - September

Hydrocotyle umbellata **MANY-FLOWERED MARSH-PENNYWORT**

DESCRIPTION: Perennial herb, growing in or near water, 1/4 to 4-1/2 inches high. Found in wet places in many plant communities.

FLOWERS: In many-flowered umbels on stems up to 4 inches long, extending above the leaves. Calyx teeth obsolete; 5 petals, white; 5 stamens. Fruit 1/16 inch long, broader than long, has corky thick ribs.

LEAVES: Alternate, circular, 1/4 to 2 inches wide. Stems attach near the center of the underside.

FLOWERING: March - July

Lomatium dasycarpum Plate 57 **WOOLLY LOMATIUM**

DESCRIPTION: Perennial herb, hairy, 4 to 16 inches high. Found on dry slopes and ridges in openings of chaparral.

FLOWERS: In compound umbels on nearly leafless stems rising well above the leaves. Subtended by bracts; 5 petals, greenish, appears white because of the hairs; 5 stamens. Fruit oblong, 1/4 to 1/2 inch long, hairy with broad membranous wings.

LEAVES: Mostly basal or alternate, 4-pinnate, to 4-1/2 inches long, finely dissected into crowded linear divisions about 1/8 inch long.

FLOWERING: March - June

APIACEAE

Lomatium lucidum Plate 176   SHINY LOMATIUM

DESCRIPTION: Perennial herb, short leafy stem, not hairy, 10 to 20 inches high. Found on slopes in Chaparral.

FLOWERS: In compound umbels on leafless stems above the leaves. Subtended by bracts; 5 petals, yellow; 5 stamens. Fruit circular in outline, notched at the ends, with thick wings.

LEAVES: Basal and alternate, consisting of 3 leaflets, each somewhat deltoid, toothed and sometimes lobed, each 5/8 to 2-1/2 inches long.

FLOWERING: January - April

Lomatium utriculatum Plate 177   HOG FENNEL

DESCRIPTION: Perennial herb, erect, leafy, purplish lower stem, 4 to 20 inches high. Found on grassy slopes.

FLOWERS: in compound umbels. Flowers subtended by bracts. 5 petals, yellow; 5 stamens. Fruit ovate to oblong, about 3/8 inch long, with broad, thin wings.

LEAVES: Alternate, finely dissected into linear segments. Leaf 1-1/4 to 6-1/2 inches long, segments 1/8 to 1 inch long.

FLOWERING: February - May

Oenanthe sarmentosa   WATER PARSLEY

DESCRIPTION: Perennial herb, succulent, lying on the ground marsh and ascending, 1-1/2 to 5 feet long. Does not have a celery odor. Found in wet shaded places. (Los Angeles River)

FLOWERS: In compound umbels in leaf axils. 5 sepals, lanceolate; 5 petals, white; 5 stamens. Fruit oblong, about 1/8 inch long, prominent ribs.

APIACEAE

LEAVES: 2-pinnate up to 1 foot long; ovate leaflets 3/8 to 2 inches long, toothed to incised.

FLOWERING: June - October

Osmorhiza brachypoda   SWEET CICELY

DESCRIPTION: Perennial herb, downy, 1 to 3 feet high. Found in Oak Woodlands. (Dead Horse Trail)

FLOWERS: In loose, compound umbels. Calyx teeth obsolete, 5 petals, white; 5 stamens. Fruit spindle-shaped, 1/2 to 3/4 inch long, with prominent bristly ribs.

LEAVES: 3 pinnate, ovate or deltoid, 3 to 10 inches long. Leaflets ovate, 3/4 to 2 inches long, saw-toothed and incised.

FLOWERING: March - May

Sanicula arguta   Plate 182   SNAKE ROOT

DESCRIPTION: Perennial herb, branching sparingly, 1/2 to 1½ feet high. Naked or few-leaved stems. Found on dry slopes in Coastal Sage Scrub and Grasslands.

FLOWERS: In compound umbels. 5 sepals, leaflike; 5 petals, yellow; 5 stamens. Fruits densely covered with hooked bristles, obovoid, about 3/16 inch long.

LEAVES: Palmately 3-5-parted, 1¼ to 4 inches long, spiny, coarsely saw-toothed. Leaves mainly basal.

FLOWERING: March - April

FIELD NOTE: *Arguta* means sharp, describing the toothed leaves.

177

APIACEAE

Sanicula bipinnata   **POISON SANICLE**

DESCRIPTION: Perennial herb, slender, erect, 4 to 24 inches high. Found in Grasslands on shaded or open slopes. Rare.

FLOWERS: In compound umbels, few and inconspicuous. Bracts 3/8 to 3/4 inch long; 5 sepals, leaf-like; 5 petals, yellow. Fruits densely covered with hooked bristles, ovoid, 1/8 inch long.

LEAVES: 1-3-pinnate, 1½ to 4 inches long. Leaflets ovate to oblong, incisely toothed. Leaves on upper part of stem reduced.

FLOWERING: April - May

Sanicula crassicaulis Plate 179   **PACIFIC SANICLE**

DESCRIPTION: Perennial herb, erect, solitary stem, branching above, 1 to 3 feet high. Found on shaded slopes in Chaparral and Oak Woodland.

FLOWERS: In compound umbels, open, subtended by leaflike bracts. 5 sepals, leaflike; 5 petals, yellow. Fruits densely covered with hooked bristles.

LEAVES: Somewhat triangular in outline, deeply palmately 3-5-lobed, each lobe incised and having spine-tipped teeth. Leaf 1¼ to 4½ inches wide, on a long stem. Upper leaves with narrower lobes.

FLOWERING: March - May

Sanicula tuberosa Plate 180   **TURKEY PEA**

DESCRIPTION: Perennial herb, simple stem or branched near base, 4 to 30 inches high. Found in Chaparral and Oak Woodland. Spicy refreshing odor.

FLOWERS: In compound umbels, scanty and irregular. 5 sepals, leaflike; 5 petals, yellow.

178

APIACEAE

Fruits densely covered with little bumps but not at all bristly.

LEAVES: Few, alternate, mostly on lower part of plant, 1¼ to 4½ inches long. Each leaf has 3 leaflets, each finely divided.

FLOWERING: March - July

Tauschia arguta   Plate 178   **SOUTHERN TAUSCHIA**

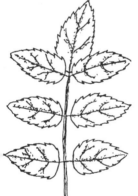

DESCRIPTION: Perennial herb, ribbed stem, 1 to 2½ feet high. Found on dry slopes in Coastal Sage Scrub and Chaparral.

FLOWERS: In compound umbels. Several bracts at the base of the flower stems. 5 sepals, evident; 5 petals, yellow. Fruits oblong, ribbed, 1/4 to 3/8 inch long.

LEAVES: Pinnately compound, mostly basal. Leaflets are ovate, sharply saw-toothed, 1¼ to 3 inches long.

FLOWERING: February - June

FIELD NOTE: *Tauschia* and *Lomatium* flowers are similar, fruits are different.

Tauschia hartwegii   **HARTWEG'S TAUSCHIA**

DESCRIPTION: Perennial herb, slightly rough to the touch, 1 to 3 feet high. Found on shaded slopes in Oak Woodland and Chaparral.   (Malibu Creek and eastward)

FLOWERS: In compound umbels. Several re-flexed leafy bracts at the base of the flower stems. 5 sepals, minute; 5 petals, yellow. Fruits nearly circular in outline, ribbed, about 1/4 inch long.

APIACEAE

LEAVES: Pinnately compound, basa1 only. Leaflets are ovate, 3/4 to 2-1/4 inches long, lobed, finely saw-toothed.

FLOWERING: March - June

FIELD NOTE: Hartweg's Tauschia reaches its southern coastal limits in disjunct Santa Monica Mountain populations.

Torilis nodosa   ***KNOTTED HEDGE-PARSLEY**

DESCRIPTION: Annual, few-branched, 7 to 12 inches high. Found in partial shade.

FLOWERS: In compound umbels on short solitary stems opposite the leaves. 5 petals, white. Fruit ovoid, with hooked spines on one side, warty on the other.

LEAVES: Pinnate compound, 2 to 8 inches long; leaflets 2-pinnate, dissected, about 3/4 inch long.

FLOWERING: April - June

Yabea microcarpa   **CALIFORNIA HEDGE-PARSLEY**

DESCRIPTION: Annual slender, erect, hairy, 4 to 16 inches high. Found in many plant communities in both shade and sun.

FLOWERS: In umbels on terminal stems and from leaf axils. 5 sepals, evident; 5 petals, white; 5 stamens. Fruit oblong 1/8 to 1-1/4 inches long, armed with several rows of hooked prickles.

LEAVES: Alternate, pinnate, compound, much dissected.

FLOWERING: April - June

APOCYNACEAE

DOGBANE FAMILY

A large family of 200 genera and 2000 species, mostly tropical. Oleander, Frangipangi, Cups of Gold, and Crape Jasmine are members. Nearly all are poisonous. 5 merous. Two genera with one species each, are found locally.

Apocynum cannabinum   INDIAN HEMP

DESCRIPTION: Perennial herb, branched above, light green, erect, 1 to 2 feet high. Found in partial shade and moist soil. (Lower Malibu Creek)

FLOWERS: In terminal cymes; small, greenish to whitish urn-shaped (or cylindrical) flowers 1/8 inch long. 5 papery calyx lobes 1/16 inch long; corolla 5-lobed; 5 stamens; 1 short stigma. The cylindrical seedpod is 5 to 8 inches long.

LEAVES: Opposite, ovate to lanceolate or oblong-lanceolate 2 to 4 inches long, with a small abrupt tip.

FLOWERING: June - August

Vinca major   *PERIWINKLE

DESCRIPTION: Perennial, evergreen vine-like plant, slightly woody. Introduced and can be found about old buildings in shaded places. Common along streams.

FLOWERS: Solitary violet or blue in the axil of leaves. Flower stems are 1 to 2 inches long. Calyx 5-parted with lobes about 1/3 inch long; corolla a 1 inch long slender tube expanding to a 5-lobed disk; 5 stamens; 1 stigma.

LEAVES: Round-ovate about 1 inch long, dark green, on a short stem.

FLOWERING: March - July

181

ASCLEPIADACEAE

MILKWEED FAMILY

Perennial herbs with milky juice. Leaves opposite or whorled. Flowers are 5-merous. Many of the milkweed flowers are unusually configured: a corolla, or crownlike cup, consisting of elements called hoods, may be above the throat of the corolla tube. Each of the 5 hoods may contain a beak-like structure. The center of the corolla contains the stamens and pistils.

Asclepias californica Plate 270 　　　　 **CALIFORNIA MILKWEED**

DESCRIPTION: Perennial herb, becumbent to ascending, 6 to 20 inches high, soft white-woolly. Found on dry slopes in chaparral.

FLOWERS: In umbels of 6-12 flowers. Calyx 5-parted, white-woolly; corolla 5-lobed, purplish, 3/8 inch long; hoods without horns on the inner surface, dark maroon, shorter than the anthers. Seedpods ovoid, covered with white down, 2 to 3 inches long.

LEAVES: Opposite, ovate to lanceolate 2 to 6 inches long. White-woolly.

FLOWERING: April - July

Asclepias eriocarpa Plate 125 　　　　 **INDIAN MILKWEED**

DESCRIPTION: Perennial herb, light green, thick leaved, woolly plant 2 feet or more high on a single, branching, main stem. Found in open, dry valleys.

FLOWERS: Many 5-lobed regular flowers on individual stems form a corymb. The main flower stem holding the head is longer than the individual flower stems. Flowers are creamy-white; hoods have a pinkish tinge and are shorter than the stamens. Each flower is about 1/3 inch across. The calyx turns back on the stem and is curved.

ASCLEPIADACEAE

LEAVES: Opposite pairs, thick, woolly; broadly oblong with blunt base and wavy edge; up to 9 inches long, on very short stem. Sometimes 3 or more leaves attached around same spot on stem.

FLOWERING: May - August

Asclepias fascicularis Plate 126   **NARROW-LEAVED MILKWEED**

DESCRIPTION: Perennial herb, erect 3-foot tall with a sparse appearance. Common in dry grassy meadows and disturbed areas, this plant is most noticed when the 3-1/2 inch long sharp pointed seedpod opens on one side and spills out hundreds of fine white hairs.

FLOWERS: Greenish-white, 5-lobed, on 1/2 inch stems rising from a single point to form an umbel. The seedpod is smooth, brown, narrow, sharp pointed and about 3-1/2 inches long. Look for the white and red spotted common Milkweed Bug (*Lygaes kalmii*).

LEAVES: Opposite, narrow, 5-inch-long leaves, in whorls of 3 or more and are not hairy.

FLOWERING: June - September

ASTERACEAE

135 species of plants in the Santa Monica Mountains belong to the sunflower family, making it the largest local family. Worldwide, 13,000 genera and 21,000 species grow in every plant community except tropical rain forests and polar regions.

In the Asteraceae family what commonly appears to be one flower is in reality many small flowers gathered together on a common receptacle. The receptacle is subtended by an involucre of many leaf-like bracts (phyllaries).

The identification of species in the Asteraceae family can be difficult. Besides the normal keying methods one must identify pappus, scales, awns, chaff, bristles, and other small structures found as parts of the flower. To make such an identification usually requires a 10-power lens and in some cases a microscope. This cannot be readily accomplished in the field. Both the Philip Munz book and the Jepson Manual have excellent keying charts that will aid in this detailed identification. The plant descriptions that are used in this book are designed for field use and for layman botanists.

However, the following information should help us name most species. A flower is necessary for identification when using this process.

We can recognize 4 distinct flower types. (Combinations of these 4 flower types gives us 5 different flower head types.) The four distinct flower types are (1) ligulate, (2) disk, (3) ray, and (4) bilabiate.

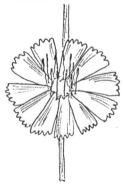

Ligulate (Latin, *ligulatus*, having a little tongue) — a flower shaped like a strap or narrow band. Ligulate flowers are bisexual and bilateral usually having a 5-lobed apex. They are always on a flower head with only other ligulate flowers. Close inspection will show that each ligule has a pistil and stamens at the base. Examples of Ligulate flower heads are found in the genera *Malacothrix, Microseris, Picris* and *Stephanomeria*.

ASTERACEAE

Disk (Latin, *discus*, a quoit) — a tubular-shaped flower not having a ligule or ray shape. Disk flowers are usually bisexual (never pistillate) with a 5-lobed corolla (sometimes 4-lobed and in the case of *Acourtia microcephala* 2-lobed on the inner lip and 3-lobed on the outer lip). Disk flowers appear on a flower head surrounded by ray flowers or on a flower head with other disk flowers only. Flower heads are designated Discoid flower heads. Examples of Discoid flower heads are found in the genera *Cirsium, Centaurea, Carduus* — all thistles — *Chaenactis,* and *Cynara.*

Ray (Latin, *radius*, the spoke of a wheel) — a flower shaped like a strap or narrow band. Ray flowers are usually pistillate or sterile (never bisexual) and bilateral often having a 3-lobed apex. They appear on a flower head surrounding central disk flowers, never alone as is the case of ligulate flowers. A flower head consisting of ray flowers surrounding disk flowers is called a Radiate flower head.

Nearly one third of the *Asteraceae* species have Radiate flower heads; most are easily recognized but some (*Achyrachaena mollis, Perityle emoryi, Pentachaeta lionii* in early bloom, and others) do not display the ray flowers and can pass as disk flowers unless observed closely. Ray flowers usually are 3-lobed at the tip.
Examples of Radiate flower heads are found in the genera *Hemizonia, Heterotheca, Grindelia,* and *Coreopsis.*

ASTERACEAE

Disciform flower heads are structurally similar to Radiate flower heads except that the ray flowers are small vestiges. This condition often makes the flower head appear as a Discoid flower head. Usually a hand lens must be used to detect the vestige of ray flowers. Disciform flower heads also can be two kinds of flowers on separate heads on the same plant or on different plants. An example of a plant having pistillate and staminate flowers in different flower heads but on the same plant is the genus *Xanthium*. An example of a plant with pistillate and staminate flower heads on different plants is the genus *Baccharis*.

Disciform flower heads give me the most identification trouble — and we have nearly 40 species locally. Look for the bisexual discoid flowers in the center of the flower head, surrounded by marginal pistillate flowers with a vestige of ray flowers (sometimes).

Bilabiate flower head. A head composed of 2-lipped disk flowers. This could be considered a special type of Discoid flower head but because of the individual flower configuration appears Radiate. Also because it is 5-lobed and is not combined with other forms it can be keyed out as Ligulate. Because it is 5-lobed (2 on one lip, 3 on the other) this book makes an exception and places the one plant in a class by itself. (Example, *Acourtia microcephala, Perezia*).

Achillea millefolium   Plate 116   **YARROW**

DESCRIPTION: Perennial herb, aromatic, cobwebby to not hairy, usually branched above, 20 to 40 inches high. Found in Riparian Woodlands and Southern Oak Woodlands. Uncommon. (Sycamore Canyon, Solstice Canyon)

FLOWERS: Radiate flower heads in a corymb-like structure, hairy, 1/4 inch high, bracts in 4 series. Ray flowers 5-6, white, 1/8 inch long. Disk flowers 25-30. Pappus none.

LEAVES: Alternate, pinnately dissected into fine segments, hairy. Lower leaves 4 to 6 inches long on long stems, upper leaves without stems.

FLOWERING: March - June

Achyrachaena mollis   Plates, 251, 452   **BLOW WIVES**

DESCRIPTION: Annual, single stem or a few branches, covered with shaggy hairs. Found in grasslands, usually clay soil. (Reagan Meadow, Malibu Creek State Park)

FLOWERS: Radiate flower heads, 5/8 to 3/4 inch high. Calyx, green, white hairs; petals white turning red. At fruit, a 1-1/2 inch globe of flat white, membranous pappus develops on maturing seedheads. Pappus is 2 whorls of 5 rays each, the outer whorl 1/2 the length of the inner whorl.

LEAVES: Opposite below, alternate above, linear, finely saw-toothed, up to 5 inches long, and 1/4 inch wide.

FLOWERING: April — May

ASTERACEAE

Acourtia microcephala Plate 321

PEREZIA

DESCRIPTION: Perennial herb with alternate leaves, stout, branching, about 3 feet high. A chaparral plant found on sunny slopes. A fire follower.

FLOWERS: Bilabiate discoid flower heads, the upper lip deeply 2-lobed, the lower broad and 3-toothed. Rose to purple or rarely white. Petals about 3/8 inch long. Flower head narrowly bell-shaped and formed of overlapping green bracts. Pappus of many rough bristles, white.

LEAVES: Alternate, 4 to 8 inches long, about 1/3 as broad, minutely hairy, finely toothed, leathery, oblong-ovate, and heart-shaped at the clasping base.

FLOWERING: June — August

Acroptilon repens

*RUSSIAN KNAPWEED

DESCRIPTION: Perennial herb, erect, open branched, woolly, cobwebby, leafy, 8 to 40 inches high. The only spines on this thistle are at the leaf tips and flower head bracts. Found in fields, pastures and along trails. Uncommon.

FLOWERS: Discoid solitary heads at the terminal of stems, forming a panicle. Heads ovate 5/8 to 3/4 inch high. Involucres thinly covered with soft hairs, bracts overlapping. Flowers many, lavender-blue to pink. Achenes 1/8 inch long, ivory-white. Pappus of many hair-like bristles to 3/8 inch long, the outer shorter and more slender, somewhat plumose.

LEAVES: Alternate. Basal leaves oblong with a wavy margin, pinnately toothed, 1-1/2 to 4 inches long. Upper leaves many, linear-

ASTERACEAE

lanceolate to oblong, smooth edged, 3/4 to 1-1/4 inches long.

FLOWERING: May — September

Ageratina adenophora   ***THOROUGHWORT**

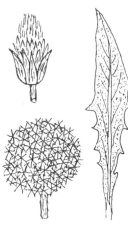

DESCRIPTION: Perennial small shrub, erect, 1-1/2 to 4 feet high. Found as an escape from cultivation in the eastern end of the mountains. (Griffith Park, Elysian Park, Lower Rustic Canyon)

FLOWERS: Discoid flower heads in dense clusters, each about 3/16 inch long, white. Involucre woolly. Disk flowers only, look like small white pincushions. Pappus of many hair-like bristles.

LEAVES: Opposite, deltoid, saw-toothed, 2 inches long, prominently 3-veined at the base.

FLOWERING: All year.

Agoseris grandiflora Plates 210, 451   **MOUNTAIN DANDELION**

DESCRIPTION: Perennial herb, from a branched root-crown, basal leaves, leafless stout flower stem, hairy, 6 to 24 inches high. Found in openings of many plant communities.

FLOWERS: A terminal ligulate flower head, 1 to 1-1/2 inches high. Exserted, yellow, 1/4 inch long. Pappus on a long beak, 50 plumose bristles, white, 1/2 inch long.

LEAVES: Basal, oblanceolate to lance-elliptic in outline, cut into narrow segments, 4 to 10 inches long.

FLOWERING: May - July

189

ASTERACEAE

Amblyopappus pusillus   COAST WEED

DESCRIPTION: Annual, aromatic, erect, leafy, branching above, sticky, yellow-green, 4 to 16 inches high. Found on sand dunes, coastal bluffs and salt-marsh borders. (Point Dume) Rare.

FLOWERS: Heads disciform or minutely radiate. Many in a compound panicle. Involucre 1/8 to 3/16 inch high. Ray flowers minute, yellow, 2-toothed. Disk flowers minute, yellow, 5-toothed. Pappus 8-12 shiny white or reddish scales.

LEAVES: Alternate except the lowest, linear, to 3/4 inch long.

FLOWERING: March - June

Ambrosia acanthicarpa   ANNUAL BUR-SAGE

DESCRIPTION: Annual, branching, sparingly bristled, 4 to 28 inches high. Found in coastal Sage Scrub, Grassland, and Southern Oak Woodlands, often in sandy creek bottoms. Common.

FLOWERING: Disciform flower heads in racemes, small, greenish or yellowish. Staminate and pistillate flowers separate but on the same plant, staminate, numerous, 1/8 inch across. Pistillate heads 1-flowered and has a rudimentary corolla. Disk flowers are staminate. Fruit has flattened straight spines. No pappus.

LEAVES: Alternate, 2-pinnate, ovate in outline, oblong segments, 3/4 to 2-1/4 inches long, on stems.

FLOWERING: August - November

ASTERACEAE

Ambrosia chamissonis   Plate 400   SILVER BEACH-BUR

DESCRIPTION: Perennial herb, matted with many stems up to 5 feet long, silvery with gray-white hairs. Found on sand dunes and sandy flats along the coast. Common.

FLOWERS: Disciform flower heads. Staminate and pistillate flowers on separate heads, but on the same plant. Staminate in dense terminal spikes about 3 inches long; pistillate flowers crowded at the base and in the upper leaf axils. Staminate heads 25-50 flowered, pistillate 1-flowered. Fruit covered with 20-30 awl-shaped spines. No pappus.

LEAVES: Alternate, ovate or oblong, 1-1/4 to 2-1/2 inches long, lobed, on stems almost as long.

FLOWERING: July - November

Ambrosia confertiflora   PERENNIAL BURWEED

DESCRIPTION: Perennial herb, erect, several stems from the base, 1 to 3 feet high. Gray-green, covered with stiff hairs pressed flat. Found in Coastal Sage Scrub.

FLOWERS: Disciform flower heads in racemes 3 inches long or less, branching at the apex. Staminate and pistillate flowers separate but on the same racemes. Pistillate 1-flowered. Fruit has broad-based hooked spines.

LEAVES: Alternate, 2-pinnate, ovate in outline, divided into oblong-linear segments, 1-1/2 to 4 inches long.

FLOWERING: May - November

191

ASTERACEAE

Ambrosia psilostachya Plate 399 **WESTERN RAGWEED**

DESCRIPTION: Perennial herb, erect, covered with short stiff hairs. 2 to 4 feet high. Aromatic. Found along roads and other disturbed areas. Common.

FLOWERS: Disciform flower heads in a raceme 12 to 25 flowered. Staminate and pistillate flowers separate but on the same plant. Pistillate 1-flowered. Involucre not spined.

LEAVES: Opposite, 1-pinnate, 1-1/2 to 5 inches long, with a short stem.

FLOWERING: July - November

Ancistrocarphus filagineus **WOOLLY FISHHOOKS**

DESCRIPTION: Annual, branching at the base, slender, grayish-white, woolly, 1 to 4 inches high. Found on dry soil in Coastal Sage Scrub and Chaparral. (Seminole Hot Springs)

FLOWERS: Disciform flower heads either solitary or in small clusters at ends of branches. Heads subtended by leafy bracts instead of a true involucre. 5-9 pistillate flowers and 3-4 staminate flowers. Each pistillate flower subtended by a woolly bract; staminate flowers subtended by a circle of 5 boat-shaped bracts with hooked tips. Pappus on some achenes, 2-5 hairlike bristles.

LEAVES: Alternate, linear to oblanceolate, 3/16 to 1/2 inch long, those surrounding the heads broader.

FLOWERING: April - May

ASTERACEAE

Anthemis cotula   Plate 114   ***MAYWEED**

DESCRIPTION: Annual, erect, branching, odorous, 4 to 20 inches high. Found in Grasslands, along trails and roadsides and open fields. Common.

FLOWERS: Radiate flower heads, terminal, each 5/8 to I inch across. Ray flowers white, 3/16 to 3/8 inch long. Disk flowers yellow. No pappus.

LEAVES: Alternate, oval in outline 3/4 to 2-1/2 inches long, pinnately dissected into fine segments.

FLOWERING: April - August

Artemisia biennis   ***BIENNIAL SAGEWORT**

DESCRIPTION: Biennial herb, erect, not woody at the base, leafy, hairless, 1 to 5 feet high. Found in moist disturbed areas. Uncommon.

FLOWERS: Discoid flower heads compact on axillary spikes. Involucre globose, 1/8 inch high. Disk flowers 15-40, minute. No Pappus.

LEAVES: Alternate, 2-pinnately parted, 2 to 6 inches long.

FLOWERING: August - October

Artemisia californica   Plate 391   **CALIFORNIA SAGEBRUSH**

DESCRIPTION: Woody shrub, freely branched, stout, light gray-green, aromatic to smell and bitter to taste, 5 to 8 feet high. Found in Coastal Sage Scrub and Chaparral.

FLOWERS: Disciform flower heads in compound racemes. Short, side branches from main branches support many nodding, globular involucres 1/8 inch high. Minute. Disk flowers 15-30. Pistillate flowers minute 6-10.

193

ASTERACEAE

LEAVES: Alternate, clustered in bunches, 3/8 to 2 inches long, 1,2,3-pinnately divided into narrow segments. Covered with minute, light gray hairs.

FLOWERING: August - December

Artemisia douglasiana Plate 393   MUGWORT

DESCRIPTION: Perennial herb, stout, sometimes branching, aromatic, 2 to 5 feet high. Found on moist soil in Riparian Woodlands, Southern Oak Woodlands, and other plant communities. Abundant near streambeds.

FLOWERS: Disciform flower heads on racemes that are axillary on main stems. Involucres bell-shaped. 1/8 inch high, woolly. Pistillate ray flowers 6-10, staminate disk flowers 10-25, both minute. No pappus.

LEAVES: Alternate, lanceolate to elliptic and smooth edged, or oblanceolate to obovate in outline and deeply lobed toward the apex. Green and usually hairless above, densely gray-woolly beneath.

FLOWERING: June - October

Artemisia dracunculus Plate 392   WILD TARRAGON,
                                                  DRAGON SAGEWORT

DESCRIPTION: Perennial herb, nearly odorless, 2 to 5 feet high. Found on dry soil in Coastal Sage Scrub and Southern Oak Woodland. (Santa Ynez Canyon)

FLOWERS: Disciform flower heads on compound panicles. Many heads, globose, 1/8 inch broad. Ray flowers 20-30, disk flowers sterile, both minute. No pappus.

194

ASTERACEAE

LEAVES: Alternate, linear, 1-1/4 to 3 inches long, usually deeply cleft.

FLOWERING: August - October

Aster subulatus
var. ligulatus

Plate 117

SLIM ASTER

DESCRIPTION: Annual, slender, erect branching, not hairy, 1 to 5 feet high. Found in wet, alkaline soil. (Point Mugu, Calleguas Creek, Franklin Canyon, near Malibu Lagoon Reservoir) Rare.

FLOWERS: Radiate flower heads in panicles. Many heads, small. Involucre 1/4 inch high, cone shaped, bracts in 3-4 series. Ray flowers, 15-40 light pink to purple. Disk flowers, many. Pappus of soft bristles, brownish-white.

LEAVES: Alternate, narrowly linear to oblanceolate, smooth edged, 2 to 4-1/2 inches long. Uppermost numerous and reduced to bracts.

FLOWERING: July - October

Baccharis brachyphylla

SHORT-LEAVED BACCHARIS

DESCRIPTION: Shrub, intricately branched, woody at base, downy throughout, branches are longitudinally grooved, 1-1/2 to 3 feet high. Found in dry, rocky, intermittent streambeds. (Malibu Creek State Park) Rare.

FLOWERS: Disciform flower heads, staminate and pistillate flowers are on separate plants. In panicles, heads loosely borne on slender stems. Pistillate heads about 3/8 inch high; the involucre about 1/4 inch, bracts in 3 rows; achenes 1/8 inch long; their pappus of many hairlike bristles, brownish-tinged, more than 1/4 inch long. Staminate heads 3/16 inch high, the involucre shorter.

195

ASTERACEAE

LEAVES: Alternate, linear, smooth-margined, without stems, rough to the touch, 3/16 to 5/8 inch long. Most leaves drop when the plant is in bloom.

FLOWERING: August - November

Baccharis douglasii   SALT MARSH BACCHARIS

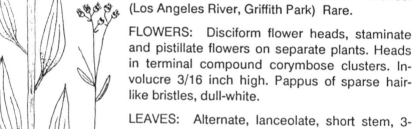

DESCRIPTION: Perennial, several stems from the base, not woody, not hairy, 3 to 6 feet high. Found in moist soil near streams and in salt marshes. (Los Angeles River, Griffith Park) Rare.

FLOWERS: Disciform flower heads, staminate and pistillate flowers on separate plants. Heads in terminal compound corymbose clusters. Involucre 3/16 inch high. Pappus of sparse hair-like bristles, dull-white.

LEAVES: Alternate, lanceolate, short stem, 3-veined, smooth edged or sometimes finely saw-toothed, 1-1/4 to 4 inches long.

FLOWERING: April - October

Baccharis pilularis Plate 134   COYOTE BRUSH

DESCRIPTION: Perennial, woody shrub, erect or rounded, much branched, 3 to 12 feet high, evergreen. Branches are longitudinally grooved. Found in Coastal Sage Scrub and Chaparral. Common.

FLOWERS: Disciform flower heads, staminate and pistillate flowers on separate plants. Many heads on small axillary and terminal cymes on leafy branchlets. Involucre 3/16 inch high, about 5 rows of bracts. Achene 1/16 inch long, 10 nerved; pappus of hair-like bristles, tawny, about 3/8 inch long. Odorous blossoms.

ASTERACEAE

LEAVES: Alternate, obovate, light green, with 5-9 coarse teeth, 5/8 to 1-1/2 inches long.

FLOWERING: August - December

Baccharis plummerae Plate 133   **PLUMMER BACCHARIS**

DESCRIPTION: Perennial herb, erect, usually not branched below the flowering area. Found in Coastal Sage Scrub, often in deep shade.

FLOWERS: Disciform flower heads, staminate and pistillate flowers on separate plants. Pistillate heads 1/4 to 5/16 inch high, about 5 rows of bracts. Pappus of many bristles, reddish-brown. Staminate heads smaller than pistillate, the pappus shorter and stouter.

LEAVES: Alternate, linear to elliptic-oblong, without stems, saw-toothed, 3-veined, 5/8 to 1-3/4 inches long. Densely covered with irregular, curly, soft hairs on the under side.

FLOWERING: August - October

Baccharis salicifolia Plate 132   **MULE FAT**

DESCRIPTION: Perennial, erect, woody shrub 6 to 12 feet high. Branches longitudinally grooved. Found along streams and in intermittent streambeds. Common.

FLOWERS: Disciform flower heads, staminate and pistillate flowers on separate plants. In terminal compound corymbs, heads are numerous on individual stems. Pistillate heads 1/4 inch high, the involucre 1/8 to 3/16 inch, bracts in 4 rows. Achenes 1/32 inch long; the pappus of hairlike bristles, whitish, 3/16 inch long. Staminate heads 3/16 inch high.

197

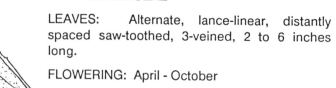

ASTERACEAE

LEAVES: Alternate, lance-linear, distantly spaced saw-toothed, 3-veined, 2 to 6 inches long.

FLOWERING: April - October

Bidens frondosa   STICKTIGHT

DESCRIPTION: Annual, erect, branching, 8 to 48 inches high, sparsely hairy. Found on damp ground in disturbed areas.

FLOWERS: Radiate or discoid flower heads. Solitary, about 3/8 inch in diameter, on irregular cymes. Composed mostly of orange disk flowers, with 1-5 small ray flowers occasionally. 8 involucre bracts; leaf-like, fringed with hairs on the margin. Achenes wedge-shaped sparsely hairy with 2 bristles at the top.

LEAVES: Opposite, on slender stems, pinnate compound, 3 or 5 lanceolate saw-toothed leaflets up to 3-1/2 inches long.

FLOWERING: August - October

Bidens laevis   BUR-MARIGOLD

DESCRIPTION: Perennial herb, erect or partially trailing, not hairy, 2 to 8 inches high. Stem is stout and smooth. Found in wet sandy places. (Los Angeles River) Rare.

ASTERACEAE

FLOWERS: Radiate flower heads, solitary, few, usually on long stems from leaf axils. Disk flowers, golden yellow; usually 8 ray flowers, golden yellow, 5/8 to 1-1/4 inches long, orange-brown tips. Achenes narrowly wedge-shaped, 4-sided, 2-4 bristles.

LEAVES: Opposite, lanceolate, saw-toothed, 2-3/4 to 6 inches long, without stems.

FLOWERING: June - October

Bidens pilosa Plates 228, 446
var. *pilosa*   *BEGGAR-TICKS

DESCRIPTION: Annual, 4-angles slender stem, branching above, 1 to 5 feet high, nearly hairless. Found along the coast and the eastern part of the mountains.

FLOWERS: Radiate or discoid flower heads, solitary, many, on irregular cymes. Composed mostly of yellow disk flowers. Ray flowers, if any, are small, yellowish white. Achenes 3/16 to 1/2 inch long, narrow, 4-angles, 2-4 bristles.

LEAVES: Opposite, on long stems, pinnate compound, 3 or 5 ovate leaflets, saw-toothed, 3/8 to 1-1/4 inches long.

FLOWERING: May - November

Brickellia californica Plate 136   BRICKELLBUSH
                                                      CALIFORNIA

DESCRIPTION: Perennial shrub, spreading from the base and branched, downy, 20 to 40 inches high. Found on dry soil in Coastal Sage Scrub and Chaparral. Common.

ASTERACEAE

FLOWERS: Discoid heads in a leafy panicle, clustered at ends of short lateral branches. Heads 1/2 inch high, 8-18 flowered. Corollas all disk flowers 5-toothed, cylindrical. Pappus of many hair-like bristles, usually white. Has a fragrant odor in the evening.

LEAVES: Alternate, deltoid-ovate, woolly both sides, edges scalloped, short-stemmed, 3/8 to 1-1/2 inches long. Upper leaves are reduced.

FLOWERING: August - October

Brickellis nevinii   Plate 137   **NEVIN'S BRICKELLBUSH**

DESCRIPTION: Perennial small shrub, branching, erect, covered with dense white wool, 1 to 2 feet high. Found on dry slopes in Coastal Sage Scrub and Chaparral. Uncommon.

FLOWERS: Discoid heads in open panicles with 1 to 3 heads at ends of short stems. Heads 5/8 inch high, about 23 flowered. Corollas all disk flowers 5-toothed, whitish to purplish. Pappus of many hair-like bristles.

LEAVES: Alternate, ovate, saw-toothed, 1/4 to 5/8 inch long, on short stems. Woolly.

FLOWERING: September - November

Carduus pycnocephalus   ***ITALIAN THISTLE**

DESCRIPTION: Annual or biennial, 1 to 6 feet tall, with prickly stems and leaves. Found along roads, in firebreaks and other disturbed areas. Uncommon.

ASTERACEAE

FLOWERS: Discoid, flower heads rose-purple, 1/2 inch diameter. All disk flowers. 2 or 3 flower heads on short stems at the ends of branches. Heads somewhat cylindrical with spine-tipped bracts covered with cobwebby wool, especially at the base. Pappus of dirty gray, hair-like bristles, 3/4 inch long.

LEAVES: Alternate, pinnately cleft into narrow lobes. Lobes and teeth spine-tipped. Leaves are green and slightly cobwebby above and white woolly beneath, 4 to 5 inches long. The bases of the leaves clasp the stem and run down, forming spiny wings. Lower leaves are 4 to 10 lobed.

FLOWERING: March - June

Centaurea melitensis Plate 229   ***YELLOW STAR-THISTLE**

DESCRIPTION: Annual, erect, openly few-branched above the base, 1 to 2-1/2 feet high. Gray-downy. Found in dry fields, along roads, trails, and other disturbed areas. Common.

FLOWERS: Discoid flower heads, solitary, 2 or 3 at ends of branching stems. Involucre ovoid, cobwebby, 3/8 inch high, the bracts tipped with branched spines not exceeding 3/8 inch long. Spines are purple or brown tinged. Disk flowers only, yellow, many. Pappus of many white, hair-like bristles, 1/8 inch long.

ASTERACEAE

LEAVES: Alternate, basal leaves pinnately cleft and with a larger terminal lobe, 2 to 4-1/2 inches long; upper leaves linear, smooth margins. All leaves without stems. The leaves extend down the main stem, wing-like.

FLOWERING: May - June

Centaurea solstitialis   ***YELLOW STAR THISTLE, BARNABY'S THISTLE**

DESCRIPTION: Annual, erect, openly branched from near the base, downy, 1 to 2-1/2 feet high. Found in dry fields, along roads and trails, and other disturbed areas. Less common than *C. melitensis*.

FLOWERS: Discoid flower heads, solitary, at the ends of branching stems. Involucre globose-ovoid, cobwebby, 1/2 to 3/4 inch high, bracts tipped with spines (the lower ones 3-pronged) 1/4 to 3/4 inch long. Disk flowers only, bright yellow. Pappus of many white, hair-like bristles 1/8 inch long.

LEAVES: Alternate. Basal leaves in a rosette, pinnately cleft and having a larger terminal lobe, 2 to 3-1/4 inches long; upper leaves linear, smooth edged, 1/4 to 1-1/4 inches long, without stems. The upper leaves extend down the main stem, wing-like.

FLOWERING: May - October

FIELD NOTE: "Morning Star" is the name of a medieval weapon of war. This was a metal ball covered with spikes and mounted on a long handle. A brush against this thistle has a lesser impact but still painful.

ASTERACEAE

Chaenactis artemisiifolia Plate 314   WHITE PINCUSHION

DESCRIPTION: Annual, stout, erect, openly branched above. Covered with mealy powder below, sticky and hairy above. Found on dry hillsides, disturbed areas, and abundant after fires in Coastal Sage Scrub and Chaparral.

FLOWERS: Discoid flower heads, solitary at the ends of stems forming a compound panicle. Heads hemispheric; involucres about 3/8 inch high, sticky and woolly. Corollas of tubular disk flowers, white or pinkish, form a domed "pincushion" when in full bloom. No pappus.

LEAVES: Alternate, broadly lanceolate in outline, 2-3-pinnately cleft into many irregular linear or oblong divisions.

FLOWERING: April - July

Chaenactis glabriuscula Plate 230   YELLOW PINCUSHION

DESCRIPTION: Annual, slender, erect, openly branched above, having occasional tufts of soft woolly hair, 4 to 16 inches high. Found on hillsides and sandy washes in Grassland, Coastal Sage Scrub, and Chaparral. Fire-follower.

FLOWERS: Discoid flower heads, solitary on the ends of upper branching stems. Involucre top-shaped, 1/4 to 3/8 inch high. The petals of the outer flowers flare into a 5-lobed corolla. Schoolbus yellow. Pappus of 4 scales.

LEAVES: Alternate, 1-2-pinnately cleft into irregular narrowly linear lobes, 1-1/4 to 3 inches long. Upper leaves becoming diminished then linear, smooth edged, less than 1/2 inch long.

FLOWERING: February - May

ASTERACEAE

Chamomilla suaveolens   Plate 398   ***PINEAPPLE WEED**

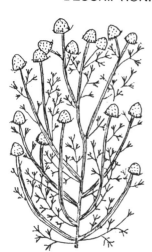

DESCRIPTION: Annual, erect, branched, aromatic, 4 to 12 inches high, leafy. Found in gardens, plowed fields and along roads or trails. Sweet-smelling. Think pineapple, then smell the flower.

FLOWERS: Discoid flower heads at the ends of branches, involucre 1/4 inch high, somewhat wider, the green bracts subtending the base of the cone-shaped receptacle. Disk flowers yellowish green. Pappus merely a crown on the achene.

LEAVES: Alternate, 3/8 to 2 inches long. Finely pinnately dissected into linear or filiform segments.

FLOWERING: May - September

Chrysanthemum coronarium   ***GARLAND CHRYSANTHEMUM**

DESCRIPTION: Annual, erect, can be either single stemmed or branched from the base, 1 to 2 feet high. Found in fields and along roads.

FLOWERS: Radiate flower heads, solitary at the ends of branches. Involucres 3/4 inch across. Ray flowers yellow, elliptic, 3/8 to 5/8 inch long; disk flowers yellow, 1/8 inch long, a slender tube with funnelform throat. No pappus.

LEAVES: Alternate, 2-pinnately cleft, obovate in outline, 1 to 2-1/2 inches long, without stems. Upper leaves slightly smaller.

FLOWERING: April - August

204

Cichorium intybus   Plate 341   ***CHICORY**

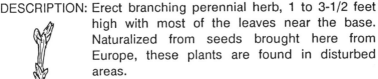

DESCRIPTION: Erect branching perennial herb, 1 to 3-1/2 feet high with most of the leaves near the base. Naturalized from seeds brought here from Europe, these plants are found in disturbed areas.

FLOWERS: Ligulate flower heads. Clusters of flat, pale blue, windmill-like flower heads attach directly to almost leafless branches. Ligulate flowers only, each tipped with 5 teeth. Heads are about 1-1/2 inches diameter. Achenes not beaked, 1/2 inch long. Pappus a minute fringed crown.

LEAVES: Lower leaves are 4 to 8 inches long, elliptic to oblanceolate, and toothed. Upper leaves are lanceolate, smaller, and clasp the branch.

FLOWERING: June - October

FIELD NOTE: Chicory came to Massachusetts from Holland in 1785. From there it spread throughout the country. Considered a common weed in most places, it is cultivated in others for the tap root which is roasted and used as a coffee additive.

Cirsium occidentale   Plate 328   **CALIFORNIA THISTLE**
   var. californicum

DESCRIPTION: Biennial herb, slender, leafy near the base and nearly bare above, branching, white-woolly, 1-1/2 to 6 feet high. Thinly cobwebby. Found throughout in Coastal Sage Scrub, Chaparral and Southern Oak Woodland. Common from Sepulveda Canyon westward. Rare along the immediate coast.

ASTERACEAE

FLOWERS: Discoid flower heads, solitary on long slender stems (1/8 inch or less diameter near head). Involucre hemispherical, woolly, cobwebby, about 1 inch high. Flowers prominently displayed above the involucre, shades of pink from lavender to white. Disk flowers only. Pappus of many white plumose bristles, 3/4 inch long.

LEAVES: Alternate, narrowly elliptic, deeply pinnately cleft, wavy margined, spine-tipped, 4 to 14 inches long.

FLOWERING: April - July

Cirsium occidentale Plate 325   **RED THISTLE,**
var. occidentale   **COBWEBBY THISTLE**

DESCRIPTION: Biennial herb, erect, leafy, woolly and cobwebby, 1 to 3 feet high. Found on sandy soil of Coastal Strand and inland to Coastal Sage Scrub and Chaparral.

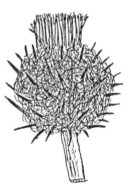

FLOWERS: Discoid flower heads, solitary on long, somewhat leafy stems. Heads 1-1/4 to 2 inches long and 2-1/2 inches broad. Stems more than 1/8 inch thick. Involucre bell-shaped to broadly hemispheric, cobwebby. Flowers purplish-red. Disk flowers only. Pappus of many white or dull plumose bristles, 1 inch long.

LEAVES: Alternate, oblanceolate-elliptic, pinnately cleft, wavy margined, toothed, spine-tipped, 4 to 12 inches long.

FLOWERING: April - July

ASTERACEAE

Cirsium vulgare   Plate 327   ***BULL THISTLE**

DESCRIPTION: Biennial herb, coarse, erect, spreading, 1-1/2 to 4 feet high. Found throughout, often in disturbed soil.

FLOWERS: Discoid flower heads, solitary, sometimes only 1 to a plant. Involucre ovoid to globose, 1-1/4 to 1-1/2 inches high. Phyllaries in many rows, turning out away from the head, spine tipped. Flowers prominent, lavender to purple. Disk flowers only. Pappus of many plumose bristles, 1 inch long.

LEAVES: Alternate, lanceolate, about 1 foot long, deeply pinnately cleft, green, bristly above, prickly, woolly underneath. Plant has a rosette of leaves, oblanceolate to elliptic, coarsely toothed. Leaves have no stems but attach and continue along the stem as long, prickly wings.

FLOWERING: June - September

Cnicus benedictus   ***BLESSED THISTLE**

DESCRIPTION: Annual, 1 to 2 feet tall, branching freely. Downy. Found in disturbed areas and valleys. Rare.

FLOWERS: Disciform flower heads. Yellow disk flowers in 1 to 1-1/2 inch tall solitary heads at the ends of branches. Leaves subtend and almost conceal the flowers. Flower head bracts are shingled. Outer bracts are tipped with a single spine, inner bracts tipped with a pinnately branched spine. Seed pappus in 2 series, brownish, the outer ring about 3/8 inch long, the inner bristles about 1/8 inch long.

LEAVES: Alternate, oblong-lanceolate in outline, 2-1/2 to 6 inches long, prominently veined,
having a wavy margin cut with spine tipped
teeth.

FLOWERING: March - June

Conyza bonariensis Plate 138   *LITTLE HORSEWEED

DESCRIPTION: Annual, erect, a simple stem often with erect
leafy branches exceeding the main axis, up to 3
feet high. Grayish-green, covered with stiff
hairs. Found on firebreaks and other disturbed
areas. Common.

FLOWERS: Disciform   flower   heads   (or
obscurely radiate) on axillary stems at the
upper end of the plant. Heads numerous. Involucre 3/16 inch high, densely hairy; pistillate
flowers 125-180, disk flowers 10-20, white.
Pappus of a few hair-like bristles, whitish or
straw-colored.

LEAVES: Alternate, lower leaves oblanceolate,
up to 4 inches long and 3/8 inch wide, on a
stem, smooth edged or saw-toothed. Upper
leaves smaller, narrower, smooth edged, without
a stem.

FLOWERING: June - August

Conyza canadensis Plate 135   HORSEWEED

DESCRIPTION: Annual, erect, simple below with many erect
branches above, leafy, 7 feet tall. Herbage
covered with stiff hairs. Found on firebreaks
and other disturbed areas. Common.

ASTERACEAE

FLOWERS: Disciform flower heads (or obscurely radiate) on side branching racemes on the upper part of the plant. Heads many. Involucre 1/8 inch high, sparsely hairy; pistillate flowers 25-40, disk flowers 7-12, white. Pappus of a few hair-like bristles, dirty white.

LEAVES: Alternate, lower leaves oblanceolate, 3/4 to 4 inches long, not over 3/8 inch wide, on a stem, most are smooth edged. Some of the lower leaves are saw-toothed. Upper leaves smaller and smooth edged.

FLOWERING: June - September

Coreopsis bigelovii   Plate 222   **ANNUAL COREOPSIS**

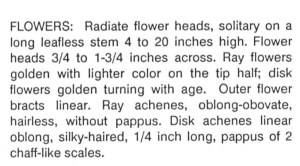

DESCRIPTION: Annual, erect, not hairy, with basal leaves and leafless flower stems, to 2 feet high. Found on dry hillsides in Coastal Sage Scrub away from the ocean. (in Malibu Creek State Park near Phantom Stagecoach Trail and Lookout Trail. Uncommon.

FLOWERS: Radiate flower heads, solitary on a long leafless stem 4 to 20 inches high. Flower heads 3/4 to 1-3/4 inches across. Ray flowers golden with lighter color on the tip half; disk flowers golden turning with age. Outer flower bracts linear. Ray achenes, oblong-obovate, hairless, without pappus. Disk achenes linear oblong, silky-haired, 1/4 inch long, pappus of 2 chaff-like scales.

LEAVES: Basal, ovate in outline, 1-2-pinnate into linear lobes.

FLOWERING: March - May

FIELD NOTE: From the Greek, koris means bedbug, because coreopsis seeds are bug-like in appearance.

Coreopsis calliopsidea   **LEAFYSTEM COREOPSIS**

DESCRIPTION: Annual, stout, erect, not hairy, 4 to 20 inches high. Found on dry soil in Grasslands and Coastal Sage Scrub. Rare.

FLOWERS: Radiate flower heads. Solitary on long stems. Flower heads 3/4 to 2-1/2 inches across (sometimes larger), golden rays and disks. Outer flower bracts ovate. Ray achenes, oval, hairless, without pappus. Disk achenes, lance-oblong, 1/4 inch long, shiny one side, silky the other, pappus of 2 yellowish chafflike scales about 3/16 inch long.

LEAVES: Basal and on lower half of stem, ovate in outline, 1-2-pinnate into linear lobes. Lower leaves 1-1/2 to 3-1/4 inches long.

FLOWERING: March - May

FIELD NOTE: Leafystem Coreopsis reaches its southern coastal limits in disjunct Santa Monica Mountain populations.

Coreopsis gigantea Plates 220, 221   **GIANT COREOPSIS**

DESCRIPTION: Perennial, stout, erect, shaggy, few-branched shrub 2 to 8 feet high, without hairs. Main trunk up to 5 inches thick. Resembles a small tree. Found along the coast in Coastal Strand and Coastal Sage Scrub. (Point Dume and west)

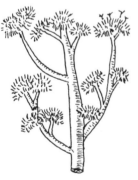

FLOWERS: Radiate flower heads showy in clusters on long leafless stems. Flowers to 3-1/4 inches across, 10-16 yellow rays, yellow disks.

LEAVES: Alternate, in dense tufts at the ends of branches. Leaves almost thread-like, 2 to 10 inches long, repeatedly pinnately divided into very narrow lobes.

ASTERACEAE

FLOWERING: February - May

FiELD NOTE: The major concentration of Giant Coreopsis is on the Channel Islands and a few limited locations along the coast. Their need for more rainfall than falls in the Santa Monica Mountains is met by fog along the immediate coast and inland along canyons such as La Jolla Valley. Moisture dripping from the plant, particularly after the rainy season has ended, adds several inches of moisture and extends the growing season.

Cotula australis   ***AUSTRALIAN BRASSBUTTON**

DESCRIPTION: Annual, slender-stemmed, branching from the base, spreading, to 8 inches high, sparsely downy, strong-scented. Found in disturbed soil, mostly in the eastern end of the mountains. Uncommon.

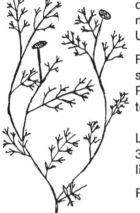

FLOWERS: Disciform flower heads, solitary on slender stems. Heads 1/8 to 3/16 inch across. Ray flowers minute, yellow. Disk flowers 4-toothed, yellow. No pappus.

LEAVES: Alternate, oblong-elliptic in outline, 3/8 to 1-1/4 inches long, pinnately divided into linear lobes.

FLOWERING: January - May

Cotula coronopifolia Plate 215   ***BRASSBUTTONS**

DESCRIPTION: Perennial herb, creeping or semi-erect, fleshy, hairless, 8 to 12 inches long. Roots from nodes. Found along streams and other wet places, and in sand near salt marshes. (Point Mugu)

ASTERACEAE

FLOWERS: Disciform flower heads, solitary on slender stems, bright yellow. Heads 3/8 inch across. No pappus.

LEAVES: alternate, linear-oblong to oblanceolate, without stems, usually deeply-toothed, 3/8 to 2-3/4 inches long.

FLOWERING: March - December

FIELD NOTE: The Greek Kotule means "small cup," and refers to the cup-like hollow at the base of the clasping leaves.

Cynara cardunculus Plate 374 ***CARDOON, WILD ARTICHOKE**

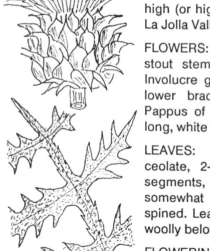

DESCRIPTION: Perennial herb, stout, thistle with a broad rosette of large basal leaves touching the ground. The thick stems and undersides of leaves covered with white wool. 1-1/2 to 3 feet high (or higher). Found in disturbed soil. (Upper La Jolla Valley)

FLOWERS: Discoid flower head, solitary on stout stems. Heads 2-3/4 to 4 inches long. Involucre globose, the bracts spine tipped, the lower bracts arch outward. Flowers purple. Pappus of many feathery bristles about 1 inch long, white to ivory.

LEAVES: Alternate, oblong or broadly oblanceolate, 2-pinnately deeply cleft into narrow segments, 1 to 2 feet long at base, and somewhat diminished above. Lobes and teeth spined. Leaves are gray-green above and white woolly below.

FLOWERING: May - July

ASTERACEAE

Dimorphotheca sinuata   ***CAPE MARIGOLD**

DESCRIPTION: Annual, loosely branched, glandular-downy. 4 to
12 inches high. Found along roads and dis-
turbed soil. (Hwy 23 near crest of mountains)
Rare.

FLOWERS: Radiate flower heads, solitary,
showy, long-stalked. Heads 1-1/2 inches across,
ray flowers orange-yellow, disk flowers yellow.
No pappus.

LEAVES: Alternate, oblong-lanceolate, toothed,
wavy margined, to 3-3/4 inches long.

FLOWERING: March - July

Eclipta prostrata   ***FALSE DAISY**

DESCRIPTION: Annual, erect or spreading, 8 to 32 inches high,
leaves in pairs all along the stem. Found in
Riparian Woodlands.

FLOWERS: Radiate flower heads, solitary on
axillary stems. Involucre hemispheric, flowers
white. Ray flowers short (1/16 inch), disk
flowers 4-toothed, greenish white. No pappus —
a thick crown on the achene is sometimes
fringed with hairs.

LEAVES: Opposite, lanceolate. Linear, or
narrow elliptic, sometimes saw-toothed, no leaf
stem, 3/4 to 4 inches long.

FLOWERING: All year

Encelia californica Plate 224   **BUSH SUNFLOWER**

DESCRIPTION: Perennial shrub, many branched, 2 to 5 feet
high. Stems covered with grayish-white, fine
hairs. Found on ocean bluffs and in Coastal
Sage Scrub and Chaparral, usually in open areas
below 1600 feet. Common.

213

ASTERACEAE

FLOWERS: Radiate flower heads, solitary, showy. The disk flowers 5/8 to 1 inch across, the ray flowers longer than the disk flowers. Disks purple with green or yellow, ray flowers deep yellow. Involucre in 2-3 rows. 3/8 to 1/2 inch high.

LEAVES: Alternate, 3-veined, lanceolate to ovate, 1-1/4 to 2-1/2 inches long, on slender stems 3/16 to 1-1/4 inches long. Leaves have a smooth edge and are wavy, green, woolly.

FLOWERING: February - June

Ericameria eriocoides   **MOCK HEATHER**

DESCRIPTION: Perennial, small shrub, leafy, branching, 1 to 2-1/2 feet high. Found on sand in Coastal Sage Scrub.

FLOWERS: Radiate flower heads in terminal clusters, yellow. Involucre top-shaped, less than 1/4 inch high, bracts tipped with a small spine. Ray flowers 2-6, slightly longer than 1/8 inch. Disk flowers 8-14. Achenes silky. Pappus of many hair-like bristles, whitish to tan. The ray flowers are difficult to detect.

LEAVES: Alternate, linear, almost tubular, many, 3/16 to 1/2 inch long. Dense clusters of smaller leaves in leaf axils.

FLOWERING: September - November

Ericameria linearifolia   **SLENDER-LEAVED GOLDENBUSH**

DESCRIPTION: Perennial, small shrub, much branched, leafy, mostly not hairy, 1-1/2 to 5 feet high. Found on dry slopes in Chaparral.

ASTERACEAE

FLOWERS: Radiate flower heads, solitary on nearly leafless stems, many, yellow. Involucre hemispheric, 3/8 to 1/2 inch high, bracts 2-3 rows. Ray flowers 13-18, 3/8 to 5/8 inch long; disk flowers many. Pappus of many hair-like bristles, white.

LEAVES: Alternate, linear, dotted with glands, 3/8 to 2 inches long, up to 1/8 inch wide, sometimes 2 or 3 in a cluster.

FLOWERING: March - May

Ericameria palmeri Plate 238   **PALMER'S GOLDENBUSH**
   var. pachylepis

DESCRIPTION: Perennial, stout small shrub, branching, leafy, 1-1/2 to 5 feet high. Found in Coastal Sage Scrub and Southern Oak Woodlands inland.(Trippet Ranch and east as well as the northwest edge of the range)

FLOWERS: Radiate flower heads in panicles, yellow. Involucre 1/4 inch high, 16-25 bracts in 4 rows. Ray flowers 1-4; disk flowers 5-10; achene densely silky. Pappus of many hair-like bristles, curved at base. The ray flowers are difficult to detect.

LEAVES: Alternate, thread-like, about 3/8 inch long.

FLOWERING: August - December

ASTERACEAE

Ericameria parishii
var. parishii

PARISH'S GOLDENBUSH

DESCRIPTION: Perennial, erect shrub, 6 to 15 feet high. Resinous, not hairy. Trunk-like stems, leafy above. Found on dry hillsides in Chaparral.

FLOWERS: Discoid flower heads in compact, terminal clusters, yellow, on short stems. Stems have scale-like bracts. Involucre about 3/16 inch high. Disk flowers only, 9-12 per head. Pappus of many fragile hair-like bristles. The ray flowers are difficult to detect.

LEAVES: Alternate, linear-oblanceolate to lance-elliptic, not toothed, 3/4 to 2-1/4 inches long, 1/8 to 3/8 inch wide, leathery.

FLOWERING: July - October

Erigeron foliosus Plate 322
var. foliosus

FLEABANE ASTER

DESCRIPTION: Perennial herb, sometimes slightly woody at the base, stout, more or less hairy, branching in upper part of plant, leafy, 16-40 inches high. Found in rock and dry rocky slopes in Coastal Sage Scrub, Chaparral, and Southern Oak Woodland.

FLOWERS: Radiate flower heads, solitary, 1/2 to 7/8 inch in diameter. Ray flowers violet-blue, disk flowers golden yellow. Pappus of 20-30 hair-like bristles, tawny.

LEAVES: Alternate, linear-filiform or narrowly linear, 1 to 2 inches long, usually 1/16 inch or less wide, sometimes oblanceolate, usually without hairs, occasionally with stiff short hairs.

FLOWERING: May - August

ASTERACEAE

Eriophyllum confertiflorum Plate 227   **GOLDEN YARROW**

DESCRIPTION: Perennial small shrub, many erect stems from the base, to 1-1/2 feet high. Found at the base of cliffs in rock and in rock crevasses. Abundant.

FLOWERS: Radiate flower heads in clusters at the ends of branches, many heads. Involucre bell-shaped, woolly, 1/8 to 1/4 inch high. Ray flowers 4-6, deep yellow, about 1/8 inch long. disk flowers yellow, tubular, 5-lobed. Pappus of several small chaffy scales on both ray and disk flowers.

LEAVES: Alternate, deeply 3-5-lobed, with narrowly linear divisions, green above, woolly below, 3/8 to 1-1/2 inches long.

FLOWERING: March - August

Euthamia occidentalis Plate 233   **WESTERN GOLDENROD**

DESCRIPTION: Perennial herb, from a rhizome, stout, branched toward the top, not hairy, 1-1/2 to 6-1/2 feet high. Found on wet meadows and stream banks in colonies of hundreds closely packed. (Upper Zuma Canyon)

FLOWERS: Radiate flower heads in small clusters at the ends of upper brackets. Involucre slightly over 1/8 inch high. Ray flowers 15-25, disk flowers 7-14, all yellow. Leaf-like bracts below the flower heads. Pappus of many hair-like bristles, white.

LEAVES: Alternate, lance-linear, without stems, 3-5 nerved, 1-1/2 to 3-1/2 inches long, 1/8 to 3/8 inch wide. Dark spots randomly spaced on the leaves. Lower leaves dry up early.

FLOWERING: August - November

217

ASTERACEAE

Filago californica Plate 85   **CALIFORNIA FILAGO**

DESCRIPTION: Annual, slender, erect, branching, leafy, up to 1 foot high. Entire plant woolly. Found in openings in Coastal Sage Scrub, Chaparral and Grassland.

FLOWERS: Disciform flower heads in small clusters, at tips of upper branches, ovoid, 1/8 inch high, subtended by densely woolly bracts. Pistillate flowers, many, in 4 to 7 series. Disk flowers 4 to 7, 4-lobed, reddish-purple.

LEAVES: Alternate, oblong-linear to spatulate, without stems, 3/8 to 3/4 inch long.

FLOWERING: March - June

Galinsoga parviflora   ***SMALL-FLOWERED GALINSOGA**
var. parviflora

DESCRIPTION: Annual, erect, slender, branching, 1/2 to 2 feet high, sparsely woolly. Long internodes, leaves paired along the stems. Found in plowed ground as an introduced weed. (Santa Monica)

FLOWERS: Radiate flower heads on small cymes from leaf axils. Ray flowers, 4 or 5, white, about 1/16 inch long. Disk flowers 8 to 50, yellow. Achenes 4-angled.

LEAVES: Opposite, ovate, 3/4 to 2 inches long, on short stems.

FLOWERING: All year

Gnaphalium bicolor Plate 83   **TWO-TONE EVERLASTING**

DESCRIPTION: Perennial herb, several stout stems, branching, leafy, 1-1/2 to 3 feet high. Pungently odorous. Found in dry open places in Coastal Sage Scrub and Chaparral. Common.

ASTERACEAE

FLOWERS: Disciform flower heads in open corymbs. Disk flowers few, 1/4 inch wide, white, on short stems. Involucre bracts white and shiny. Pappus of many hair-like bristles. Pistillate flowers in several series.

LEAVES: Alternate, lanceolate with ear-shaped appendages at the base. The 1-1/2 to 2-3/4 inch long leaves clasp the plant's stem. Leaves green on top and white woolly below.

FLOWERING: January - April

Gnaphalium californicum Plate 84   CALIFORNIA EVERLASTING
GREEN EVERLASTING

DESCRIPTION: Biennial herb, somewhat stout, erect, branching at the summit, leafy, green, sticky, smells strongly of maple sugar, 16 to 32 inches high. Found in open places throughout the area. Common.

FLOWERS: Disciform flower heads in a large terminal corymb-like cluster. Involucre 1/4 inch high, involucre bracts white. Disk flowers and pistillate flowers, white. Pappus of many hair-like bristles.

LEAVES: Alternate, oblong-lanceolate, 1-1/2 to 4 inches long. Upper leaves reduced. All leaves hairy, sticky, and green on both sides. No stems, the leaves joining the main stem and running down in narrow wings.

FLOWERING: January - July

ASTERACEAE

Gnaphalium canescens ssp. *beneolens*   FRAGRANT EVERLASTING

DESCRIPTION: Perennial herb, erect stems usually branching only near the top, white-woolly, often with a greenish-yellow cast, 1-1/2 to 3-1/2 feet high. Found in Chaparral and Coastal Sage Scrub.

FLOWERS: Disciform flower heads in small open clusters at ends of branches. Disk flowers slightly yellowish, 3/16 inch long. Pappus of many hair-like bristles that fall separately. Pistillate flowers small.

LEAVES: Alternate, lance-linear, 3/4 to 2-3/4 inches long, white-woolly both above and below. The lowest leaves are narrowly spatulate-oblong. The base of the leaves runs down the stem from point of attachment.

FLOWERING: July - November

Gnaphalium canescens Plate 81 ssp. *microcephalum*   FELT-LEAF EVERLASTING WHITE EVERLASTING

DESCRIPTION: Perennial herb, erect, branching, chalky white, woolly, 2 to 3-1/2 feet high, nearly odorless. Found in dry soil of Grasslands, Coastal Sage Scrub, Southern Oak Woodlands and open places in Chaparral.

FLOWERS: Disciform flower heads in small clusters at the ends of branches of a 3/4 to 6 inch long panicle. Involucre 1/4 inch high. Involucre bracts whitish. Disk flowers very pale green, about 35-40 in each head. Pappus of many hair-like bristles that fall separately. Pistillate flowers small.

LEAVES: Alternate, oblanceolate to spatulate, without stem, 3/4 to 2 inches long, 3/16 to 3/8 inch wide. White and wooily both sides.

FLOWERING: June - October

ASTERACEAE

Gnaphalium leucocephalum   SONORA EVERLASTING

DESCRIPTION: Perennial herb, erect, woolly, few leafy stems to 2 feet high. Found in sandy creek beds. (Calleguas Creek)

FLOWERS: Disciform flower heads of compact clusters at the end of each stem. Involucre pearly white, 1/4 inch high. Involucre bracts papery. Disk flowers yellow. Pappus of many hair-like bristles.

LEAVES: Alternate, narrow-linear gradually tapering, green above, white-woolly beneath, no stem, 3/4 to 3 inches long.

FLOWERING: August - September

Gnaphalium luteo-album   Plate 87   *WEEDY CUDWEED

DESCRIPTION: Annual, branching at the base, somewhat decumbent, leafy, densely white-woolly, lightly fragrant, 1/2 to 1-1/2 feet high. Found in moist soil near ponds and streams.

FLOWERS: Disciform flower heads in several cymose clusters. 3/16 inch high. Involucre bracts greenish or straw-colored. Disk flowers few. Pappus of a few hair-like bristles. Pistillate flowers many.

LEAVES: Alternate, linear-oblanceolate, 3/4-1-1/2 inches long, white-woolly both above and below.

FLOWERING: All year

ASTERACEAE

Gnaphalium palustre   LOWLAND CUDWEED

DESCRIPTION: Annual, usually branched at the base, gray-woolly, 4 to 11 inches high. Stems are silky. Found in wet places about vernal ponds and along streambeds from Topanga Canyon and west. (Pond at Rocky Oaks)

FLOWERS: Disciform flower heads in loose clusters usually surpassed by the subtending leaves. Involucre 1/8 inch high, densely woolly. Disk flowers whitish. Pappus of many hair-like bristles that fall separately. Pistillate flowers small.

LEAVES: Alternate, spatulate, clasping, white-woolly on both sides, up to 1-1/4 inches long, the top leaves extend above the flower heads.

FLOWERING: May - October

Gnaphalium ramosissimum   PINK EVERLASTING

DESCRIPTION: Biennial herb, slender, erect, branching above, sometimes one stem but often several, green and somewhat downy, sticky, strong pleasant odor, 1-1/2 to 4 feet high. Found in Chaparral, Coastal Sage Scrub and Coastal Strand.

FLOWERS: Disciform flower heads on panicles up to 1-1/2 feet long. Involucre top-shaped about 3/16 inch high. Involucre bracts pink, rarely white. Disk flowers few, corollas yellowish. Pappus of many hair-like bristles. Pistillate flowers small.

LEAVES: Alternate, lance linear to lanceolate, often wavy-margined, leaves 1-1/4 to 2-1/4 inches long. Green both above and beneath. Leaves have no stalk, and extend down the stem below the insertion. Sticky and downy.

FLOWERING: March - September

Gnaphalium stramineum   **COTTON-BATTING PLANT**

DESCRIPTION: Biennial herb, erect, several stems, woolly with a greenish-yellow cast, leafy, 1/2 to 2 feet high. Found on damp soil in many plant communities. (Griffith Park) Uncommon.

FLOWERS: Disciform flower heads, closely compacted in a cluster at the end of each stem. Involucre bracts are greenish-yellow. Disk flowers, yellow. Pappus of many hair-like bristles. Pistillate flowers small and many.

LEAVES: Alternate, lanceolate to narrow spatulate, 3/4 to 2 inches long, white-woolly both above and below. Upper leaves reduced. The base of the leaves run down the stem from point of attachment.

FLOWERING: June - October

Grindelia camporum Plate 225   **GUMPLANT**
var. bracteosum

DESCRIPTION: Perennial herb, erect, branching near the top, sticky, resinous, not hairy, 1-1/2 to 4 feet high. Found in open fields and meadows of Coastal Sage Scrub and Chaparral. Common.

FLOWERS: Radiate flower heads solitary at ends of stout branches. Heads strongly resinous, 1-1/4 to 2 inches across. Involucre bracts recurved, sticky. Ray flowers many, bright yellow, 3/8 to 5/8 inch long. Disk flowers many, tubular, 5-lobed, yellow. Pappus of 3 or 4 narrow chaffy scales.

LEAVES: Alternate; basal leaves oblanceolate, usually sharply toothed, up to 7 inches long; upper leaves ovate-lanceolate to linear-oblong, reduced in size.

FLOWERING: March - September

223

ASTERACEAE

Gutierrezia californica   SNAKEWEED

DESCRIPTION: Perennial, globuse small shrub, much branched, 1 to 2 feet high. Found on dry slopes in Chaparral and Grassland.

FLOWERS: Radiate flower heads solitary at the ends of branchlets in a panicle. Involucre top-shaped, 1/4 inch high, the bracts in 3 rows. Ray flowers usually 5, 1/4 to 5/16 inch long; disk flowers usually 4. Achenes hairy. Pappus of 10-12 chaffy scales.

LEAVES: Alternate, narrow-linear, 2 inches long, about 1/32 inch wide.

FLOWERING: May - October

Hazardia squarrosa Plate 236   SAWTOOTH GOLDENBUSH
  var. grindelioides

DESCRIPTION: Perennial, many-stemmed small shrub, woody at base, densely covered with small hairs, white, woolly near the flower heads, 1 to 3-1/2 feet high. Found in Coastal Sage Scrub and Chaparral. Common.

FLOWERS: Discoid flower heads, 2 or 3 clustered on spikes. Involucre top-shaped about 3/8 inch high, bracts ash-gray on both faces, in 8 to 10 rows. Disk flowers with only a vestige of ray flowers. 15-30 flowered, yellow. Pappus of many hair-like bristles, red-brown.

LEAVES: Alternate, oblong, sharply toothed, stiff, clasping at the base, woolly underneath on the midrib, upper side of leaves somewhat hairy. 5/8 to 1-1/2 inches long.

FLOWERING: July - October

ASTERACEAE

Hedypnois cretica   *HEDYPNOIS

DESCRIPTION: Annual, branching, hairy, 4 to 12 inches high. Found in disturbed areas and near streams.

FLOWERS: Ligulate flower heads on long stems. Involucre 3/8 inch high. Ligulate flowers only, yellowish with purple tip. Pappus of few 3/16 inch long bristles flattened near their base.

LEAVES: Basal leaves are often lobed, upper leaves oblanceolate, 1-1/4 to 4 inches long. Lower leaves have stems, upper leaves clasp the branch.

FLOWERING: March - May

Helenium puberulum   SNEEZEWEED

DESCRIPTION: Perennial herb, minutely downy, branching, 1 to 5 feet high. Found on damp soil in meadows and marshes. (Malibu Creek, Los Angeles River)

FLOWERS: Radiate flower heads solitary at the end of long, slender branches. Ray flowers 5-10, 1/8 to 5/16 inches long; disk flowers in globose form, 3/8 to 5/8 inch wide. Pappus of 5 or 6 chaffy scales, ovate, sharp tipped.

LEAVES: Alternate. Basal and lower stem leaves are gone before flowering. Upper leaves lance-oblong to linear, 1-1/4 to 6 inches long, 1/4 to 1-1/4 inches wide, without stems and prominently extend down the stem below the insertion.

FLOWERING: June - September

ASTERACEAE

Helianthus annuus Plate 216

**COMMON SUNFLOWER
PRAIRIE SUNFLOWER**

DESCRIPTION: Annual, stout, branching, rough with stiff hairs, 1 to 8 feet high. Found alongside trails and disturbed places. Common.

FLOWERS: Radiate flower heads, terminal on long stems. Heads large and showy, the disk flowers purplish-brown, the ray flowers yellow. Flower size varies, 2 to 6 inches across is usual.

LEAVES: Lower leaves opposite, ovate, saw-toothed, 6 inches or longer, on long stems. Upper leaves alternate, sometimes smooth margined, ovate. All leaves and stems are rough and hairy.

FLOWERING: February - October

Helianthus gracilentus Plate 217

SLENDER SUNFLOWER

DESCRIPTION: Perennial herb, shrubby, rough with stiff hairs, 3 to 6 feet high. Found along roadsides, in dry fields and openings in Chaparral.

FLOWERS: Radiate flower heads, solitary or in corymbs on long stems, showy, yellow ray flowers and a red-purple to yellow center of disk flowers.

LEAVES: Lanceolate, usually smooth margined, sometimes saw-toothed. 1-1/4 to 5 inches long, on short stems, rough and hairy.

FLOWERING: May - October

ASTERACEAE

Hemizonia fasciculata Plate 213   SLENDER TARWEED

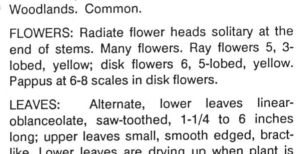

DESCRIPTION: Annual, erect, branching, sometimes hairy, 8 to 40 inches high, sharply aromatic. Found on dry ridges and slopes in openings of Coastal Sage Scrub, Chaparral, Grasslands and Southern Oak Woodlands. Common.

FLOWERS: Radiate flower heads solitary at the end of stems. Many flowers. Ray flowers 5, 3-lobed, yellow; disk flowers 6, 5-lobed, yellow. Pappus at 6-8 scales in disk flowers.

LEAVES: Alternate, lower leaves linear-oblanceolate, saw-toothed, 1-1/4 to 6 inches long; upper leaves small, smooth edged, bract-like. Lower leaves are drying up when plant is in flower.

FLOWERING: May - August

Hemizonia minthornii Plate 214   SANTA SUSANA TARWEED

DESCRIPTION: Perennial leafy small shrub 1-1/2 to 3 feet high, 3 to 10 feet wide, many (up to 500) stiff stems ascending from base. Stems and leaves rough, covered with short hairs, sticky, fragrantly resinous. Found in openings in Chaparral and exposed ridges. (Ridge near the north end of Corral Canyon Road, Calabasas Motorway, Charmlee Park) Uncommon.

FLOWERS: Radiate flower heads solitary on long stems in compound racemes. Involucre 1/4 inch high; 8 ray flowers, yellow, 1/4 inch long; 18-23 disk flowers. Pappus of 8-12 bristles in disk flowers.

LEAVES: Alternate, linear, thick.

FLOWERING: July - October

ASTERACEAE

Hemizonia pungens   COMMON SPIKEWEED

DESCRIPTION: Annual, robust, branching, leafy, hairy, 4 to 48 inches high. Leaves and stems yellowish-green. Found in valleys and Grassland. (Near the Los Angeles River) Rare.

FLOWERS: Radiate flower heads in upper axils, and terminal. Involucre usually overtopped by bracts. Ray flowers 2-lobed; disk flowers 5-lobed. No pappus.

LEAVES: Alternate. Basal leaves linear-lanceolate in outline, bipinnately divided into segments, 2 to 6 inches long. Upper leaves small, smooth edged, fringed with stiff hairs, spine-tipped.

FLOWERING: April - October

FIELD NOTE: Spikeweed reaches its southern coastal limits in disjunct Santa Monica Mountain populations.

Heterotheca grandiflora Plate 219   TELEGRAPH WEED

DESCRIPTION: Biennial herb, stout, simple stem below, branching above, densely hairy, strongly aromatic having a "camphor" odor, sticky, up to 7 feet high. Found in Coastal Sage Scrub, Chaparral, and Southern Oak Woodland, particularly on firebreaks and other disturbed areas. Common.

FLOWERS: Radiate flower heads in panicles on 1 to 2 inch stems. Involucre 5/16 inch high. Ray flowers 25-35, 1/4 to 5/16 inch long, yellow; disk flowers 50-65, yellow. Pappus in 2 rows, inner row hair-like, outer row shorter, brick red.

ASTERACEAE

LEAVES: Alternate, ovate to oblong or oblanceolate, the lower ones with a petal, and often with a pair of lobes at the base. Leaves are hairy and sticky, 3/4 to 2-3/4 inches long. Much reduced above.

FLOWERING: All twelve months of the year.

Heterotheca sessiflora
ssp. fastigiata

HAIRY GOLDEN-ASTER

DESCRIPTION: Perennial herb, usually branched, leafy, 1 to 3 feet high. Found on dry slopes and intermittent streams in Coastal Sage Scrub and Chaparral.

FLOWERS: Radiate flower heads solitary in branched clusters. More flowers than the *Heterotheca* species below. Involucres 1/4 to 3/8 inch high. Ray flowers 10-16, about 1 inch across, yellow; disk flowers 20-40, yellow. Pappus when present are short bristles.

LEAVES: Alternate, linear-oblong to elliptic, covered with silky wool, 3/8 to 1-1/4 inches long, margins irregularly curled.

FLOWERING: July - November

Heterotheca sessiliflora
ssp. sessiliflora

HAIRY GOLDEN-ASTER

DESCRIPTION: Perennial herb, few or several stems from a woody root crown, 1-1/3 to 2 feet high. Herbage hairy and somewhat sticky. Found on slopes and washes in Coastal Sage Scrub and Chaparral.

229

FLOWERS: Solitary heads in branched clusters on leafy stems. Radiate flower heads fewer than the species above. Ray flowers, 20-30, 1/4 to 3/8 inch long, yellow. Disk flowers 30-50 yellow. Achene densely covered with hairs. Pappus of slender scales.

LEAVES: Alternate, oblong or spatulate, 3/8 to 3/4 inch long.

FLOWERING: July - September

Hieracium argutum Plate 212   HAWKWEED

DESCRIPTION: Perennial herb, erect, sparsely leaved stem, leafy below in a rosette, 1 to 5-1/2 feet high. Found on rocky soil in Chaparral. (Roadcut on Castro Motorway) Rare.

FLOWERS: Ligulate flower heads on a raceme. Ligulate flowers only, yellowish, about 5/16 inch long. Involucre 1/4 to 3/8 inch long, with both light and dark stalked glands. Pappus of many hair-like bristles, whitish.

LEAVES: In a basal rosette and alternate on the stem, oblong to oblanceolate, toothed at spaced intervals. Lower leaves 3-1/4 to 6-1/2 inches wide, covered with shaggy brown hairs. Upper leaves reduced.

FLOWERING: June - August

FIELD NOTE: The Hawkweed population in the Santa Monica Moutains is a significant disjunction.

ASTERACEAE

Hypochoeris glabra   *ANNUAL CAT'S EAR

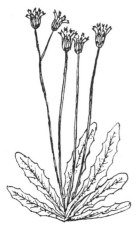

DESCRIPTION: Annual, several branching, flowering stems 4 to 16 inches tall. Leaves in a basal rosette. Not hairy. Found in meadows and disturbed areas. Common.

FLOWERS: Ligulate flower heads, yellow, 1/2 to 5/8 inch high, somewhat bell-shaped. Ligules short, barely exceeding the phyllaries. Flower stems branched with each branch supporting a flower head. Pappus feathery. Inner achenes beaked; outer achenes not beaked.

LEAVES: Spatulate-oblong, 1 to 5 inches long, mostly broadly toothed. Leaves in a basal rosette.

FLOWERING: March - June

Hypochoeris radicata   *PERENNIAL CAT'S EAR

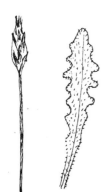

DESCRIPTION: Perennial herb with several stems, from a fleshy root. Leaves in a basal rosette. Hairy, found on ocean facing slopes and other open areas.

FLOWERS: Ligulate flower heads, yellow. Each 5-toothed. Ligules are showy in comparison with *H. glabra*. Flower stems 1-1/2 to 3 feet high. Pappus feathery. Achenes beaked.

LEAVES: Basal rosette, spatulate shaped, pinnately cleft into shallow lobes, 2-1/2 to 5-1/2 inches long. Rough with bristly hairs.

FLOWERING: May - November

ASTERACEAE

Isocoma menziesii var. sedoides

COAST GOLDENBUSH

DESCRIPTION: Perennial shrub, prostrate or with the tips ascending, not hairy, stout. Found along the immediate coast.

FLOWERS: Discoid flower heads aggregated into a very dense cluster of heads, yellow. Disk flowers only. Involucres 1/2 inch high, 3/8 inch diameter, phyllaries in 3-6 series.

LEAVES: Alternate, obovate, toothed, succulent, 3/4 to 1-1/2 inches long.

FLOWERING: April - December

Isocoma menziesii var. vernonioides   Plate 239

COAST GOLDENBUSH

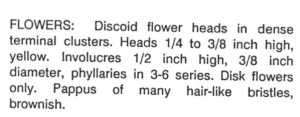

DESCRIPTION: Perennial, shrub, erect, branching from the base, leafy, 1-1/2 to 4 feet high. Found in Coastal Sage Scrub and Southern Oak Woodland.
Common.

FLOWERS: Discoid flower heads in dense terminal clusters. Heads 1/4 to 3/8 inch high, yellow. Involucres 1/2 inch high, 3/8 inch diameter, phyllaries in 3-6 series. Disk flowers only. Pappus of many hair-like bristles, brownish.

LEAVES: Alternate, linear to spatulate-oblong, toothed, tipped with small spines, 3/8 to 1-1/2 inches long. Upper leaves diminished, less likely to be toothed, and often in small clusters.

FLOWERING: April - December

ASTERACEAE

Iva axillaris
ssp. robustior

POVERTY WEED

DESCRIPTION: Perennial herb from rhizome, several stemmed, covered with rigid hairs, 8 to 24 inches high. Found in Coastal Salt Marsh.

FLOWERS: Disciform flower head solitary in leaf axils, 1/4 inch wide, greenish-white, inconspicuous. Heads in a lobed cup, nodding. The pistillate flowers around the margin, the disk flowers are sterile, have a tubular corolla and stamens.

LEAVES: Opposite below, alternate above, oblanceolate with very short stems. 3/8 to 1-1/2 inches long, thick, 3-nerved, woolly.

FLOWERING: May - September

Jaumea carnosa Plate 201

MARSH JAUMEA

DESCRIPTION: Perennial herb, fleshy, with several stems 4 to 10 inches high. Some stems lie on the ground and root at the nodes. Found along the coast in damp soil of salt marshes. (Mugu Lagoon)

FLOWERS: Radiate flower heads in terminal heads on short stems, involucre 3/8 inch or more high. Ray flowers yellow, 6 to 10, 3-toothed, 1/8 to 3/16 inch long. Disk flowers yellow. No pappus.

LEAVES: Opposite, linear-oblanceolate, fleshy, without a stem, 3/4 to 1-1/2 inches long, 1/8 to 3/16 inch long.

FLOWERING: May - October

233

ASTERACEAE

Lactuca serriola Plate 209

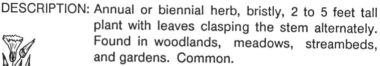

*PRICKLY LETTUCE

DESCRIPTION: Annual or biennial herb, bristly, 2 to 5 feet tall plant with leaves clasping the stem alternately. Found in woodlands, meadows, streambeds, and gardens. Common.

FLOWERS: Ligulate flower heads, yellow, each 5-toothed. Flower heads 3/8 to 1/2 inch high, clustered in short stems; bracts in about 4 rows. Pappus thread-like, white. Achenes beaked.

LEAVES: Alternate, 1-1/2 to 6-1/2 inches long, prickly along the midrib. Slightly toothed and spined.

FLOWERING: May - September

FIELD NOTE: In Latin, lacta means "milk." Break off a lettuce stem and milky fluid is seen.

Lagophylla ramosissima

HARELEAF

DESCRIPTION: Annual, branching, grayish or dull green, covered with white hairs, 8 to 40 inches high. Found on clay soil in open fields. Rare.

FLOWERS: Radiate flower heads growing along and at the ends of branches. Flowers open in the evening, close in the morning. Dense soft hairs cover the heads. Ray flowers 5, yellow, 3-lobed disk flowers 6, sterile. No pappus.

LEAVES: Alternate. Lower leaves linear-lanceolate to spatulate, 1-1/4 to 5 inches long. Upper leaves smaller, some fascicles, reduced to bracts toward the top.

FLOWERING: May

ASTERACEAE

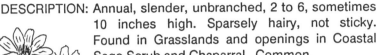

Lasthenia californica Plate 234   COAST GOLDFIELDS

DESCRIPTION: Annual, slender, unbranched, 2 to 6, sometimes 10 inches high. Sparsely hairy, not sticky. Found in Grasslands and openings in Coastal Sage Scrub and Chaparral. Common.

FLOWERS: Radiate flower heads terminal on stems 1-1/4 to 4 inches long. Involucre broadly hemispheric. Ray flowers yellow, 1/4 to 3/8 inch long. Disk flowers yellow. Pappus sometimes of 2 to 7 clear to brownish, chaffy scales; often no pappus.

LEAVES: Opposite, narrowly linear, 1 to 2-1/4 inches long, 1/32 to 1/8 inch wide.

FLOWERING: March - May

Lasthenia coronaria   SOUTHERN GOLDFIELDS

DESCRIPTION: Annual, sweet-scented, usually branched above, sometimes branching from the base, sparsely hairy, 4 to 12 inches high. Covered with short-stalked sticky glands. Found on sand in sun in Coastal Sage Scrub, Grassland and Chaparral. (Boney Mountains) Not as common as Coast Goldfields.

FLOWERS: Radiate flower heads terminal on slender stems. Involucre hemispheric. Ray flowers yellow, 3/16 to 3/8 inch long. Disk flowers yellow. Pappus sometimes of 8 to 12 chaffy scales; often no pappus.

LEAVES: Opposite, pinnately parted, narrowly linear, 3/8 to 1-1/4 inches long.

FLOWERING: March - May

Layia platyglossa   Plate 203   TIDY TIPS

DESCRIPTION: Annual, trailing on the ground to erect, stout, succulent, branched, 4 to 12 inches long. Found in Grasslands.

FLOWERS: Radiate flower heads solitary on long stems. Flower head bracts are covered by many short hairs. Ray flowers 3-lobed, yellow with white tips, 1/4 to 5/8 inch long; disk flowers 5-lobed, yellow. Pappus of 18-32 bristles, white or tawny.

LEAVES: Alternate, hairy. Basal and lower leaves are coarsely saw-toothed to projecting lobes.

FLOWERING: March - June

Lepidospartum squamatum   Plate 242   SCALE BROOM

DESCRIPTION: Perennial shrub, round-topped, many ascending branches, leafy, young growth woolly, older growth not woolly, green, 3 to 6 feet high. Found on sand and gravel along intermittent streams in Coastal Sage Scrub, Chaparral, and Southern Oak Woodlands. (A substantial stand in Sullivan Canyon at the 1225' level)

FLOWERS: Discoid flower heads on spikes, many of which are short branches from main stems. Involucre bell-shaped, 3/16 inch high. Disk flowers only, yellow. Pappus of many hair-like bristles, white.

LEAVES: Alternate, obovate, about 3/8 inch long. Upper leaves become reduced to scales. Leaves fall in late summer.

FLOWERING: August - November

ASTERACEAE

Lessingia filaginifolia Plate 323   WOOLLY ASTER
var. filaginifolia

DESCRIPTION: Perennial, small shrub, 1 to 2 feet high, erect, open, widely branching. Entire plant is white woolly when flowering. Common along trails in Coastal Sage Scrub, Oak Woodland.

FLOWERS: Radiate flower heads, terminal. Disk flowers many, yellow, tubular. Ray flowers about 25, lavender, showy, to 1/2 inch long, 3-lobed. Involucre top shaped, 5-tiered, to 3/8 inch high.

LEAVES: Alternate, oblong 1/2 to 1-1/2 inches long, 1/4 to 1/2 inch wide.

FLOWERING: June - December

Madia elegans Plate 202   COMMON MADIA

DESCRIPTION: Annual, branching above, hairy, 8 to 32 inches high. Found on slopes and meadows in Grasslands, open Chaparral and Southern Oak Woodland. (Upper Zuma Canyon)

FLOWERS: Radiate flower heads solitary on long stems, terminal and axillary. Bud of flower is hemispheric. Involucre urn-shaped, 3/8 inch long, hairy, sticky. Ray flowers 3-lobed, 8-16, 1/4 to 5/8 inch long, yellow; disk flowers 25 or more, yellow to maroon, staminate, no pappus.

LEAVES: Alternate, linear to broadly lanceolate, 3/4 inch to 7-1/2 inches. Lower leaves are often crowded, upper leaves well spaced.

FLOWERING: June - August

237

Madia exigua   **PYGMY MADIA**

DESCRIPTION: Annual, erect, hairy, branched above, 2 to 12 inches high. Aromatic. Found in dry Grassland and Southern Oak Woodland. Rare.

FLOWERS: Radiate flower heads, solitary on thread-like, widely diverging stems. Involucre flattened, 1/8 to 1/4 inch high. Ray flowers 3-lobed, 5-8, 1/32 to 1/16 inch long, inconspicuous. Disk flower 1. (sometimes 2) Fertile, no pappus.

LEAVES: Alternate, linear, covered with sharp hairs, 3/4 to 1-1/2 inches long.

FLOWERING: May - July

Madia gracilis   Plate 204   **STICKY MADIA, GUMWEED**

DESCRIPTION: Annual, erect, slender stem, sticky, sometimes branching from the middle, 4 to 40 inches high. Found in openings in Chaparral and Southern Oak Woodland from Topanga Canyon westward. Common.

FLOWERS: Radiate flower heads in racemes. Involucre globe-like, 1/4 to 3/8 inch high, covered with stout gland-tipped hairs. Ray flowers 3-lobed, 5-9, 1/8 to 5/16 inch long. Disk flowers 15-35, fertile. Pappus none.

LEAVES: Alternate, linear, without a stem, hairy, sticky, to 4 inches long.

FLOWERING: April - June

Malacothrix clevelandii Plate 211   **ANNUAL MALACOTHRIX**

DESCRIPTION: Annual, 1 to 2 feet high, spreading from branches near the base. Found in burns and disturbed areas in Coastal Sage Scrub and Chaparral.

FLOWERS: Ligulate flower heads about 1/4 inch high. Involucre bell-shaped, 1/4 inch high, 1 series of bracts. Ligulate flowers only, yellow, tipped with 5 teeth. Achenes not beaked, not flattened. Pappus of many hair-like bristles, most deciduous, 1 persistent.

LEAVES: Alternate, mostly near the base, 1-1/2 to 4 inches long, pinnately cleft into 1/8 inch wide lobes not reaching to the midrib.

FLOWERING: April - June

Malacothrix saxatilis Plate 112   **CLIFF-ASTER**

DESCRIPTION: Perennial herb, 2 to 6 feet tall, sparsely branched. Usually several stems growing at an angle from the root crown rather than erect. Found along roadcuts, cliffs, and open places in Coastal Sage Scrub and Chaparral. Abundant.

FLOWERS: Ligulate flower heads about 1/2 inch high, solitary, and not very many on each plant. Ligulate flowers only, white with a rose tint, tipped with 5 teeth. Flower head about 1-1/4 inch in diameter. Achenes not beaked, not flattened. Pappus bristles drop early, leaving a slightly toothed crown at the top of achene.

LEAVES: 1 to 4 inches long, linear-lanceolate. Lower leaves usually coarse toothed or pinnately cleft; upper leaves with smooth margins.

FLOWERING: March - September

FIELD NOTE: *Saxatilis* in Latin means "rock dwelling;" the plant often is found among rocks.

ASTERACEAE

Micropus californicus   **SLENDER COTTONWEED**

DESCRIPTION: Annual, slender, erect, gray-woolly, leafy, branched or unbranched, 2 to 14 inches high. Found in dry open places.

FLOWERS: Disciform flower heads in small, dense, axillary and terminal clusters. About 1/8 inch high and 3/16 inch wide. Involucre of about 8 bracts. Densely woolly bracts enclose each of the 5-6 pistillate flowers. Disk flowers staminate, inconspicuous. No pappus.

LEAVES: Alternate, linear-oblong, 3/16 to 5/8 inch long.

FLOWERING: April - June

Microseris douglasii   **MICROSERIS**
ssp. douglasii and tenella

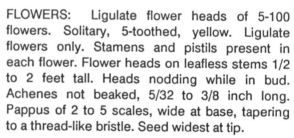

DESCRIPTION: Annual herb with basal leaves and leafless flower stems. Several slender stems, curved at the base, rise from the center of the basal rosette. Found in grassy areas throughout, in clay soil. Uncommon.

FLOWERS: Ligulate flower heads of 5-100 flowers. Solitary, 5-toothed, yellow. Ligulate flowers only. Stamens and pistils present in each flower. Flower heads on leafless stems 1/2 to 2 feet tall. Heads nodding while in bud. Achenes not beaked, 5/32 to 3/8 inch long. Pappus of 2 to 5 scales, wide at base, tapering to a thread-like bristle. Seed widest at tip.

LEAVES: Basal, 2 to 10 inches long, oblanceolate, coarsely pinnately cleft to leaves with nearly continuous margins. Leaves never hairy, but sometimes covered with bran-like scales.

FLOWERING: March - April

ASTERACEAE

FIELD NOTE: *M.d. ssp tenella* is also found locally. It is at its southern coastal limit as a disjunct population. Similar to *ssp dougasia* but seed is widest at the middle, and the pappus scales are 1/32 inch (where *ssp. douglasii* pappus scales are larger — up to 1/4 inch).

Microseris elegans   **ELEGANT MICROSERIS**

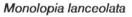

DESCRIPTION: Annual herb with basal leaves and leafless flower stems. Several slender stems curved at the base rise from the center of the basal rosette. Found in grassy flats and hillsides in clay soil. Uncommon.

FLOWERS: Ligulate flower heads of 10-100 flowers. Ligulate flowers only, 5-toothed, yellow or yellow-orange. Stamens and pistils present in each flower. Flower heads on slender leafless stems 4 to 14 inches high. Heads nodding in bud. Achenes not beaked, 1/6 to 1/8 inch long. Pappus of 5 scales, wide at the base, tapering to thread-like bristles.

LEAVES: Basal, 2 to 8 inches long, linear or narrowly oblanceolate, toothed or pinnatifid, not hairy, sometimes covered with bran-like scales.

FLOWERING: April - May

Monolopia lanceolata   **MONOLOPIA**

DESCRIPTION: Annual, white-woolly, erect, branching toward the top, 4 to 24 inches high. Found on grassy slopes and bottoms in Grassland, Chaparral and Southern Oak Woodland. Uncommon.

ASTERACEAE

FLOWERS: Radiate flower heads terminal on stems 1-1/4 to 5 inches long. Involucre bell-shaped 1/4 to 3/8 inch high. 8 involucre bracts free, distinct, densely white-woolly below, and black-woolly at the tips. Ray flowers usually 8, bright yellow, 3-toothed, 3/8 to 3/4 inch long. Disk flowers yellow. No pappus.

LEAVES: Opposite below, alternate above. Lanceolate, the lower leaves broadly so, the upper leaves narrowly so, 1-1/4 to 4 inches long. Leaf edges are smooth to toothed, sometimes wavy.

FLOWERING: March - May

Pentachaeta, lyonii Plate 232   **LYON'S PENTACHAETA**

DESCRIPTION: Annual, one stem or branching, 1/2 to 1-1/2 feet high. Found on heavy soil in Grassland and Coastal Sage Scrub. (Rocky Oaks, Westlake) Rare.

FLOWERS: Radiate flower heads solitary at the end of branching stems. Involucre hairy, 3/16 inch high. 20-45 ray flowers; 20-90 disk flowers. All flowers golden-yellow. Pappus of 10-12 fragile bristles, flared at base.

LEAVES: Alternate, linear or spatulate-linear, 3/4 to 2 inches long. Leaf margins are hairy.

FLOWERING: March - April

FIELD NOTE: Endangered

Perityle emoryi   **ROCK DAISY**

DESCRIPTION: Annual, branching, stout but brittle branches, minutely downy and sticky, 4 to 16 inches high. Found in crevices of cliffs and on rocky soil in Coastal Sage Scrub. Rare.

242

ASTERACEAE

FLOWERS: Radiate flower heads solitary on the ends of short stems. Involucre about 1/4 inch high, minutely downy and sticky. Ray flowers 10-13, white, about 3/32 inch long. Disk flowers yellow. Pappus of a crown of very small scales and 1 bristle.

LEAVES: Alternate, broadly cordate to ovate, deeply toothed to lobed, 3/4 to 4 inches long with stems as long.

FLOWERING: February - June

Picris echioides   Plate 206   ***BRISTLY OX-TONGUE**

DESCRIPTION: Biennial herb, coarse rough-bristly, branched, 1-1/2 to 4 feet high. Found in grassy fields, disturbed soil, and even in gardens. Prefers moist soil. Common.

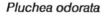

FLOWERS: Ligulate flower heads, yellow, on axillary braches 2 to 3 inches long. Involucre of 2 series of bracts: the outer leaf-like, ovate with a heart shape; the inner slender, 5/8 to 3/4 inch long and tapering to a point. Achenes beaked. Pappus of densely plumose bristles.

LEAVES: Alternate, oblong to oblanceolate, without stem, coarse toothed, 2 to 8 inches long. Short spines on the upper surface.

FLOWERING: June - December

Pluchea odorata   SALT MARSH FLEABANE

DESCRIPTION: Perennial herb, erect, branched above, covered with soft hairs, leafy, 1 to 4 feet high. Heavy-scented. Stem is stout and marked with fine longitudinal furrows. Found in alkaline wet places. (Los Angeles River) Rare.

ASTERACEAE

FLOWERS: Disciform flower heads, many in terminal corymbs. Involucres broadly bell-shaped, 3/16 inch high. Disk flowers purple. Pistillate flowers are numerous and hair-like; about 10 tubular flowers with both stamens and pistils. Pappus of many hair-like bristles.

LEAVES: Alternate, ovate to lanceolate toothed, dull green. Lower leaves on short stems, upper leaves without a stem. 1 to 4-1/2 in. long.

FLOWERING: July - November

Psilocarphus tenellus   **WOOLLY-HEADS**

DESCRIPTION: Annual, slender, branched, prostrate, woolly, 1-1/2 to 6 inches long. Found along streams and in dried mudflats. (Upper Malibu Creek, Griffith Park)

FLOWERS: Disciform flower heads, solitary, mostly at tips of stems and branches. Heads subtended by bracts rather than an involucre. Disk flowers staminate; pistillate flowers enclosed by chaff scales. Many small flowers in each head. No pappus.

LEAVES: Opposite, spatulate to oblong, 3/16 to 1/2 inch long.

FLOWERING: April - June

Rafinesquia californica Plate 113   **CALIFORNIA CHICORY**

DESCRIPTION: Annual, 1 to 5 feet tall, branching particularly toward the top. Found in recently burned areas and firebreaks in Coastal Sage Scrub and Chaparral.

244

ASTERACEAE

FLOWERS: Ligulate flower heads nearly 3/4 inch high, solitary at branch ends. Ligulate flowers only, white, tipped with 5 teeth. Achenes beaked. Pappus of 10-15 plumed bristles, dull or brownish.

LEAVES: 2 to 8 inches long, pinnately cleft into narrow lobes not reaching to the midrib. The larger leaves have stems; the others are clasping.

FLOWERING: April - July

Senecio aphanactis   **CALIFORNIA GROUNDSEL**

DESCRIPTION: Annual, slender, single stem or branched, not hairy except for the flowers, 4 to 10 inches high. Found in dry open places in Chaparral and Coastal Sage Scrub. (Northeast slope of Conejo Mountain, the ridge east of Decker Road) Rare.

FLOWERS: Radiate flower heads at the ends of axillary and terminal branches. Involucre narrow, slightly constricted above, 3/16 inch high, about 8 bracts — not black-tipped. Ray flowers few and inconspicuous; disk flowers yellow. Flower head somewhat cobwebby. Pappus of many hair-like bristles, white. Flower heads look discoid.

LEAVES: Alternate, linear to oblong in outline, pinnately cleft or coarsely toothed, 3/8 to 1-1/2 inches long, without stems.

FLOWERING: February - March

245

ASTERACEAE

Senecio breweri   Plate 244   **BREWER'S BUTTERWEED**

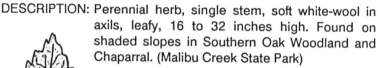

DESCRIPTION: Perennial herb, single stem, soft white-wool in axils, leafy, 16 to 32 inches high. Found on shaded slopes in Southern Oak Woodland and Chaparral. (Malibu Creek State Park)

FLOWERS: Radiate flower heads in a flat-topped cluster. Involucre about 3/8 inch high. Ray flowers about 1/2 inch long, yellow, conspicuous. Disk flowers yellow. Pappus of many hair-like bristles.

LEAVES: Alternate, spatulate to obovate in outline, pinnately cleft with pairs of lateral segments, the terminal segment large and toothed, 1-1/2 to 3 inches long, on stems.

FLOWERING: April - June

FIELD NOTE: Brewer's Butterweed reaches its southern coastal limits in disjunct Santa Monica Mountain populations.

Senecio californicus   **CALIFORNIA BUTTERWEED**

DESCRIPTION: Annual, single stem or brached from the base, mostly hairless with some soft shaggy hairs, 4 to 20 inches high. Found in dry open spaces of Coastal Strand, Coastal Sage Scrub and Chaparral.

FLOWERS: Radiate flower heads in an open corymb. Involucre 1/4 inch high, naked at the base; bracts usually black-tipped. Ray flowers 14-20, 3/8 inch long, yellow, conspicuous. Disk flowers yellow. Pappus of hair-like bristles.

LEAVES: Alternate, narrow lanceolate to oblong, occasionally toothed to cleft, 3/4 to 2-1/4 inches long, clasping.

FLOWERING: March - May

Senecio flaccidus Plate 240   **BUSH SENECIO**
var. douglasii

DESCRIPTION: Perennial shrub, branched, bushy, gray-green, leafy until blooming, 3 to 4-1/2 feet high. Woolly. Found in Coastal Sage Scrub and Chaparral. Common along roads, trails, and dry creek beds.

FLOWERS: Radiate flower heads at ends of slender branches. Involucre broadly top-shaped 3/8 inch high; about 20 narrow bracts and some shorter base bracts enclose the flowers. Ray flowers, 10-13, yellow, showy, 3/8 to 5/8 inch long. Disk flowers many, yellow. Pappus of many hair-like bristles, white.

LEAVES: Alternate, pinnately branched into narrowly linear segments. Leaf 1-1/4 to 4 in. long, segments 3/4 to 2-1/4 inches long. Small leaves often in axils of principal leaves.

FLOWERING: June - November

Senecio mikanioides Plate 241   *GERMAN IVY

DESCRIPTION: Perennial vine, climbing or covering the ground, leafy, hairless, shiny, ivy-like, 15 to 20 foot vines. Found in canyons and gullies as a naturalized plant. (Temescal Canyon)

FLOWERS: Discoid flower heads in compact clusters on axillary stems. Involucre 1/8 inch high. Disk flowers only, yellow. Pappus of many hair-like bristles.

LEAVES: Alternate, round-cordate, sharply lobe-angled, 3/8 to 3 inches long, with long stems.

FLOWERING: December - March

247

Senecio vulgaris Plate 243   *COMMON GROUNDSEL

DESCRIPTION: Annual, single stem or branched from the base, leafy, sparsely covered with minute hairs or hairless, 4 to 20 inches high. Found in disturbed places. Common.

FLOWERS: Discoid flower heads in clusters on short stems. Involucre about 1/4 inch high subtended by short bracteoles. Involucre bracts black tipped. Disk flowers only, yellow. Pappus of many hair-like bristles.

LEAVES: Alternate, lanceolate in outline, coarsely and irregularly toothed, often deeply cleft, 3/4 to 4 inches long, 3/16 to 1-3/4 inches wide. The lower leaves tapering to a stem base, the upper clasping.

FLOWERING: Spring through fall.

Silybum marianum Plate 326   *MILK THISTLE

DESCRIPTION: Biennial herb, stout, erect, branched, with large, mottled leaves, to 6 feet high. Found in pastures and other disturbed soil, often in large impenetrable masses. Invasive, crowds other vegetation. (Sycamore Canyon)

FLOWERS: Discoid flower heads on bracted stems. Involucre 1 to 2 inches across; bristly receptacle, spiny edged and tipped with a 3/8 to 3/4 inch long spine. Disk flowers only, many, red-violet. Pappus of many hair-like bristles in several rows, 3/8 to 3/4 inch long, ivory-white.

LEAVES: Alternate on the stem, basal leaves in the form of a rosette. Lower leaves are oblanceolate or elliptic, spiny-toothed or pinnately cleft and spine tipped, on stems. Wavy

ASTERACEAE

edged. Upper leaves are clasping. Leaves are up to 2-1/2 feet long, 1 foot wide; upper leaves diminished. Many yellow prickles on leaves.

FLOWERING: April - August

Solidago californica Plate 235   **CALIFORNIA GOLDENROD**

DESCRIPTION: Perennial herb, robust, erect, single stem, ashy-gray colored, dense downy stems and leaves, 8 to 48 inches high. Found on wet meadows and stream banks in colonies of plants.

FLOWERS: Radiate flower heads in a compact ovate panicle. Involucre 1/8 to 3/16 inch high. Ray flowers 8-13, disk flowers 4-12, all yellow. Pappus of many hair-like bristles, white.

LEAVES: Alternate; lower leaves spatulate to obovate or oval, saw-toothed or scalloped, 2 to 4-1/2 inches long, 3/8 to 1-3/8 inches wide; the upper leaves reduced, elliptic, smooth edged. Gray-green.

FLOWERING: August - November

Soliva sessilis   ***COMMON SOLIVA**

DESCRIPTION: Annual, branching from the base, spreading, woolly, 2 to 10 inches across. Found in Coastal Strand on bluffs above the beaches, also in lawns.

FLOWERS: Disciform flower heads attached without stems to the plant in the basal rosette and at the nodes. Involucre 1/8 inch high. Disk flowers 4 to 6, pistillate flowers 10 to 12, greenish. No pappus, but a minute apical tooth projects from the top of the achene.

ASTERACEAE

LEAVES: Alternate, orbicular to oval in outline, finely dissected into narrow oblanceolate lobes, 3/8 to 1-1/4 inches long, on longer stems.

FLOWERING: April - July

Sonchus asper Plate 205   ***PRICKLY SOW-THISTLE**

DESCRIPTION: Annual, single stem, erect, robust, leafy, mostly hairless, 3 to 8 feet high. Found in disturbed soil throughout.

FLOWERS: Ligulate flower heads on a few stems branching from the top of the plant. Involucre 3/8 to 5/8 inch high. Ligulate flowers only, yellow. Achene somewhat flattened, plainly 3-nerved on each side. Pappus of many soft, hairy bristles, white.

LEAVES: Alternate, lower leaves obovate to spatulate and on stems, the margins deeply cleft into sharp lobes, each lobe being spiny toothed. Upper leaves are clasping. Base of the leaves have ears that are rounded in outline and deeply toothed. Leaves are glossy.

FLOWERING: All year

Sonchus oleraceus Plate 207   ***SOW-THISTLE**

DESCRIPTION: Annual, single stem, erect, somewhat stout, sparingly leafy, hairless, 1-1/2 to 4 feet high. Found in disturbed soil throughout. Abundant.

FLOWERS: Ligulate flower heads on a few stems branching from the top of the plant. Involucre 3/8 to 5/8 inch high. Ligulate flowers only, yellow. Achene somewhat flattened, longitudinally striate, not beaked. Pappus of many soft hairy bristles, white.

ASTERACEAE

LEAVES: Alternate, lanceolate to oblanceolate, up to 12 inches long, variable, deeply cleft into lobes, the terminal lobe large. Edges toothed and tipped with small spines. Lower leaves on a stem; upper leaves clasping. Base of the leaf has pointed ears that extend around the main stem. Leaves are light green and not shiny.

FLOWERING: All year.

Stebbinsoseris heterocarpa Plate 450

BROWN MICROSERIS

DESCRIPTION: Annual herb with basal leaves and leafless flower stems. Several slender stems curved at the base rise from the center of the basal rosette. Found in grasslands on clay soil.

FLOWERS: Ligulate flower heads of 5-125 flowers. Ligulate flowers only, 5-toothed, yellow. Stamens and pistils present in each flower. Flower heads on leafless stems 4 to 24 inches tall. Flower head receptacle 3/8 to 1-1/4 inches high. Achenes 3/16 to 3/8 inches long, not beaked. Pappus of 5 parts, wide at the base, tapering to threadlike bristles.

LEAVES: Basal, 2 to 12 inches long, linear to narrow-elliptic. Some leaves have continuous margins; some are pinnatifid. Covered with bran-like scales.

FLOWERING: March - May

FIELD NOTE: This is a hybrid, *uropappus lindleyi X Microseris douglasii.*

ASTERACEAE

Stephanomeria cichoriacea Plate 324   TEJON MILK-ASTER

DESCRIPTION: Perennial herb, erect, 1-1/2 to 4 feet high, woody based. Milky sap. Found on rocky slopes and in canyons in open areas of Chaparral and Coastal Sage. Uncommon.

FLOWERS: Ligulate flower heads on short stems bracted along the main stems. Ligulate flowers only, 5-toothed, purplish-pink about 1-1/4 inches in diameter. Stamens and pistils present in each flower. Flower heads 1/2 to 5/8 inch high, with overlapping bracts. Achenes not beaked. Pappus of plumose bristles, dull gray, 1/2 to 5/8 inch long.

LEAVES: Alternate, oblong to oblanceolate, 2 to 8 inches long. Backwards pointed teeth at intervals along leaf edge. Some leaves do not have teeth. White-woolly when young. Leaves remain on plant through flowering time.

FLOWERING: August - October

Stephanomeria virgata Plate 115   WAND CHICORY

DESCRIPTION: Annual, stiff and erect, branching, 2 to 8 feet tall, and green stemmed. Found in burned over Chaparral, openings in Coastal Sage Scrub and disturbed areas.

FLOWERS: Ligulate flower heads. Ligulate flowers only, to pinkish above, purplish on the back, head about 3/4 to 1 inch in diameter. Stamens and pistils present in each flower. Flower heads about 1/4 inch high, directly attached to the plant. Achenes not beaked. Pappus of many plumose bristles, white, 3/16 inch long.

ASTERACEAE

LEAVES: Alternate. Lower leaves oblong, 4 to 8 inches long, with a wavy margin. Upper leaves smaller, linear, with a continuous margin with no indentations or teeth. Leaves wither before the flowering season. Basal rosette.

FLOWERING: July - September

Stylocline gnaphalioides   **EVERLASTING NEST-STRAW**

DESCRIPTION: Annual, branching from the base, gray-woolly, 2 to 6 inches high. Found on dry soil in Coastal Sage Scrub and Chaparral. (West of Triunfo Pass at 2100 ft. elevation)

FLOWERS: Disciform flower heads clustered at the tips of stems and branches, dry and thin, not green. Involucre of about 5 thin bracts with sparse woolly green center. Disk flowers 2 to 6, staminate; pistillate flowers tubular in several series. Each flower subtended by a woolly bract. Staminate flowers have pappus of few bristles; Pistillate flowers have no pappus.

LEAVES: Alternate, narrowly oblong to spatulate-linear, 3/16 to 1/2 inch long.

FLOWERING: March - May

Taraxacum officionale Plate 208   ***DANDELION**

DESCRIPTION: Perennial herb having a rosette of leaves at the base and single flower stems. This is the dandelion found in lawns, gardens, and other damp cultivated areas.

FLOWERS: Ligulate flower head yellow, each flower toothed. flower heads 1 to 2 inches in diameter, solitary on leafless hollow stems. Outer bracts bend outward and back; the inner bracts a single row, erect. Achenes beaked. Pappus of many hair-like bristles, white.

ASTERACEAE

LEAVES: In a basal tuft, spatulate-oblong, 2 to 12 inches long; some leaves pinnately cleft into narrow lobes not reaching the mid-vein; others with almost smooth edges.

FLOWERING: January - December

Tragopogon porrifolius Plate 273   ***OYSTER PLANT, SALSIFY**

DESCRIPTION: Biennial or perennial herb growing 2 to 4 feet high. Very leafy low on the stem. Milky sap. Found in grassy areas, meadows and fields.

FLOWERS: Ligulate flower heads on axillary stems, about 90 purple ligulate flowers in each head. Flowers have 5 points at the terminal end. Flower head bracts about 2 inches long in 1 series, lanceolate, longer than the flowers. Flower head stem swollen and hollow. Upon going to seed, flower heads become round, brown balls of plumed achenes. Achenes beaked, 1-1/4 to 1-3/8 inches long (including the beak). Pappus of plumose bristles, brown.

LEAVES: Alternate, linear-lanceolate to 1 foot long, clasping the stem. Nearly succulent.

FLOWERING: April - July

Uropappus lindleyi Plate 449   **SILVER PUFFS**

DESCRIPTION: Annual herb with basal leaves and leafless flower stems. Several slender stems rising from a short leafy stem. Found in grassy areas on clay soil.

ASTERACEAE

FLOWERS: Ligulate flower heads of 5-150 flowers. Ligulate flowers only, 5-toothed, yellow. Stamens and pistils present in each flower. Heads always erect, terminal, on 4 to 24 inch stems. Flower head receptacle 1/2 to 1-1/4 inches high. Pappus of 5 narrow scales tapering to thread-like bristles. Achenes not beaked.

LEAVES: Basal, and a few alternate on a short main stem, 1-1/4 to 10 inches long, linear to narrow-elliptic, often reddish. Some leaves have continuous margins, some pinnatifid, and some with teeth bent backward.

FLOWERING: March - June

Venegazia carpesioides Plates 218, 223

CANYON
SUNFLOWER

DESCRIPTION: Perennial small shrub, widely branched, leafy, coarse, from a woody base. 3 to 7-1/2 feet high, not hairy. Found in shade on slopes, rocky canyon walls, and stream banks in Southern Oak Woodland, Coastal Sage Scrub and Chaparral. Common.

FLOWERS: Radiate flower heads, solitary on stems that are terminal or from upper leaf axils. Involucre hemispheric. Ray flowers 13-21, yellow, 5/8 to 3/4 inch long. Disk flowers many, yellow. No pappus.

LEAVES: Alternate, deltoid-ovate, edges almost smooth to toothed and wavy, gland-dotted underneath, 2 to 6 inches long, on stems 1-1/4 to 2 inches long.

FLOWERING: February - September

ASTERACEAE

Verbesina encelioides
var. *exauciculata*

*GOLDEN CROWNBEARD

DESCRIPTION: Annual, erect, much-branched, 1 to 4 feet high. Stems covered with grayish-white, fine hairs. Found in fields and Grassland.

FLOWERS: Radiate flower heads, solitary, showy, 1 to 1-3/4 inches wide. Disk flowers yellow turning dark with age. 10-12 golden-yellow ray flowers, 3 lobed, 3/8 to 5/8 inch long. Achenes broadly 2-winged. Involucre in 2 rows, 1/4 to 1/2 inch high, 3/8 to 5/8 inch wide. Pappus of 2 short bristles.

LEAVES: Alternate, on slender stems, narrowly lanceolate to deltoid-ovate, 3-veined from base, 1-1/2 to 4 inches long, conspicuously saw-toothed, covered with stiff, white hairs lying flat. Upper surface greener than lower. Lowest leaves are opposite.

FLOWERING: May - December

Xanthium spinosum Plate 454

SPINY COCKLEBUR

DESCRIPTION: Annual, erect, branching, 1 to 4 feet high, spiny in leaf axils. Found near habitations, along stream banks, and cultivated areas.

FLOWERS: Disciform flower heads in terminal and axillary clusters. Pistillate and staminate flowers are in different flower heads, both types of heads are found on the same plant. Staminate heads above, rust colored and downy; the pistillate heads below. The involucre of the pistillate heads encloses 2 flowers, becoming a hardened burr covered with hooked prickles. Burr is elliptic, about 3/8 inch long. No pappus.

ASTERACEAE

LEAVES: Alternate, lanceolate, few-toothed or lobed, 1-1/4 to 3 inches long, small stiff hairs on top or hairless, woolly below. Leaf axils armed with yellow 3-forked spines, 1-1/4 inch long or less.

FLOWERING: July - October

Xanthium strumarium   COCKLEBUR
   var. canadense and var. glabratum

DESCRIPTION: Coarse, vigorous, 4 foot annual often found in grassy areas near dry - or wet streambeds or other moist, fertile soil. Usually noticed because of the burr-like seedpod.

FLOWERS: Disciform flower heads. Pistillate and staminate flowers are in different flower heads, both types of heads are found on the same plant. Pistillate heads are clustered below staminate heads. Seedpods: Burr 3/4 to 1-1/2 inches long with many stout prickles. Two incurved hooks at the end of the burr. No pappus. *var. glabratum* differs mainly in the burrs: mostly less than 3/4 inch long and without bristly hairs.

LEAVES: Alternate, deltoid or heart-shaped, 4 inches long, green on both sides. Irregularly toothed and often 3-lobed, the leaves are thick and sandpapery. Leaf stems are about the same length as the leaves.

FLOWERING: July - October

FIELD NOTE: *Xanthium* is Greek for "yellow" — a color in hair dye made from the plant.

BATIDACEAE

SALTWORT FAMILY

This family species of 1 is found in tropical and subtropical areas of the Western Hemisphere and the Hawaiian Islands. On the Pacific Coast it is found from Point Mugu south, on the Atlantic Coast from North Carolina south, in the Caribbean and down the coast of South America to Brazil.

Recognition characteristics: An indicator plant in Coastal Salt Marsh, adapted to grow in a salt water environment. Opposite fleshy leaves. Pistillate and staminate flowers are on separate plants. Flowers in axillary, sessile, catkin-like spikes. Flower has no petals and only the staminate flower has sepals.

Batis maritima   SALTWORT

DESCRIPTION: Sprawling perennial, herb, woody at base only, strong scented. Found in the Coastal Strand Community at salt marshes. (Mugu Lagoon)

FLOWERS: In catkin-like spikes. Staminate and pistillate flowers are on separate plants. Staminate flower spikes sessile, about 3/8 inch long and look like a cone with overlapping bracts which hide the spikes; 8 stamens (4 are sterile) extend beyond the bracts. Pistillate flower spikes about 3/8 inch long, on short stems and in a bracted catkin. No calyx or corolla; the end of the pistil and stigma protrude beyond the bracts.

LEAVES: Opposite, fleshy, linear-oblanceolate, almost cylindrical, about 1/2 to 3/4 inch long.

FLOWERING: April - October

BERBERIDACEAE

BARBERRY FAMILY

A rather large family of 9 genera and 590 species, only 1 of which is found in the Santa Monica Mountains, and then only rarely.

BERBERIDACEAE

Berberis pinnata Plate 412   **CALIFORNIA BARBERRY**

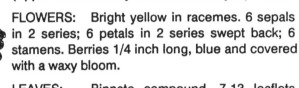

DESCRIPTION: This small evergreen shrub is easily identified by its glossy green prickly leaves. Found in shade of trees, not necessarily in canyons. (Upper Carlisle Canyon, Newton Canyon) Rare.

FLOWERS: Bright yellow in racemes. 6 sepals in 2 series; 6 petals in 2 series swept back; 6 stamens. Berries 1/4 inch long, blue and covered with a waxy bloom.

LEAVES: Pinnate compound. 7-13 leaflets crowded, overlap along leaf stem. Each leaflet is spiny, glossy and 1 to 2 inches long.

FLOWERING: March - May

BETULACEAE
BIRCH FAMILY

Deciduous trees and shrubs. Birch, beech, alder, ironwood, and hazelnut trees are all members of this family of about 150 species. White Alder is the only local member.

Alnus rhombifolia Plate 466   **WHITE ALDER**

DESCRIPTION: The only member of the Alder family found in the Santa Monicas, can grow to 90 feet tall but usually found as a thicket of small trees along a permanent stream. (Upper Zuma Canyon, Topanga Canyon)

FLOWERS: Catkins appear in the fall and flower in early spring before the new leaves appear. Male catkins are scalelike and pendulous; female catkins are spikelike and develop into woody cones about 5/8 inch long.

LEAVES: Alternate, small — not more than 4 inches long — ovate, prominently veined, and single toothed along the margin. They drop late in the fall while still green.

BETULACEAE

The straight leaf veins are characteristic, and from the midvein the veins run to the leaf margin. Pith chamber of twigs is distinctly triangular.

FLOWERING: January - March

BORAGINACEAE

BORAGE FAMILY, FORGET-ME-NOT FAMILY

This family of 100 genera and 2000 species is found in tropical and temperate zones. 5 genera and 13 species are found locally, all native to the Santa Monica Mountains.

Recognition characteristics: Alternate leaves, round stems, coiled racemes, 5-merous flowers, radially symmetrical, corolla a narrow tube abruptly flared at the top, 4-lobed superior ovary. Herbal plant covered with stiff hairs, except Heliotropium. The 4 nutlets or achenes must be present in order to key out.

Amsinckia menziesii   Plate 188   **SMALL-FLOWERED FIDDLENECK**

DESCRIPTION: Annual, erect, ascending branches above, 4 to 24 inches high. Bristly. Found on grassy hillsides. Not as common as Fiddleneck.

FLOWERS: In coiled racemes 2 to 6 inches long; corolla tubular, pale yellow, 1/4 inch long. 4 nutlets without spines, triangular-ovoid to ovoid, slightly mealy, bumpy.

LEAVES: Alternate, hairy on both sides, 1¼ to 4½ inches long; lower leaves linear, on long stems; upper leaves lanceolate.

FLOWERING: April - June

260

BORAGINACEAE

Amsinckia menziesii Plate 189   **COMMON FIDDLENECK**
Var. intermedia

DESCRIPTION: Annual, erect, slender, sometimes widely branched, 8 to 32 inches high. Sparsely bristled. Found on grassy hillsides and on burned areas. Common.

FLOWERS: In coiled racemes 2 to 8 inches long. Leafy bracts subtending golden yellow flowers. 5 sepals attached at the base; corolla tubular, 5-lobed, 3/8 inch long. 4 nutlets without spines, triangular ovoid to ovoid, bumpy, about 1/8 inch long.

LEAVES: Alternate, linear to linear-lanceolate, usually clasping at the base, sparsely hairy both sides, 3/4 to 6 inches long.

FLOWERING: February - May

Cryptantha clevelandii   **WHITE FORGET-ME-NOT**

DESCRIPTION: Annual, branched, erect or sometimes trailing, 4 to 20 inches long, hairy. Found in Coastal Sage Scrub and Chaparral.

FLOWERS: In slender spikes, bractless, 1½ to 4 inches long; 5 sepals attached at the base, hairy; corolla tubular, 5-lobed, white, tiny. 1 to 4 nutlets without spines, smooth, shiny, oblong-ovoid to broadly lanceolate.

LEAVES: Alternate, many at base, lance-linear to linear, 3/8 to 2 inches long, hairy. Bristly along margins. Sparse above.

FLOWERING: April - June

BORAGINACEAE

Cryptantha intermedia Plate 127

**POPCORN FLOWER
LARGE-FLOWERED**

DESCRIPTION: Annual, erect, stiff, branched, 6 to 20 inches high. Found in Coastal Sage Scrub and Chaparral. Fire follower. Common.

FLOWERS: In bractless spikes 2, 3 or more from a node. Spikes 2 to 6 inches long; 5 sepals attached at the base, about 3/16 inch long, hairy; corolla tubular, 5-lobed, white, 1/8 to 1/4 inch broad. Usually 4 nutlets, without spines, bumpy, lance-ovoid much shorter than the calyx.

LEAVES: Alternate, lanceolate to linear, hairy, 5/8 to 2 inches long.

FLOWERING: March - July

Cryptantha micromeres Plate 128

**POPCORN FLOWER
MINUTE-FLOWERED**

DESCRIPTION: Annual, slender, branching from the base, erect, dull green, 4 to 20 inches high, covered with short hairs. Found in open places in Chaparral and on burned over slopes.

FLOWERS: In bractless spikes, usually 3 from a node, slender, 3/4 to 3 inches long; 5 sepals attached at the base, 1/16 inch long; corolla 5-lobed, white, about 1/32 inch broad. 4 nutlets without spines, bumpy, triangular-ovoid, 1/32 inch long.

LEAVES: Alternate, linear or oblong-linear, 3/8 to 1½ inch long, covered with short bristly hairs.

FLOWERING: March - June

262

BORAGINACEAE

Cryptantha microstachys

**POPCORN FLOWER
TEJON CRYPTANTHA**

DESCRIPTION: Annual, erect, slender-branched from the base and above, hairy, 3 to 12 inches high. Found in openings in Chaparral.

FLOWERS: In spikes, 2 or 3 from a node, very slender, 1 to 3 inches long; 5 sepals attached at the base, 1/16 inch long; corolla 5-lobed, white, 1/32 inch broad. 1 nutlet without spines, smooth and polished, lanceolate, 1/16 inch long.

LEAVES: Alternate, linear to linear-lanceolate, hairy, 3/8 to 1½ inches long. Sparsely bristled along margins.

FLOWERING: April - June

Cryptantha muricata

PRICKLY POPCORN FLOWER

DESCRIPTION: Annual, erect, stout, hairy, branching, 4 to 32 inches high. Found on rocky open slopes.

FLOWERS: In spikes at the terminals of main branches in 2, 3, or 4 from a node, 1½ to 4 inches long; 5 sepals attached at the base, 1/8 inch long; corolla tubular, 5-lobed, 1/8 to 1/4 inch broad. 4 nutlets without spines, bumpy, ovoid-triangular.

LEAVES: Alternate, linear, 5/8 to 1¼ inches long. Covered with short, gray bristles.

FLOWERING: March - June

Heliotropium curassavicum Plate 131
   var. oculatum

WILD HELIOTROPE

DESCRIPTION: Perennial herb, fleshy, not hairy, branching, trailing, 4 to 24 inches long. Found in marshes, streambeds, and alkali flats in Coastal Wetlands (Point Mugu) and inland on both wet and dry soil.

BORAGINACEAE

FLOWERS: In coiled spikes mostly in pairs, 2¼ to 4½ inches long; 5 sepals fused at the base, 1/8 inch long; corolla white with yellow at the throat, usually becoming purple about the center, 1/8 to 1/4 inch broad. Fruit rounded, not hairy, 4 nutlets.

LEAVES: Alternate, succulent, oblanceolate to spatulate, 3/8 to 1½ inches long, on short stems.

FLOWERING: March - October

Pectocarya linearis
ssp. ferocula

SLENDER PECTOCARYA

DESCRIPTION: Annual, low spreading, slender stems, about 5 inches high, covered with small, stiff, grayish-white hairs. Found on grassy slopes in Coastal Sage Scrub and Chaparral. (Boney Mountain, Triunfo Pass)

FLOWERS: On sparsely leaved spikes; 5 sepals united, hairy, 1/16 inch long; corolla, 5-lobed, tubular, white. 4 nutlets widely spreading with prominent spines, margin toothed.

LEAVES: Alternate, filiform-linear to oblance-linear, 3/8 to 1½ inches long, covered with stiff hairs. Basal leaves many and large, diminishing in size higher on the plant.

FLOWERING: March - May

Pectocarya penicillata

WINGED PECTOCARYA

DESCRIPTION: Annual, spreading, slender, branching stems 2 to 8 inches long, covered with small stiff grayish-white hairs. (Vermont Canyon, Griffith Park)

FLOWERS: On sparsely leaved spikes; 5 sepals united, hairy, 1/16 inch long; corolla 5-lobed, tubular, 1/16 inch long. 4 nutlets widely spreading, prominent hooked spines at apex.

264

BORAGINACEAE

LEAVES: Alternate, linear to narrow-spatulate, 3/8 to 1-1/4 inches long.

FLOWERING: February - June

Plagiobothrys acanthocarpus   ADOBE POPCORN FLOWER

DESCRIPTION: Annual, slender-stemmed, branching, covered with stiff hairs, 4 to 16 inch long stems. Found on moist clay flats in Chaparral and Grasslands. (Upper Zuma Canyon) Rare.

FLOWERS: In loose racemes, bracted, on short stems; 5 sepals dull brownish-yellow, 1/8 to 1/4 inch long; corolla 5-lobed, less than 1/8 inch across, white. 4 nutlets with spines, ovoid wrinkled.

LEAVES: Opposite, linear to oblanceolate, 3/4 to 2¼ inches long.

FLOWERING: March - May

Plagiobothrys canescens   VALLEY POPCORN FLOWER

DESCRIPTION: Annual, branching from the base, usually trailing on the ground, 4 to 24 inches long, with shaggy hairs. Purple dye showing on roots, stems and other parts. (Malibu Creek and east) Rare.

FLOWERS: In a raceme, loosely flowered, subtended by leafy bracts; 5 sepals, 1/4 inch long, densely hairy, united at midpoint; corolla tubular, 3/16 inch across, white. 4 nutlets without spines, ovoid abruptly narrowed to a pointed apex.

LEAVES: Alternate, mostly basal in a rosette, linear-oblanceolate, 5/8 to 2 inches long. Upper leaves few, smaller and linear.

FLOWERING: March - May

265

BORAGINACEAE

Plagiobothrys nothofulvus   Plate 129   POPCORN FLOWER

DESCRIPTION: Annual, slender, erect, hairy, with most leaves at base, 8 to 20 inches high. Purple dye noticeable on roots, stems, leaf midrib and margins, and stipules. Found on grassy hillsides. (Eastern part of mountains)

FLOWERS: In a raceme, loosely flowered; 5 sepals; narrow brownish-hairy lobes; corolla 5-lobed, tubular, 1/4 inch wide, white. 1 to 4 nutlets without spines, ovoid abruptly constricted to a pointed apex.

LEAVES: Alternate, mostly basal in a rosette, oblanceolate, 1¼ to 4 inches long, sparsely hairy. Upper leaves are few, smaller, and lance-linear.

FLOWERING: March - May

BRASSICACEAE
MUSTARD FAMILY

These plants are widely distributed in the Santa Monicas, and with 26 genera and 43 species, the family is well represented. About 40% of the species are introduced.

Flowers are bisexual with 4 sepals, 4 petals, 6 stamens (4 long, 2 short), and 2 united pistils.

Arabis glabra   Plate 106   TOWER MUSTARD

DESCRIPTION: Biennial or perennial herb, erect without branching, 1½ to 4 feet high. Found in Grassland and Southern Oak Woodlands.

FLOWERS: On a long, straight, erect raceme; 4 oblong, yellowish sepals; 4 narrow, yellow-white (or sometimes purplish) petals; 6 stamens. Seedpods slender, erect, 1½ to 4 inches long.

BRASSICACEAE

LEAVES: Alternate, oblanceolate to ovate, 3½ to 6 inches long, 1/5 as wide. Lower leaves on stems form a rosette; upper leaves sessile and with earlike lobes.

FLOWERING: March - July

Arabis sparsiflora var. californica

ELEGANT ROCK ROSE

DESCRIPTION: Perennial herb, 1 to 3 feet high. Often branched at the woody base. Hairy stems and leaves. Grows in openings in Chaparral. Rare.

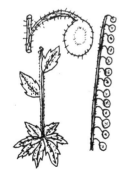

FLOWERS: In racemes, bractless; 4 sepals; 4 pink to purple petals, each about 1/2 inch long; 6 stamens. Seedpods 2½ to 5 inches long, arching downward.

LEAVES: Alternate. Lower leaves do not form a rosette, grow to 4 inches long, 1/10 as wide, linear-oblanceolate on stems; upper leaves linear-oblong 1/4 to 3/4 inches long, sessile, with earlike wings at the base.

FLOWERING: February - April

Athysanus pusillus

DWARF ATHYSANUS

DESCRIPTION: Annual, branched from near the base, 4 to 12 inches high. Inconspicuous, in meadows and brushy areas of most plant communities. Rare.

FLOWERS: Minute in a raceme where all flowers are on one side of the stem. 4 sepals, 4 petals, 6 stamens. Flat, small seedpod.

LEAVES: Alternate, ovate-oblong, up to 3/4 inch long. All near the base.

FLOWERING; March - June

BRASSICACEAE

Barbarea orthoceras Plate 162   **WINTER CRESS**

DESCRIPTION: Biennial or perennial herb, stout stems, 8 to 16 inches tall. Basal rosette overwinters. Found in meadows and along stream banks.

FLOWERS: In racemes; 4 sepals yellow-green, 4 petals pale yellow, 6 stamens.

LEAVES: Alternate. Basal leaves 1 to 4 inches long, on stems, elliptic to circular. Upper leaves cleft into narrow lobes not reaching the midrib.

FLOWERING: May - September

Brassica nigra Plate 168   ***BLACK MUSTARD**

DESCRIPTION: Annual, erect, branching above, 2 to 8 feet tall. Grows in meadows, disturbed areas, and along trails and roads.

FLOWERS: 4 sepals, 4 bright yellow petals, 6 stamens.

LEAVES: Alternate. Lower leaves 4 to 8 inches long, deeply cleft. Upper leaves smaller, on shorter stems, and not clasping.

FLOWERING: February - July

Brassica rapa   ***FIELD MUSTARD**

DESCRIPTION: Annual, erect, 1 to 4 feet tall. Grows in disturbed areas, in meadows, and along trails and roads.

FLOWERS: 4 yellowish, narrow-oblong sepals, 4 yellow spatulate petals, 6 stamens.

LEAVES: Alternate. Lower leaves 4 to 8 inches long, lobed to an extent, and on stems. Upper leaves clasping, with earlike lobes.

FLOWERING: January - December

FIELD NOTE: The Latin name for cabbage is brassica. Cabbage, broccoli, cauliflower and other food plants belong to this genus.

BRASSICACEAE

Cakile maritima Plate 108   ***SEA ROCKET**

DESCRIPTION: Annual succulent, branching from the base, and trailing on the ground, but not rooting. Grows in beach sand. (Point Mugu State Park)

FLOWERS: 4 sepals, 4 petals 3/8 inch long, pink to whitish; 6 stamens. Seedpods 4-sided; 1/4 inch diameter and 3/4 inch long. The pods break transversely so that some seeds will be dispersed away from the plant and others stay in the plant's vicinity.

LEAVES: Alternate, 1½ to 3 inches long, deeply cleft into oblong lobes.

FLOWERING: March - November

Capsella bursa-pastoris Plate 109   ***SHEPHERD'S PURSE**

DESCRIPTION: Annual, erect, 8 to 20 inches tall. Grows in moist shaded places.

FLOWERS: 4 sepals, 4 small white petals, 6 stamens. Seedpods heart-shaped and flattened, about 1/4 inch diameter.

LEAVES: Alternate. Basal leaves in a rosette, sharply incised, the lobes pointing downward. Upper leaves lanceolate, attached directly by the base, and have earlike lobes.

FLOWERING; All year.

Cardamine californica Plate 107   **MILKMAIDS**

DESCRIPTION: Perennial herb from ovoid rhizomes. Stems to 16 inches high. Grows on shady banks and slopes most often in southern Oak and Riparian Woodland communities.

FLOWERS: Many flowered racemes; 4 sepals; 4 petals pale rose to white, about 1/2 inch long; 6 stamens.

269

BRASSICACEAE

LEAVES: Alternate, 3-foliate with each leaflet broadly ovate, sometimes heart-shaped, 1 to 2 inches broad. Wavy margins, sometimes saw-toothed.

FLOWERING: January - April

Cardamine oligosperma   **BITTER-CRESS**

DESCRIPTION: Annual or biennial herb, with a slender tap-root. 4 to 12 inches high. Grows .in moist Oak Woodlands and in canyons. Rare.

FLOWERS: 2 to 10 flowers on each raceme; 4 sepals, tiny; 4 petals, small, white; 6 stamens.

LEAVES: Alternate. Compound leaves in basal rosette and also leaves along the stem, each 1/2 to 1-1/2 inches long. 5 to 11 small, narrow leaflets to each leaf.

FLOWERING: March - July

Cardaria draba Plate 105   ***HOARY CRESS**

DESCRIPTION: Perennial herb, several-stemmed, hairy, 12 to 16 inches high, leafy plant. Found in fields and disturbed places. Rare.

FLOWERS: Flowers in a terminal raceme; 4 sepals; 4 petals, small, white; 6 stamens.

LEAVES: Alternate, 1 to 2½ inches long, upper leaves clasping with earlike lobes.

FLOWERING: March - June

Caulanthus heterophyllus Plate 163   **JEWEL FLOWER**

DESCRIPTION: Annual, hairy — especially the lower parts, erect, sometimes branched. 1 to 3 feet high. Found in open places in Chaparral. Look for it after a fire.

BRASSICACEAE

FLOWERS: In racemes 8 to 16 inches long. White flowers about 1 inch diameter; 4 sepals greenish or purplish; 4 petals yellowish with purple veining; 6 stamens, 1 style having a 2-lobed stigma. Seedpods pendent, straight, 2 to 3 inches long, 1/16 inch wide.

LEAVES: Alternate, clasping main stem. Linear to lanceolate, 1½ to 3½ inches long. Pinnatifid with widely divergent lobes. Upper leaves smaller and not toothed.

FLOWERING: March - May

Coronopus didymus   ***WART CRESS**

DESCRIPTION: Heavily scented annual. Numerous leafy stems 6 to 8 inches long, prostrate or ascending. Hairy. A naturalized weed found in disturbed areas.

FLOWERS: 4 sepals, 4 small petals, 6 stamens.

LEAVES: Alternate, 3/8 to 3/4 inch long with narrow divisions.

FLOWERING: March - July

Descurainia pinnata Plate 164   **TANSY MUSTARD**

DESCRIPTION: Annual, 3/4 foot to 2 feet tall, having a single stem with short branches. Found on dry slopes in many plant communities.

FLOWERS: 4 sepals, 4 petals greenish yellow, about the same length as the sepals, 6 stamens. Seedpod short-tipped, two rows of seeds; seedpod stems at right angles to the main stem.

LEAVES: Alternate. Lower leaves 1 to 3½ inches long, bipinnate, the small segments obovate. Upper leaves pinnate to bipinnate, the small segments linear to oblanceolate.

FLOWERING: March - June

271

BRASSICACEAE

Descurainia sophia   *FLIX-WEED

DESCRIPTION: Annual, leafy, branched plant, 10 inches to 2 feet high. Found in Southern Oak Woodland.

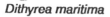

FLOWERS: 4 sepals equal to or exceeding in length the 4 greenish-yellow petals. 6 stamens. Narrow pods 3/4 to 1-1/4 inches long. Seeds in one row.

LEAVES: Alternate, 3/4 to 3-1/2 inches long, 2-3 pinnate with fine segments.

FLOWERING: May - August

Diplotaxis tenuifolia   *WALL ROCKET

DESCRIPTION: Perennial herb, bushy, leafy, 1 to 2 feet tall. Grows in disturbed areas.

FLOWERS: In loose racemes; 4 sepals, 4 yellow petals, 6 stamens.

LEAVES: Alternate, lanceolate, 2½ to 5 inches long, mostly pinnately cleft into narrow lobes.

FLOWERING: March - June

Dithyrea maritima   SPECTACLE POD

DESCRIPTION: Perennial herb, branching from the base, with leaves basal along 4 to 12 inch long stems. Found growing in sand along the coast. Rare.

FLOWERS: In racemes; 4 sepals; 4 petals, white; 6 stamens. Seedpod 2-lobed, flat, more than 1/2 inch across.

LEAVES: Alternate, slightly longer than orbicular, fleshy, not quite lobed, 1-1/2 to 4 inches long. Upper leaves reduced.

FLOWERING: March - May

FIELD NOTE: *Dithyrea* (dis thureos) is Greek meaning "two shields" and refers here to the double, spectacle-like seedpods.

BRASSICACEAE

Draba cuneifolia   ROCK CRESS

DESCRIPTION: Annual, 2 to 10 inches tall. Grows in Coastal Sage Scrub and Chaparral. (Along the trail between Nicholas Flat and Leo Carrillo Beach)

FLOWERS: 10-70 flowers in dense racemes borne on leafless stems; 4 sepals, 4 white petals, 6 stamens. Seedpods 1/4 to 5/8 inch long, about 3/32 inch wide.

LEAVES: Alternate, ovate to obovate or oblanceolate, wedge-shaped from the base, to 2 inches long. Usually toothed. Mostly basal.

FLOWERING: February - May

FIELD NOTE: *Draba*, from the Greek, means "sharp" and refers to the burning taste of the leaves.

Erysimum capitatum Plate 253   WESTERN WALLFLOWER

DESCRIPTION: Biennial herb, leafy, covered with stiff hairs, 1 to 2½ feet high, on a stout stem. Usually found in dry, rocky places, but also on moist canyon slopes.

FLOWERS: Few on a short raceme; 4 sepals, 4 petals prominent, yellow-orange; 6 stamens. Seedpods 2 to 4 inches long.

LEAVES: Alternate. Basal leaves lanceolate, 1½ to 6 inches long and to 3/8 inch wide, toothed. Upper leaves shorter.

FLOWERING: March - July

BRASSICACEAE

Erysimum insulare Plate 161 **COAST WALLFLOWER**

DESCRIPTION: Perennial herb branching, with 1-1/2 to 3-1/2 foot long succulent branches. Found in Coastal Strand and Coastal Sage Scrub. (Point Mugu State Park) Rare.

FLOWERS: Few on a short raceme. 4 sepals, 4 petals bright yellow, 1/2 to 3/4 inch long. Seedpods coarse with a square cross section, 2 to 2-1/4 inches long.

LEAVES: Alternate, narrowly linear-lanceolate 1-1/4 to 2-3/4 inches long. 1/8 inch wide, gray.

FLOWERING: January - May

Guillenia lasiophylla Plate 111 **CALIFORNIA MUSTARD**

DESCRIPTION: Annual, erect, sometimes branching, 1 to 5 feet high. Grows in Grasslands and open places in Woodlands.

FLOWERS: In racemes; 4 sepals greenish; 4 petals yellowish-white, spatulate; 6 stamens. Seedpods deflex down the stem, 1-1/4 to 2-1/4 inches long.

LEAVES: Alternate. Lower leaves oblong or oblanceolate, irregularly pinnatifid with strongly wavy leaf margins, 1-1/4 to 4-1/2 inches long. Upper leaves reduced.

FLOWERING: March - June

Hirschfeldia incana Plate 160 ***MEDITERRANEAN MUSTARD**

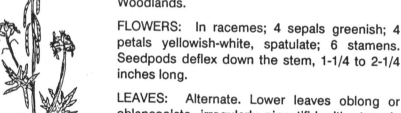

DESCRIPTION Perennial herb, 16 to 32 inches high, covered with grayish-white fine hairs. A common weed in disturbed areas and along trails and roads.

FLOWERS: On many terminal racemes; 4 sepals, 4 light yellow petals, 6 stamens.

BRASSICACEAE

LEAVES: Alternate. Basal leaves lyre shaped, pinnate, 1-1/2 to 5 inches long, with a large terminal lobe. Upper stem leaves dentate to lobed, smaller, not clasping.

FLOWERING: May - October

Lepidium lasiocarpum   HAIRY PEPPERGRASS

DESCRIPTION: Annual, branched and spreading, hairy, 2 to 10 inches long. Grows on grassy slopes.

FLOWERS: 1 to 3 inch racemes; 4 purple sepals, 4 petals small, narrow; 6 stamens. Flower stems flattened. Seedpods circular, 3/16 inch across.

LEAVES: Alternate, linear to oblanceolate, 3/8 to 3/4 inch long, toothed to pinnately cleft. Lower leaves can be over 2 inches long.

FLOWERING: April - May

FIELD NOTE: *Lepidium*, from the Greek, means "a little scale," describing the shape of the pods.

Lepidium latifolium   *PERENNIAL PEPPERGRASS

DESCRIPTION: Perennial herb from a well developed root system. 1 to 3 feet tall. Grows in waste places.

FLOWERS: Many flowered racemes; 4 sepals, 4 white petals, 6 stamens. Seedpods round-ovate, 1/16 to 1/2 inch long.

LEAVES: Basal leaves oblong, 4 to 12 inches long on stems. Upper leaves smaller and sessile.

FLOWERING: June - August

BRASSICACEAE

Lepidium latipes   DWARF PEPPERGRASS

DESCRIPTION: Annual, low spreading, hairy, 4 inch long stout stems branched from the base. Grows in alkaline flats and Grasslands.

FLOWERS: Congested in dense racemes, 3/4 to 2-1/4 inches long. Individual flowers on wide flat stems; 4 sepals downy; 4 petals greenish, 6 stamens. Pods broadly oval, 1/4 inch long, winged at the apex.

LEAVES: Alternate, linear, 2 to 4 inches long, basal leaves pinnately cleft into narrow lobes; upper leaves smooth margined and linear.

FLOWERING: March - May

Lepidium nitidum   Plate 445   SHINY PEPPERGRASS

DESCRIPTION: Annual, usually erect, sometimes spreading from the base, 2 to 16 inches long. Grows in Coastal Sage Scrub, Chaparral, and Grassland, often on shallow soil and rocky places. Common.

FLOWERS: In loose racemes on flattened stems; 4 sepals ovate; 4 petals spatulate, white; 6 stamens. Seedpods oval, smooth and shiny.

LEAVES: Alternate. Lower leaves 1 to 4 inches long, pinnately cleft into narrow segments. Upper leaves smaller, some not cleft.

FLOWERING: January - May

Lepidium perfoliatum   *SHIELD CRESS

DESCRIPTION: Biennial herb, erect, not hairy, covered with a whitish bloom. 8 to 24 inches high. Found in disturbed soil.

FLOWERS: On terminal racemes with many flowers on slender cylindrical stems. 4 hairy sepals, 4 yellow petals, 6 stamens.

BRASSICACEAE

LEAVES: Basal leaves are 2-pinnate with linear segments. Upper leaves are heart-shaped and entirely surround the stem. (perfoliate)

FLOWERING: March - May

Lepidium virginicum var. pubescens

*PEPPERGRASS

DESCRIPTION: Branching annual 1 to 2 feet tall. Grows in Coastal Sage Scrub, Chaparral and other plant communities.

FLOWERS: Many racemes with many flowers on slender, cylindrical stems; 4 sepals, 4 white petals, 6 stamens. Seedpods oval, about 1/8 inch long, shallowly notched at apex.

LEAVES: Basal leaves incised to pinnate, 2 to 6 inches long. Upper leaves alternate, lanceolate to linear, some with incised margins, others smooth.

FLOWERING: March - August

Lobularia maritima

*SWEET ALYSSUM

DESCRIPTION: Spreading annual herb 6 to 10 inches high. Often cultivated, becomes a garden escape, remaining long after the original garden is gone. Found on the beaches, base of cliffs, stream banks and slopes.

FLOWERS: Small, white, in a terminal raceme; 4 sepals, 4 petals, 6 stamens (4 long, 2 short). Sweet-smelling.

LEAVES: Alternate, linear, smooth edged, about 1/2 inch long.

FLOWERING: January - December

277

BRASSICACEAE

Matthiola incana   ***GARDEN STOCK**

DESCRIPTION: Biennial herb, stout, erect, 20 inches tall, branches at the top. Found near seashore bluffs.

FLOWERS: Usually purple, individual petals with a stemlike base, about 1-1/4 inch diameter; 4 sepals, 4 petals, 6 stamens. Seedpods 3 to 6 inches long.

LEAVES: Alternate, 2 to 6 inches long, smooth edged to wavy and some saw-toothed.

FLOWERING: March - May

Raphanus raphanistrum   ***JOINTED CHARLOCK**

DESCRIPTION: Biennial herb, widely branching, 1 to 4 feet high with scattered, bristly hairs on stems and foliage. Grows in fields and meadows.

FLOWERS: In a raceme, yellow aging to white, 1/2 to 1 inch in diameter; 4 sepals, narrow; 4 petals, each with a stemlike base; 6 stamens. Seedpods 3 to 4 inches long, each with 4-10 seeds. Pod longitudinally grooved.

LEAVES: Alternate. Lower leaves pinnately divided, 4 to 8 inches long, with a rounded terminal segment. Upper leaves toothed.

FLOWERING: April - June

Raphanus sativus Plate 309   ***WILD RADISH**

DESCRIPTION: Biennial herb, widely branching, 1 to 4 feet high with scattered bristly hairs on stems and foliage. Grows in fields and meadows.

FLOWERS: In a terminal raceme. Flowers about 1 inch in diameter, white or yellow with rose or purple veins. 4 sepals, narrow; 4 petals, each with a stemlike base; 6 stamens. Seedpod not longitudinally grooved, 3/4 to 1-1/4 inch long including the conical beak, 2-3 seeds in each.

BRASSICACEAE

LEAVES: Alternate. Lower leaves pinnately divided, 4 to 8 inches long, with a rounded terminal segment. Upper leaves toothed.

FLOWERING: February - July

Rorippa curvisilique   YELLOW CRESS

DESCRIPTION: Biennial herb. Several stems branching from the base, 4 inches to 1 foot long. Grows in stream-beds, marshy areas and pond margins.

FLOWERS: In loose racemes at the end of axillary branches, 1/8 inch diameter; 4 sepals, 4 petals yellow, 6 stamens. Seedpods round in cross-section, curved, 1/4 to 3/8 inch long, 1/16 inch thick.

LEAVES: Alternate, oblong-lanceolate in outline, pinnately divided into lobes. Lower leaves 1 to 3 inches long. Upper leaves slightly reduced.

FLOWERING: April - September

Rorippa nasturtium-aquaticum Plate 110   *WATER CRESS

DESCRIPTION: Perennial herb, aquatic, with stems 2 feet long, free-rooting at the nodes. Usually grows in quiet flowing water and on wet banks.

FLOWERS: In racemes at the ends of axillary branches, small, white; 4 sepals, 4 petals, 6 stamens.

LEAVES: Alternate, pinnate, up to 4 inches long, not hairy, with 3-11 ovate leaflets.

FLOWERING: March - November

279

BRASSICACEAE

Sinapis arvensis   *FIELD CHARLOCK

DESCRIPTION: Annual, erect, stiff hairs at the base. 1 to 3 feet high. Found in fields and disturbed places.

FLOWERS: In racemes, showy; 4 sepals 3/16 inch long; 4 petals yellow, 5/16 inch long; 6 stamens. Seedpods, cylindric and tapering, 3/4 to 1 inch long.

LEAVES: Alternate. Lower leaves obovate, pinnately divided, the terminal segment larger and rounded, 2 to 6 inches long. Upper leaves oblong to lanceolate, toothed, reduced in size.

FLOWERING: March - October

Sisymbrium altissimum   *TUMBLE MUSTARD

DESCRIPTION: Annual, stems erect, many branches, 2 to 3 feet high. Grows in disturbed ground.

FLOWERS: In terminal racemes; 4 sepals, 4 petals yellowish-white, 1/4 inch long; 6 stamens. Seedpods 2 to 4 inches long, less than 1/16 inch thick.

LEAVES: Alternate, narrowly elliptic in outline. Lower leaves, 4 to 6 inches long, sharply pinnatifid, the lobes pointing downward. Upper leaves smaller.

FLOWERING: May - July

Sisymbrium irio Plate 167   *LONDON ROCKET

DESCRIPTION: Erect annual, 8 to 24 inches tall, branching above. Found in gardens and disturbed areas.

FLOWERS: On long, many-flowered racemes; 4 sepals, 4 petals yellow, 1/8 inch long; 6 stamens. Seedpods 1-1/4 to 1-3/4 inches long, about 1/32 inch thick.

BRASSICACEAE

LEAVES: Alternate. Lower leaves sharply pinnatifid, lobes pointing downward, 4 to 6 inches long. Upper leaves smaller.

FLOWERING: January - April

Sisymbrium officionale Plate 166   *HEDGE MUSTARD

DESCRIPTION: Annual, rigid, erect stem with few widely divergent branches, 1 to 4 feet tall. Plant is somewhat hairy, especially near the base. Common in disturbed areas.

FLOWERS: In long, narrow racemes; 4 sepals, 4 petals yellowish, 1/8 inch long; 6 stamens. Seedpods, 3/8 to 5/8 inches long, lie along the stem.

LEAVES: A basal rosette of lyrate-pinnatifid, hairy leaves, 2 to 4 inches long. Upper leaves hastate shaped, alternate.

FLOWERING: April - July

Sisymbrium orientale Plate 165   *ORIENTAL MUSTARD

DESCRIPTION: Annual or biennial herb, 1 to 2 feet high, somewhat hairy. Found in disturbed soil.

FLOWERS: In terminal racemes; 4 sepals, 4 petals yellowish, 1/4 inch long; 6 stamens. Seedpods 1½ to 3½ inches long, diverging from stem, and ascending.

LEAVES: Alternate, pinnate, 1¼ to 5 inches long, with a hastate terminal lobe.

FLOWERING: May

BRASSICACEAE

Stanleya pinnata   GOLDEN PRINCE'S PLUME

DESCRIPTION: Small shrub, woody, 1½ to 5 foot tall stem, usually branched above. Found in Coastal Sage Scrub facing the ocean. (Cheseboro Canyon) Rare.

FLOWERS: In many-flowered racemes 1 to 2 feet long; yellow; 4 linear sepals; 4 petals 1/2 to 5/8 inch long; 6 stamens. Seedpods 1-1/4 to 2-3/4 inches long.

LEAVES: Alternate. Lower leaves pinnatifid into lanceolate segments, 2 to 8 inches long, on stems. Upper leaves oblanceolate, smooth edged or divided, 1 to 2-1/4 inches long.

FLOWERING: January - December

Thysanocarpus curvipes Plate 448   LACE-POD

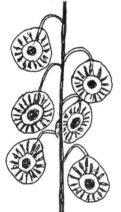

DESCRIPTION: Annual, slender, erect, 1 to 1-1/2 feet high, somewhat hairy at the base. Found in Grasslands, Coastal Sage Scrub, and Chaparral.

FLOWERS: In racemes, small white or purplish; 4 sepals ovate; 4 petals; 6 stamens. Pods round-obovate about 1/4 inch in diameter including the circular membranous wing.

LEAVES: Basal leaves in a rosette, toothed with a wavy margin, oblong in outline, 1 to 2 inches long. Upper leaves alternate, lanceolate, clasping in the stem, and with earshaped appendages at the base.

FLOWERING: March - May

Thysanocarpus laciniatus Plate 104   NARROW-LEAVED
                                                    FRINGE-POD

DESCRIPTION: Annual, slender, erect, branching, 4 to 16 inches high. Found in Grasslands, Coastal Sage Scrub and Chaparral.

282

BRASSICACEAE

FLOWERS: In long open racemes; 4 sepals, 4 petals, 6 stamens. Pods obovate, oval or circular, about 1/8 inch across.

LEAVES: Alternate, not in a rosette at base, 1/2 to 2 inches long. Lower leaves pinnatifid into narrow segments, some almost undivided. Upper leaves narrowly linear, usually not hairy, no ear-shaped appendages.

FLOWERING: March - May

Tropidocarpum gracile Plate 157   DOBIE-POD

DESCRIPTION: Slender annual with branches nearly lying on the ground, 12 inches long. Plant is covered with soft, short hairs. Grows in Grasslands. Uncommon.

FLOWERS: Small in loose, leafy racemes on stems 1/4 to 5/8 inch long; 4 spreading sepals, 4 yellow petals, 6 stamens, 4 long 3 short. Seedpods linear, 3/4 to 2 inches long; seeds in 2 rows.

LEAVES: Mostly basal, pinnatifid, 3/8 to 2 inches long. Upper leaves alternate, reduced.

FLOWERING: March - May

BUDDLEJACEAE
BUDDLEJA FAMILY

The two species of this family found locally are escapees from cultivation. Summer Lilac came from China, Butterfly Bush from South Africa. Other plants of this family of 32 genera and 800 species have been cultivated for their beauty in the garden. These two, and probably others, have been able to escape and survive in the wild because they are very tolerant of poor, dry gravel soil.

BUDDLEJACEAE

Buddleja davidii   ***SUMMER LILAC**

DESCRIPTION: Deciduous or semi-evergreen shrub, 15 feet high. Found as an escape in moist soil. (Near the mouth of Malibu Creek)

FLOWERS: In dense, spikelike clusters, 6 to 12 inches long, at branch ends. Smaller clusters at ends of side branches; small fragrant, tubular, lilac colored with orange at the throat.

LEAVES: Opposite, lanceolate, flat, finely serrate, 4 to 12 inches long; dark green above, white felted beneath.

FLOWERING: June - July

Buddleja saligna   ***BUTTERFLY BUSH**

DESCRIPTION: Deciduous shrub, 9 to 12 feet high. Found in disturbed areas in Chaparral. (Near Saddle Peak)

FLOWERS: Many branched, expanding panicles; fragrant, cream-colored, 1 inch long; calyx bell-shaped.

LEAVES: Alternate, narrowly lanceolate to ob-lanceolate, margins entire and rolled back, 4 inches long or less.

FLOWERING: June - October

CACTACEAE

CACTUS FAMILY

Cactus family members total 2000, 4 of which are native to our local mountains. Cacti are western hemisphere plants even though they are scattered throughout the world today, having been carried about by explorers and other travelers. Identifying characteristics include spine size, shape, and color. The *Opuntia* genus of the Santa Monica Mountains has a pocket of glochids (microscopic barbed hair-like spines) near the bases of spines. *Opuntia* flowers have many sepals, many petals, many stamens and an inferior ovary.

CACTACEAE

Areoles which are specialized structures situated in leaf-axils, are the location for the growth of spines, flowers, and branches. Flowers appear on joints grown during the previous year.

All of the local native cactus species have very small tapering leaves that fall off early in the season.

Opuntia basilaris   BEAVER-TAIL CACTUS

DESCRIPTION: Perennial, woody at the base, herbaceous succulent, low spreading (8 to 20 inches high), spineless plant with flattened 3 to 6 inch long obovate joint. Many short, brown glochids. Found inland on dry slopes and ridges.

FLOWERS: On upper margins of joints, several clustered, each 4 to 6 inches across, rose to rose-purple, with a velvet sheen on the petals.

LEAVES: Small, fleshy, and awl-shaped, appear on new growth and fall off in 2 to 3 months.

FLOWERING: March - June

Opuntia littoralis   COAST PRICKLY PEAR

DESCRIPTION: Plant with fleshy, flat joints grows prostrate to ascending and spreads to a large mass. Very spiny. Joints longer than wide, sometimes twice as long. Spines 5/8 to 1-3/8 inches long, not barbed, and nearly round in cross section, white with red-brown base. Found near the coast and inland to elevations of 500 feet.

FLOWERS: Yellow, 2 to 3 inches in diameter. Petals 1-1/2 times longer than wide; stamens yellow, 3/8 to 1/2 inch long; style pink. Fruit red to red-purple, pear-shaped with attachment at the large end; flat scar where flower was attached.

CACTACEAE

LEAVES: Small, fleshy, awl-shaped appear on new growth and fall off in 2 to 3 months.

FLOWERING: May - June

Opuntia oricola Plate 159   PRICKLY PEAR

DESCRIPTION: Plant with fleshy, flat joints ascending or erect and spreading to large masses. Sometimes tree-like, 3 to 10 feet high. Very spiny. Joints almost round. Spines yellow aging to brownish-gray, 3/4 inch long, flattened and somewhat hooked. Plant grows inland as well as on the coast but at low elevations.

FLOWERS: Yellow, 2 to 2-1/4 inches in diameter. Petals twice as long as wide; stamens yellow, about 3/8 inch long. Green stigmas atop purplish-red styles. Fruit is red, almost globular; deeply depressed scar where flower was attached.

LEAVES: Small, fleshy, awl-shaped, appear on new growth and fall off in 2 to 3 months.

FLOWERING: May - June

Opuntia prolifera Plate 413   COAST CHOLLA

DESCRIPTION: Plant erect and bushy, very spiny; can grow to 6 feet high, branching several times, fleshy cylindrical joints. The 5-inch-long end joints will fall off and attach to animals or clothing. Dislodged joints root as the principal method of reproduction. Spines are reddish-brown, aging to dark gray. Not barbed. A coastal plant of low elevations, prefers good soil, Grasslands. (Point Mugu State Park) Rare.

FLOWERS: Rose to red-purple, inner petals about 1/2 inch long. Fruit green, globe-shaped, about 1 inch in diameter.

CACTACEAE

LEAVES: Small, fleshy, awl-shaped, appear on new growth and fall off in 2 to 3 months.

FLOWERING: April - June

CALLITRICHACEAE

WATER STARWORT FAMILY

This family has 1 genus and 25 species widely distributed throughout the world. 1 species is native to the Santa Monica Mountains.

Recognition characteristics: Aquatic herb with slender stems, leaves opposite with a smooth margin. Flowers are small with both calyx and corolla missing; 1 lone stamen on staminate flowers, 2 fused carpels forming 1 pistil on pistillate flowers.

FIELD NOTE: From the Greek, *kallos*, beautiful and *trichos*, hair.

Callitriche marginata   CALIFORNIA WATER-STARWORT

DESCRIPTION: Herbal plant with slender stems 2 to 4 inches high, forming mats. Found growing in mud or at the margins of ponds.

FLOWERS: Axillary, either staminate or pistillate, on stems shorter than leaf length. Calyx and corolla missing. 1 stamen or 1 pistil. Fruit slightly over 1/32 inch long, slightly wider than long, notched at both base and apex. Thin perimeter margin.

LEAVES: Opposite, spatulate, 1/8 to 5/16 inch long.

FLOWERING: March - June

CAMPANULACEAE

BLUEBELL FAMILY

Seventy genera and 2000 species of this family grow worldwide in tropical, subtropical, and temperate zones. 4 native species, each in a different genus, are found in the Santa Monica Mountains.

Recognition Characteristics: Flowers are 5-merous, the calyx divided into 5 separate sepals, the corolla 5-lobed.

Githopsis diffusa   SOUTHERN BLUE-CUP

DESCRIPTION: Annual, slender, branching, mostly without hairs, about 6 inches high. Found on moist shady places in Chaparral. Rare.

FLOWERS: Axillary, solitary, few, scattered, without a stem; 5 sepals linear, to 1/4 inch long; corolla regular, nearly cylindrical, 5-lobed —lobes pointed — light purple.

LEAVES: Alternate, without stipules, obovate, finely saw-toothed, 1/8 to 1/4 inch long.

FLOWERING: April - June

Lobelia dunnii   ROTHROCK'S LOBELIA

DESCRIPTION: Perennial herb, prostrate to ascending. 1 to 2 feet high. Found in moist canyons in Coastal Sage Scrub and Chaparral. Rare.

FLOWERS: In a headlike raceme, few to several flowers on stems 3/16 to 3/8 inch long. Linear bracts 1/16 inch long (lower longer); sepals linear-awl-shaped to 1/2 inch long; corolla downy, blue, to 3/4 inch long, the tube split on the side away from the stem to about half way, upper lip erect, lower lip spreading and 3-lobed.

LEAVES: Alternate, without stipules, oblanceolate low on the stem, linear-lanceolate above;

288

not hairy, 1-1/4 to 2-3/4 inches long, saw-toothed. Lower leaves on stems, upper leaves without stems.

FLOWERING: July - September

Nemacladus ramosissimus   **NUTTALL'S NEMACLADUS**

DESCRIPTION: Annual, slender, intricately branched stems, not hairy, 2 to 10 inches high. Found on dry soil in Chaparral and Coastal Sage Scrub. Rare.

FLOWERS: In Leaf axils on hairlike stems spreading nearly horizontally and curved upward near the apex. Stems 1/4 to 3/4 inch long. Flower bracts linear, 1/8 to 1/4 inch long; 5 sepals lanceolate, 1/32 inch long; corolla white. Small seeds almost spherical with rows of rounded pits.

LEAVES: Alternate, without stipules. Basal leaves in a rosette, oblanceolate, saw-toothed, 1/4 to 5/8 inch long. Leaves higher on the stem reduced to awl-like bracts.

FLOWERING: April - May

Triodanus biflora   **LITTLE VENUS' LOOKING GLASS**

DESCRIPTION: Annual, slender single stem, 1/2 to 2 feet high. Slightly hairy below, rough with short hairs above. Found in many plant communities, after a fire and in open disturbed places.

FLOWERS: In a spike, each flower on a very short stem in a leaf axil. Calyx 3 to 5 lobes, earlier blooming flowers more likely to have 3; corolla 5-lobed, blue to violet or lilac. The flowers in lower axils do not open. Capsule 1/4 to 3/8 inch long.

LEAVES: Alternate, ovate to oblong, sessile, 3/8 to 1-1/4 inch long, smooth edged, sometimes barely toothed.   FLOWERING: April - June

CANNABACEAE

HEMP FAMILY

The family includes 2 genera: *Cannabis* — hemp, marijuana; and *Humulus* — hops. Only *Cannabis* is known to grow in the local area.

Recognition Characteristics: Erect Annual herbs or climbing perennial herbs with watery juice. Leaves opposite. *Cannabis* has palmate leaves. Pistillate and staminate flowers are on separate plants. Flowers are 5-merous and without petals.

Cannabis sativa

*MARIJUANA

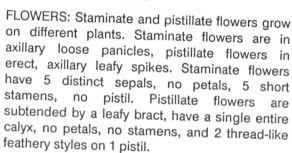

DESCRIPTION: Annual, robust, erect, branching 3 to 16 feet high. The plant is sticky, has an odor, and is covered with fine hair. Found along major streams, but rarely so. This escape from cultivation has been about eradicated from the Santa Monica Mountains.

FLOWERS: Staminate and pistillate flowers grow on different plants. Staminate flowers are in axillary loose panicles, pistillate flowers in erect, axillary leafy spikes. Staminate flowers have 5 distinct sepals, no petals, 5 short stamens, no pistil. Pistillate flowers are subtended by a leafy bract, have a single entire calyx, no petals, no stamens, and 2 thread-like feathery styles on 1 pistil.

LEAVES: Opposite below, alternate above, compound, finger-like, with 5 to 11 linear-lanceolate serrate leaflets.

CAPPARACEAE

CAPER FAMILY

A large family of tropical, subtropical, and desert plants, only 1 of which grows locally.

Flower recognition characteristics: 4-cleft calyx, 4 petals, 4 to many stamens (6 for genus *Isomeris*), and 2 united carpels forming 1 pistil. *Isomeris arborea* is easily identified by the 1 to 2 inch long, inflated seedpod.

Isomeris arborea Plate 149   BLADDERPOD

DESCRIPTION: Ill-smelling shrub widely branched, erect, 5 feet high. Covered with a bloom, branches minutely downy. Found in Coastal Sage Scrub and on coastal bluffs and hills. Common.

FLOWERS: Yellow in a dense raceme. Calyx 4-cleft, about 1/4 inch long; 4 petals, each 1/2 inch or more long; 6 stamens. The fruit is a large, inflated capsule 1 to 2 inches long.

LEAVES: Alternate, trifoliolate, stemmed. Leaflets are 1/2 to 1-3/8 inches long and 1/4 as wide, with a small, abrupt, pointed tip.

FLOWERING: January - December

CAPRIFOLIACEAE

HONEYSUCKLE FAMILY

Trees, shrubs, or vines with opposite leaves. Flowers are bisexual, 5 sepals, 5 petals, 5 stamens, 2-3-5-8 united carpels forming 1 pistil. The family is easily confused with the *Rubiaceae* (Madder family). A distinguishing characteristic is the presence of stipules in *Rubiaceae* and their absence in *Caprifoliaceae.*

CAPRIFOLIACEAE

Lonicera hispidula var. vacillans
CALIFORNIA HONEYSUCKLE

DESCRIPTION: Climbing vine to 20 feet high, sometimes found in Chaparral in canyons and along streams. (Malibu Canyon downstream of Piuma Road) Rare.

FLOWERS: In whorls of spikes or panicles, hairy. Calyx tube ovoid; corolla tube strongly 2-lipped, the upper lip 4-lobed, the lower lobe, reddish purple outside, yellow inside, 3/4 to 1 inch long; 5 stamens exserted; 1 exserted pistil. The flower is minutely hairy (*hispidulous*) on the outside and very hairy inside.

LEAVES: Opposite, elliptic to oblong-ovate, 1-1/2 to 3-1/2 inches long, white and downy on the underside, green above. Several upper pairs are united at their bases surrounding the stem of the vine.

FLOWERING: May - June

FIELD NOTE: California honeysuckle reaches its southern coastal limits in disjunct Santa Monica populations.

Lonicera subspicata var. denudada   Plates 181, 426
CHAPARRAL HONEYSUCKLE

DESCRIPTION: Evergreen shrub to 8 feet tall, straggling, woody-based.   Grows in shaded areas at the edge of   Oak Woodlands and on Chaparral slopes. Common throughout.

FLOWERS: In whorls on short, leafy spikes 3/4 to 4-1/2 inches long. Calyx tube ovoid, minutely 5-cleft; corolla tube strongly 2-lipped, the upper lip 4-lobed, the lower a lobe, cream or yellowish, 1/2 to 7/16 inch long. Fruit a yellowish to red berry.

292

CAPRIFOLIACEAE

LEAVES: Opposite, oblong-ovate to roundish, 1 inch long and curve inward. Soft, white fuzz on the underside. Smaller than on (*L. hispidula*).

FLOWERING: April - June

FIELD NOTE: Chaparral honeysuckle is found nearly nearly everywhere in the Santa Monica Mountains.

Sambucus mexicana   Plates 25, 423   **ELDERBERRY**

DESCRIPTION: Small tree, usually found in a Southern Live Oak Woodland plant community. It needs more moisture than is found in Chaparral and can tolerate some shade. Common.

FLOWERS: Small (1/4 inch diameter), white flowers in a flat-topped cluster. 5 sepals, 5 petals fused at the base, 5 stamens, 1 pistil. Berries are blue or almost black, with a whitish bloom; ripen in late summer.

LEAVES: Opposite odd-pinnate leaves. Opposite leaflets with serrate borders. Leaflets lanceolate to elliptic.

FLOWERING: April - August

Symphoricarpos mollis   Plates 300, 425   **SNOWBERRY**

DESCRIPTION: Widely spread, branching bush 1 to 3 feet high, found in Southern Oak Woodland or Chaparral, nearly always in shade. Common.

FLOWERS: Pairs or small clusters of pink flowers toward the ends of branches. Calyx 5-cleft corolla, bell-like, 5-lobed, pink; 5 stamens; 1 pistil. Fruit is a white berry, 1/4 inch in diameter. Berries often stay on the bush into winter, long after the leaves have dropped.

293

CAPRIFOLIACEAE

LEAVES: Opposite, thin, round-oval, 1/2 to 1-1/2 inch long, attached along all the stems.

FLOWERING: April - May

CARYOPHYLLACEAE

PINK FAMILY

Eighty genera and 2000 species of this family are native to northern hemisphere temperate and cool regions. 9 genera and 17 species are found in the Santa Monica Mountains. 6 species are introduced.

Recognition characteristics: The flowers of this family generally have 5 sepals, sometimes fused into a tube or ovoid shaped, sometimes free. The 5 petals are often notched, occasionally so deeply as to appear 10 petalled. The number of stamens is nearly always 10, a few species having 5, and others between 5 and 10. 2-5 united carpels form 1 pistil, with 1 to 5 styles. The ovary is usually 1-celled. The fruit is normally a capsule, occasionally a utricle.

Cardionema ramosissimum   SAND MAT

DESCRIPTION: Perennial herb, forming dense mats 5 to 18 inches across, woolly, leafy. Found at the seacoast. (Point Dume)

FLOWERS: 5 sepals, woolly; petals absent. Fruit a utricle.

LEAVES: Opposite, 1/4 to 1/2 inch long.

FLOWERING: April - May

FIELD NOTE: The Greek *cardia* means "heart" and *nema*, "thread," so the name refers to the inversely heart-shaped stamens.

CARYOPHYLLACEAE

Cerastium glomeratum Plate 17

*MOUSE-EARED CHICKWEED

DESCRIPTION: Annual, erect, sticky, downy, 4 to 12 inches high. Found in fields and along trails.

FLOWERS: In clusters; 5 sepals lanceolate, 3/16 inch long; 5 petals deeply notched at the apex, white; 10 stamens.

LEAVES: Opposite, elliptic, hairy, 3/8 to 1 inch long, without stems.

FLOWERING: February - May

Herniaria hirsuta
ssp. hirsuta

*HERNERIA

DESCRIPTION: Annual, branching and trailing on the ground, forming mats, bristly, 2 to 8 inches across, 1 to 2-1/2 inches high. Found on disturbed slopes in Chaparral. (Triunfo Pass)

FLOWERS: In all axils, minute, green, in clusters, without stems; 5 sepals; petals absent.

LEAVES: Opposite oblong-oblanceolate, 1/8 to 1/4 inch long. Many leaves, bristly.

FLOWERING: April - June

Minuartia douglasii Plate 19

DOUGLAS' SANDWORT

DESCRIPTION: Annual, slender, branching, 2 to 12 inches high. Found in dry places on sandy or rocky soil.

FLOWERS: In loose cymes, on threadlike stems 1/4 to 1 inch long; 5 sepals ovate, 1/8 inch long; 5 petals obovate, white, conspicuous, 1/8 to 1/4 inch long. Fruit a dry capsule.

LEAVES: Opposite, threadlike, 3/8 to 3/4 inch long.

FLOWERING: April - June

CARYOPHYLLACEAE

Polycarpon depressum   CALIFORNIA POLYCARP

DESCRIPTION: Annual, branching from the base, slender stems, 3/8 to 2 inches long. Found in sandy soil in Coastal Sage Scrub and Chaparral.

FLOWERS: In loose cymes; 5 sepals 1/32 inch long; 5 petals smaller than sepals, linear, white. Capsule globose.

LEAVES: Opposite, spatulate, 1/8 to 1/4 inch long, membranous stipules.

FLOWERING: April - June

Polycarpon tetraphyllum   *FOUR-LEAVED POLYCARP

DESCRIPTION: Annual, much branched from the base, 3 to 5-1/2 inches long, not hairy. Found along trails.

FLOWERS: In cymes, leafless, many flowered; 5 sepals 1/16 inch long, green or purplish. Capsule ovoid.

LEAVES: Opposite, often in 4's, oblong to obovate, 3/16 to 1/2 inch long. Membranous stipules.

FLOWERING: May - July

Silene antirrhina   SLEEPY CATCHFLY
SNAPDRAGON CATCHFLY

DESCRIPTION: Annual, erect; sparingly branched, 8 to 52 inches high. Upper internodes often have reddish-brown, sticky bands. Uncommon.

FLOWERS: In loose umbels. Calyx ovoid, 10-nerved, contracted at apex, 5-toothed, 3/16 to 5/16 inch long; 5 petals cleft, white to pink, slightly longer than sepals; 10 stamens.

CARYOPHYLLACEAE

LEAVES: Opposite, basal leaves oblanceolate to spatulate, upper leaves oblanceolate to linear, 1-1/4 to 2-1/2 inches long, without stems.

FLOWERING: April - August

Silene gallica   Plate 22   ***WINDMILL PINK**

DESCRIPTION: Annual, hairy, erect, simple or sometimes branched, 4 to 20 inches high. Found in Grasslands, fields, and along trails. Common.

FLOWERS: In racemes on short stems, leafy-bracted, mostly on one side of the stem. Calyx 5-cleft, tubular becoming inflated with age, 10 conspicuous ribs, 1/4 to 3/8 inch long, hairy, constricted at apex; 5 petals open, twisted (windmill-like), pink turning white; 10 stamens.

LEAVES: Opposite, basal leaves are spatulate or oblanceolate, upper leaves are narrower. 3/8 to 1-1/2 inches long.

FLOWERING: February - June

Silene laciniata   Plate 269   **INDIAN PINK**

DESCRIPTION: Perennial herb, branching from the base, 1 to 4 feet high, finely woolly. Found on grassy slopes in shade in Coastal Sage Scrub Chaparral, and Southern Oak Woodlands.

FLOWERS: Terminal on branches of a panicle, sometimes in clusters. Stems 3/4 to 1-1/2 inches long. Calyx tubular, 5-cleft, 5/8 to 3/4 inch long; 5 petals, each blade deeply cleft into 4 linear lobes, open, scarlet; 10 stamens.

LEAVES: Opposite, narrowly linear to lanceo-elliptic, 2 to 4 inches long, 3/32 to 1/2 inch wide, downy.

FLOWERING: May - July

CARYOPHYLLACEAE

Silene multinervia Plate 20   **MANY-NERVED CATCHFLY**

DESCRIPTION: Annual, erect, simple or branching, 8 to 24 inches high, shaggy haired, sticky. Found on disturbed soil and burns in Chaparral.

FLOWERS: On cymosely forked, uneven branches. Bracts 1/4 to 1/2 inch long, calyx ovoid 5/16 to 1/2 inch long, 25 nerved, 5-cleft; 5 petals cleft at the apex, white to pinkish, open; 10 stamens.

LEAVES: Opposite, linear to lanceolate, 1 to 2-1/2 inches long.

FLOWERING: April - May

Silene verecunda Plate 18   **DOLORES CAMPION**
ssp. platyota

DESCRIPTION: Perennial herb, slender, branching above into an open panicle. Found on rock outcroppings in Chaparral. (East of Castro Peak) Rare.

FLOWERS: On panicles, scattered flowers on long stems, sometimes in 3-flowered clusters. Calyx 5-cleft, lightly woolly; 5 petals, bi-lobed, white, greenish or rose; 10 stamens.

LEAVES: Opposite, linear-oblanceolate to obovate, 2 to 3-1/2 inches long.

FLOWERING: June - August

FIELD NOTE: The Dolores Campion population in the Santa Monica Mountains is a significant disjunction.

Spergula arvensis   ***CORN SPURRY**

DESCRIPTION: Annual, erect, branched at base, usually not hairy, 4 to 16 inches high. Found on sandy flats near the coast. Common.

298

CARYOPHYLLACEAE

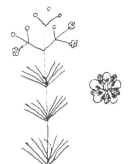

FLOWERS: In terminal cymose panicles, on slender stems; 5 sepals ovate, 3/16 inch long; 5 petals white, slightly exceeding the sepals; 10 stamens, but on rare occasions, only 5.

LEAVES: Whorled, linear, 3/8 to 1-1/4 inches long.

FLOWERING: April - August

Spergularia macrotheca   **LARGE-FLOWERED
SAND SPURRY**

DESCRIPTION: Perennial herb from a stout fleshy root, stems ascending. 4 to 16 inches high, hairy and sticky. Found along the coast in salt marshes and occasionally inland. Common.

FLOWERS: In irregular terminal cymes; 5 sepals broadly lanceolate, lightly woolly, 3/16 to 3/8 inch long; 5 petals ovate, pink, 1/8 to 1/4 inch long; 10 stamens; 3 styles. Seeds usually winged.

LEAVES: Opposite, usually bunched, linear, cylindrical, 5/8 to 1-1/2 inches long. Stipules conspicuous, awl-shaped, 3/16 to 3/8 inch long.

FLOWERING: All year.

Spergularia marina Plate 332   **SALT-MARSH
SAND SPURRY**

DESCRIPTION: Annual, widely spread, stems 2 to 12 inches long, fleshy, downy. Found along the coast in salt marshes and occasionally inland. Common.

FLOWERS: In irregular, terminal, racemose cymes; 5 sepals ovate, 5/32 to 3/16 inch long; 5 petals ovate, white to pink, slightly shorter than sepals; 2-5 stamens; 3 styles. Seeds usually not winged.

CARYOPHYLLACEAE

LEAVES: Opposite, not fascicled, scarcely linear, cylindrical, fleshy, 3/4 to 1-1/2 inches long. Stipules deltoid, 1/8 inch long.

FLOWERING: All year.

Spergularia villosa *SAND SPURRY

DESCRIPTION: Perennial herb, branching from a taproot, stems sticky and hairy, 4 to 12 inches long. Found occasionally along the coast and inland.

FLOWERS: In many-flowered cymes; 5 sepals linear-lanceolate, 1/8 to 3/16 inch long; 5 petals ovate, white, 1/8 to 3/16 inch long; 7 - 10 stamens.

LEAVES: Opposite, fascicled, linear, cylindrical, 3/8 to 1-1/2 inch long. Stipules broadly lanceolate, 1/8 to 5/16 inch long.

FLOWERING: April - July

Stellaria media Plate 21 *CHICKWEED

DESCRIPTION: Annual with trailing stems, 4 to 16 inches long. A longitudinal line of hairs runs along the stems. Found in Southern Oak Woodlands, cultivated areas, and burned out areas. Common.

FLOWERS: In leafy cymes; 5 sepals ovate, woolly, 3/16 inch long; 5 petals white, each one cleft, giving the appearance of 10 petals.

LEAVES: Opposite, ovate, 3/8 to 1-1/4 inches long. Lower leaves short stemmed, upper leaves without a stem.

FLOWERING: February - September

CARYOPHYLLACEAE

Stellaria nitens   SHINY CHICKWEED

DESCRIPTION: Annual, erect, forked slender stems, 4 to 8 inches high, not hairy. Found in Grasslands. Common.

FLOWERS: Terminal in cymes; 5 sepals lanceolate, 1/8 inch long; 5 petals each one cleft, 1/16 inch long.

LEAVES: Opposite, linear to lance-linear, 3/16 to 3/8 inch long; very few leaves, mostly on lower part of plant.

FLOWERING: March - June

CHENOPODIACEAE
GOOSEFOOT FAMILY

Worldwide, 102 genera and 1500 species belong to the Goosefoot family; 7 genera and 26 species are found in the Santa Monica Mountains. Characteristically grows on salty soil, in an arid environment.

Recognition characteristics: Minute green flowers, 5 sepals, no petals, 5 free stamens, 2 (rarely 3-5) carpels unite to form 1 pistil. Goosefoot is sometimes mistaken for the family Amaranthaceae but differs by having somewhat fleshy bracts rather than being dry and papery, and by having free stamens rather than fused.

FIELD NOTE: From the Greek, *chen* means "goose," and *pous*, "foot," referring to the leaf shape.

Atriplex californica   CALIFORNIA SALTBUSH

DESCRIPTION: Perennial herb, many branched, prostrate, leafy, 8 to 20 inches long, covered with white, bran-like scales. Found at the edge of Coastal Salt Marsh, in Coastal Strand and Coastal Sage Scrub.

CHENOPODIACEAE

FLOWERS: Green, in axillary clusters, staminate and pistillate flowers separate but in the same cluster or the staminate in terminal spikes. 5 sepals, no petals, 5 stamens, or 2 stigmas.

LEAVES: Alternate (or the lowest opposite) lanceolate to oblanceolate, 3/16 to 3/4 inch long, sessile, covered with gray bran-like scales.

FLOWERING: April - November

Atriplex coulteri   COULTER'S SALTBUSH

DESCRIPTION: Perennial herb, spreading, leafy, branched, 1 to 3 feet high. Found on alkaline soil in Grassland and Coastal Sage Scrub.

FLOWERS: Green, Pistillate flowers in lower axils, staminate flowers in small clusters in upper axils and short terminal spikes. Bracts subtending pistillate flowers are united to the middle, sharply dentate above. Seed brown.

LEAVES: Alternate, elliptic to lanceolate to ovate, smooth margined, 1/4 to 3/4 inch.

FLOWERING: March - October

Atriplex lentiformis Plate 409   QUAIL BUSH

DESCRIPTION: Perennial small shrub, erect, widely spreading, 3 to 9 feet high and often wider. Small stems are cylindrical, with gray bran-like scales when young. Found on alkaline soil in Coastal Sage Scrub in the west end of the mountains, also along the coastal bluffs.

FLOWERS: In abundant terminal panicles, green. Staminate and pistillate flowers on separate plants. Bracts subtending pistillate flowers are united to the middle. Seed brown.

CHENOPODIACEAE

LEAVES: Alternate, oblong to ovate-deltoid, 5/8 to 1-1/4 inches long, on short stems. Smooth margined.

FLOWERING: August - October

Atriplex leucophylla Plate 408   **BEACH SALTBUSH**

DESCRIPTION: Perennial herb, woody at the base, many branched, prostrate, 1 to 2 feet long, covered with white, bran-like scales. Found along the beach in Coastal Strand. (near Point Mugu)

FLOWERS: Green. Pistillate flowers clustered in axils, staminate flowers in dense terminal spikes. Bracts subtending pistillate flowers united, with bumps on the outer faces. 5 sepals, no petals, 5 stamens.

LEAVES: Alternate, round-ovate to oblong, 3/8 to 1-1/4 inches long, smooth margined.

FLOWERING: April - October

Atriplex patula
var. hastata   ***ARROW-LEAF SALTBUSH**

DESCRIPTION: Annual branching, trailing to erect, 1 to 3 feet high. Found in damp saline soil along the coast.

FLOWERS: In dense panicles, green. Calyx 5-cleft, petals none, stamens 5. Bracts subtending pistillate flowers are united at the base.

LEAVES: Alternate. Lower leaves triangular, hastate to deltoid, toothed and wavy margined, 1-1/2 to 2-3/4 inches long.

FLOWERING: June - November

CHENOPODIACEAE

Atriplex rosea   ***REDSCALE**

DESCRIPTION Annual, erect, branched, 1 to 3 feet high, herbage green, sometimes mealy. Found on alkaline soil in many plant communities.

FLOWERS: In axillary clusters and terminal spikes, green. Calyx 5-cleft, petals none, stamens 5. Bracts subtending pistillate flowers united to about the middle.

LEAVES: Alternate, ovate, 3/4 to 2 inches long. Toothed and wavy margined.

FLOWERING: July - October

Atriplex semibaccata Plate 435   ***AUSTRALIAN SALTBUSH**

DESCRIPTION: Perennial low shrub, many branched, prostrate, leafy, 8 to 48 inches long, when young covered with bran-like scales, with age not hairy nor covered with scales. Found in disturbed areas near roads and marshes.

FLOWERS: Green. Pistillate flowers in axils, staminate flowers in small terminal clusters. Bracts subtending pistillate flowers are fleshy, become red with age, sepals 5, petals none, stamens 5.

LEAVES: Alternate, elliptic-oblong 3/8 to 1-1/4 inches long, short stems. Somewhat toothed and wavy margined.

FLOWERING: April - December

Atriplex serenana   **ANNUAL SALTBUSH**

DESCRIPTION: Annual, branched, leafy, spreading, 2 to 6 feet across and 1 to 3 feet high. Found on alkaline soil in many plant communities.

CHENOPODIACEAE

FLOWERS: Green. Staminate flowers in terminal panicles, pistillate flowers in small axillary clusters. Bracts subtending pistillate flowers united to the middle, toothed above. Seed brown.

LEAVES: Alternate, lanceolate to oval, dentate or smooth margined, 3/4 to 1-1/4 inches long, on very short stems.

FLOWERING: May - October

Bassia hyssopifolia   ***FIVE-HOOK BASSIA**

DESCRIPTION: Annual, branching from base, hairy, 1 to 2 feet long. Found on disturbed soil near the coast.

FLOWERS: In small axillary clusters, green, hairy. Calyx 5-lobed, incurved with a hook on the back of each sepal; petals none; stamens 5, pistil 1 or in pistillate flowers — stamens 0, pistil 1.

LEAVES: Alternate, linear-lanceolate, 3/4 to 1¼ inches long, hairy.

FLOWERING: May - October

Beta vulgaris   ***GARDEN BEET**

DESCRIPTION: Annual, with a beet for a taproot, several stems, or 1, rising from the crown, leafy, not hairy, 1 to 4 feet high. Found as an escape from gardens and has become established in low moist ground near the coast.

FLOWERS: In clusters in panicled spikes, green. Calyx 5-parted, petals none, stamens 5, styles 2-3. Each flower has both stamens and pistil.

LEAVES: Alternate, deltoid to ovate-oblong, 4 to 8 inches long on long stems.

FLOWERING: July - October

305

CHENOPODIACEAE

Chenopodium album   *LAMBS' QUARTERS

DESCRIPTION: Annual, erect, branching, mealy, pale green, red veined, 1 to 6 feet high. Found in disturbed soil throughout.

FLOWERS: In clusters on dense upper axillary spikes, green. Calyx deeply 5-cleft, mealy, the sepals with a central longitudinal ridge; petals none; stamens 5. Seeds black and shiny, horizontal.

LEAVES: Alternate, rhombic-ovate to lanceolate, irregularly toothed and wavy margined, 3/8 to 2 inches long. Whiter below than above.

FLOWERING: June - November

Chenopodium ambrosioides   *MEXICAN TEA

DESCRIPTION: Perennial herb, erect, usually branched, 1-1/2 to 5-1/2 feet high. Odorous. Sometimes woolly when young, not mealy. Found along streams and in disturbed moist places throughout. Common.

FLOWERS: Green. On spikes that are axillary, forming a pyramidal panicle at the top of the plant. Flowers are intermixed with leaves. Calyx deeply 5-cleft, dotted, sticky; petals none; stamens 5, pistil 1. Seed horizontal, reddish.

LEAVES: Alternate, oblong to lanceolate, wavy margined, sometimes toothed, 3/4 to 4 inches long, smaller high on the plant.

FLOWERING: June - December

Chenopodium berlandieri   *GOOSEFOOT

DESCRIPTION: Annual, erect, mealy, to 4-1/2 feet high. Found on disturbed soil throughout.

CHENOPODIACEAE

FLOWERS: In clusters in terminal panicles, green. Calyx 5-parted, sepals, strongly keeled, not sticky, petals none, stamens 5. Seeds 1/16 inch in diameter, horizontal. Covering is densely and evenly pitted.

LEAVES: Alternate, rhombic-ovate to lanceolate, irregularly toothed and wavy margined, dull on upper surface.

FLOWERING: June - November

Chenopodium botrys   *JERUSALEM OAK
                                        FEATHER GERANIUM

DESCRIPTION: Annual, erect, branching, hairy, sticky, fragrant, 8 to 24 inches high, not mealy. Found in sandy soil.

FLOWERS: In many flowered cymes, green, downy, calyx deeply 5-parted, petals none, stamens 5. The stems to the cymes axillary from the main stem. Seed dull dark brown.

LEAVES: Alternate, oblong to oval in outline, lobed, 3/8 to 2 inches long. Pinnately cleft, the lobe usually toothed.

FLOWERING: June - October

Chenopodium californicum   CALIFORNIA GOOSEFOOT
                                        SOAP PLANT

DESCRIPTION: Perennial herb, several stems rising obliquely or erect, sparsely mealy on young herbage, 1 to 3 feet long. Found in Grassland, Coastal Sage Scrub, and Southern Oak Woodland.

FLOWERS: In clusters in long dense terminal spikes, green, calyx 5-cleft to the middle, petals none, stamens 5. Seeds vertical.

CHENOPODIACEAE

LEAVES: Alternate, deltoid, sharply and unequally toothed and wavy margined, 1-1/4 to 4 inches long. Lower leaf stems as long as the leaves.

FLOWERING: March - June

FIELD NOTE: The root of the plant has been grated on a rock and used as a soap.

Chenopodium macrospermum Plate 402   COAST GOOSEFOOT
var. *Halophilum*

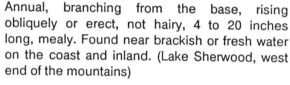

DESCRIPTION: Annual, branching from the base, rising obliquely or erect, not hairy, 4 to 20 inches long, mealy. Found near brackish or fresh water on the coast and inland. (Lake Sherwood, west end of the mountains)

FLOWERS: In crowded terminal clusters on spikes from axils of reduced upper leaves, green, small, calyx 5-lobed, petals none, stamens 5. Seeds vertical.

LEAVES: Alternate, deltoid, not hairy, mealy below, coarsely toothed and wavy margined, 5/8 to 2 inches long. Stems not longer than the leaf blades.

FLOWERING: July - October

Chenopodium multifidum   *CUT-LEAVED GOOSEFOOT

DESCRIPTION: Annual, branching from the base, prostrate, 8 to 28 inches long, more or less fleshy, sticky, not mealy. Found in disturbed areas, mostly near the coast.

FLOWERS: In axils, 1-3 sessile flowers, green; calyx urn-shaped, shallowly 3-5 pointed; petals none; stamens 5; styles 3 on 1 pistil. Seed is dotted.

CHENOPODIACEAE

LEAVES: Alternate, oblong in outline, pinnately cleft, 3/8 to 1-1/4 inches long.

FLOWERING: June - November

Chenopodium murale   ***NETTLE-LEAF GOOSEFOOT**
SOWBANE

DESCRIPTION: Annual, stout, succulent, mealy, branching at the base and rising obliquely, dark green, 8 to 15 inches long. Found in disturbed areas as a common weed.

FLOWERS: In dense axillary or terminal leafless panicles, green, bractless, sessile and clustered. Calyx deeply 5-cleft, not sticky; petals none; stamens 5. Seeds horizontal.

LEAVES: Alternate, rhombic-ovate, irregularly and sharply toothed. Shiny on upper surface, 1 to 1-3/4 inch long.

FLOWERING: All year, mostly in the spring.

Chenopodium pumilio   ***TASMANIAN GOOSEFOOT**

DESCRIPTION: Annual, branching from the base, hairy, sticky, low or ascending, 8 to 16 inches long, not mealy. Found on sandy soils in fields and as a weed in gardens. (West Los Angeles)

FLOWERS: In small headlike clusters, all axillary, green, sticky; calyx deeply 5-parted sticky; petals none; stamen 1. Seed vertical.

LEAVES: Alternate, oblong to ovate, 3/8 to 3/4 inch long. Coarsely toothed and wavy margined. Stems almost as long as the leaves.

FLOWERING: June - September

CHENOPODIACEAE

Chenopodium strictum   ***WHITE GOOSEFOOT**
var. glaucophyllum

DESCRIPTION: Annual, mealy, not sticky. Found in disturbed soil, occasionally in low places.

FLOWERS: In straight axillary spikes or terminal panicles, green; calyx deeply 5-cleft, the sepals with a central longitudinal ridge; petals none; stamens 5. Seed less than 1/16 inch in diameter, horizontal; seed covering smooth or finely and irregularly pitted.

LEAVES: Alternate, lower leaves ovate, dentate or serrate, upper leaves lanceolate, 3/8 to 2 inches long. Dull on upper surface.

FLOWERING: August - October

Salicornia europaea   **ANNUAL PICKLEWEED**
SLENDER GLASSWORT

DESCRIPTION: Annual succulent herb, 3 to 9 inches high, jointed stems, opposite branches from the main branch. Joints longer than broad. Flowering spikes, or horns, 3/4 to 2-1/4 inches long. Found in salt-marsh mudflats. (Point Mugu)

FLOWERS: In opposite clusters of 3 with middle flower highest, green, in axils of scales of the thickened upper joints; calyx small, petals none, stamens 2, pistil 1 with 2 or 3 styles.

LEAVES: Opposite, reduced to scales at the nodes.

FLOWERING: July - November

Salicornia subterminalis   **PARISH'S GLASSWORT**

DESCRIPTION: Perennial small shrub, stems spreading to erect, jointed, 1/2 to 1 foot high. Many crowded branchlets. Flowering spikes 3/4 to 1-1/2 inches long. Found in salt marshes along the coast. (Malibu Lagoon, Mugu Lagoon)

CHENOPODIACEAE

FLOWERS: Low on the spike, sterile ones above, green; calyx bladder-like with an opening on the side away from the stem, petals none, stamens 2. Seeds brown, hairless.

LEAVES: Opposite, reduced to scales at the nodes.

FLOWERING: April - September

Salicornia virginica

WOODY GLASSWORT, PICKLEWEED

DESCRIPTION: Perennial, shrubby with several stems, decumbant, 8 to 24 inches long. Jointed stems, joints longer than broad. Fruiting spikes, or horns, 5/8 to 2 inches long. 1/8 inch thick. Found in colonies all along the coast on upper beaches and in salt marshes.

FLOWERS: In opposite clusters, green, in axils of scales of the thickened upper joints. Seeds brown, downy.

LEAVES: Opposite, scale-like, at the nodes.

FLOWERING: August - November

Salsola tragus Plate 254
[Salsola pestifer]

*RUSSIAN THISTLE, TUMBLEWEED

DESCRIPTION: Annual, densely branched, soft and fleshy when young, rigid when dry. Globe-shaped to 6 feet in diameter. Uprooted by the strong fall winds, the plant tumbles along roads and open fields, dropping seeds along its route. Found along fences and in cultivated fields.

FLOWERS: Looks like a membranous saucer, reddish or greenish, small, subtended by 3 bracts in leaf axils, no petals.

311

CHENOPODIACEAE

LEAVES: Alternate, slender, almost threadlike, lower ones 1-1/4 to 2-1/4 inches long, the upper shorter and broader.

FLOWERING: May - November

Suaeda californica   **CALIFORNIA SEA BLITE**

DESCRIPTION: Perennial low shrub, branching, ascending or decumbent, leafy, stout, covered with a bloom, 1 to 3 feet long. Found in salt marshes along the coast.

FLOWERS: 1 or 2 in leaf axils, green; calyx 5-lobed, cleft halfway; petals none; stamens 5. Seeds black, shining.

LEAVES: Alternate, narrowly linear, fleshy, tubular. 5/8 to 1-1/4 inches long.

FLOWERING: July - October

Suaeda calceoliformis   **SEA BLITE**

DESCRIPTION: Annual, leafy, not hairy, stout erect branches, 1 to 2 feet high. Found in salt marshes along the coast. (Pacific Palisades)

FLOWERS: Solitary or clustered in leaf axils, green; calyx 5-lobed, each lobe backed with a horn-like appendage; petals none, stamens 5. Seeds black.

LEAVES: Alternate, linear to narrow lanceolate, tubular, smooth margined, 3/4 to 2 inches long.

FLOWERING: July - October

CISTACEAE
ROCK-ROSE FAMILY

Of the 8 genera and 200 species found worldwide, 2 are found locally, 1 native, 1 introduced.

CISTACEAE

Recognition characteristics: Sepals 5, petals 5, stamens many, carpels united to form 1 pistil, fruit a capsule. Both of the local species are shrubs.

Cistus ladanifer   ***CRIMSON-SPOT ROCKROSE**

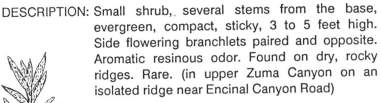

DESCRIPTION: Small shrub, several stems from the base, evergreen, compact, sticky, 3 to 5 feet high. Side flowering branchlets paired and opposite. Aromatic resinous odor. Found on dry, rocky ridges. Rare. (in upper Zuma Canyon on an isolated ridge near Encinal Canyon Road)

FLOWERS: Showy in terminal cymes, aromatic; 5 sepals; 5 petals, white with a dark crimson spot up from the base; stamens many, bright yellow; ovary superior. Seedpod globular, slightly flattened, 1/2 inch in diameter, in 10 segments.

LEAVES: Opposite, clasping, narrowly elliptic to broadly linear, shiny, sticky, 1-1/2 to 2-1/2 inches long.

FLOWERING: March - August

FIELD NOTE: This is the stickiest plant in the mountains. Some species produce a resin used in perfume. I don't know if this species can be so used, but one method of collecting the resin without destroying the plant sounds ingenious. In the Mediterranean area sheep are driven through the field of plants and the resin sticks to the wool. My research is incomplete; I don't know how to get the resin off the sheep.

Helianthemum scoparium Plate 139   **ROCK-ROSE**
  var. vulgare

DESCRIPTION: Shrubby plant with many green ascending stems about 1-1/2 feet tall. Found in chaparral openings, often on ridges that have a view of the ocean.

313

CISTACEAE

FLOWERS: Many individual stems in a narrow panicle. 5 sepals about 1/8 inch long (2 are small and bract-like); 5 petals yellow, about 1/4 inch long; about 20 stamens; 1 pistil.

LEAVES: Alternate, narrowly linear, roll backward from the main vein, 3/8 to 1 inch long. Leaves drop from the plant in early summer.

FLOWERING: March - June

FIELD NOTE: The name of the genus *Helianthe* comes from the Greek words *helios* (sun) and *antheon* (flower). The flowers open only in the sun.

CONVOLVULACEAE

MORNING GLORY FAMILY

This family of 1500 species, more or less, and 50 genera includes the sweet potato, dichondra (a lawn plant), and trees, shrubs, herbs, and vines. The 7 local species are herbaceous or vinelike. All have similar flower parts: 5 distinct sepals, corolla of 5 united petals, and 5 stamens each attached at the base to the corolla.

Calystegia macrostegia Plate 63   **MORNING GLORY**
  ssp cyclostegia

DESCRIPTION: Perennial vine with twining stems 12 feet long. Stems often woody below. Grows in Coastal Sage Scrub and Chaparral. Common. Abundant after fires.

FLOWERS: White, often with purple stripes on the outside along the folds, usually solitary but sometimes 2 flowers together. Membranous, purplish, involucre bracts about 1/2 inch long, closely subtending the calyx. 5-lobed calyx, 5-lobed corolla 1 to 1-3/4 inches long, 3 stamens, and 2 broadly linear stigmas.

CONVOLVULACEAE

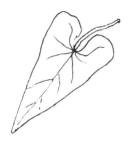

LEAVES: Alternate, triangular-lanceolate to ovate 2/3 to 2 inches long, the basal leaves usually angled. Stems shorter than the blades.

FLOWERING: March - August

Calystegia soldonella   Plate 62   **BEACH MORNING GLORY**

DESCRIPTION: Perennial, fleshy, 20 inch long stems growing from a strong root system. Grows on sand dunes near the ocean in Coastal Strand.

FLOWERS: Funnelform, rose to purple, on short stems, low to the ground. 1/4 to 1/2 inch membranous bracts subtend the 5 sepals, a 5-lobed corolla, 5 stamens, 2 more or less cylindrical stigmas. Stigma and style are distinct.

LEAVES: Alternate, heart-shaped, shiny green, 3/4 to 2 inches long and as broad.

FLOWERING: April - August

Convolvulus arvensis   ***BINDWEED**

DESCRIPTION: Deep-rooted perennial with 40-inch twining stems. Introduced, found in cultivated fields and other open places.

FLOWERS: Usually solitary on a stem with bracts well below the sepals; 5 sepals about 1/8 inch long; 5-lobed corolla white (sometimes with some pink), about 3/4 inch long; 5 stamens.

LEAVES: Alternate, arrowhead to ovate shaped about 1-1/2 inches long. Leaf stems slender and shorter than the blade.

FLOWERING: May - July

CONVOLVULACEAE

Cressa truxillensis
var. vallicola   ALKALI WEED

DESCRIPTION: Low branching perennial herb that colonizes an area. Found in salt flats and clay mudflats in Coastal Salt Marsh.

FLOWERS: Small, white, solitary in the upper axils; 5 sepals covered with fine, grayish-white hairs; 5-lobed corolla about 1/4 inch long; 5 stamens exserted. 2 styles.

LEAVES: Alternate, oblong-ovate, 3/8 inch long, not stalked.

Dichondra occidentalis   WESTERN DICHONDRA

DESCRIPTION: Creeping perennial herb, forms mats, sometimes cultivated as a lawn. Found on dry, sandy stream banks and under trees. Coastal Sage Scrub, Chaparral, Southern Oak Woodland.

FLOWERS: Solitary, white to purplish, on axillary stems; 5-lobed calyx 1/16 inch long; 5-lobed corolla 1/8 inch long; 5 stamens; 2 styles.

LEAVES: 3/4 to 2 inches across, singly on slender stems at rooting nodes.

FLOWERING: March - May

Ipomoea purpurea   *COMMON MORNING GLORY

DESCRIPTION: Annual with twining hairy stems. A garden escape found near habitation.

FLOWERS: In clusters of 1-5, purple, blue, pink or white. 5 pointed sepals 1/2 to 5/8 inches long. 5-lobed corolla funnel shaped, 2 to 2-1/4 inches long; 5 stamens, 1 pistil.

LEAVES: Alternate, broadly heart-shaped, ovate leaves, 4-1/2 inches long. Downy.

FLOWERING: June - November

CORNACEAE

DOGWOOD FAMILY

One species of tree represents the Dogwood family in our mountains, and it is rare. Dogwoods need cool canyons and moisture, so are found in just a few places.

Cornus glabrata   **BROWN DOGWOOD**

DESCRIPTION: 15 to 20 foot tree, usually in a thicket because it grows from underground shoots. Found along mountain streams. Rare.

FLOWERS: Dull white flowers, 1 to 1-3/4 inches across; calyx a small, pointed tube; 4 petals, 4 stamens, 1 pistil.

LEAVES: Opposite, lanceolate to elliptic, 1 to 2 inches long and half as wide, on short stems, simple, same color of green on both sides.

FLOWERING: May - June

CRASSULACEAE

STONECROP FAMILY

Three genera of the Stonecrop family are found in the Santa Monica Mountains: Crassula, an annual; Dudleya and Sedum, perennials. They are all succulent herbs. Our Crassula has minute opposite leaves, flowers are 4 merous. Dudleyas have basal rosette leaves; flowers are 5 merous. Our Sedum has loose basal rosette leaves, flowers are 5 merous.

Crassula erecta Plate 252   **PIGMY WEED**

DESCRIPTION: A small (1 to 2 inches tall) erect, branching annual, often reddish tinged. Found in shallow soil, often sandy. Common.

CRASSULACEAE

FLOWERS: In small, axillary bracted clusters, red, 4 sepals 1/32 inch long. 4 petals 1/32 inch long.

LEAVES: Opposite, joining at the base, fleshy, ovate, about 1/8 inch long.

FLOWERING: February - May

**Dudleya abramsii
ssp. parva**   DUDLEYA

DESCRIPTION: Perennial herb, succulent, with a small rosette, 2 to 4 inches high. The leaves die back early in the season. Found in open Grassland on clayey rocky slopes. (Conejo Grade)

FLOWERS: 10-20, on curled simple cymes, on stem to 6 inches high; 5-cleft calyx rounded below, pointed above; 5 petals pale yellow, sometimes with red flecks.

LEAVES: Linear to oblanceolate leaves in a 2-1/2 inch diameter rosette. A light white bloom but not chalky. Small, sparsely distributed leaves on the flower stem, lanceolate to tri-angular-ovate, 3/16 to 5/8 inch long.

FLOWERING: May - June

Dudleya blochmaniae   BLOCKMAN'S LIVE-FOREVER

DESCRIPTION: Perennial herb, succulent, rising from a corm. 1 or more stems to 6 inches high, basal rosette of 5 to 8 leaves. Found on dry rocky slopes in Coastal Sage Scrub. Uncommon.

FLOWERS: On a cyme of 2 or more branches. Flowers on very short stems; 5-cleft calyx 1/8-3/16 inch long; 5 petals to 3/8 inch long, red or purple; stamens exserted. Sweet odor.

CRASSULACEAE

LEAVES: Yellow-green to 2-1/2 inches long in a basal rosette of 5-8 leaves. Linear-oblanceolate to linear-spatulate. Some leaves on the flower stem, deltoid-lanceolate to broadly ovate, 3/16 to 1 inch long.

FLOWERING: May - June

Dudleya caespitosa **Plate 250**   LIVE-FOREVER

DESCRIPTION: Green succulent perennial, sometimes with a whitish bloom, growing 1/2 to 1-1/2 feet tall. Found near the coast on sandy bluffs from Point Dume west, usually in clumps.

FLOWERS: In curled cymes on 1/8 inch stems; 5-lobed calyx 1/4 to 5/16 inch high and to 3/8 inch broad; 5 petals yellow to red, up to 5/8 inch long.

LEAVES: The basal rosette leaves shiny, up to 8 inches long and 2 inches wide, lanceolate. Alternate leaves along the stem, triangular-ovate, 3/8 to 1 inch long. Herbage is not powdery.

FLOWERING: April - July

Dudleya cymosa
ssp. marcescens   MARCESCENT DUDLEYA

DESCRIPTION: Perennial herb, succulent, with a dense basal rosette 1-1/2 to 3 inches in diameter. Plant not over 4 inches high with a woody base up to 1/4 inch thick. Found on rocky slopes and cliffs in shade. Chaparral. (Little Sycamore Canyon)

FLOWERS: On curled simple cymes, each 3-5 flowered, on a stem to 4 inches high. Individual flowers on stems 3/16 to 1/2 inch long; 5-cleft; 5 petals bright yellow often with red markings, about 1/2 inch long.

CRASSULACEAE

LEAVES: In a dense basal rosette, lanceolate, thick, 5/8 to 1-3/8 inches long, 3/16 to 1/2 inch wide; alternate leaves along the stem, much reduced. Leaves wither in summer.

FLOWERING: May - June

FIELD NOTE: This Dudleya is endemic to the Santa Monica Mountains.

Dudleya cymosa Plate 171
ssp. ovatifolia

SANTA MONICA
MOUNTAINS DUDLEYA

DESCRIPTION: Perennial herb, succulent, with a dense basal rosette 2 to 4-1/4 inches in diameter. Plant not over 6 inches high with a woody base 3/8 to 5/8 inch thick. Found on open rocky slopes and cliffs, often in shade, in Coastal Sage Scrub and Chaparral, from Topanga Canyon west to Arroyo Sequit.

FLOWERS: On curled simple cymes, each 3-5 flowered on a stem to 6 inches high; 5-cleft calyx 1/8 inch high; 5 petals bright yellow, 3/8 inch long.

LEAVES: A dense basal rosette of 6-10 shining ovate to elliptic leaves 3/4 to 2 inches long. Smaller alternate leaves on the flower stem. Leaves are not powdery.

FLOWERING: March - May

FIELD NOTE: Agoura Live-forever (*ssp. agourensis*) grows on an outcrop of conglomerate rock on the north side of Ladyface Peak.)

Dudleya lanceolata Plate 416

LANCE-LEAF
LIVE-FOREVER

DESCRIPTION: Perennial herb, succulent with a rosette of pale green leaves. 4 to 16 inches in diameter; 8 to 24 inches high. Found on dry rocky slopes in Chaparral and Coastal Sage Scrub. Common.

320

CRASSULACEAE

FLOWERS: On curled simple cymes, many flowers on an 8 to 24 inch, reddish stem; 5-cleft calyx; 5 petals pale green tinged with red or orange, 3/8 to 5/8 inch long.

LEAVES: Pale green lanceolate leaves 2 to 8 inches long in a rosette. Smaller leaves sessile on the flowering stem. Herbage is not powdery.

FLOWERING: May - July

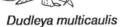

Dudleya multicaulis

LONG-STEMMED HASSEANTHUS

DESCRIPTION: Perennial herb, succulent, rising from a corm, 1 or more stems to 14 inches high. Basal tuft of leaves. Found on slopes of Coastal Sage Scrub and in openings in Chaparral. Uncommon.

FLOWERS: On a cyme of elongated racemes, many flowers, on very short stems; 5-cleft calyx; 5 petals yellow, often flocked with red; stamens exserted.

LEAVES: A basal rosette of as many as 15 linear leaves. Leaves tubular, up to 6 inches long. Smaller leaves on flower stem, alternate, clasping, turgid, tinged with purple.

FLOWERING: May - June

Dudleya pulverulenta Plates 268, 415   **CHALK LIVE-FOREVER**

DESCRIPTION: Perennial herb, succulent, with a basal rosette up to 20 inches in diameter. Largest of the Dudleyas, sometimes 2-1/2 feet high, completely covered with a thick layer of white, mealy powder. Has a short woody stem 1-1/2 to 3-1/2 inches thick. Found on rocky cliffs and canyons in Coastal Sage Scrub and Chaparral. Common.

CRASSULACEAE

FLOWERS: On curled simple cymes. Stout 30 inch main flower stems carry 10-30 flowers on 1 inch stems; 5-cleft calyx chalky, about 3/8 inch long; 5 petals red and pink vertically striped, about 3/4 inch long.

LEAVES: About 30 obovate-spatulate thick leaves form a heavy rosette to 20 inches in diameter. Many clasping leaves on the flower stem.

FLOWERING: May - July

Dudleya verityi   DUDLEYA

DESCRIPTION: Perennial, succulent herb, usually with several small rosettes, evergreen. Found on north facing volcanic rock between Conejo Mountain and Long Grade.

FLOWERS: On curled simple cymes to 6 inches high; 5-cleft calyx; 5 petals tubular, united less than 1/3 their length, pale lemon-yellow, tips spreading 90° or more.

LEAVES: In several small tufted rosettes white-waxy when young. Leaves oblong to oblanceolate, 3/4 to 2 inches long.

FLOWERING: May - June

Sedum spathulifolium Plate 226   STONECROP

DESCRIPTION: Perennial, succulent herb, 2 to 6 inches high. Propagates by lateral offshoots. Found on north and east facing cliffs. (Malibu Creek State Park)

FLOWERS: 15-20, in terminal cymes, simple to compound, 3-parted; 5 sepals; 5 petals yellow, narrow lanceolate, 3/8 inch long, spreading.

CRASSULACEAE

LEAVES: Alternate on stems, spatulate; basal leaves broadly spatulate, 3/16 to 1-1/4 inches long. Basal rosettes at ends of lateral offshoots root to establish new plants.

FLOWERING: April - May

FIELD NOTE: This stonecrop reaches its southern coast limit in disjunct Santa Monica Mountains populations.

CUCURBITACEAE

GOURD FAMILY

The 2 members of the Gourd Family found in the Santa Monica Mountains are vines — one stays on the ground, the other climbs into trees and on bushes. They both have an immense perennial root. Male and female flowers are separate, but on the same plant. Calyx and corolla are 5-lobed.

Cucurbita foetidissima   Plates 172, 447   **GOURD**
                                                          CALABAZILLA

DESCRIPTION: Perennial herb, dies back in winter, and in the spring grows as a rank vine that covers an area 25 feet in diameter. Found on Coastal Strand, Coastal Sage Scrub, and Grassland.

FLOWERS: Male and female separate but on the same plant. Male flowers about 4-1/2 inches long, bell-shaped, ribbed and veiny; 5 prominent stamens. Female flowers slightly smaller, pistil thick, short structure. Both flowers are yellow, 5-lobed, and downy. 5 sepals pointed. The fruit is a gourd.

LEAVES: Triangular-ovate, 10 inches long, on sturdy stems.

FLOWERING: June - August

CUCURBITACEAE

Marah macrocarpus   Plates 51, 419

WILD CUCUMBER
MAN-ROOT

DESCRIPTION: Perennial herb, dies back in the summer, and every winter the large woody root (sometimes weighing 100 lbs.) sends up rapidly growing shoots. We usually first notice it in December, and again later when the prickly seedpods are formed. Found in Coastal Sage Scrub, Chaparral, and Southern Oak Woodland.

FLOWERS: Male and female separate but on same plant, often from same leaf axil. Staminate flowers in racemes; pistillate solitary. Sepals are rudimentary; 5 petals. Large seeds in a 5 inch long, spiny, ovoid pod.

LEAVES: Palmately lobed, alternate, not hairy. Tendrils opposite the leaves.

FLOWERING: January - April

CUPRESSACEAE

CYPRESS FAMILY

World wide, the Cypress family includes 19 genera and 130 species. 5 genera are native to the United States. 2 species are found in the Santa Monica Mountains, probably neither truly native. The *Juniperus californica* colony that was south of Cornell Corners until the fire of 1978 burned them is of unknown ancestry. The many individuals of *Cupressus forbesii* established throughout are the result of reseeding after a fire.

Other conifers that have been planted in the area have not successfully reproduced and are not considered as natural populations.

Cupressus forbesii

*TECATE CYPRESS

DESCRIPTION: A small evergreen tree. Native to Santa Ana Mountains in Orange County and in San Diego County. Found on Mt. Tecate.

CUPRESSACEAE

Plantings of individual trees and reseeding after fires have scattered a few cypresses in unexpected places— usually in Chaparral at higher elevations.

FLOWERS: Male cones about 1/8 inch long carry pollen. Seed cones globular, dull gray-brown and about 1 inch in diameter.

LEAVES: Foliage in light green, scale-like leaves, each almost 1/16 inch long and sharply pointed. A small resin pit on most leaves. White, waxy film gives an overall grayish appearance. Crushed leaves have a strong resinous odor.

FIELD NOTE: Tecate Cypress cones hang on a tree for many years and open only as a result of fire. Although not plentiful, these trees can compete in chaparral that is periodically subjected to fire.

Juniperus californica   CALIFORNIA JUNIPER

DESCRIPTION: Aromatic evergreen shrub, tree-like, 12 feet tall, occasionally to 30 feet; fluted straight trunk; outer bark gray, thin and shredding. (Can be seen from the north end of Cornell Road) Rare.

FLOWERS: Male and female separate but on same tree. Staminate cones minute, scaly; pistillate berrylike. Fruit is a blue berry, with dense bloom, aging to reddish-brown, 1/2 inch in diameter, maturing early in September of the second year.

LEAVES: Scale-like, pale yellow-green, 1/8 inch long, resinous, overlapping one another to form stemlike structures.

FLOWERING: January - March

CUSCUTACEAE

Parasitic plants, leafless, rootless, viney. The slender yellow or orange stems are fastened to the host plant by *haustoria*, a knoblike organ that penetrates and draws nourishment. Calyx is 4-5 lobed; corolla is 4-5 lobed, 4-5 stamens, 2 united carpels form 1 pistil.

Cuscuta californica   Plate 64   DODDER

DESCRIPTION: Annual, medium yellow stems, parasitic on a wide variety of plants throughout the mountains. Favorite hosts are Sage Buckwheat, Deerweed, and some of the composites.

FLOWERS: 3/16 inch long or less, clustered in loose panicles. Corolla narrowly bell-shaped with narrow pointed lobes turned back at the tip.

LEAVES: None.

FLOWERING: May - August

Cuscuta pentagonia   DODDER

DESCRIPTION: Annual, yellow thread-like stems covering host plant (cockle bur and other streamside plants.)

FLOWERS: 3/32 inch-long in dense clusters about 1/2 inch thick. Calyx and corolla tube about equal length.

LEAVES: None

FLOWERING: July - November

Cuscuta salina   DODDER

DESCRIPTION: Annual, slender orange stems, parasitic to saltbush and other salt marsh plants.

CUSCUTACEAE

FLOWERS: 3/32 inch long, in a more or less flat cluster; 5 sepals; 5-lobed, bell-like corolla about the length of the sepals.

LEAVES: None

FLOWERING: May - September

Cuscuta subinclusa   CANYON DODDER

DESCRIPTION: Annual, coarse orange stems, parasitic to Laurel Sumac, Ceanothus, Bush Monkey Flower, Willow, Oaks, and others.

FLOWERS: 3/16 inch long, scattered or in clusters; calyx less than 1/2 the length of the cylindrical corolla.

LEAVES: None

FLOWERING: June-October
Illustration: Dodder on Laurel sumac.

CYPERACEAE

SEDGE FAMILY

The Sedges are usually grass-like herbs with solid stems, 3 sided, mostly with alternate basal leaves. Found in wet and marshy areas. 4 genera and 21 species are known in the Santa Monica Mountains. They are not individually described here.

DATISCACEAE

DATISCA FAMILY

One species in one genera, found only in California, is the total representative of the Datisca family in the United States and is native to the Santa Monica Mountains.

DATISCACEAE

Datisca glomerata Plate 401   **DURANGO ROOT**

DESCRIPTION: Clusters of stout, hollow stems reaching 8 feet grow from a perennial root. Usually grows on banks of intermittent streams.

FLOWERS: Several in each leaf axil along the raceme. Staminate (male) and pistillate (female) on different plants. The calyx of staminate flowers is 1/16 inch long and 4-9 lobed. The calyx of pistillate flowers is about 1/4 inch long and 3-toothed. No petals, about 10 stamens.

LEAVES: Alternate, 6 inches long, incised, and sharply sawlike, on a 1 inch stem.

FLOWERING: May - July

ELATINACEAE

WATERWORT FAMILY

The 1 member of this family in our area is *Elatine californica*, a semi-aquatic plant. Worldwide, 2 genera and 40 species are found. All are annuals. Characteristically, the waterworts are small plants with opposite leaves and membranous stipules between them. The flowers are small, symmetrical, solitary, and 2 to 5 merous. Our local plant is 4 merous.

Elatine californica   **CALIFORNIA WATERWORT**

DESCRIPTION: A low matted, small leaved plant, found in fresh water and mud flats.

FLOWERS: About 1/16 inch diameter; 4 sepals, 4 obovate petals, 8 stamens, 1 pistil with 4 styles. The small, curved seeds are pitted in rows.

LEAVES: Opposite, narrow spatulate, about 1/8 inch long.

FLOWERING: March - August

EQUISETACEAE

HORSETAIL FAMILY

Rushlike, fluted, cylindrical, stems rising from a perennial underground rhizome. 2 species of 1 genus found in swampy places and along streams.

Equisetum laevigatum Plate 480   SMOOTH SCOURING
                                                        RUSH

DESCRIPTION: Slender, green, reed-like plant grows to 3 feet along waterways in wet sand or clay. Rootstalk creeping, widely branching, perennial; above ground shoots die back annually; stems smooth to the touch.

FLOWERS: A solitary cone (strobilus) develops at the top of each fertile stem.

LEAVES: The nearest this plant comes to a leaf is a 1/3 inch leaf-sheath that spreads over the stem node in a clasping manner. The green bamboo-like stem performs photosynthesis.

FLOWERING: April - July

Equisetum telmateia   GIANT HORSETAIL
ssp. braunii

DESCRIPTION: Tall, slender stem to 8 feet high; found along waterways throughout. Infertile branches green, branched at nodes; fertile stems brownish, shorter, do not branch.

FLOWERS: 2 to 3 inch spike at top of 1-1/2 foot high fertile stem.

LEAVES: None. The cylindrical green stem, furrowed with about 30 grooves, performs photosynthesis.

FLOWERING: February - April

FIELD NOTE: From the Latin, *equus*, horse, and *seta*, bristle.

329

ERICACEAE

HEATH FAMILY

The Heath family includes many perennial shrubs. Leaves are mostly alternate, simple, and leathery. Most of the 25 genera indigenous to the United States prefer acid soils and more rain than found locally. 2 genera and 3 species grow in the Santa Monica Mountains in Chaparral, away from the coast and rarely below 500 feet.

Arctostaphylos glandulosa Plate 437   EASTWOOD MANZANITA

DESCRIPTION: A woody, erect shrub, grows 8 feet high; stems crooked, smooth, and reddish colored; bark peels off in layers. Has a basal burl, and root-crown sprouts after a fire. A chaparral plant found on dry, rocky ridges and slopes. Grows with Bigberry Manzanita.

FLOWERS: Small, urn-shaped, white, 1/4 inch long. Fruit is red-brown, about 5/16 inch in diameter, and sticky when developing, becoming dry by mid-summer.

LEAVES: Ovate to lanceolate, dull green 1 to 2 inches long. Branchlets are hairy, leaves somewhat hairy with hairy stems. Evergreen.

FLOWERING: January - April

Arctostaphylos glauca Plate 440 Plate 52   BIGBERRY MANZANITA

DESCRIPTION: Sturdy, more tree-like than Eastwood Manzanita, 15-20 feet high. Trunk and branches reddish-colored, smooth and crooked; No basal burl. Grows with Eastwood Manzanita. Reseeds after fire.

FLOWERS: In a panicle, sometimes in a raceme, white to pink, small urn-shaped, 3/8 inch long. Fruit brownish, about 1/2 inch in diameter, and sticky when developing, dry by mid-summer.

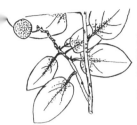

ERICACEAE

LEAVES: Oblong, elliptic or ovate, 1 to 1-3/4 inches long. Both branchlets and leaves are hairless.

FLOWERING: December - March

Comarostaphylis diversifolia Plate 50   **SUMMER HOLLY**
ssp. planifolia

DESCRIPTION: Shrub 6 to 15 feet high. Bark on main stems shredded; leaves leather-like, evergreen. Found in Chaparral. (Upper Carlisle Canyon, Santa Ynez Canyon) Rare.

FLOWERS: Urn shaped in 2 to 5 inch racemes, white,1/4 inch long. Berry red, one seed.

LEAVES: Oblong-ovate, saw-toothed, shiny green above, whitish downy below, 1-1/2 to 3 inches long.

FLOWERING: May - June

FIELD NOTE: *Comarostaphylis diversifolia* is usually considered a Channel Island species that has relic occurrences to the Santa Monica Mountains. The amount of rainfall in the Santa Monicas is marginal for Summer-Holly but it has survived in canyons where fog-shrouded periods in late spring not only increase the moisture in the soil but extend the "rainy" season.

EUPHORBIACEAE
SPURGE FAMILY

This family of 290 genera and 7500 species is well represented in the tropics and semi-tropics. 4 genera and 11 species grow in the Santa Monica Mountains. Many species have products of economic value such as rubber, castor oil, tung oil, cassava and tapioca. Most of the plants characteristically have a milky, latex-like juice. All of the spurge family should be considered poisonous and contact of the juice, particularly with the eyes and the lining of mouth and throat, should be avoided.

EUPHORBIACEAE

The floral structure in the Euphorbia genus is both unique and unusual. Individual flowers are contained in a cyathium (Greek for wine cup), which is a complex of several staminate flowers and one pistillate flower within a parianthlike involucre; the whole looks like a single flower. The other Santa Monica Mountains' genera are characterized by a 5-merous perianth, regular flowers with either sepals or petals or with neither. Pistillate and staminate flowers are separate.

Recognition characteristics of all species: Herbs and shrubs with milky latex. Seeds mottled and have a corky bump. 3-parted pistillate flower. The individual flowers are either pistillate or staminate.

Chamaesyce albomarginata   RATTLESNAKE WEED

DESCRIPTION: Perennial herb, prostrate, not hairy, 2 to 10 inches long. Found on dry slopes near cultivated fields. (Point Dume)

FLOWERS: In a bell-shaped cyathium, solitary from leaf axils. 4-lobed, maroon at the base, white margined. 1 central pistillate flower and 15-30 staminate flowers within the small cyathium. Seed capsule 3-angled, not hairy. Seeds white.

LEAVES: Opposite, orbicular to oblong, 1/8 to 1/4 inch long, on short stems.

FLOWERING: April - November

Chamaesyce maculata   *SPOTTED SPURGE

DESCRIPTION: Annual herb, erect or rising obliquely, usually radiately branching, hairless except for the young tips, 4 to 36 inches high. Found as a weed in disturbed soil.

EUPHORBIACEAE

FLOWERS: In a cyathium, congested at the branch tips, 4-lobed, about 1/32 inch across, white margins; 1 central pistillate flower becoming exserted; 5-11 staminate flowers within the small cyathium. Seed capsules hairy. Seeds gray to brown.

LEAVES: Opposite, oblong, toothed, 3/8 to 1-1/4 inches long, on very short stems.

FLOWERING: April - October

Chamaesyce melanadenia Plate 97　　　　SQUAW SPURGE

DESCRIPTION: Perennial herb, woolly, matted, forking stems, 3 to 8 inches long. Found throughout the area on dry soil.

FLOWERS: In a cyathium at ends of branches, wide bell-shaped, dark red spots at base of lobes, white margined; 1 central pistillate flower becoming exserted; 15-20 staminate flowers within the small cyathium. Seed capsules hairy. Seed 4-angled, white.

LEAVES: Opposite, ovate, smooth margined, 1/8 to 5/16 inch long.

FLOWERING: December - May

Chamaesyce polycarpa　　　　　　　　GOLONDRINA
var. hirtella

DESCRIPTION: Perennial herb, prostrate or obliquely ascending, branching, 2 to 10 inches long; erect hairs on leaves and stems. Found on sand dunes near Point Mugu.

FLOWERS: In a cyathium, solitary at nodes, bell-shaped; lobes white margined, maroon spots at base; 1 central pistillate flower becoming exserted; 15-32 staminate flowers within the small cyathium. Seed capsules hairy. Seeds whitish, 4-angled.

333

EUPHORBIACEAE

LEAVES: Opposite, oblong to round, smooth margined, 1/8 to 5/32 inch long.

FLOWERING: April - October

Chamaesyce serpyllifolia   THYME-LEAVED SPURGE

DESCRIPTION: Annual herb, branching, prostrate, not hairy, 2-14 inches long. Found in disturbed soil near streams and lakes. North slope of west end of the mountains.

FLOWERS: In a cyathium, bell-shaped; white margined. Lobes not horned. 1 central pistillate flower becoming exserted; 5-18 staminate flowers within the small cyathium. Seed capsules not hairy.

LEAVES: Opposite, ovate to obovate, fine teeth at the apex. 1/8 to 1/2 inch long.

FLOWERING: August - October

Croton californicus   CROTON

DESCRIPTION: Perennial herb, branched, downy, 8 to 40 inches high. Found on dry sand in Coastal Sage Scrub and Chaparral.

FLOWERS: On racemes, greenish. Staminate and pistillate flowers on separate plants. Many staminate flowers on 3/8 to 5/8 inch long racemes; calyx 5-parted; 5 petals; 12-15 stamens. Few pistillate flowers on short racemes. Calyx 5-parted, pistil 1, style 3.

LEAVES: Alternate, oblong-elliptic, smooth margined, 5/8 to 1-1/2 inches long, 3/8 to 3/4 inch wide, on stems.

FLOWERING: March - October

334

EUPHORBIACEAE

Eremocarpus setigerus Plate 98   TURKEY MULLEIN

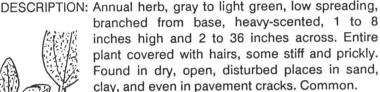

DESCRIPTION: Annual herb, gray to light green, low spreading, branched from base, heavy-scented, 1 to 8 inches high and 2 to 36 inches across. Entire plant covered with hairs, some stiff and prickly. Found in dry, open, disturbed places in sand, clay, and even in pavement cracks. Common.

FLOWERS: Pistillate flowers sessile in axils of upper branches, no calyx, no corolla. Staminate flowers on 1/8 inch long stems in axils of lower branches, calyx of 5-6 sepals; No corolla; 6-7 stamens exserted.

LEAVES: Alternate, entire, 3-veined, ovate to about round. 3/8 to 2 inches long on stems almost as long.

FLOWERING: May - October

FIELD NOTE: The Greek *eremos*, (lonely) and *karpos* (fruit) refers to the solitary carpel of the pistillate flower.

Euphorbia crenulata Plate 169   CHINESE CAPS

DESCRIPTION: Annual herb, not hairy, erect, 1 or more stems branching below and again at the umbel, 5 to 20 inches high. Found on dry soil in many plant communities. (Serrano Canyon)

FLOWERS: In a cyathium 1/16 to 1/8 inch high, on an umbel. Lobes 2-horned; 1 central pistillate flower becoming exserted; several staminate flowers within the small cyathium. Seed capsules not hairy. Seeds brown, globose, narrowly ridged.

LEAVES: Alternate, narrowed at the base, stem-leaves obovate to spatulate smooth-margined; umbel-leaves obovate to rhombic-obovate, sessile, 5/8 to 1-3/8 inches long.

EUPHORBIACEAE

Floral-leaves, opposite or in 3's, deltoid to rhombic-ovate, 3/16 to 5/8 inch long.

FLOWERING: March - August

Euphorbia peplus   *PETTY SPURGE

DESCRIPTION: Annual herb, not hairy, erect, 4 to 18 inches high, 1 or more stems branching below and again at the umbel. Found in moist soil. Is a garden weed.

FLOWERS: In a cyathium 1/16 inch high, bell-shaped, on an umbel. Lobes 2-horned, yellow. Seed capsules not hairy. Seeds gray, oblong, pitted.

LEAVES: Alternate, on stems, round to obovate, smooth-margined, 3/8 to 1-3/8 inches long. Floral-leaves ovate, 1/4 to 5/8 inch long.

FLOWERING: February - August

Ricinis communis Plate 444   *CASTOR-BEAN

DESCRIPTION: Perennial large shrub, often tree-like, with large leaves, 3 to 10 feet high. Found in disturbed areas throughout.

FLOWERS: In clusters on racemes, staminate and pistillate flowers on same plant, with pistillate higher on the plant. Staminate with color of staminate calyx 3-5-parted; no petals; many stamens. Pistillate with calyx 3-5-parted; no petals; 1 pistil; 3 styles bifid, red. Seedpod spiny, 3-celled. Seeds mottled silvery and brown, 3/8 to 1/2 inch long.

LEAVES: Alternate, palmately 5-11-lobed, 4 to 16 inches broad.

FLOWERING: All year.

FABACEAE

This large family of 600 genera and 13,000 species is represented in the Santa Monica Mountains by 14 genera and 62 species. Some botanists recognize the three subfamilies as separate families. They are *Mimosaceae, Caesalpiniaceae,* and *Papilionaceae.* All of the Fabaceae species in the Santa Monica Mountains are in the subspecies *Papilionaceae.*

Recognition characteristics: Herbs, or shrubs. Leaves alternate, palmately or pinnately compound. Flowers pea-shaped with a calyx of 3-5 united sepals; a corolla of 5 unequal petals (except Amortha), the upper petal outside the 2 lateral ones, the lower 2 petals united; 10 stamens, usually 1 is free and the other 9 are united (all 10 stamens are free in *Pickerengia* and united in *Lupinus)*; 1 pistil. Fruit is a legume but variable in appearance.

Amorpha californica   FALSE INDIGO

DESCRIPTION: Shrub 4-1/2 to 9 feet high, downy, heavy-scented. Found in Southern Oak Woodland on the north side of the mountains in the western half.

FLOWERS: In racemes 2-10 inches long; 5-lobed calyx, downy; corolla of 1 petal, reddish-purple, about 3/16 inch long; 10 stamens. Pod 1/4 inch long, curved.

LEAVES: Alternate, odd-pinnate, 4 to 8 inches long on short petioles. 11-27 oblong-elliptical leaflets to each leaf. Each leaflet 3/8 to 1 inch long, downy on both sides. Glandular. Deciduous.

FLOWERING: May - July

Astragalus brauntonii Plate 288   BRAUNTON'S
                                                     RATTLE-WEED

DESCRIPTION: Perennial shrub, erect, hollow-stemmed, 3 to 4½ feet high. Entire plant densely woolly. Found in dry soil in Coastal Sage Scrub and Chaparral. Very rare.

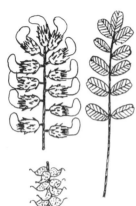

FABACEAE

FLOWERS: Pea-like in dense racemes, 1-1/2 to 3-1/2 inches long; 5-toothed calyx 1/8 inch long, hairy; corolla rose-purple, 3/8 inch long; stamens 9 united; 1 free; pistil 1. Seedpod sessile, hairy, 3/8 inch long.

LEAVES: Alternate, odd-pinnate, 1-1/2 to 5-1/2 inches long. 25-41 leaflets, each to 3/4 inch long, oblong to oblong-elliptic.

FLOWERING: February - June

Astragalus didymocarpus   COMMON DWARF LOCOWEED

DESCRIPTION: Annual herb, 4 inches to 1 foot high, branching from the base. Found in Coastal Sage Scrub and grassy slopes.

FLOWERS: Pea-like in globose heads, cream-white or tinged with purple; 5-toothed calyx, hairy; corolla 1/4 inch long; stamens 9 united, 1 free; pistil 1. Pods erect, about 3/16 inch long, 2-seeded.

LEAVES: Alternate, odd-pinnate 3/4 to 2-1/4 inches long, 7-17 leaflets, linear to linear-oblong, each up to 1/2 inch long.

FLOWERING: March - April

Astragalus gambelianus   GAMBELL'S DWARF LOCOWEED

Description: Annual herb, thinly covered with soft gray or green hairs, 1-1/2 to 8 inches high, branching from the base. Found in Coastal Sage Scrub, Grassland, and Southern Oak Woodlands.

FLOWERS: Pea-like in racemes 1/4 to 3/4 inch long, 4-15 flowers, whitish tinged with violet; 5-toothed calyx, hairy; corolla up to 1/4 inch long; stamens 9 united, 1 free. Pods deflexed, sessile, about 3/16 inch long, 2-seeded.

FABACEAE

LEAVES: Alternate, odd-pinnate, 1/2 to 1-1/4 inches long, 9-13 leaflets, linear, notched, each about 1/4 inch long.

FLOWERING: March - April

Astragalus tener   **SLENDER RATTLE-WEED**

DESCRIPTION: Annual herb, branching from the base, stems angled at nodes, about 1 foot high. Found in grassy alkaline vernal flats near the coast.

FLOWERS: Pea-like, 2 or more in loose heads, sessile; 5-toothed calyx; corolla purple, to 1/2 inch long; stamens 9 united, 1 free. Pods 3/8 inch long, 5 or more seeds.

LEAVES: Alternate, odd-pinnate. 7-17 leaflets, narrowly obovate to linear, 1/4 to 1/2 inch long.

FLOWERING: March - April

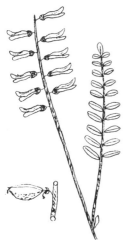

Astragalus trichopodus Plate 199   **SOUTHERN**
var. lonchus   **CALIFORNIA LOCOWEED**

DESCRIPTION: Perennial shrub, bushy branched, 8 to 24 inches high, covered with soft straight hairs. Found in Coastal Strand and Coastal Sage Scrub, on bluffs and low hills near the coast. Point Mugu is the northern limit of this plant. Abundant on Mugu Peak.

FLOWERS: In racemes 1-1/4 to 4-1/4 inches long, 12-36 flowers. Calyx 5-toothed; corolla greenish-white, 1/2 inch long; stamens 9 united, 1 free. Seedpods inflated, 3/4 to 1-3/4 inches long, hairy.

LEAVES: Alternate, odd-pinnate, 2 to 6 inches long, with 21-39 ovate-oblong to oblanceolate leaflets, each 1/4 to 3/4 inch long.

FLOWERING: February - June

FABACEAE

Astragalus trichopodus Plate 197
  var. phoxus

SANTA BARBARA
LOCOWEED

DESCRIPTION: Perennial shrub 3-1/2 feet high. Grows on dry hillsides in Chaparral and Coastal Sage Scrub. (Caballero Canyon)

FLOWERS: Pea-like in 3 to 4 inch racemes crowded with up to 50 flowers about 1/2 inch long. 5-toothed calyx a bell-shaped tube, 3/16 inch long; corolla greenish-yellow; stamens 9 united, 1 free. Pod 5/8 to 1-1/2 inches long, up to 3/8 inch wide and not inflated.

LEAVES: Alternate, up to 7 inches long, odd-pinnate, with a terminal leaflet. 21-39 leaflets oblong, about 5/16 inch long, each on a short stem.

FLOWERING: February - June

Genista monspessulana Plate 191

*FRENCH BROOM

DESCRIPTION: A shrub growing to 10 feet tall alongside roads and other disturbed areas. Many small flowers and small leaves. (Musch Ranch). Uncommon.

FLOWERS: About 8-12 clustered in a dense head at the end of short branches, yellow, about 1/2 inch long, fragrant; 3-pointed calyx hairy; petals pea-like, 10 stamens fused into a tube about half way; 1 pistil. Seedpod about 1 inch long, shaggy haired.

LEAVES: Alternate, on 1/8 inch leaf stalk; 3 leaflets, obovate, 3/8 to 3/4 inch long, free of hairs on top and downy underneath.

FLOWERING: March - May

340

FABACEAE

Glycyrrhiza lepidota   **WILD LICORICE**

DESCRIPTION: Perennial herb with a sweet root, 1 to 3-1/2 feet high, somewhat sticky. Found in moist, disturbed places. (Malibu Creek)

FLOWERS: On axillary spikes, less than 1 inch long; 5-toothed calyx sticky; corolla yellowish-white, about 3/8 inch long; stamens 9 united, 1 free. Pod oblong, 1/2 inch long, burlike with hooked prickles.

LEAVES: Alternate, odd-pinnate about 5 inches long. 11-19 leaflets, oblong to ovate-lanceolate, about 1 inch long.

FLOWERING: May - July

Hoita macrostachya Plate 371   **LEATHER ROOT**

DESCRIPTION: Perennial shrub, 3 to 10 feet high. Heavy-scented. Found in moist ground along streams.

FLOWERS: In silky spikes 3 to 4-1/2 inches long; pea-like, purple, about 3/8 inch long; 5-toothed calyx, hairy, 1/4 to 5/16 inch long; stamens 9 united, 1 free. Pod 1/4 inch long, downy.

LEAVES: Alternate. Pinnately 3-foliolate; leaflets broadly lanceolate to ovate, 3/4 to 3 inches long. Stems 1-1/2 to 4 inches long. Stipules awl-shaped, 1/8 to 3/16 inches long.

FLOWERING: May - August

Lathyrus vestitus Plate 287   **WILD SWEET PEA**
  var. vestitus

DESCRIPTION: Perennial herb, climbing, 3 to 10 feet long, branching. Found in Coastal Sage Scrub, Chaparral, Southern Oak Woodlands and along the streambed. Common.

341

FABACEAE

FLOWERS: 5-12 in a raceme, pale pink to lavender with a rose-veined banner, 5/8 to 7/8 inch long; 5-toothed calyx 1/2 inch long; stamens 9 united, 1 free; style curved, flattened, hairy on the inner side. Pods 1-1/2 to 3 inches long, about 1/4 inch wide, many seeded.

LEAVES: Even-pinnate with a terminal tendril, about 5 inches long. Leaflets 6-12, oblong to ovate, 3/4 to 2 inches long. Stipules lanceolate to lance-ovate, usually toothed, smaller than the leaflets.

FLOWERING: February - June

FIELD NOTE: At first glance vetch (*Vicia*) and wild pea (*Lathyrus*) look closely enough alike to be in the same genus. They are not. Many technical points separate them. One difference requires the use of a hand lens: the style of a vetch is terminated by a microscopic "shaving brush" while the style of the pea has hairs on one side only, like a "toothbrush."

Lotus argophyllus Plate 194   SILVER LOTUS

DESCRIPTION: Perennial, woody at the base, lying on the ground, many-branched, silver woolly, stems 8 to 20 inches long. Found on dry hills and sandstone rocks in Chaparral and Coastal Sage Scrub. (Cathedral Rock, Eagle Rock)

FLOWERS: Pea-like, 3-8 in an umbel; 5-toothed calyx hairy; corolla yellow, 3/8 inch long; stamens 9 united, 1 free. Seedpod body barely exserted beyond the calyx. Pod 1-seeded.

LEAVES: Alternate, odd-pinnate, 3-5 leaflets, broadly oblanceolate to obovate, 3/8 inch long or less, woolly.

FLOWERING: March - June

FABACEAE

Lotus corniculatus   ***BIRDFOOT TREFOIL**

DESCRIPTION: Perennial, trailing on the ground, branched, stems 4 to 20 inches long. Found in disturbed areas.

FLOWERS: Pea-like, 3 to 6 in an umbel; 5-toothed calyx; corolla bright yellow, 3/8 inch long; stamens 9 united, 1 free. Seedpod 1 inch long, straight, cylindrical.

LEAVES: Alternate, trifoliate; leaflets obovate to oblong, about 1/2 inch long. Leaf-like stipules.

FLOWERING: May - September

Lotus grandiflorus   Plate 195   **LARGE-FLOWERED LOTUS**

DESCRIPTION: Perennial shrub from a woody base 8 to 24 inches high, hairy, growing in sunny spots in canyons and openings in chaparral.

FLOWERS: Several in an umbel, on a 3-6 inch long stem; 5-toothed calyx tube, about 3/16 inch long; corolla, yellow, aging red; stamens 9 united, 1 free. Seedpods straight, cylindrical, 2 inches long, radiate from end of stem. Pod opens up and twists, throwing out many dark brown, ovoid seeds when ripe.

LEAVES: Alternate, 7-9 obovate to elliptical leaflets, about 1/2 to 3/4 inch long, each with small soft point on the end (mucronate). Stipules gland-like, not leafy.

FLOWERING: February - June

Lotus hamatus   **SAN DIEGO LOTUS**

DESCRIPTION: Annual herb, branching from the base, 6 to 24 inches long, sparsely leafy. Found on dry slopes in Coastal Sage Scrub and Chaparral. Rare.

343

FABACEAE

FLOWERS: Pea-like, 3 to 9 in bractless umbels, yellow or pinkish; 5-toothed calyx sparsely hairy; corolla 1-3/8 inch long; stamens 9 united, 1 free. Pod covered with stiff hairs, body curved, 2 seeds.

LEAVES: Alternate, pinnately compound; leaflets 3-5, oblong, 3/16 to 3/8 inch long.

FLOWERING: March - June

Lotus micranthus   **SMALL-FLOWERED LOTUS**

DESCRIPTION: Annual herb, slender stemmed, branching mostly from the base, 4 to 12 inches high. Found on open slopes of many plant communities.

FLOWERS: Single on 1/2 inch stems, pea-like, pinkish or pale salmon, tinged or turning red; bract of 1-3 leaflets; 5-toothed calyx corolla 3/16 inch long; stamens 9 united, 1 free. Pods 5/8 to 3/4 inch long.

LEAVES: Alternate, pinnately compound 3/8 to 5/8 inches long. 3-5 leaflets, elliptical or oblanceolate, 3/8 inch long or less.

FLOWERING: March - May

Lotus oblongifolius   **NARROW-LEAVED LOTUS**

DESCRIPTION: Perennial, 8 to 20 inches high, covered with stiff hairs. Found in wet places in Chaparral.

FLOWERS: 1-4 in an umbel with 1-3 leaf-like bracts at base; pea-like, yellow, occasionally tinged with purple; 5-toothed calyx; corolla 3/8 to 5/8 inch long; stamens 9 united, 1 free. Pod 1 to 1-1/2 inches long.

FABACEAE

LEAVES: Alternate, pinnately compound about 2-1/4 inches long, 7-11 leaflets, lance-linear, pointed at both ends, 3/4 inch long or less. Stipules membranous.

FLOWERING: May - September

Lotus purshianus Plate 291   **SPANISH CLOVER**

DESCRIPTION: Annual, branching stems, 8 to 24 inches high, many pale gray hairs. Found in Southern Oak Woodlands, dry fields and disturbed places. Common.

FLOWERS: Solitary (with 1 leaflike bract) on 2 inch stem, pea-like; 5-toothed calyx; corolla white, tinged with rose, 1/4 inch long; stamens 9 united, 1 free. Seedpod about 1 inch long, deflexed.

LEAVES: Alternate, trifoliolte. Leaflets oblong-lanceolate to elliptical, 3/8 to 5/8 inch long.

FLOWERING: May - September

Lotus salsuginosus Plate 196   **COASTAL LOTUS**

DESCRIPTION: Annual, prostrate stems, 4 to 12 inches long, somewhat succulent, slightly hairy. Found on beaches, sea bluffs, stream banks and in Coastal Sage Scrub and Chaparral. (Malibu Creek bank near Mott Adobe) Abundant after fires.

FLOWERS: 1-5 in umbels, pea-like, subtended by a leaflike bract; 5-toothed calyx; corolla yellow, 1/4 to 3/8 inch long; stamens 9 united, 1 free. Pods 5/8 to 1-1/4 inches long.

LEAVES: Alternate, 1-1/2 inches long, 5-8 leaflets, obovate, 3/16 to 1/2 inch long.

FLOWERING: March - June

345

FABACEAE

Lotus scoparius   Plates 190, 192   **DEERWEED**

DESCRIPTION: Perennial bush, 1-1/2 to 4 feet high, branching, green branches. Found in Coastal Sage Scrub and Chaparral. Sometimes covers dry hillsides after a fire. Dominant shrub second year after a fire.

FLOWERS: 1-4 in axils, pea-like, stemless; 5-toothed calyx; corolla yellow, aging to red, 1/4 to 3/8 inch long; stamens 9 united, 1 free, 2-seeded pod, slightly curved, does not split open to disperse the seeds.

LEAVES: Alternate, 3 leaflets oblong to oblanceolate, 1/8 to 3/8 inches long.

FLOWERING: January - December

Lotus strigosus   Plate 198   **STRIGOSE LOTUS**

DESCRIPTION: Annual, slender-stemmed, branching, to 1 foot high. Hairy. Grows on coastal bluffs and in Coastal Sage Scrub on south side of the Santa Monicas.

FLOWERS: 1-3 in umbels, pea-like, yellow, turning rose-red; 5-toothed calyx; corolla 1/4 to 3/8 inch long; stamens 9 united, 1 free. Pods about 1 inch long.

LEAVES: Alternate, 3/8 to 1 inch long; 6-10 leaflets, linear-oblong to elliptic, 3/16 to 1/2 inch long. Stipules gland-like.

FLOWERING: March - June

Lotus wrangelianus   **CHILE LOTUS**

DESCRIPTION: Annual, diffusely branched, prostrate stems, 4 to 12 inches long. Can be hairy. Found on dry grassy slopes.

FABACEAE

FLOWERS: Solitary in leaf axils, pea-like; 5-toothed calyx; corolla yellow, tinged red-purple in age, 1/4 inch long; stamens 9 united, 1 free. Pod 3/8 to 5/8 inch long.

LEAVES: Alternate, about 1 inch long; 3-5 leaflets, obovate, 3/16 to 5/8 inch long.

FLOWERING: March - June

Lupinus bicolor Plate 354   **DOVE LUPINE**

DESCRIPTION: Annual, one or several stems from the base, 4 to 16 inches high, covered with stiff appressed and long soft hairs. Found in open sandy and gravelly places in Coastal Sage Scrub and Chaparral. Fire-follower.

FLOWERS: In terminal racemes 3/8 to 3 inches long with 2-7 indistinct whorls; pea-like, deep blue with purple dots on a white spot on the banner; 2-lipped calyx, upper lip cleft, lower 3-toothed; lower and upper margins of keel are not hairy except near the tip, banner is longer than wide; stamens 10 united into a tube surrounding the pistil, anthers alternately long and short. Pods 3/4 inch long, hairy.

LEAVES: Alternate, palmately compound; 5-7 leaflets; narrow oblanceolate to linear; 5/8 to 1-1/4 inches long, sparsely hairy, if at all, above, stiff hairs beneath, on a 1/2 to 3 inch stem. Narrow stipules.

FLOWERING: March - June

Lupinus chamissonis   **DUNE BUSH LUPINE**

DESCRIPTION: Woody stemmed shrub, 1-1/2 to 3-1/2 feet high, sometimes taller, covered with silky hairs. Found on beaches and sand dunes to Coastal Strand. Rare.

FABACEAE

FLOWERS: In terminal racemes 1/4 to 5/8 inch long, in whorls; blue or lavender with a yellow spot, banner hairy on back; 2-lipped calyx, upper-lip cleft, lower entire; stamens 10 united into a tube surrounding the pistil, anthers alternately long and short. Pods 1 to 1-3/8 inches long.

LEAVES: Palmately compound; 6-9 leaflets, oblanceolate, 3/8 to 1 inch long, 3/16 inch wide. Silvery. Narrow stipules.

FLOWERING: March - July

FIELD NOTE: Becoming rare because of sand dune disturbance.

Lupinus concinnus Plate 292   BAJADA LUPINE

DESCRIPTION: Annual, prostrate, much branched, slender stems, 2 to 8 inches high, sparsely covered with shaggy hairs. Found on dry, open, disturbed places.

FLOWERS: In terminal racemes but not whorled, pea-like, lilac, edged with red-purple, banner has yellow center, keel not hairy; upper calyx lip cleft, the lower 3-toothed; stamens 10 united into a tube surrounding the pistil; anthers alternately long and short. Pods 3/8 to 5/8 inch long.

LEAVES: Alternate, palmately compound; 5-9 leaflets, narrow-oblanceolate, 3/8 to 3/4 inch long. Narrow stipules.

FLOWERING: March - May

348

FABACEAE

Lupinus formosus   **SUMMER LUPINE**

DESCRIPTION: Perennial herb, stems several from the root crown, 1 to 3 feet high, silky haired. Found in dry fields of many plant communities.

FLOWERS: In racemes 4 to 10 inches long, somewhat whorled; pea-like, about 1/2 inch long, violet or blue to lilac or white; 2-lipped; stamens 10 united into a tube surrounding the pistil; anthers alternately long and short. Pods about 1-3/8 inches long, silky.

LEAVES: Alternate, palmately compound; 7-9 oblanceolate leaflets, 1-1/4 to 2-3/4 inches long, silky both sides. Narrow stipules.

FLOWERING: May - July

Lupinus hirsutissimus Plate 295   **STINGING LUPINE**

DESCRIPTION: Robust annual, branching from the base, 8 inches to 2-1/2 feet high, covered with stiff, yellowish, nettlelike hairs. Painful to touch. Found in open places of Coastal Sage Scrub and Chaparral. Dominant fire-follower.

FLOWERS: In terminal racemes 4 to 10 inches long but not whorled; pea-like 1/2 to 5/8 inch long, red-violet to magenta, the banner nearly circular, often with a yellow blotch; keel fringed with hairs on lower edge; 2-lipped calyx, the upper lip cleft, the lower not cleft or sometimes 3-toothed; stamens 10 united into a tube surrounding the pistil; anthers alternately long and short. Pods 1 to 1-3/8 inches long, bristly.

LEAVES: Alternate, palmately compound; 5-8 broadly cuneate-obovate leaflets, 1 to 2 inches long, with nettlelike hairs. Narrow stipules

FLOWERING: March - May

349

FABACEAE

Lupinus latifolius Plate 293   **BROAD-LEAVED LUPINE**

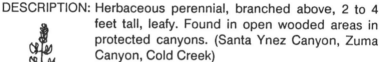

DESCRIPTION: Herbaceous perennial, branched above, 2 to 4 feet tall, leafy. Found in open wooded areas in protected canyons. (Santa Ynez Canyon, Zuma Canyon, Cold Creek)

FLOWERS: In terminal racemes 6 to 18 inches long with whorls or scattered blooms; pea-like, 3/8 to 5/8 inch long, blue or purplish or with some pink, white center; 2-lipped calyx, upper lip notched, lower not notched; stamens 10 united into a tube surrounding the pistil; anthers alternately long and short. Pods about 1-1/4 inch long, hairy, brown.

LEAVES: Alternate, palmately compound; 7-9 broadly oblanceolate leaflets, 1-1/2 to 4 inches long, bright green on upper surface. Largest leaves on midstem, basal leaves often dry at flowering. Narrow stipules.

FLOWERING: April - July

Lupinus longifolius Plates 289, 290   **BUSH LUPINE**

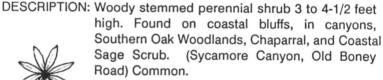

DESCRIPTION: Woody stemmed perennial shrub 3 to 4-1/2 feet high. Found on coastal bluffs, in canyons, Southern Oak Woodlands, Chaparral, and Coastal Sage Scrub. (Sycamore Canyon, Old Boney Road) Common.

FLOWERS: In racemes 8 to 16 inches long with blooms scattered to somewhat whorled; pea-like, about 5/8 inch long, blue to violet, banner nearly circular with a center yellow spot, keel fringed with hairs along upper edges; 2-lipped calyx, upper lip cleft, lower entire or minutely 2-toothed; stamens 10 united into a tube surrounding the pistil, anthers alternately long and short. Pods 1-1/2 to 2-1/4 inches long, brownish.

FABACEAE

LEAVES: Alternate, palmately compound; 6-9 elliptic- or oblong-oblanceolate leaflets, 1 to 2-1/4 inches long, somewhat silky both sides. Narrow stipules.

FLOWERING: April - June

Lupinus luteolus   **BUTTER LUPINE**

DESCRIPTION: Annual, 1 to 3 feet high, branched, covered with stiff appressed hairs. Found on dry slopes.

FLOWERS: In terminal racemes 2 to 8 inches long with crowded whorls; pea-like, about 1/2 inch long, light to pale yellow, sometimes pale lilac at first, banner ovate, keel fringed with hairs on upper and lower margins of base; 2-lipped calyx, hairy, 3/8 inch long; stamens 10 united into a tube surrounding the pistil, anthers alternately long and short. Pods 5/8 inch long, hairy.

LEAVES: Alternate, palmately compound; 7-9 cuneate-oblanceolate leaflets, 3/4 to 1-1/4 inches long, stiff hairs on both sides or only below. Narrow stipules.

FLOWERING: May - August

Lupinus luteus   ***YELLOW LUPINE**

DESCRIPTION: Reported growing along Decker Road: Koutnik and Dawes 490 (DAV). Not described.

Lupinus nanus   **SKY LUPINE**

DESCRIPTION: Annual, 1/2 to 2 feet high, single stemmed or sometimes branched at base, hairy. Found in grassy fields and brushy slopes in Coastal Sage Scrub and Grassland. Rare.

FABACEAE

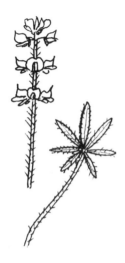

FLOWERS: In terminal racemes 2 to 7 inches long with well-separated whorls; pea-like, blue with a white or yellowish spot on circular banner; 2-lipped calyx, upper calyx cleft, lower 2 or 3-toothed; stamens 10 united into a tube surrounding the pistil, anthers alternately long and short. Pods 1-1/4 to 1-1/2 inch long.

LEAVES: Alternate, palmately compound; 5-7 oblanceolate leaflets, 1/2 to 1-1/4 inches long. Narrow stipules.

FLOWERING: April - May

Lupinus sparsiflorus　Plate 355　　　　COULTER'S LUPINE

DESCRIPTION: Annual, slender-stemmed, erect, branched, 8 to 16 inches high, covered with stiff hairs and soft hairs. Found in open places in Coastal Sage Scrub and Chaparral. Fire-follower.

FLOWERS: In terminal racemes 3 to 8 inches long, not whorled and not crowded; pea-like light blue to lilac, 3/8 to 1/2 inch long banner nearly circular with a yellow spot; 2-lipped calyx, upper lip cleft, lower 3-toothed; stamens 10 united into a tube surrounding the pistil, anthers alternately long and short. Pods 3/8 to 3/4 inch long, bristly.

LEAVES: Alternate, palmately compound; 5-9 linear to oblanceolate leaflets, 3/8 to 3/4 inch long. Narrow stipules.

FLOWERING: March - May

FIELD NOTE: Quick to recover after a fire.

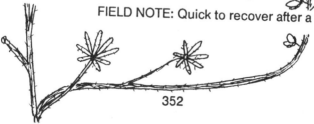

FABACEAE

Lupinus microcarpus Plate 65   **VALLEY LUPINE**
var. microcarpus

DESCRIPTION: Annual, 1 stem usually branched, shaggy haired, 6 to 16 inches high. Found on dry slopes, in Grassland and Southern Oak Woodland. Prefers clay soil. (Liberty Canyon) Rare.

FLOWERS: In terminal racemes 2 to 6 inches long with 3 to 9 whorls; pea-like, white, lilac, or rose pink, 1/2 to 5/8 inch long; keel fringed with hairs above near the base; 2-lipped calyx 3/8 inch long, hairy; stamens 10 united into a tube surrounding the pistil, anthers alternately long and short. Bracts persistent, reflexed during flowering. Pods 5/8 inch long.

LEAVES: Alternate, palmately compound, mostly on the lower half of the plant; 5-9 oblanceolate leaflets, 5/8 to 1-1/2 inches long, hairless above, soft hairs beneath. Leaves basal or on lower and middle stem.

FLOWERING: April - May

FIELD NOTE: The Liberty Canyon colony is in jeopardy because of construction activity along Liberty Canyon road into Malibu Creek State Park.

This variety reaches its southern coastal limit in the Santa Monica Mountains as a disjunct.

Lupinus succulentus Plate 356   **ARROYO LUPINE,**
                                                    FOOTHILL LUPINE

DESCRIPTION: Annual, stout, branching stem, 8 to 24 inches high. Found in heavy clay soil on grassy slopes, in Grasslands, and Coastal Sage Scrub. Dominant fire-follower.

FABACEAE

FLOWERS: In terminal racemes 2-1/2 to 12 inches long with whorls; pea-like, deep purple-blue, 1/2 to 5/8 inch long, keel fringed with hairs on both edges near base; 2-lipped calyx, the upper lip deeply cleft, the lower entire to 3-toothed; stamens 10 united into a tube surrounding the pistil; anthers alternately long and short. Pods 1-1/2 to 2 inches long.

LEAVES: Alternate, palmately compound; 7-9 cuneate-obovate leaflets, 3/4 to 2-3/4 inches long, dark green, hairless above, short, stiff, appressed hairs below.'

FLOWERING: February - May

FIELD NOTE: Quick to recover after a fire. The Dayton Canyon fire of October 1982 burned the Great Meadow (Reagan Ranch) and the Coastal Sage Scrub hillside and the Chaparral. Four months later the sage hillside and part of the meadow were densely covered with blooming Foothill Lupines.

Lupinus truncatus Plate 294

COLLAR LUPINE

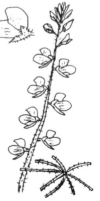

DESCRIPTION: Annual, branched, 1 to 2-1/2 feet high. Found in grassy areas in Coastal Sage Scrub and Chaparral.

FLOWERS: In terminal racemes 2 to 6 inches long but not with whorls; pea-like, purplish-blue, redder with age, 3/8 to 1/2 inch long, keel fringed with hairs on upper edge near base, slightly on lower edge; 2-lipped calyx, the upper lip cleft, the lower entire to 3-toothed; stamens 10 united into a tube surrounding the pistil, anthers alternately long and short. Pods about 1-1/4 inches long.

FABACEAE

LEAVES: Alternate, palmately compound; 5-7 linear leaflets, deep green 3/8 to 1-1/4 inches long, cut off squarely at the ends (truncate), sometimes notched.

FLOWERING: March - May

FIELD NOTE: Quick to recover after a fire.

Medicago lupulina   ***BLACK MEDICK**

DESCRIPTION: Annual, branched at the base, 1 to 2 feet high, downy. Found in disturbed areas.

FLOWERS: In short, dense racemes, pea-like, yellow, less than 1/8 inch long; calyx 5-toothed; stamens 9 united, 1 free, style awl-shaped. Pods smooth, somewhat kidney-shaped, 1-seeded.

LEAVES: Alternate, pinnately 3-foliolate; leaflets obovate to roundish, 1/4 to 5/8 inch long. Stipules leaflike.

FLOWERING: April - July

Medicago polymorpha Plate 173   ***BUR-CLOVER**
ssp. hispida

DESCRIPTION: Annual, branched at the base, trailing on the ground, 4 to 16 inches long. Found in grassy areas, even in lawns.

FLOWERS: 2-5 on axillary 1 inch stems; pea-like, about 3/16 inch long; 5-toothed calyx, slightly hairy; stamens 9 united, 1 free. Pods spirally coiled with 2 rows of hook prickles rising from the outer edge.

LEAVES: Alternate, pinnately 3-foliolate;leaflets obovate or obcordate, finally toothed, 3/8 to 3/4 inch long. Stipules deeply divided.

FLOWERING: March - June

FABACEAE

Medicago sativa Plate 367   *ALFALFA

DESCRIPTION: Perennial herb, branching, bushy, 1 to 2-1/2 feet high, not hairy. Found in cultivated fields and along roadsides and trails.

FLOWERS: In dense, short racemes; pea-like, 3/8 inch long, blue-violet to purple; calyx 5-toothed; stamens 9 united, 1 free. Pods spirally coiled, downy.

LEAVES: Alternate, pinnately 3-foliolate; leaflets oblanceolate or obovate, 3/8 to 1 inch long.

FLOWERING: April - October

Melilotus alba Plate 72   *WHITE SWEETCLOVER

DESCRIPTION: Annual, erect, 3 to 6 feet high. Found in disturbed areas. Prefers damp soil.

FLOWERS: In racemes 2 to 4 inches long; pea-like, white, about 1/4 inch long; calyx 5-toothed; stamens 9 united, 1 free. Pods ovoid, 3/16 inch long.

LEAVES: Alternate, pinnately 3-foliolate; leaflets oblong-oblanceolate, 3/8 to 3/4 inch long, serrate. Stipules, in pairs, awl-shaped, 1/4 inch long.

FLOWERING: May - September

Melilotus indica   SOURCLOVER

DESCRIPTION: Annual, not hairy, erect, branching 8 to 30 inches high. Found in disturbed areas.

FLOWERS: In racemes 3/4 to 4 inches long; pea-like, yellow, about 1/8 inch long; calyx 5-toothed; stamens 9 united, 1 free. Pods ovoid, about 1/8 inch long.

FABACEAE

LEAVES: Alternate, pinnately 3-foliolate; 3/16 to 3/4 inch stem; leaflets cuneate-oblong to obovate, 3/4 to 1 inch long. finely toothed. Stipules, in pairs at the leaf stem base, are awl-shaped, 1/4 inch long.

FLOWERING: April - October

Melilotus officinalis   *YELLOW SWEETCLOVER

DESCRIPTION: Similar to *M. albus* except flowers are yellow.

Pickeringia montana Plate 297   CHAPARRAL PEA

DESCRIPTION: Evergreen shrub with stiff, widely spreading branches, spiny, 8 to 10 feet high. Found on slopes and ridges in Chaparral. The broad ridge between peaks 2793 and 2854, south of Hidden Valley, supports a small forest of *Pickeringia montana*. Scattered individuals in Saddle Peak area and Rustic Canyon.

FLOWERS: Solitary, pea-like, showy, reddish-purple, 1/2 to 3/4 inch long; 5-toothed calyx bell-shaped; stamens 10 free. Pod 1-1/4 to 2 inches long, straight, several-seeded.

LEAVES: Alternate, palmately 3-foliolate; leaflets oblanceolate to obovate 3/8 to 5/8 inch long, firm, pale green.

FLOWERING: May - August

FIELD NOTE: Root-crown-sprouts and makes a quick recovery after a fire.

357

FABACEAE

Pisum sativum   *GARDEN PEA

DESCRIPTION: Annual, vine-like, up to 6 feet long. Found as a garden escape.

FLOWERS: Solitary or in clusters of 2 or 3; pea-like, white or colored 5/8 inch or more long; calyx 5-toothed; stamens 9 united, 1 free. Pods flattened, several seeded, 2 to 4 inches long.

LEAVES: Alternate, pinnate in 1-3 pairs with a tendril at the end, leaflets oval to oblong, 3/4 to 2 inches long. Very small stipules at base of leaf stem.

FLOWERING: March - May

Rupertia physodes   Plate 35   CALIFORNIA TEA

DESCRIPTION: Perennial herb, 1 to 2-1/2 feet high. Heavy-scented. Found in open places of many plant communities. Rare.

FLOWERS: In dense racemes, 1/2 to 1 inch long covered with shaggy black hair; pea-like, whitish or yellow-white, 3/8 to 1/2 inch long; 5-toothed calyx, black-and-white-hairy; stamens 9 united, 1 free. Pod 1/4 inch long, ovoid, hairy.

LEAVES: Alternate, pinnately 3-foliolate; leaflets ovate, 3/4 to 2-1/4 inches long, sparsely downy. Stems 3/4 to 2 inches long. Stipules lanceolate 3/16 inch long.

FLOWERING: April - June

FABACEAE

Spartium junceum   Plate 193

*SPANISH BROOM

DESCRIPTION: Upwards branching, almost leafless shrub, erect, green-stemmed, to 10 feet high. Found along roads, trails, and other disturbed areas.

FLOWERS: In terminal racemes, pea-like, yellow, 3/4 to 1 inch long; fragrant; calyx split on upper side, 5 minute teeth; stamens 10 united about the pistil. Pod 2 to 4 inches long, many seeded.

LEAVES: Few, alternate, oblanceolate - oblong or narrower, 1/2 to 1 inch long.

FLOWERING: April - June

Trifolium albopurpureum

RANCHERIA CLOVER

DESCRIPTION: Annual, sprawling, hairy, 4 to 16 inches long. Found in grassy areas. (Triunfo Pass, Lake Eleanor) Rare.

FLOWERS: In ovoid heads without an involucre, 1/4 to 5/8 inch long; pea-like, purple, 1/4 inch long; 5-toothed calyx covered with long plumed hairs; stamens 9 united, 1 free. Pods 1-seeded, hairy at the apex.

LEAVES: Alternate, palmately 3-foliolate; leaflets cuneate-oblong, blunt or rounded at the end, finely toothed above the middle, 1/4 to 3/4 inch long. Stipules not toothed.

FLOWERING: March - June

Trifolium ciliolatum

TREE CLOVER

DESCRIPTION: Annual, pale green, not hairy, hollow stemmed, erect 8 to 20 inches high. Found in open areas and grassy slopes, inland. Malibu Creek and eastward.

FABACEAE

FLOWERS: In ovoid heads without an involucre, 1/2 to 3/4 inch long; pea-like, pinkish-purple, 1/4 inch long; calyx 5-toothed; stamens 9 united, 1 free. Pods 1- or 2- seeded.

LEAVES: Alternate, palmately 3-foliolate; leaflets oblong to obovate, smooth edged or finely saw-toothed, 3/8 to 1-1/4 inches long. Stipules not toothed, 5/8 to 1-1/4 inch long.

FLOWERING: March - June

Trifolium depauperatum   PALE SACK CLOVER
   var. amplectans

DESCRIPTION: Annual, light green, not hairy, sprawling, slender, 4 to 10 inches long. Found in grassy areas and Coastal Sage Scrub.

FLOWERS: In round heads with an involucre at the base; pea-like, white, reddish or purple, 1/4 inch long; calyx 5-toothed; stamens 9 united, 1 free.

LEAVES: Alternate, palmately 3-foliolate; leaflets obovate to oblanceolate, finely saw-toothed, 1/4 to 3/4 inch long. Stipules not toothed.

FLOWERING: April - June

Trifolium fucatum   Plate 298   SOUR CLOVER

DESCRIPTION: Annual, not hairy, hollow stemmed, spreading, 8 to 32 inches long. Found in moist places.

FLOWERS: In heads 1 to 1-1/2 inches in diameter with an involucre at the base; pea-like, cream-colored with dark purple keel, 1 inch long, become inflated with age; calyx 5-toothed; stamens 9 united, 1 free. Pods 3-8 seeded.

FABACEAE

LEAVES: Alternate, palmately 3-foliolate; leaflets broadly obovate, finely saw-toothed, 3/8 to 1-1/4 inch long. Stipules not toothed, 5/8 to 3/4 inch long.

FLOWERING: April - June

Trifolium gracilentum   **PIN-POINT CLOVER**

DESCRIPTION: Annual, erect or spreading, 4 to 16 inches long. Found in grassy slopes.

FLOWERS: In heads without an involucre, 1/4 to 3/8 inch long; pea-like, pink to reddish-purple, 1/4 inch long; calyx 5-toothed; stamens 9 united, 1 free. Pods 1- or 2- seeded.

LEAVES: Alternate, palmately 3-foliolate; leaflets obovate, finely saw-toothed, notched at the apex, 1/4 to 5/8 inch long. Stipules not toothed.

FLOWERING: April - June

Trifolium incarnatum   ***CRIMSON CLOVER**

DESCRIPTION: Annual, erect, 1/2 to 2-1/2 feet high, covered with soft hairs. Found in disturbed areas. (Oak Woodland near Lake Sherwood)

FLOWERS: In spike-like heads without an involucre, 1-1/8 to 2-1/4 inches long; pea-like, crimson, about 1/2 inch long; 5-toothed calyx hairy; stamens 9 united, 1 free.

LEAVES: Alternate, palmately 3-foliolate; leaflets obovate to obcordate 5/8 to 1 inch long. Stipules not toothed.

FLOWERING: May - August

FABACEAE

Trifolium microcephalum   SMALL-HEADED CLOVER

DESCRIPTION: Annual, trailing on the ground or ascending, 8 to 16 inches long, covered with soft hairs. Found in open grassy areas in damp soil. (Saddle Peak)

FLOWERS: In heads about 1/2 inch in diameter, with a hairy involucre at the base; pea-like, rose to white, 1/4 inch long; 5-toothed calyx downy; stamens 9 united, 1 free. Pods 1 or 2-seeded.

LEAVES: Alternate, palmately 3-foliolate; leaflets obcordate to oblanceolate, saw-toothed, notched at the apex, 1/4 to 5/8 inch long. Stipules toothed.

FLOWERING: April - August

Trifolium obtusiflorum   CREEK CLOVER

DESCRIPTION: Annual, more or less ascending, 12 to 20 inches high, stem stout and hollow, woolly. Found in creek bottoms and other moist places. (Near Lake Sherwood)

FLOWERS: In heads about 1 inch in diameter with woolly involucre at the base; pea-like, white or pale rose with a dark center spot, 1/2 inch long; calyx 5-toothed; stamens 9 united, 1 free. Pods 2-seeded.

LEAVES: alternate, palmately 3-foliolate; leaflets lance-linear to narrow-obovate, saw-toothed, about 1 inch long. Stipules toothed.

FLOWERING: April - July

Trifolium repens   *WHITE CLOVER

DESCRIPTION: Perennial herb, not hairy, with creeping stems branching from the base, 4 to 12 inches long. Rooting at nodes. Found in lawns and damp wayside places.

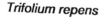

362

FABACEAE

FLOWERS: In globose heads without an involucre, 5/8 to 1 inch broad; pea-like, white to pale pink, 1/4 to 3/8 inch long; calyx 5-toothed; stamens 9 united, 1 free.

LEAVES: Alternate, palmately 3-foliolate; leaflets obovate, finely saw-toothed, 3/8 to 3/4 inch long. Stipules not toothed, small.

FLOWERING: April - December

Trifolium variegatum   **WHITE-TIPPED CLOVER**

DESCRIPTION: Annual, branching from the base, trailing to ascending, 1/2 to 2 feet long. Found in moist places.

FLOWERS: In heads 1/4 to 1/2 inch broad with an involucre at the base; pea-like, purple, white-tipped, 1/4 inch long; 5-toothed calyx equally cleft; stamens 9 united, 1 free. Pods 2-seeded.

LEAVES: Alternate, palmately 3-foliolate; leaflets obovate or oblong-lanceolate, finely saw-toothed, 1/4 to 5/8 inch long.

FLOWERING: April - July

Trifolium willdenovii Plate 299   **TOMCAT CLOVER**

DESCRIPTION: Annual, not hairy, often branching from the base, 4 to 18 inches high. Found in grassy places and Southern Oak Woodlands.

FLOWERS: In heads 5/8 to 3/4 inch broad, with an involucre at the base; pea-like, red-purple, 1/2 inch long; 5-toothed calyx not equally cleft; stamens 9 united, 1 free. Pods usually 2-seeded.

LEAVES: Alternate, palmately 3-foliolate; leaflets linear to lance-oblong, finely saw-toothed, 5/8 to 1-1/2 inches long. Stipules fringed with hairs.

FLOWERING: March - June

FABACEAE

Vicia americana var. *americana*   AMERICAN VETCH

DESCRIPTION: Perennial herb, trailing or climbing, sparsely downy, 2 to 4 feet long. Found in grassy areas. (Lower Malibu Creek) Rare.

FLOWERS: 4-9 in racemes; pea-like, purplish aging blue, 5/8 inch long; calyx 5-toothed; stamens 9 united, 1 free; style tufted at the apex. Pods, not hairy; 1-1/4 to 1-1/2 inches long, more or less downy. Stipules segmented.

FLOWERING; April - June

Vicia ludoviciana var. *ludoviciana*   SLENDER VETCH

DESCRIPTION: Annual, slender-stemmed, climbing, 1 to 2 feet long. Found in grassy, brushy, or woody slopes. (Monte Nido) Rare.

FLOWERS: 1 or 2 on threadlike stems; near tip, pea-like, white to pale blue, about 3/8 inch long; calyx 5-toothed; stamens 9 united, 1 free; style tufted at the apex. Pods 3/4 to 1-1/4 inches long.

LEAVES: Alternate, pinnately compound, having a tendril at the apex; 2-6 pairs of leaflets, linear, 3/8 to 1 inch long.

FLOWERING: April - June

Vicia sativa Plate 296   *SPRING VETCH

DESCRIPTION: Annual, climbing, 1 to 3 feet long. Found in disturbed areas.

FLOWERS: 1 or 2 in leaf axils; pea-like, violet-purple, 3/4 to 1 inch long; calyx 5-toothed; stamens 9 united, 1 free; style tufted at the apex. Pods 1-1/2 to 3 inches long.

364

FABACEAE

LEAVES: Alternate, pinnately compound, having a tendril at the apex; 4-8 pairs of leaflets, linear to wedge-shaped, squared or notched at the apex, mucrunate, 3/8 to 1-1/4 inches long. Stipules segmented.

FLOWERING: April - July

Vicia villosa   Plate 357   ***WINTER VETCH**

DESCRIPTION: Annual or biennial herb, trailing, 2 to 4 feet long. Found in grassy areas and disturbed places.

FLOWERING: More than 10 in 1-sided racemes, 3/8 to 3/4 inch long; pea-like, violet and white, 1/2 to 5/8 inch long; calyx 5-toothed; stamens 9 united, 1 free; style tufted at the apex. Pods oblong, 3/4 to 1-1/4 inch long.

LEAVES: Alternate, pinnately compound, having a tendril at the apex; 6-9 pairs of leaflets, linear to narrow-oblong, tip rounded, 3/8 to 1 inch long. Stipules narrow, not toothed.

FLOWERING: April - July

Vicia villosa
  ssp. varia   ***PURPLE VETCH**

DESCRIPTION: Annual or biennial herb, trailing, 2 to 4 feet long, not hairy. Found in grassy areas and disturbed places.

FLOWERS: Ten to twenty in 1-sided racemes; pea-like, purplish-violet, 1/2 to 5/8 inch long; calyx 5-toothed; stamens 9 united, 1 free; style tufted at the apex. Pods 3/4 to 1-1/2 inches long.

365

FABACEAE

LEAVES: Alternate, pinnately compound, having a tendril at the apex; 6-9 pairs of leaflets, linear to narrow-oblong, 3/8 to 3/4 inch long.

FLOWERING: April - July

FAGACEAE

OAK FAMILY

One genus and all four species are oaks. Worldwide the 8 genera and 900 species include Beeches, Chestnuts, Chinquapin, Tanbark Oak, and about 450 species of Oaks. Local oak trees often display galls on the twigs. Galls are green at first, then turn red or brown and grow to 4 inches in diameter. They are caused when an "Oak Gall Wasp" inserts eggs into soft young twigs. Upon hatching, larvae tunnel into the twig and release an enzyme that causes the tree to form a gall. The soft tissue is food for the one or more larvae that chew exit tunnels before pupating. Damage to the tree is minimal.

Recognition characteristics: All are catkin bearing, have buds clustered at the tips of twigs, and a fruit that is to some degree enclosed by a cup. Fruit is a nut.

Quercus agrifolia Plates 456, 458

COAST LIVE OAK
ENCINA

DESCRIPTION: Evergreen tree, 75 foot tall, broad crowned, dense. The dominant plant in Southern Oak Woodland, and an important plant along streamsides. Thick moist bark is a protection against fires, and many very old oaks survive repeated burning of the area.

FAGACEAE

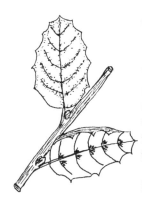

FLOWERS: Male and female separate but on the same tree; staminate catkins about 1-1/4 to 2-1/2 inches long; small sepals, no petals. Acorns long, pointed, 1 to 1-3/8 inches long; mature in one season.

LEAVES: Oblong to oval, 1 to 2-1/4 inches long, convex. The upper sides are often dotted with light-colored minute star-shaped hairs and the paler green underside has brownish hairs in the vein axils.

FLOWERING: February - April

Queracus dumosa   Plates 455, 469   **SCRUB OAK**

DESCRIPTION: Chaparral shrub, 10 feet tall. Grows on dry slopes. It is low growing, impenetrable, and thicketlike.

FLOWERS: Male and female separate but on same tree; staminate and pistillate catkins small, bud-like bodies in leaf axils; small sepals, no petals. Acorns mature in one season.

LEAVES: Oblong to elliptic to roundish, stiff, leathery, spine tipped edges; 1/2 to 1 inch long, shiny green above, paler below. Evergreen.

FLOWERING: March - May

Quercus lobata Plates 457, 468   **VALLEY OAK**

DESCRIPTION: Stately tree — largest of the oaks — occurs in a scattered pattern, often alone, mostly in open valleys. Tapia Park, Malibu Creek State Park, and Hidden Valley support spectacular Valley Oaks.

FAGACEAE

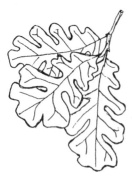

FLOWERS: Male and female separate but on the same tree; staminate catkins 1 to 3 inches long; pistillate small, budlike bodies in leaf axils, develop into 1-1/4 to 2 inch long acorns, maturing the first autumn.

LEAVES: 2 to 4 inches long, distinctly divided with 3-5 pairs of obtuse lobes. Deciduous.

FLOWERING: March - April

Quercus wislizenii
var. frutescens

INTERIOR LIVE OAK

DESCRIPTION: Shrub about 10 feet tall found in valleys and on slopes. The rarest of the oaks in the Santa Monica Mountains. (Cold Creek, north slope of Saddle Peak, north slope of Boney Mountain.)

FLOWERS: Male and female separate but on the same tree; staminate catkins, about 1-1/4 to 2-1/2 inches long; pistillate small, budlike bodies develop late 3/4 to 1-1/2 inch long.

LEAVES: 3/4 to 1-1/2 inches long, oblong, stiff and shiny. Evergreen.

FLOWERING: March - May

FERNS

Fern is the common name for a group of plants bearing only spores without the ovules, seeds, or bulblets common to other plants described in this book. Ferns don't bear flowers.

The ferns are lumped together alphabetically, here, without regard to their family relationship. Of the thousands of ferns worldwide 15 are known in the Santa Monica Mountains. Escapes from habitations may have been overlooked but are not known in significant populations.

FERNS

Recognition characteristics: Leafy plants, the fronds originating at the base more or less in a rosette. Fronds are pinnately formed having 1, 2 or 3 divisions. Fronds are in a coil when young. Root is a rhizome. Sporangia are borne on the underside of fertile blades in a pattern distinct with the species. Sori are a distinct cluster of spores.

Adiantum capillis-veneris Plate 471   **VENUS-HAIR FERN**

DESCRIPTION: This 2 foot fern with round, black, shiny stalks often arches down a moist cliff face. Delicate looking with individual leaves that widen gradually from a pointed base. Each leaf is cleft into distinct unsymmetrical lobes (differing from *Adiantum jordanii)*. Leaves are light green on both sides and about 3/4 inch wide. 2-3-pinnate. Rhizome scales are small, thin, and light-brown. Found near waterfalls and other moist cliff faces. Often found in calcium laden seepages.

SORI: Borne on the lower surface of the leaves, at the outer margin, in single spots, the covering membranous flaps of leaf tissue curl down in crescent shapes. Spores mature March -May.

Adiantum jordanii   **MAIDEN-HAIR FERN**

DESCRIPTION: This 2-pinnate delicate looking fern has broadly fan-shaped leaves, is 8 to 18 inches high. The outer edge of the leaves is rounded and not lobed (or slightly lobed on fertile leaves where the edge turns down to cover the sori). Some segments are finely serrated. The leaf segment is 1/2 inch across and is light green on both sides. Stalks are dark grown, rising along a creeping rootstock. Stalks shorter than *Adiantum capilus-veneris,* which resembles this plant. Thizome scales are large, rigid, and dark-brown. Found on shaded slopes in Southern Oak Woodland. Common.

FERNS

SORI: Borne on the lower surface of leaves, at the outer edge, in single spots. Membranous flaps of leaf tissue curl down hiding the sori. Spores mature March - May.

FIELD NOTE: Greek a, (not) and *diaino*, (to wet), refers to the characteristic of the foliage to shed water rather than a wet habitat.

Aspidotis californica Plate 477   CALIFORNIA LACE-FERN

DESCRIPTION: 3-pinnate, delicately structured, clustered fronds, 1 foot long. Densely tufted, dull, dark brown stalks. Frond outline is broadly triangular to pentagular. Ultimate leaf segments are small and incised. Found in the shade on rocky hillsides. Usually in dry areas, mostly east of Topanga Canyon. Uncommon.

SORI: Small, solitary spots on leaflet edges at the ends of enlarged veins. The crescent-shaped indusia are at the bases of the teeth segments. Spores mature March - April.

Asplenium vespertinum   WESTERN SPLEENWORT

DESCRIPTION: Evergreen fronds on shiny, purplish-brown stalks, in a clump. Blades linear or oblanceolate-linear in outline, 1-1/2 to 8 inches long. 1-pinnate, the 20 to 30 pairs of leaflets almost opposite to alternate, attached to the main stalk with very short stems. Each leaflet oblong or linear-oblong from an inequilateral broad base. Found in moist shady places in Southern Oak Woodland, Coastal Sage Scrub and Chaparral. Rare.

SORI: Small, oblong, and aligned at an angle to the midrib of the leaf segments. The indusium is attached to the leaf along one edge. No more than 6 sori on each leaflet.

FERNS

Azolla filiculoides   WATER FERN

DESCRIPTION: Small moss-like, free-floating, compact aquatic
plant. Found in slow moving fresh water. Green
or reddish. Leaves 3 per node, one of which is
finely divided into rootlike segments and is
submerged. Reproduction is by sporangia, thin-
walled and soft, borne in pairs beneath the
stem.

LEAVES: Ovate, about 1/32 inch long, 2-lobed.

Chilanthes covillei   COVILLES LIP FERN

DESCRIPTION: Many fronds 4 to 12 inches long from a short-
creeping rhizome. Stems are brown to dark
purplish. Leaf blades oblong to ovate-deltoid in
outline, 2 to 6 inches long, 3-pinnate, scaly on
the underside. Found on rocky places in Chaparral. (Boney Mountain)

SORI: Borne within the recurved outer border
of the leaflets.

Dryopteris arguta Plate 479   COASTAL WOOD-FERN

DESCRIPTION: Several fronds on stout stems up to 2-1/2 feet
long come from a woody root-crown. Most of
the fronds arch over with the ends almost
touching the ground. 2-pinnate. Dark, evergreen
leaf segments with spiny teeth. Found in moist
shade of Southern Oak Woodland. Common.

SORI: A row of large, round sori parallel either
side of the vein of each ultimate leaf. Indusia
circular and deeply cleft. Spores mature April-
November.

FIELD NOTES: Greek: *drys* for oak, and *pteris*
for fern, refers to the plant's habitat.

FERNS

Notholaena californica   CLOAK FERN

DESCRIPTION: Several to many erect fronds, 1-1/2 to 6 inches high, densely woolly, covering some of the leaf detail. Brownish or dull white under; whiter above. Leaf blades are deltoid-pentagonal in outline. 3/4 to 2 inches long. 3-pinnate. The ultimate leaflets are very small — less than 1/8 inch long, and curve down. Found in rock crevices and cliffs in Coastal Sage Scrub. Rare.

SORI: In a continuous line near the margin of leaflets, blackish color, and hidden by the woolly covering but not otherwise covered.

Notholaena newberri   COTTON FERN

DESCRIPTION: The 4 to 9 inch tall fronds are clustered and grow erect on shiny dark-brown stalks covered with hairs. The narrow-oblong to oblong-lanceolate frond is 3-pinnate. The ultimate leaf segment has no stem and is minute. The entire plant is woolly. Found on dry rocky slopes in Coastal Sage Scrub and Chaparral. Rare.

SORI: Relatively large for the size of the leaf, blackish, hidden from view by the woolly covering when the frond is growing, but emerging at maturity. Spores mature March - May.

Pellaea andromedifolia Plate 478   COFFEE FERN

DESCRIPTION: Evergreen, sparsely leaved, open, one to two feet tall. Stalks are hard, wiry, straw-colored. Leaflets are oval-shaped, dark, dull green on top, light green underneath. Opposite, lateral leaflets attach to the branch without a stem, 2 and 3 pinnate. Sterile leaves are flat; fertile leaves have revolute edges. Found on dry, rocky soil, usually in part shade. Common.

FERNS

SORI: The spores are borne in a line along the leaf margin. Leaf edge turns down, hiding the sori. Spores mature January - April

Pellaea mucronata Plate 472   **BIRD'S-FOOT FERN**

DESCRIPTION: Open fronds 1-1/2 feet high having a characteristic leaf pattern resembling a bird's foot. Dark brown, dull, stalks. 2-pinnate at branch ends and 3-pinnate lower on the frond. The ultimate leaflet is on a very short stem, is 4 times longer than wide, has a soft point, and curls under from the midvein. The very small (3/16-inch long) leaflets are a lead color. Found on dry rocky slopes in Coastal Sage Scrub and Chaparral. Common.

SORI: Near the leaf edge near lateral veins. The leaf edges curl under and hide the sori. Spores mature December - June.

Pentagramma triangularis Plate 475   **GOLDBACK FERN**

DESCRIPTION: Dark green clusters of leaves on stout stems, 4 to 16 inches high. 2-pinnate frond occasionally 3-pinnate on the bottom of the lowest segment. Leaf stalks longer than the blade, dark brown and shiny. The underside of the entire frond is covered with yellow spores. Frond outline is triangular to pentagular. Found on rocky dry slopes in Southern Oak Woodland, Coastal Sage Scrub and Chaparral. Common.

SORI: Completely covers the underside of the frond. Gold color. Indusium lacking. Spores mature December - April.

FERNS

Polypodium californicum Plate 476   **CALIFORNIA POLYPODY**

DESCRIPTION: Light-green lance-shaped fronds are 1-pinnate,1 to 2 feet long. Fronds are spaced along the rootstock rather than coming up in bunches. Found on moist rocky soils and in crevices of rock cliffs. Prefers north or east facing slopes. Found in most of the canyons and protected places in Oak Woodlands. Common.

Pteridium aquilinum Plate 474   **WESTERN BRACKEN FERN**
var. pubescens

DESCRIPTION: Coarse, deciduous fronds 4 feet high grow singly from along a strong, woody, underground rootstalk. The many stout fronds may be erect or reclining. The frond outline shape is deltoid. Leaves are slightly hairy on the underside. 2- and 3-pinnate. Found in shady or sunny locations in both damp and dry places. Shaded canyons on the coast side of the mountains from Temescal Canyon westward. Uncommon.

SORI: In a continuous line near the leaf margin, covered by indusium as well as by infolding of the leaf edge. Spores mature September-November.

Thelypteris puberula   **DOWNY WOODFERN**
[Lastria augescens]

DESCRIPTION: Few stout fronds, stems straw-colored, 1 to 3 feet high. Leaf blades are broadly oblong 1 to 2 feet long, pinnately cleft into narrow lobes, downy on the underside. Found in moist canyons in Chaparral. (Encinal Canyon) Rare.

SORI: Small, close together near the center.

FERNS

Woodwardia fimbriata Plate 473   GIANT CHAIN-FERN

DESCRIPTION: This coarse, large fern grows in masses of 6 to 8 foot high fronds, 8 to 20 inches wide. Oblong in outline, pinnate, deeply cleft, the segments lanceolate. Found deep in cool, well-shaded canyons that are always wet. Uncommon.

SORI: The oblong-linear sori form a chainlike row on either side of the vein of each ultimate leaf. Each indusium is convex and attached to the leaf on the outer side of the sorus.

FRANKENIACEAE
FRANKENIA FAMILY

This family of herbaceous plants consists of about 90 species, only 1 of which lives in our area. Prefers saline and dry sites.

Recognition characteristics of the *Frankenia* genus: Opposite leaves, small, entire. Flowers sessile, solitary. Calyx 4 or 5 toothed, petals 4 or 5, stamens 4 to 7, style 2 or 3 cleft. Seed a capsule.

Frankenia salina   ALKALI HEATH

DESCRIPTION: Perennial herbaceous plant, 1 foot high, bushy. Found in salt marshes along the coast from Mugu Lagoon to Malibu Creek.

FLOWERS: Solitary, tubular, rose-purple, about 3/8 inch long and 5/16 inch wide at the flared tube attached at stem axils without a stem; 5-cleft calyx, pointed teeth; corolla 5-lobed, stamens 6 (4-7); style 3-cleft.

LEAVES: Opposite lower leaves obovate, up to 5/8 inch long; upper leaves narrow.

FLOWERING: June - October

GARRYACEAE

The worldwide distribution of this family consists of 18 species, one of which is found locally. Our species is found on dry, rocky slopes in Chaparral.

Recognition characteristics: Evergreen shrubs with opposite leaves. Flowers in catkins, fruit a berry.

Garrya veatchii Plate 442

SILK-TASSEL BUSH

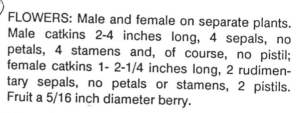

DESCRIPTION: Chaparral shrub ten feet high, evergreen, root-crown sprouts after fires. Found on dry slopes. Plentiful along Carslisle Creek at the 2500' level. Some along the trail from Tapia Park to Malibu Creek State Park, at 600'.

FLOWERS: Male and female on separate plants. Male catkins 2-4 inches long, 4 sepals, no petals, 4 stamens and, of course, no pistil; female catkins 1- 2-1/4 inches long, 2 rudimentary sepals, no petals or stamens, 2 pistils. Fruit a 5/16 inch diameter berry.

LEAVES: Opposite, lanceolate to ovate, broadly tapering to a point, 1 to 2-1/4 inches long, green above, woolly below. Slightly rolled under.

FLOWERING: December - March

GENTIANACEAE

GENTIAN FAMILY

Only 1 member of this 1100 species family is found in the Santa Monica Mountains. A dry hillside plant of Coastal Sage Scrub or Chaparral plant communities.

Recognition characteristics: Annual or perennial herbs. Leaves opposite, entire, without stipules. Calyx of 4 (sometimes 5) sepals, corolla of 4 or 5 united petals, the same number of stamens, 2 united carpels form 1 pistil.

GENTIANACEAE

Centaurium venustum Plate 313   CANCHALAGUA

DESCRIPTION: Annual, single stem branching above, not hairy, 4 to 12 inches high. Found on dry slopes in Coastal Sage Scrub and Chaparral.

FLOWERS: Solitary at the ends of branches; calyx in 5 segments, about 3/8 inch long; corolla a tube, flaring, 5-lobed, rose with red spots and a white throat, the tube 5/16 to 1/2 inch high, the petals 5/16 to 5/8 inch long; stamens 5.

LEAVES: Opposite, ovate to oblong, sessile, 3/8 to 1 inch long.

FLOWERING: March - July

GERANIACEAE

GERANIUM FAMILY

The worldwide Geranium family consists of 11 genera and 780 species. 2 genera and 8 species are found in the Santa Monica Mountains, 2 of which are native.

Recognition characteristics: The flowers are 5-merous. Each flower has 5 seeds with tails that split apart and roll or spiral up a central beak.

Erodium botrys Plate 303   *LONG-BEAKED FILAREE

DESCRIPTION: Annual, semiprostrate, some branches as long as 3 feet. Stems and leaves are hairy and downy. Found in grassy areas.

FLOWERS: Solitary on hairy stems; 5 reddish tipped sepals 5/16 inch long, growing longer when the seeds appear, hairy; 5 petals about 5/8 inch long, lavender with purple veins; style-column is often 5 inches long.

377

GERANIACEAE

LEAVES: In a basal rosette and opposite on the stem, ovate to oblong-ovate, deeply lobed, 3 inches long and 1 inch wide, bristly along the veins and margins, on long stems. Stipules ovate. Often deep reddish-green.

FLOWERING: March - May

FIELD NOTE: Filarees plant their own seeds. After the petals drop and the seeds mature, the style splits into 5 sections, with one seed at the base of each. The style coils like a corkscrew when dry and uncoils when damp. This action screws the seed into the ground and plants it.

Erodium brachycarpum   *FILAREE

DESCRIPTION: Annual, branches curving upward to 16 inches. Entire plant covered with hairs. Found in open grasslands.

FLOWERS: Solitary, on hairy stems 1/2 inch long; 5 sepals 5/16 inch long; 5 petals about 3/8 inch long, lavender; style-column 2-1/4 to 3-3/8 inches long.

LEAVES: In a basal rosette and opposite on the stem, oblong-ovate to 3 inches long. Lower leaves 3-7 shallow rounded lobes; upper leaves deeply pinnately cleft. Stipules ovate.

FLOWERING: April - August

Erodium cicutarium Plate 305   *RED-STEM FILAREE

DESCRIPTION: Annual, decumbent slender stems up to 18 inches long. The 1-1/2 inch "storksbill" seeds are on the plant while buds and blowers are developing at the tip. The hairy stems are usually red-tinted. Found in open cultivated places. Most noticeable in spring because it gets a quick start. Common.

GERANIACEAE

FLOWERS: Solitary in umbel-like clusters high on a main stem; 5 sepals green, prominently ribbed, 3/16 inch long; 5 petals rose-lavender, 1/4 inch long; style-coumn 3/4 to 1-1/2 inch long.

LEAVES: In a basal rosette, fernlike, pinnately cleft into leaflets that are again pinnately cleft into narrow lobes. Hairy on the undersides and on stems.

FLOWERING: January - May

FIELD NOTE: Remains of filaree plants have been found in adobe bricks of the Mission San Antonio Padua, dated 1771, San Juan bautista 1797, and several others. Some botanists reported this filaree as a native because of its widespread distribution in the early 1800's. It is now agreed that it was one of the earliest introduced plants.

Erodium macrophyllum Plate 42   WHITE-FLOWERED FILAREE

DESCRIPTION: Annual, shallowly lobed, palmately leaved, downy. Found in grasslands and fields. Our only native Erodium. (Malibu Creek State Park) Rare.

FLOWERS: Solitary on 1/4-3/4 inch stems; 5 sepals 3/8 inch long; 5 petals, white, 3/8-5/8 inch long; style-column 2 inches long.

LEAVES: In a basal rosette, broadly ovat-cordate, palmately lobed, 1 to 2 inches broad on stems 1-1/4 to 4-1/2 inches long.

FLOWERING: March - May

GERANIACEAE

Erodium moschatum   WHITE-STEM FILAREE

DESCRIPTION: Annual, decumbent fleshy stems, 4 to 24 inches long. The entire plant is hairy. Found on cultivated land, orchards and gardens.

FLOWERS: In a cluster of 6-12 on 1/4-3/4 inch long stems; 5 sepals; 5 petals rose-violet; style-column 3/4 to 1-1/2 inches long.

LEAVES: Opposite pinnate, 2-13 inches long; individual ovate leaflets in slightly unequal pairs, about 1 inch long, serrate. Stipules round-ovate.

FLOWERING: February - May

Geranium carolinianum Plate 302   CAROLINA GERANIUM

DESCRIPTION: Annual or biennial herb, densely hairy, branching, erect or rising obliquely, 16 inches high. Found in shady grass areas throughout.

FLOWERS: In clusters on short stems at the end of branches, small and pink; 5 sepals, bristle tipped; 5 petals ntoched, 1/4 inch long; 10 stamens; style-column 3/8 to 1/2 inch long, yellow-green tip.

LEAVES: Opposite, reinform-orbicular in outline, palmately lobed, deeply 5-cleft and round-tipped, 2-1/4 inches across.

FLOWERING: March - July

Geranium molle   *DOVE'S FOOT GERANIUM

DESCRIPTION: Annual or biennial herb, nearly prostrate, branching stems, covered with soft hairs. Found in grassy, brushy and waste places.

GERANIACEAE

FLOWERS: In pairs on slender stems, rose-pink, tiny; 5 sepals pointed but without a bristle; 5 notched petals; 10 stamens; style-column 3/8 inch long. Seedpod stems reflexed.

LEAVES: Opposite, palmately lobed, 5-7 cleft; somewhat rounded, 1 to 2-1/4 inches wide.

FLOWERING: April - July

GROSSULARIACEAE

GOOSEBERRY FAMILY

The Genue Ribes has been segregated from the Saxifrage family. The *Grossulriaceae* family now consists of one genus consisting of about 120 species and subspecies. The five species found in the Santa Monica Mountains are native.

Recognition characteristics: Perennial shrub usually more than 6 feet high at maturity. Flowers are 5-merous, radial, bisexual, small; fruit is a berry. Leaves simple, alternate.

Ribes aureum   Plates 151, 432   GOLDEN CURRANT
   var. gracillimum

DESCRIPTION: Shrub, erect, 3 to 6 feet high, not hairy. (Along the creek below the pond in the Reagan meadow, Malibu Creek State Park; on the south side of Muholland Drive about 2-1/2 miles east of Topanga Canyon Blvd.) Not common.

FLOWERS: 5-15 in racemes 1-1/4 to 2-3/4 inches long, subtended at base of flower stems by bracts; floral tube (including ovary) 1/4 to 3/8 inch long, slender, yellow; 5 sepals pointed, about 3/16 inch long; 5 petals red in age, oblong, irregularly toothed, about 1/8 inch long. Orange or yellow berry, 1/4 inch diameter.

GROSSULARIACEAE

LEAVES: Alternate, palmately veined, usually 3-lobed, the lobes rounded, 5/8 to 2 inches wide, on stems about as long as blades. Deciduous.

FLOWERING: February - April

Ribes californicum Plate 47
var. hesperium

HILLSIDE GOOSEBERRY

DESCRIPTION: Shrub 4-1/2 feet high or less, intricately branched and compact, usually with 3 spines at nodes. Found in Chaparral, in canyons and open slopes. Rare.

FLOWERS: On stems from leaf axils, floral tube (including ovary) bristly, about 1/8 inch long; 5 sepals reddish, bent back, about 1/4 inch long; 5 petals white, 1/4 inch long; 5 stamens exserted. Berry reddish, 3/8 inch diameter, bristly.

LEAVES: Roundish, thin, 3-5-cleft, rounded lobes, 3/8 to 1-1/4 inches wide.

FLOWERING: February - March

Ribes indecorum Plate 45

WHITE CHAPARRAL CURRANT

DESCRIPTION: Shrub 4-1/2 to 7-1/2 feet high, erect and open; leaves drop during the summer and come into bud in early November when the flowers begin blooming; new growth is sticky and downy. Found in Coastal Sage Scrub and Chaparral.

FLOWERS: In arching or drooping racemes 3/4 to 1-1/4 inches long, on 1/16 inch long stems subtended by longer bracts; cup bell-shaped; 5 sepals; 5 petals white sometimes with a rose tint. Berry sticky and hairy.

GROSSULARIACEAE

LEAVES: Alternate, 3-lobed, finely crenate on the margins, finely wrinkled, sticky, downy above, white-woolly below, 3/4 to 1-1/2 inches broad.

FLOWERING: November - March

FIELD NOTE: Distinguished from Chaparral Currant by the smaller leaves and white flower.

Ribes malvaceum Plates 275, 434   **CHAPARRAL CURRANT**
ssp. viridifolium

DESCRIPTION: Shrub, erect, 3 to 6 feet high; leaves drop during summer and come into bud in October and November. Found in Chaparral and Southern Oak Woodland. Common.

FLOWERS: 10-25 rose colored in drooping racemes; hairy; bracts 1/4 to 3/8 inch long; floral tube (including ovary) about 3/8 inch long; 5 sepals spreading, 1/8 inch long; 5 petals erect, short. Berry purple-black, 1/4 inch diameter, hairy, with a bloom.

LEAVES: Alternate, roundish in outline, thick, wrinkled, rough, 3/4 to 2-1/4 inches wide, bright green above, less green, coarsely downy below, 3-5-lobed. Deciduous.

FLOWERING: October - March

FIELD NOTE: Distinguished from White-flowered Currant by the larger leaves and rose-colored flowers.

GROSSULARIACEAE

Ribes speciosum   Plates 259, 436

FUCHSIA-FLOWERED
GOOSEBERRY

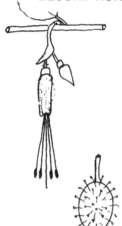

DESCRIPTION: Shrub, evergreen, 3 to 6 feet high, with long, spreading branches, usually with 3 spines at nodes. Found in Coastal Sage Scrub and Chaparral in shaded canyons. Common.

FLOWERS: 1-4 attached to stems in raceme-like pattern; bracts red; floral tube (including ovary) bristly, red; 4 sepals, erect, about 1/32 inch long; 4 petals barely as long as sepals; 4 stamens well exserted. Berry bristly, red, 3/8 inch diameter.

LEAVES: Alternate, roundish, 3/8 to 1-1/2 inches across, dark green, shiny above, lighter below.

FLOWERING: January - May

HYDROPHYLLACEAE

PHACELIA FAMILY

20 genera and 270 species are found world-wide nearly everywhere except Australia. 16 genera are indigenous to the U.S., 7 in the Santa Monica Mountains. None are introduced here.

Recognition characteristics: Bristly herbs (*Eriodictyon* is the only shrub), flowers with 5 united sepals, 5 united petals, and 5 stamens attached to the corolla base. Almost all species in this family are fire-followers.

Emmananthe penduliflora   Plate 170

WHISPERING BELLS

DESCRIPTION: Erect branching annual with a pleasant odor, 4-20 inches high. Found in Grasslands and openings in Chaparral. Dominant fire-follower.

HYDROPHYLLACEAE

FLOWERS: In loose racemes, pendulous, cream-colored; calyx of 5 united sepals, divided almost to the base; corolla bell-shaped and 5-lobed; 5 equal stamens; apparent 2-celled ovary.

LEAVES: Alternate linear-oblong, pinnately cleft but not to the midrib, 1 to 4 inches long. Upper leaves have no stem.

FLOWERING: April - July

Eriodictylon crassifolium Plate 342   **YERBA SANTA**

DESCRIPTION: Perennial shrub, hairy, leafy, 3 to 6 feet high, woody base. Found in Chaparral and Coastal Sage Scrub growing in dry, rocky places. Most often found at higher elevations on the north side and western part of the mountains. A colony of plants grows at the 750' level in the arroyo 1/2 mile east of the Diamond X Ranch and others also grow along Castro Peak Motorway.

FLOWERS: 5-lobed calyx; 5-lobed corolla tubular, lavender; 5 stamens.

LEAVES: Alternate lance-ovate to oval, 2 to 6 inches long, margin scalloped or saw-toothed; woolly, soft hairs growing on both sides.

FLOWERING: April - June

Eucrypta chrysanthemifolia Plate 41   **EUCRYPTA**

DESCRIPTION: Erect annual, slightly hairy, 18 inches tall, with characteristic unpleasant odor. Dominant fire-follower.

FLOWERS: In loose clusters on long stems; yellowish-white, open bell-shaped, about 1/4 inch across; 5-lobed calyx; 5-lobed corolla; 5 stamens not visible from outside the flower.

HYDROPHYLLACEAE

LEAVES: Lower leaves opposite; upper leaves alternate; 1 to 4 inches long. Upper leaves sessile.

FLOWERING: February - June

Nama stenocarpum

MUD NAMA

DESCRIPTION: Annual, many stems, most of which lie on the ground, leafy, 4 to 12 inches long, hairy. Found on damp heavy soil. Rare.

FLOWERS: In terminal leafy clusters and at nodes; 5-lobed calyx divided about 3/4 its length; 5-lobed corolla funnelform, pale violet; 5 stamens; 1 style divided about 1/3.

LEAVES: Alternate, oblanceolate, 3/8 to 1 inch long; lower leaves on stems; upper leaves sessile.

FLOWERING: March - May

Nemophila menziesii Plate 349

BABY BLUE-EYES

DESCRIPTION: Annual, somewhat succulent, covered with short, soft hairs, angled and spreading stems, 4 to 12 inches long. Grows with other plants on moist flats and slopes in most plant communities. Uncommon.

FLOWERS: Saucer to bowl-shaped, 1/2 to 1-1/2 inches wide; calyx deeply divided into 5 lanceolate lobes; 5-lobed corolla divided about 3/4 of the way to base, bright blue with a light blue center; 5 stamens. The cleft between lobes of the calyx supports ear-like appendages.

LEAVES: Opposite, 1 to 2 inches long, pinnately divided.

FLOWERING: February - June

HYDROPHYLLACEAE

Nemophila pedunculata Plate 350 MEADOW NEMOPHILA

DESCRIPTION: Annual, spreading, weak-stemmed, and sparsely covered with short, soft hairs, stems 4 to 12 inches long. Grows in moist soil, shade or sun, in most plant communities. Occasional fire-follower.

FLOWERS: 5-calyx lobes lanceolate, up to 1/8 inch long; 5-lobed corolla bell-shaped, about 1/4 inch broad, white to pale blue with purple blotch on each lobe. The cleft between calyx lobes supports ear-like appendages that are about as long as the lobes.

LEAVES: Opposite, 3/8 to 1-1/4 inches long, deeply pinnately divided.

FLOWERING: March - July

Phacelia brachyloba Plate 36 YELLOW-THROATED PHACELIA

DESCRIPTION: Annual, 6 to 24 inches high, with many branches from the base or none, covered with downy hairs. Found in burned-over or disturbed areas of Chaparral or Coastal Sage Scrub. Fire follower. (On the ridge west of the crest of Chaparral Trail in Malibu Creek State Park, Saddle Peak, Castro Crest)

FLOWERS: Many in panicles along upper half of main stem; 5-lobed calyx hairy; 5-lobed corolla bell-shaped, usually white, sometimes pink, yellow center; 5 stamens.

LEAVES: Alternate, oblanceolate to narrow elliptical in outline, 1 to 2-1/2 inches long, pinnate or with clefts not reaching the midrib. Few leaves on upper part of plant.

FLOWERING: May - June

Phacelia cicutaria Plate 39 var. *hispida*   CATERPILLAR PHACELIA

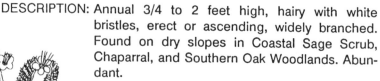

DESCRIPTION: Annual 3/4 to 2 feet high, hairy with white bristles, erect or ascending, widely branched. Found on dry slopes in Coastal Sage Scrub, Chaparral, and Southern Oak Woodlands. Abundant.

FLOWERS: Crowded in coiled racemes that loosen upon maturity; 5-narrow-lobed calyx, hairy; 5-moderately-lobed petals, open bell-shape, pale blue or lavender; 5 stamens; style cleft to the middle.

LEAVES: Alternate, ovate to oblong-ovate in outline, 1 to 4 inches long, pinnately divided with the divisions further divided. Upper leaves smaller and may be only toothed or incised. Leaves are dark green appearing somewhat grayish because of the white hairs.

FLOWERING: March - June

Phacelia cicutaria Plate 40 var. *hubbyi*   CATERPILLAR PHACELIA

DESCRIPTION: Annual, shaggy hairy, stout, erect to ascending, widely branched, 2 to 3 feet high. Found away from the immediate coast in Coastal Sage Scrub, Southern Oak Woodlands, and Chaparral. Less common than var. hispida.

FLOWERS: Crowded in dense coiled racemes, shaggy hairs; 5-lobed calyx; 5-lobed corolla, open bell-shaped, lavender; 5 stamens.

LEAVES: Alternate, 2-1/4 to 6-1/4 inches long, pinnately divided; the segments 1 to 2-1/4 inches long, incised and toothed.

FLOWERING: March - June

HYDROPHYLLACEAE

Phacelia distans Plate 345   **FERN-LEAF PHACELIA**

DESCRIPTION: Annual, 8 to 30 inch high, branched, hairy. Found on dry slopes. Fire-follower.

FLOWERS: 5-lobed calyx, hairy, unequal; 5-lobed corolla open bell-shaped, blue-violet; 5 short stamens; style deeply cleft.

LEAVES: Alternate, ovate to ovate-oblong in outline, 3/4 to 4 inches long, pinnately divided with the divisions further divided.

FLOWERING: March - June

Phacelia douglasii   **DOUGLAS' PHACELIA**

DESCRIPTION: Annual, 2 to 16 inches high, usually several stems branch from the base, covered with soft hairs. Grows in sandy soil at low elevations. Rare.

FLOWERS: Mostly solitary at branch ends; 5-lobed calyx; 5-lobed corolla open bell-shaped blue to purplish; 5 short stamens; 1 short pistil, 10-20 seeds.

LEAVES: Mostly basal, upper leaves alternate, oblong in outline, 1-1/4 to 3 inches long, pinnately divided, sometimes not all the way to the midvein.

FLOWERING: March - May

Phacelia egena   **CALIFORNIA PHACELIA**

DESCRIPTION: Perennial herb, with a branched base from a woody root-crown. 8 to 24 inches high; stem and foliage covered with dense minute hairs. Plant is gray colored. Found on rocky slopes of Chaparral in either shade or sun and at margins of Southern Oak Woodlands. Western half of the Santa Monica Mountains away from the ocean. Rare.

HYDROPHYLLACEAE

FLOWERS: In dense cymes; 5-lobed, each lobe linear-lanceolate to linear, hairy, less than 1/16 inch wide, not overlapping; 5-lobed corolla bell-shaped, with spreading lobes about 3/4 inch in diameter, white; 5 stamens.

LEAVES: Mostly basal, 2 to 5 inches long, on stout stem almost as long as the blade, ovate in outline, pinnately lobed into 3-7 sharply pointed leaflets; terminal leaflet longer than the others; stiff hairs cover and press flat against the leaf. Prominently veined.

FLOWERING: May - June

FIELD NOTE: California Phacelia reaches its southern coastal limits in disjunct Santa Monica Mountain populations.

Phacelia grandiflora Plates 348, 352   **LARGE-FLOWERED PHACELIA**

DESCRIPTION: Annual, robust, hairy with sticky, amber-colored globules at ends of hairs, 20 to 40 inches high. Pleasant odor. Found on burned areas and other disturbed places in Chaparral and Riparian Woodlands. The most abundant of the fire-followers.

FLOWERS: In dense cymes, deeply saucer-shaped, 1-1/4 to 2 inches in diameter; 5 sepals hairy, spatulate; 5-lobed corolla, purple to bluish with a lighter center, 1/2 to 1-1/4 inches long, showy; pistil 1/2 to 1 inch long, cleft 3/4 of its length.

LEAVES: Alternate, ovate, saw-toothed, more or less cordate at base, 2 to 6 inches long, stems less than 3/8 inch long. Upper leaves have a shorter stem.

FLOWERING: April - June

HYDROPHYLLACEAE

FIELD NOTE: The sticky amber-colored globules cause an itchy rash on some people a few hours after exposure.

Phacelia imbricata   Plate 37   **MOUNTAIN PHACELIA**

DESCRIPTION: Perennial herb, with a branched base from a woody root-crown, 8 to 16 inches high; stems and foliage covered with dense, minute hairs. Plant is gray colored. Found on rocky slopes of Chaparral in either shade or sun and at margins of Southern Oak Woodlands.

FLOWERS: In dense cymes; 5-lobed calyx broadly lanceolate to ovate, overlapping, hairy, 1/16 inch or wider; 5-lobed corolla about 1/2 inch in diameter, white, tubular, conspicuously incurved as flower fades; 5 stamens; pistil about 1/2 inch long, cleft.

LEAVES: Mostly basal, 2 to 5 inches long, pinnately lobed into 5-9 sharply pointed leaf-lets, the terminal leaflet longer than the others. Leaf stem slender and at least as long as the blade. Stiff hairs cover and press flat against the leaf. Prominently veined.

FLOWERING: April - June

FIELD NOTE: Mountain Phacelia reaches its southern coastal limits in disjunct Santa Monica Mountain populations.

Phacelia longipes   **LONG-STALKED PHACELIA**

DESCRIPTION: Annual, branching at base, 4 to 15 inches high, hairy. Found in Chaparral. Rare.

FLOWERS: In open cymes, 5 linear-oblong calyx-lobes; 5-lobed corolla, shallow bell-like, white to bluish; 5 stamens exserted; 1 pistil divided halfway.

391

HYDROPHYLLACEAE

LEAVES: Alternate ovate to rounded, 1/2 to 1-1/2 inches long, with rounded margin lobes, cordate at the base, on very long stems.

FLOWERING: April - July

FIELD NOTE: Long-stalked Phacelia reaches its southern coastal limits in disjunct Santa Monica Mountain populations.

Phacelia minor   CALIFORNIA BELLS

DESCRIPTION: Annual, 8 to 24 inches high, hairy, sticky. Found in burned-over areas and other disturbed places in Chaparral and Coastal Sage Scrub. Uncommon.

FLOWERS: 3/4 to 1-1/4 inches long in a loose cyme; calyx deeply 5-lobed, lobes linear-oblong; corolla tubular, bell-like, purple; 5 stamens; 1 pistil divided at the terminal.

LEAVES: Alternate, lower leaves ovate to oblong, more or less cordate at base, saw-toothed, 3/4 to 3 inches long on longer stems. Upper leaves reduced in size.

FLOWERING: March - June

Phacelia parryi Plates 343, 353   PARRY'S PHACELIA

DESCRIPTION: Annual, 1/2 to 1-1/2 feet high, hairy, and sticky, single stem or sparsely branched. Found on dry slopes in burned-over or disturbed areas of Chaparral and Coastal Sage Scrub. Rarely found east of Topanga Canyon.

FLOWERS: Few, in open cymes; open bell-shaped, 5 linear sepals; 5-lobed corolla, cleft below the middle, royal purple with a yellowish or whitish 5-rayed center; 5 stamens, 3/8 to 3/4 inch long; pistil cleft 1/3 from the end.

392

HYDROPHYLLACEAE

LEAVES: Alternate ovate to oblong, 3/4 to 2 inches long, irregularly double toothed or lobed, somewhat cordate at the base. Lower leaves on longer stems than upper leaves.

FLOWERING: March - May

Phacelia ramosissima   Plate 38   **BRANCHING PHACELIA**

DESCRIPTION: Perennial herb, has a woody root-crown with several branching stems, 1-1/2 to 3-1/2 feet long, covered with minute hairs. Found on dry rocky slopes of many plant communities.

FLOWERS: In dense, short cymes, many; 5-lobed calyx, lobes spatulate, hairy and sticky; 5-lobed corolla, bell-like, dirty-white to bluish; 5 stamens exserted, 1 pistil deeply cleft.

LEAVES: Alternate, pinnately lobed, oblong to broadly ovate in outline, pinnately lobed, each lobe oval to oblong and toothed to deeply cleft. Each leaf 1-1/2 to 4 inches long, on a short stem. Upper leaves smaller and sometimes sessile.

FLOWERING: May - July

Phacelia tanacetifolia   Plate 346   **FERN-LEAF PHACELIA**

DESCRIPTION: Annual, stout-stemmed, hairy, 1-1/4 to 4 feet high. Grows in open areas of most plant communities. Uncommon.

FLOWERS: In compact cymes; 5-lobed calyx bristly, each lobe linear; 5-lobed corolla open bell-shaped, blue; 5 stamens 1-1/2 to 2 times as long as the corolla; pistil deeply cleft.

LEAVES: Alternate, oblong-oval to ovate in outline, pinnately divided, the divisions incised. Short stem.

FLOWERING: March - May

393

Phacelia viscida   Plate 344   STICKY PHACELIA

DESCRIPTION: Annual, 2/3 to 2 feet high, without branches or slightly branching, hairy, sticky. Found in open areas, sandy soil, in Chaparral, Coastal Sage Scrub, and Riparian Woodlands. Fire-follower.

FLOWERS: Many flowers, dense in panicles at branch terminals; 5 calyx-lobes linear-spatulate, hairy; 5-lobed corolla, deep saucer-shape, blue with purple or white center, 5 stamens.

LEAVES: Alternate, broadly ovate or rounded, 1-1/2 to 3-1/2 inches long, doubly saw-toothed, somewhat cordate at the base, stem usually shorter than blade. Upper leaves sometimes sessile.

FLOWERING: March - June

FIELD NOTE: A small, sticky globule of brown viscid liquid is on the ends of hairs on the stem. The pleasant odor is deceptive because the brown stains that come from handling the plant soon turn to an itchy rash.

Pholistoma auritum   Plate 347   FIESTA FLOWER

DESCRIPTION: Annual, succulent, straggling coarse branches, 1 to 3-1/2 feet long. Prickles bend back on the stem. Found on shaded slopes in canyons in many plant communities. Fire-follower. Common.

FLOWERS: Solitary in cymes; calyx 5-lobed nearly to base with an ear-shaped appendage between each lobe; 5-lobed corolla, 3/8 to 1-1/4 inches broad, lavender to purple with dark markings; 5 stamens; pistil cleft less than half way.

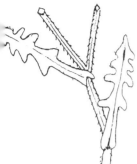

HYDROPHYLLACEAE

LEAVES: Lower leaves oblong to lance-ovate in outline, 2 to 6 inches long, irregularly and unequally pinnately cleft, leaf stems broadly winged and bear ear-shaped appendages at the point of clasping the main stem. Covered with small bristly hairs on both sides.

FLOWERING: March - May

Pholistoma racemosum   WHITE FIESTA FLOWER

DESCRIPTION: Annual, straggling, weak stems, 1/2 to 2 feet long. Prickles bend back on the stem. Found in shaded places in Coastal Sage Scrub, Chaparral and Oak Woodland. (Little Sycamore Canyon) Rare.

FLOWERS: Solitary in cymes; calyx 5-lobed nearly to base with an ear-shaped appendage between each lobe; 5-lobed corolla, 1/4 to 3/8 inch broad, white to bluish; 5 stamens.

LEAVES: Opposite, ovate or deltoid-ovate in outline, thin, 1 to 4 inches long, pinnately cleft. Has some small bristly hairs on both surfaces. Leaf stems are narrowly winged and do not have ear-shaped appendages.

FLOWERING: March - May

IRIDACEAE

IRIS FAMILY

Of the 1500 species of this family throughout the world, only 1 is native to our mountains. Cultivated, introduced species are also found locally, such as in the marshy area of Cold Creek. The fire of 1970 burned the buildings, but left a thriving iris patch that may last forever - and also propagate downstream.

Recognition characteristics: 3 sepals petal-like, fused at the base; 3 petals fused at the base; 3 stamens; 3 united carpels form 1 pistil.

IRIDACEAE

Sisyrinchium bellum Plate 351   BLUE-EYED GRASS

DESCRIPTION: These plants grow in colonies and are most noticeable during the spring flowering season. Found in grass meadows and other open places. Common.

FLOWERS: On top of 16-inch branching stems; 3 sepals and 3 petals joined together at the base, forming a curved tube and a 6-lobed flower, purple with yellow center.

LEAVES: Grass-like leaves originate at the base of the plant as well as alternately along the stem. The tips of the leaves rarely exceed the height of the flowers.

FLOWERING: February - May

JUGLANDACEAE

WALNUT FAMILY

Counting the Walnuts, Pecans, Hickories, Butternuts, and Mockernuts, the world knows 70 species of the Walnut family. 1 native species lives in our mountains. A few abandoned English walnut groves can still be found, but I've seen no evidence of continued reproduction.

Juglans californica Plates 461, 462   CALIFORNIA
                                                             BLACK WALNUT

DESCRIPTION: A low tree, usually not more than 30 feet tall, with several trunks. Found along streambeds, in Southern Oak Woodlands, and on dry slopes. Usually does not compete in Chaparral.

FLOWERS: Male and female separate but on the same tree; staminate catkins 2-3 inches long, with a lobed calyx and many stamens; pistillate spikes small, 4 pointed sepals and 2 arching yellow stigmas. The fruit is a 1 inch globose, thick-shelled walnut.

JUGLANDACEAE

LEAVES: Alternate leaves about 10 inches long, each having opposite leaflets plus a terminal leaflet from 1 to 2-1/2 inches long. Leaflets lanceolate shaped with saw-tooth edges.

FLOWERING: March - April

JUNCACEAE
RUSH FAMILY

Rushes are grass-like herbs, usually found in moist places. The world-wide distribution of this family of 9 genera and 400 species is mostly in cool temperate and subarctic climates. 1 genera (Juncus) and 10 species are native to the Santa Monica Mountains. These rushes are found in salt marshes, canyons, lakes, ponds, and meadows throughout.

Recognition characteristics: Inconspicuous green flowers with 6 sepaloid tepals in 2 rows; normally 6 stamens, and 3 united carpels forming 1 pistil.

JUNCAGINACEAE
ARROW-GRASS FAMILY

The Arrow-Grass family consists of perennial herbs found in salt marshes and fresh water. World-wide, 4 genera and 26 species are found in most climatic zones. 1 species represents the family locally.

Recognition characteristics: Grasslike, basal leaves, inconspicuous flowers, 6 sepaloid tepals in 2 rows, 6 stamens, 3-6 pistils (our local species has 6 united).

Triglochin concinna   **ARROW-GRASS**
   var. concinna

DESCRIPTION: Perennial herb, grasslike, 4 to 16 inches high. Found in Coastal Salt Marsh. (Mugu Lagoon, Malibu Lagoon)

LAMIACEAE

FLOWERS: In racemes 2 to 6 inches long; small, on stems about 1/8 inch long; 6 perianth segments in 2 rows; 6 stamens, 1 pistil formed of 6 united carpels.

LEAVES: Basal, long cylindrical, 1/16 inch in diameter.

FLOWERING: March - August

LAMIACEAE

MINT FAMILY

Of the 180 genera and 3500 species in the mint family, only 11 genera and 21 species are found in the Santa Monica Mountains. They are aromatic herbs — sometimes shrubs — with square stems, a "minty" odor, 5 sepals, 5 irregular petals, 2 or 4 stamens, 2 united carpels form 1 pistil, opposite leaves.

This family has similarities with *Boraginaceae, Scrophulariaceae,* and *Verbenaceae.* They can be distinguished from these families: *Boraginaceae* have alternate leaves and regular flowers; *Scrophulariaceae* have alternate leaves; and *Verbenaceae* usually have 1 pistil.

Lamium amplexicaule Plate 286   *HENBIT

DESCRIPTION: Annual, branching from the base, somewhat straggling, 1/2 to 1-1/2 feet long. Found in cultivated fields and other disturbed places.

FLOWERS: In axillary and terminal clusters; 5-lobed calyx, hairy; 2-lipped corolla purple-red, with a slender tube; 4 stamens.

LEAVES: Opposite, ovate to round 3/4 to 1 inch wide, coarsely toothed. Short stems on lower leaves, none on upper.

FLOWERING: April - September

LAMIACEAE

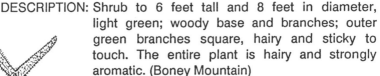

Lepechinia fragrans Plate 70   PITCHER SAGE

DESCRIPTION: Shrub to 6 feet tall and 8 feet in diameter, light green; woody base and branches; outer green branches square, hairy and sticky to touch. The entire plant is hairy and strongly aromatic. (Boney Mountain)

FLOWERS: Opposite pairs spaced 1 inch or more apart along the terminal end of branches; each on a 3/4 inch stem in a leaf axil, white to a slight rose tint with age, 1-1/2 inch. Calyx woolly, 7/8 inch long, divided about 1/2 way into 5 lanceolate segments; 5-lobed corolla; open tube, fuzzy, with lower lobe extending beyond the others; 4 stamens; anthers positioned in upper part of the corolla tube; 1 pistil slender, with a cleft at the tip.

LEAVES: Opposite, hairy and aromatic. Lower leaves deltoid, up to 4 inches long, on a stem. Upper leaves lanceolate and clasping. All leaves show a strong netting pattern from below.

FLOWERING: April - June

Marrubium vulgare Plate 69   *HOREHOUND

DESCRIPTION: Perennial, branched from the base, woolly, 1 to 2 feet tall. Found in disturbed soil. Common.

FLOWERS: In whorls; calyx with 10 spined teeth; corolla 1/4 inch long, white, 2-lipped, the upper lip 2-lobed, the lower lip 3-lobed; 4 stamens.

LEAVES: Opposite, wrinkled, scalloped on the edges, thick, woolly, ovate to round, 1/2 to 1-1/2 inches long. Stems as long as the blades.

FLOWERING: April - August

LAMIACEAE

Mentha arvensis   TULE MINT

DESCRIPTION: Perennial, stems usually branched, to 2-1/2 feet high. Wet soil.

FLOWERS: Axillary clusters in whorls; calyx 5-lobed; corolla lilac-pink to purplish, 1/4 inch long, nearly regular 5-lobed; 4 stamens.

LEAVES: Opposite, light green, lanceolate to ovate, saw-toothed, 3/4 to 2-3/4 inches long.

FLOWERING: July - October

Mentha pulegium Plate 373   *PENNYROYAL

DESCRIPTION: Perennial herb, with a mint odor, erect or more or less decumbent, slender, white-downy, 8 to 20 inches long. Found on damp soil in many plant communities. (Malibu Creek)

FLOWERS: In whorls, subtended by reduced leaves, calyx 10-nerved, 5-toothed, short-hairy on nerves and teeth; 2-lipped corolla twice as long as calyx, lavender; stamens 4.

LEAVES: Opposite on square stems, elliptic to oblong-ovate, serrate or smooth margined, covered with grayish-white hairs, 3/8 to 3/4 inch long.

FLOWERING: June - September

Mentha spicata Plate 71   *SPEARMINT
var. *spicata*

DESCRIPTION: Erect stem, 1 to 4 feet high. Wet soil.

FLOWERS: Dense clusters along a spike about 2 inches long; 5-lobed calyx; 5-lobed nearly regular corolla pale lavender, narrow tube; 4 stamens.

400

LAMIACEAE

LEAVES: Opposite, oblong or ovate-lanceolate, 3/4 to 2-1/4 inches long, saw-toothed, short leaf stem or none.

FLOWERING: July - October

Monardella hypoleuca Plate 370   **MONARDELLA**

DESCRIPTION: Perennial, 1 to 2 feet high, woolly, simple or branched. Found in dry soil.

FLOWERS: Many flowers in terminal heads 1-1/4 to 1-1/2 inches broad, surrounded by ovate bracts 1/4 to 3/8 inch long; 5-lobed nearly regular calyx; 5-lobed nearly regular corolla pale lavender, 5/8 inch long; 4 stamens exserted beyond corolla rim.

LEAVES: Opposite, ovate — lanceolate, 3/4 to 1-1/2 inches long, green on top, white and felt-textured underneath.

FLOWERING: July - September

Monardella lanceolata   **MUSTANG MINT**

DESCRIPTION: Annual, 1/2 to 1-1/2 feet high, simple or branched, downy above, without hairs below. Found in dry soil. Rare.

FLOWERS: Many in terminal heads 5/8 to 1-1/4 inches broad, surrounded by rough bracts often purplish tipped, to 5/8 inch long; 5-lobed calyx woolly; 5-lobed nearly regular corolla rose-purple, tube downy; 4 stamens exserted beyond corolla rim.

LEAVES: Opposite, lanceolate to lance-oblong, 1/2 to 2 inches long.

FLOWERING: May - August

401

LAMIACEAE

Salvia apiana   Plate 66   **WHITE SAGE**

DESCRIPTION: Perennial, woody at the base, 3 to 6 feet high, whitish with hairs that lie along the stem. Found on dry slopes.

FLOWERS: Few in open panicles, subtended by bracts; 5-lobed calyx, lower teeth free, upper united; corolla white tinted with lavender, 1/2 to 1 inch long; 2 stamens, well exserted beyond the corolla rim.

LEAVES: Opposite, crowded at the base, lance-oblong 1-1/4 to 4 inches long, scalloped edges.

FLOWERING: April - July

Salvia columbariae   Plate 380   **CHIA**

DESCRIPTION: Annual, unbranched or branching near the base, 4 to 20 inches high. Found in dry, disturbed places. Major fire-follower.

FLOWERS: In headlike cymes subtended by bracts; 5-lobed calyx; 2-lipped corolla dark blue.

LEAVES: Opposite, mostly basal, downy, pinnately divided, 3/4 to 4 inches long; on stems as long as the blades.

FLOWERING: March - June

Salvia leucophylla   Plate 285   **PURPLE SAGE**

DESCRIPTION: Perennial shrub, many-branched, woolly, 3 to 4-1/2 feet high. Found on dry slopes in Coastal Sage Scrub.

FLOWERS: In headlike whorls spaced 2 or 3 inches apart along main stems; 2-lipped calyx; 2-lipped corolla rose-pink, about 3/4 inch long; 2 stamens exserted.

402

LAMIACEAE

LEAVES: Opposite, lance-oblong, grayish, white, wrinkled, wavy edged, 3/4 to 2-1/2 inches long; Woolly underneath.

FLOWERING: May - July

Salvia mellifera Plate 379   **BLACK SAGE**

DESCRIPTION: Perennial shrub, 3 to 6 feet high, openly branched. Found on dry slopes in Coastal Sage Scrub and Chaparral.

FLOWERS: Many in headlike compact whorls spaced 2 or 3 inches apart along main stems, subtended by bracts covered with a meal-like powder; 2-lipped calyx, the lower lip very short; 2-lipped corolla, the lower lip twice as long as the upper, pale blue or whitish, about 1/2 inch long; 2 stamens.

LEAVES: Opposite, elliptical, rounded teeth, green, wrinkled, 3/4 to 2-1/4 inches long. Strong odor when crushed.

FLOWERING: April - July

Salvia spathacea Plate 271   **CRIMSON PITCHER-SAGE**

DESCRIPTION: Perennial, stout stem, 1 to 2-1/2 feet high. Found in Southern Oak Woodlands and Riparian Woodlands.

FLOWERS: 5 or more in whorls subtended by purplish bracts; 2-lipped calyx, bristly, 1 inch long; 2-lipped corolla, upper lip nearly erect, lower lip spreading, crimson, 1-1/4 to 1-1/2 inches long; 2 stamens exserted.

403

LAMIACEAE

LEAVES: Opposite, mostly basal, broadly oblong-ovate, with rounded teeth, arrowhead shaped, 3 to 8 inches long, on 2 to 3 inch stems. Upper surface dark green and wrinkled; under surface woolly white.

FLOWERING: March - May

Satureja douglasii   YERBA BUENA

DESCRIPTION: Shrubby, perennial, trailing, evergreen herb, 1 to 2 feet long. Found in Southern Oak Woodlands. Uncommon.

FLOWERS: Solitary in leaf axils on stems about 1/2 inch long; 5-toothed calyx tubular; corolla white or purplish, downy; 4 stamens.

LEAVES: Opposite, round-ovate, downy, 5/8 to 1 inch long, scalloped edges.

FLOWERING: April - September

Scutellaria tuberosa Plate 381   SKULLCAP

DESCRIPTION: Perennial, 2 to 8 inches tall, branching at the base. Dry slopes in Chaparral. Major fire-follower.

FLOWERS: Solitary in axils, on short stems; 2-lipped calyx bell-shaped, soft hairy; 2-lipped corolla tubular, 1/2 to 3/4 inch long.

LEAVES: Opposite, ovate, 3/8 to 3/4 inch long, slightly crenate or entire.

FLOWERING: March - June

Stachys ajugoides Plate 67
  var. *rigida*

RIGID HEDGE NETTLE

DESCRIPTION: Perennial herb, 2 to 3-1/2 feet high, hairy. Square stem. Found in moist, shady places. Not nearly as common as *S. bullata*. Is significantly aromatic.

FLOWERS: On open spikes 4 to 8 inches long; 1 to 3 flowers in axil of each bract (usually appears as a whorl of 6); 5-toothed calyx, the teeth triangular and spreading at apex, soft spine-tipped; 2-lipped corolla pinkish or tinted white, mottled with rose-purple; 4 stamens under the upper lip; exserted pistil.

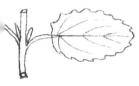

LEAVES: Opposite, oblong ovate to ovate, crenate-serrate edges, 2 to 4 inches long. Leaves higher on the stem are smaller.

FLOWERING: March - August

Stachys albens Plate 68

WHITE HEDGE NETTLE

DESCRIPTION: Perennial, stout, densely white-woolly, 1 to 3½ feet high. Square stem. Found in moist soil of Grasslands and Coastal Sage Scrub, primarily along streams.

FLOWERS: On 4 to 8 inch long spikes in whorls; 5-toothed calyx 1/4 inch long, woolly, pointed; 2-lipped corolla lower lip slightly longer than upper lip, white or pinkish with purple veins; 4 stamens; 1 pistil exserted.

LEAVES: Opposite, ovate, 1 to 4-1/2 inches long, scalloped edges. Densely covered with soft hairs on the underside. Petioles up to 2 inches long.

FLOWERING: May - October

405

LAMIACEAE

Stachys bullata Plate 284   HEDGE NETTLE

DESCRIPTION: Perennial, stem base trails on the ground, slender, 1-1/4 to 2-1/2 feet long. Square stem. Grows in partial shade on slopes and in canyons. Common.

FLOWERS: 6 in whorls, separated; 5-toothed calyx, hairy, teeth triangular spine tipped; 2-lipped corolla, lower lip twice as long as upper lip; 4 stamens exserted.

LEAVES: Opposite, ovate to oblong-ovate, 1-1/4 to 7 inches long, scalloped edges, the base heart-shaped. Leaf stems up to 2-1/4 inches long.

FLOWERING: March - September

Trichostema lanatum Plate 378   WOOLLY BLUE-CURLS

DESCRIPTION: Shrub, many branched, 1-1/2 feet high, minutely hairy. Found on dry Chaparral slopes. Common.

FLOWERS: In a spike of uneven clusters, along the stem; woolly with blue, purple, or whitish hairs 1/8 inch long; 5-lobed calyx hairy; corolla tube slender, deeply 5-cleft, blue; 4 stamens greatly exserted, arched, 1 pistil with a cleft style.

LEAVES: Opposite, lance-linear, 1-1/4 to 3 inches long, green above, woolly beneath, without stems and usually with a bundle of smaller leaves in the axil.

FLOWERING: March - August

406

LAMIACEAE

Trichostema lanceolatum Plate 382   **VINEGAR WEED**

DESCRIPTION: Annual, branching from the base, 1/2 to 2 feet high, strong-smelling. Grows in dry fields in full sun.

FLOWERS: In axils of leaves; 5-toothed; 2-lipped corolla tube, the lower lip as long as the tube and deflexed, light blue; 4 stamens 1/2 to 3/4 inch long, exserted and arched.

LEAVES: Opposite, lanceolate to lance-ovate, 3/4 to 2 inches long, 3/16 to 1/2 inches wide, on a short stem.

FLOWERING: August - October

LAURACEAE
LAUREL FAMILY

California-Bay is the sole representative of the laurel family in our mountains. Mostly a family of the tropics, the family includes Sassafras, Avocado, Camphor, Cinnamon, and Spicebush.

Umbellularia californica Plate 459   **CALIFORNIA LAUREL, BAY**

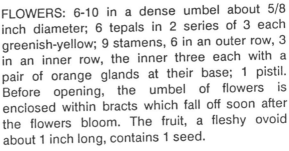

DESCRIPTION: Evergreen tree, pungently aromatic, grows to 30 feet high. Found in canyons and on damp slopes.

FLOWERS: 6-10 in a dense umbel about 5/8 inch diameter; 6 tepals in 2 series of 3 each greenish-yellow; 9 stamens, 6 in an outer row, 3 in an inner row, the inner three each with a pair of orange glands at their base; 1 pistil. Before opening, the umbel of flowers is enclosed within bracts which fall off soon after the flowers bloom. The fruit, a fleshy ovoid about 1 inch long, contains 1 seed.

LEAVES: Alternate, lanceolate, 2 to 4 inches long.

FLOWERING: December - May

LEMNACEAE

DUCKWEED FAMILY

These plants are free-floating aquatics in freshwater. The plant is a very small oval or globose body which does not have recognizable roots, stems, or leaves. The plants are 3/8 inch long or less. 2 genera and 4 species are known in the Santa Monica Mountains. They are not individually described here.

LILIACEAE

LILY FAMILY

This family of 250 genera and 6500 species consists mostly of perennial herbs growing from bulbs, rhizomes, or corms. This book includes *Amaryllidaceae* and *Agavaceae* in *Liliaceae*. 10 genera and 17 species of the Lily Family are found in the Santa Monica Mountains.

Recognizable characteristics: Perianth of 6 distinct segments, 3 classed as petaloid sepals and 3 classed as petals. With the exception of Calochortus, the physical difference of sepals and petals is not readily evident. 6 stamens, 3-valved seed capsule. Leaves are parallel veined and linear.

Allium haematochiton Plate 75　　　　　**RED-SKINNED ONION**

DESCRIPTION: Perennial herb grows in clumps of a dozen or so plants, 4 to 16 inches high. The 1 inch bulbs are oblong and in clusters; the outer membranous layers are reddish purple. Smells like onion. Found in sandy soil near running water or on hillsides.

FLOWERS: 10-30 flowers on 1/2 inch stems in a compact umbel. The sepals and petals are white or occasionally pink with a darker mid-vein. 3 sepals (look like petals), 3 petals, 6 stamens, 1 pistil. The main stem is slightly 2-edged.

LEAVES: Flat and narrow up to 8 inches long.

FLOWERING: March - May

LILIACEAE

Allium lacunosum   PITTED ONION

DESCRIPTION: Perennial herb 4 to 8 inches high, light colored ovoid bulb. Smells like onion. Found on open slopes and flatlands. (Near Saddle Rock) Rare.

FLOWERS: Borne on 4-8 inch tall main stems, the 8-25 flowers are in a close umbel. Sepals and petals are white to pinkish with green or red mid-veins. 3 sepals that look like petals, 3 petals, 6 stamens, 1 pistil.

LEAVES: Cylindrical, slender, reed-like leaves up to 5 inches long.

FLOWERING: April - May

FIELD NOTE: The Pitted Onion population in the Santa Monica Mountains is a significant disjunction.

Allium peninsulare Plate 331   PENINSULAR ONION

DESCRIPTION: Perennial herb 8 to 12 inches high, gray-brown bulb ovoid, 5/8 inch long. Smells like onion. Grows on dry hillsides and grassy, open, wooded slopes. Not nearly as common as Red-skinned onion.

FLOWERS: Few to 25 in open umbel, on 1 inch long, slender stems. Sepals and petals are deep rose-purple, 3/8 to 1/3 inch long. 3 sepals (look like petals), 3 petals, 6 stamens, 1 pistil with a 3-lobed stigma.

LEAVES: Long, narrow, flat leaves grow to 12 inches tall. Leaves and flowering heads grow to about the same height.

FLOWERING: March - June

LILIACEAE

Bloomeria crocea Plate 174   **GOLDENSTAR**

DESCRIPTION: Perennial herb 8 to 20 inches high. Bulb 5/8 inch diameter, covered with brown fibers. Usually found on grassy slopes and broad ridges. Likes heavy clay soil on dry flats and hillsides. (Topanga Meadows) Common.

FLOWERS: Orange-yellow, star-like flowers with dark brown lines on 1 to 2-1/2 inch long stems in a loose umbel. The main flower stem is usually 1 to 1-1/2 feet tall, sometimes 2 feet. 3 sepals that look like petals, 3 petals, 6 stamens (notched at the tips), 1 pistil.

LEAVES: One basal, grasslike leaf about 1/2 as long as the flower stalk.

FLOWERING: April - June

Brodiaea jolonensis Plate 369   **WILD BRODIAEA**

DESCRIPTION: Perennial herb, 1-1/2 to 8 inches high. This elusive flower can be found hidden in grass on dry slopes and broad ridges. Prefers a heavy clay soil.

FLOWERS: Violet, 1 inch long, flared, tube-shaped flowers in a loose umbel. 6 perianth segments, cleft more than half way, 3 stamens (and 3 sterile stamens), 1 pistil, stigma 3-parted.

LEAVES: Usually longer than height of flower. Narrow, rounded.

FLOWERING: April - May

LILIACEAE

Calochortus albus Plate 120

**FAIRY LANTERN,
GLOBE LILY**

DESCRIPTION: Slender stemmed, branching plant. Found in shady places in open woods. Common after fires.

FLOWERS: Solitary, white, globose, nodding, about 1 inch across; 3 sepals; 3 petals; 36 stamens; 3 united carpels form 1 pistil; 3 stigmas; pedicel subtended by pair of 5/8 to 2 inch long bracts. Seedpod elliptic-oblong, 3-winged, 1 to 1-1/2 inches long.

LEAVES: Basal leaves 8 to 20 inches long, grasslike. Upper leaves 2 to 10 inches long, lanceolate.

FLOWERING: April - June

FIELD NOTE: *Calochortus* in Greek means "beautiful grass."

Calochortus catalinae Plates 121, 335

**CATALINA
MARIPOSA LILY**

DESCRIPTION: Stem erect. 8 to 24 inches high. Found on grassy slopes in heavy soil. Major fire-follower.

FLOWERS: Solitary, white tinged with lilac, a purple spot near the base of each sepal and petal, 3 sepals; 3 petals; 6 stamens; 3 united carpels form 1 pistil; 3 stigmas, pedicel subtended by 3/4 to 4 inch-long bracts.

LEAVES: Linear, 4 to 10 inches long; basal leaves usually withered at flowering time.

FLOWERING: March - May

411

LILIACEAE

Calochortus clavatus Plates 185, 186
ssp. pallidus

YELLOW
MARIPOSA LILY

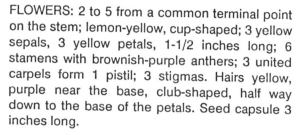

DESCRIPTION: Perennial from a bulb, having a coarse zigzag stem 1-1/2 to 3 feet high. Found on dry slopes in Chaparral. Fire-follower.

FLOWERS: 2 to 5 from a common terminal point on the stem; lemon-yellow, cup-shaped; 3 yellow sepals, 3 yellow petals, 1-1/2 inches long; 6 stamens with brownish-purple anthers; 3 united carpels form 1 pistil; 3 stigmas. Hairs yellow, purple near the base, club-shaped, half way down to the base of the petals. Seed capsule 3 inches long.

LEAVES: Lower leaves 4 to 8 inches long, upper shorter.

FLOWERING: April - June

Calochortus plummerae Plates 337, 338

PLUMMER'S
MARIPOSA LILY

DESCRIPTION: Perennial from a bulb, with slender, branched stem 1 to 2 feet high. Found in openings in Chaparral.

FLOWERS: 2 or 4 erect, white to pink to rose, bowl-shaped; 3 sepals; 3 petals irregularly toothed, sometimes fringed with hairs, inner side of petal covered with long yellow hairs often brown tipped; 6 stamens; 3 united carpels form 1 pistil; 3 stigmas.

LEAVES: Lower leaves 8 to 16 inches long, usually withered when the plant is in bloom. Upper leaves shorter.

FLOWERING: May - July

LILIACEAE

Calochortus splendens Plate 336 **LILAC MARIPOSA LILY**

DESCRIPTION: Perennial from a bulb, sparingly branched, 1-1/2 to 2 feet high. Found on hillsides in Chaparral and Grassland. Uncommon.

FLOWERS: 2 or more usually terminating the branches, deep lilac, often with a purple spot at the base of he sepals and petals, bowl-shaped; 3 sepals; 3 petals with a few hairs near the base; 5 stamens with blue to lilac anthers; 3 united carpels form 1 pistil; 3 stigmas.

LEAVES: Lower leaves 4 to 6 inches long, 1/4 inch wide. Upper leaves smaller.

FLOWERING: May - June

Calochortus venustus Plate 122 **BUTTERFULY MARIPOSA LILY**

DESCRIPTION: Perennial from a bulb, usually branched, 1/2 to 2-1/2 feet high. Found in Grasslands. Uncommon.

FLOWERS: 1 to 3 erect, bell-shaped, white to yellow, 3 green sepals, usually reflexed, 3 petals each with a pale red spot in the upper part, and a lower darker one with yellowish border, scattered hairs on the lower part of petals; 6 stamens; 3 united carpels form 1 pistil.

LEAVES: 1 or 2 lower leaves 4 to 8 inches long, 1/16 to 3/16 inch wide. Upper leaves smaller.

FLOWERING: May - July

FIELD NOTE: Butterfly Mariposa Lily reaches its southern coastal limits in disjunct Santa Monica Mountain populations.

LILIACEAE

Chlorogalum pomeridianum   Plate 123   SOAP PLANT

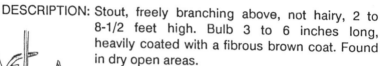

DESCRIPTION: Stout, freely branching above, not hairy, 2 to 8-1/2 feet high. Bulb 3 to 6 inches long, heavily coated with a fibrous brown coat. Found in dry open areas.

FLOWERS: In an elongate raceme, widely spaced, 3 sepals and 3 linear petals look alike, all 6 segments with 3 purple or green nerves down the middle; 6 stamens; 1 pistil 3-cleft at the apex. Flowers open on cloudy days or late in the day.

LEAVES: Wavy, 8 to 28 inches long, mostly basal.

FLOWERING: May - August

Dichelostemma capitatum   Plate 368   BLUE DICKS
ssp. pauciflorum

DESCRIPTION: Perennial herb 1 to 2 feet high. This widely distributed plant is seen in openings in Chaparral, in Coastal Sage Scrub, and Grasslands. The colorful umbel of flowers on a long stem make it an early spring favorite.

FLOWERS: A tight umbel of 6 to 20 flowers at the terminal of a 2-foot-long slender stem. Violet floral tube of 6 perianth segments, cleft less than halfway, flared. 3 stamens (and 3 sterile stamens), 1 pistil.

LEAVES: Basal, grasslike, slender leaves up to 15 inches long.

FLOWERING: March - May

LILIACEAE

Fritillaria biflora Plate 383   **CHOCOLATE LILY**

DESCRIPTION: Stout, light green stem, 6 to 16 inches high. Found on clay soil on grassy slopes.

FLOWERS: 1-4, occasionally more, in an elongate raceme, widely spaced, nodding, bell-shaped, dark brownish-purple tinged with green; 3 sepals and 3 petals look alike; 6 stamens; 1 pistil, cleft about halfway.

LEAVES: Alternate, 3-7, just above ground level, oblong to ovate-lanceolate, 2 to 5 inches long, 1/3 to 1 inch wide.

FLOWERING: February - June

Lilium humboldtii Plate 249   **HUMBOLDT LILY**
ssp. ocellatum

DESCRIPTION: Stout stem, 3 to 8 feet high. Found along intermittent streams in Chaparral and Southern Oak Woodland.

FLOWERS: Few to 40, in an elongate raceme, nodding, orange, spotted maroon margined with red, about 3 inches long; 3 sepals and 3 petals look alike; 6 stamens 2 inches long, with 1/2 inch, orange colored anthers; 3 united carpels form 1 pistil.

LEAVES: In whorls of 10-20 each, 3-1/2 to 5 inches long, oblanceolate, minutely hairy on margins and larger veins underside.

FLOWERING: June - July

Yucca whipplei Plate 101   **CHAPARRAL YUCCA;**
ssp. intermedia   **OUR LORD'S CANDLE**

DESCRIPTION: Small shrub, found on dry Coastal Sage Scrub or Chaparral slopes. The plant sits flush on the ground with its leaf-spears pointing outward in all directions.

LILIACEAE

FLOWERS: Creamy-white bisexual flowers, each 1 to 1-1/2 inches long, in a compact panicle on a single 8 to 10 foot stem. The plant blooms once and dies, leaving several small plants at the base.

LEAVES: 3 feet long bayonet-like leaves in a dense basal rosette. The ends are needle sharp.

FLOWERING: April - June

FIELD NOTE: Yucca and a moth *Tegeticula maculata* have a symbiotic relationship: the yucca moth lays its eggs only in the yucca seedpod, and except for rare and random happenings, all pollinization of the Yucca is performed by the moth. The mouth parts of the female moth gather pollen and form it into a ball which is scraped across the next plant's stigma. No other insect does that. Many insects visit the flower but do not pollinate. Without each other, both life forms would be in jeopardy.

Zygadenus fremontii   Plate 124   STAR LILY

DESCRIPTION: Stout, light-green main stem with branching flowering stems on upper 2/3 of plant, 1-1/2 to 3 feet high. Found in Chaparral, especially after a fire.

FLOWERS: Numerous, in compound racemes up to 1 foot long; 3 sepals and 3 petals look somewhat alike, yellowish-white, about 1/2 inch long; 6 stamens.

LEAVES: Basal leaves are 8 to 24 inches long, 1/3 to 1 inch wide, folded and arched. Upper leaves smaller.

FLOWERING: March - May

LINACEAE

FLAX FAMILY

The flax family consists of 12 genera and 290 species. 2 genera and 2 species are found in the Santa Monica Mountains. The family has economic importance because of flax fibers, linseed oil, and its ornamental flowers.

Recognition characteristics: Regular radiating flowers, 5 distinct sepals, 5 petals, 5, 10, or more stamens, and 5 united carpels form 1 pistil.

Hesperolinon micranthum   SMALL-FLOWERED
                                               DWARF FLAX

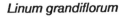

DESCRIPTION: Annual, slender, dichotomously branching, 8 to 16 inches high. Found in open areas.

FLOWERS: Solitary on slender 1/2 inch stems; 5 sepals; 5 petals, white tinged with pink; 10 stamens.

LEAVES: Alternate, linear, 3/8 to 1 inch long.

FLOWERING: April - July

Linum grandiflorum   *FLOWERING FLAX

DESCRIPTION: Annual, branching 8 to 20 inches high. Found as an escape from cultivation.

FLOWERS: Solitary on a slender stalk 3/4 to 2-3/4 inches long; 5 sepals with stiff hairs; 5 petals, rich red, 5/8 to 3/4 inch long; 1 pistil.

LEAVES: Lanceolate, 3/8 to 3/4 inch long.

FLOWERING: April - June

417

LOASACEAE

The Loasa family is mainly of tropic and temperate America. 15 genera and 250 species compose the family; 1 species is found as native in the Santa Monica Mountains.

Recognition characteristics: Sepals 5, petals 5 (sometimes 10), stamens 5 to many, 3 to 7 inferior ovaries, style simple or 3-cleft.

Mentzelia micrantha Plate 150

STICK-LEAF,
BLAZING STAR

DESCRIPTION: Annual, branched; 1 to 2 feet high, hairy. Found in disturbed or burned areas in Chaparral.

FLOWERS: At branch ends in clusters, pale yellow, about 1/4 inch wide and smaller than the broadly ovate bracts; 5 sepals; 5 petals; many stamens with outer 5 petal-like.

LEAVES: Alternate, ovate, wavy toothed, 1 to 2 inches long.

FLOWERING: April - July

FIELD NOTE: All parts of plant are covered with minute barbs that tenaciously grab on to clothing and are difficult to remove.

LYTHRACEAE

Of the 25 genera and 550 species of the Loosestrife family, only 2 genera, each represented by 1 species, grow in the local mountains. They are small-flowered, purple-petalled, and grow in damp soil.

LYTHRACEAE

Ammannia coccinea   **LONG-LEAVED AMMANIA**

DESCRIPTION: Annual, 4 to 16 inches high, not hairy. Found in wet places. (Los Angeles River)

FLOWERS: In leaf axils, 2-5, rarely 1, about 1/8 inch across, purple; 4 sepals, 4-angled floral tube; 4 petals; 4-8 stamens; 1 pistil.

LEAVES: Opposite, linear-lanceolate 3/4 to 2 inches long.

FLOWERING: May - October

Lythrum californicum   **CALIFORNIA LOOSESTRIFE**

DESCRIPTION: Perennial, branching above, 1-1/2 to 5 feet high, pale green, not hairy. Found in moist soil, near vernal pools or streams. (Topanga Creek, Cold Creek)

FLOWERS: Solitary in leaf-axils; calyx tubular, 6 purple petals.

LEAVES: Alternate, narrowly linear to linear-oblong, 3/8 to 1-1/4 inches long.

FLOWERING: April - October

MALVACEAE

MALLOW FAMILY

World-wide, the mallow family is represented by 85 genera and 1500 species. In the Santa Monicas we have 5 genera and 6 species. The Bush Mallow, Alkali Mallow, and Checkerbloom are native to the mountains. Bull Mallow, and Cheeseweed are naturalized from Europe and are usually found near towns. Bristly Mallow was introduced by way of the southeastern United States and is established where white clover plantings have been made.

419

MALVACEAE

Malacothamnus fasciculatus   Plate 277   BUSH MALLOW

DESCRIPTION: Shrub, open-branching, 3 to 15 feet high, with long, sparsely leaved branches; covered with soft hairs. Found on dry slopes throughout in Chaparral and Coastal Sage Scrub, often in colonies. Native. Common.

FLOWERS: In clusters in axils of upper leaves; 5 sepals united at base; 5 lavender petals; many stamens fused into a central tube. Flower 1 to 1-1/2 inches across.

LEAVES: Round-ovate, shallowly 3-5 lobed, 3/4 to 1-1/2 inches long, covered with grayish hairs below, less so above. Scalloped edges.

FLOWERING: April - September

Malva nicaeensis   *BULL MALLOW

DESCRIPTION: Annual, branched, 8 to 24 inches high, downy or sometimes the stems hairless. Found in waste places.

FLOWERS: In axillary clusters; 5 sepals united at base; 5 petals pink to blue-violet; many pistils: fruit discoid; calyx lobes close over the fruit.

LEAVES: Round, shallowly 5-7-lobed, saw-toothed, 1 to 4 inches broad. Petioles 2 to 6 inches long.

FLOWERING: March - November

Malva parviflora   *CHEESEWEED

DESCRIPTION: Annual, branched, 12 to 30 inches high, sparsely hairy to hairless. Found in waste places and as ground cover in orchards.

MALVACEAE

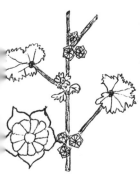

FLOWERS: In dense clusters in leaf axils; linear bractlets at base; 5-lobed calyx enlarges to spread under the circular fruit; 5 pinkish petals.

LEAVES: Somewhat round, sharply lobed, saw-toothed, 1 to 5 inches broad, with a red spot at the base and long leaf-stalks.

FLOWERING: January - December

Modiola caroliniana   ***BRISTLY MALLOW**

DESCRIPTION: Perennial, somewhat prostrate, 8 to 20 inches long; roots at nodes. Found along roadsides and in fields.

FLOWERS: Solitary in leaf axils; 2-3 4 narrow bractlets; calyx 5-cleft. Fruit is a circle of 15-30 bristly carpels.

LEAVES: Rounded, coarsely-toothed, deeply palmately-lobed, 1 to 1-1/2 inches broad.

FLOWERING: April - September

Sida hederacea   **ALKALI MALLOW**

DESCRIPTION: Perennial, low-growing, hairy, 1/2 to 1 foot long. Found in alkali soils but is also common in damp sand.

FLOWERS: Singly or in small clusters in leaf axils; calyx 5-pointed; 5 petals; cream-colored, about 1/2 inch long.

LEAVES: Round-kidney-shaped to broad deltoid, toothed, 5/8 to 1-1/2 inches wide.

FLOWERING: May - October

MALVACEAE

Sida malvaeflora Plate 281
ssp. sparsifolia

CHECKER BLOOM

DESCRIPTION: Perennial, hairy, 1/2 to 2 feet high. Found in meadows and near streams along north slope of the mountains. Scattered in upper Zuma Creek watershed and upper Malibu Creek watershed.

FLOWERS: Few, in racemes; 5 petals, white veined, rose-pink, 1/2 to 1 inch long. Staminate and pistillate on separate plants.

LEAVES: Basal leaves roundish, shallowly lobed, coarsely toothed, 3/4 to 2-1/4 inches broad. Upper leaves deeply cleft with 3 to 5 narrow lobes.

FLOWERING: March - June

MARTYNIACEAE

UNICORN-PLANT FAMILY

A small plant family of warm areas. Prominent for its large, woody seedpod with curved horns, and large showy flowers. Rare in the Santa Monicas.

Proboscidea parviflora

*UNICORN-PLANT

DESCRIPTION: Annual, sticky, hairy, spreading to matted plants with stems 2-1/2 feet long. Found in dry river bottoms. Native to SW United States, rare in the Santa Monica Mountains.

FLOWERS: Showy, in terminal racemes; calyx 5-lobed; red-purple corolla funnelform, 5-lobed, bilabiate with an oblique rim; 4 stamens; 1 pistil. Seedpod is 2 to 3 inches long with 2 curved horns 4 to 6 inches long.

MYRICACEAE

LEAVES: More or less opposite, the upper sometimes alternate, broadly triangular to round-ovate; 5-7 rounded lobes or no lobes, 3 to 5 inches wide.

FLOWERING: June - August

MYRICACEAE
WAX-MYRTLE FAMILY

Shrubs or trees widely distributed throughout the world in 2 genera and 40 species. One species is found (rarely) in the Santa Monica Mountains.

Recognition characteristics: Alternate, aromatic, resinous-dotted leaves, without stipules. Flowers have no sepals or petals. Staminate and pistillate flowers are in separate catkins, sometimes both on the same plant, as with *M. californica*; sometimes on separate plants.

Myrica californica   **CALIFORNIA WAX-MYRTLE**

DESCRIPTION: Evergreen shrub, 6 to 12 feet high, occasionally 30 feet. Found in canyons and moist slopes at low elevations. Uncommon.

FLOWERS: Staminate and pistillate on the same plant; staminate in 3/4 inch long catkins, in lower leaf axils; no sepals; no petals; 7 to 16 stamens. Pistillate on rigid 1/2 inch long catkins ovoid, in upper leaf axils; no sepals; ovoid ovary. Fruit 1/3 inch diameter, brown-purple, covered with whitish wax.

LEAVES: Alternate, oblong to oblanceolate, dark green, glossy, 2 to 4 inches long, serrate.

FLOWERING: March - April

MYRTACEAE

MYRTLE FAMILY

Most of the 100 genera and 3000 species of this family are native to Australia and tropical America. The Myrtle family includes Eucalyptus, Bottlebrush, Eugenia, Guava and others. From the 605 Eucalyptus species we have chosen to illustrate the most prominent introduced member that continues to prosper.

Eucalyptus globulus   *BLUE GUM

DESCRIPTION: A large tree with shedding bark, growing to 200 feet high. This species, as well as other Eucalyptus species, has been widely introduced in the area. Reseeding near a parent tree is common on moist soils.

FLOWERS: White to cream, 2 inches wide in leaf axils; consists mainly of hundreds of radiating stamens; sepals and petals united, forming a thick cap on the bud that drops off as the flower opens. Fruit, a woody capsule.

LEAVES: Alternate, linear-lanceolate; 6 to 8 inches long.

FLOWERING: December - May

NAJADACEAE

WATER-NYMPH FAMILY

Fifty species, all in the genus *Najas*, are found throughout the world. 1 is found in the Santa Monica Mountains. The plants of the Water Nymph family spend their entire existence in water from germination to pollination.

Recognition characteristics: Annuals submerged in water. Leaves are opposite or whorled, linear, toothed, sheathed at the base. Flowers are either staminate or pistillate. Perianth is missing, the single stamen or single pistil enclosed by a small membranous bract.

424

NAJADACEAE

Najas flexilis   WATER-NYMPH

DESCRIPTION: Annual aquatic herb, submerged, branching,
slender, 3 to 6 feet long. Found in streams and
ponds. Uncommon.

FLOWERS: Solitary in axils, minute; pistillate
and staminate separate but on the same plant;
pistillate 1/8 inch long, usually 3 stigmas;
staminate with 1 stamen and a 2-lipped
perianth.

LEAVES: Opposite, linear, minutely toothed. 5/8
to 1 inch long, 1/32 inch wide. Sessile with a
sheathing base.

FLOWERING: July

FIELD NOTE: *Najas* (Greek, *Naias*, water
nymph).

NYTAGINACEAE

FOUR-O-CLOCK FAMILY

In the tropics most members of this family are trees or shrubs,
but in the Santa Monica Mountains, they are herbaceous.

Recognition characteristics: Opposite leaves. Bracts are sepal-like,
sepals are petal-like (sometimes brightly colored), no petals, 5
stamens, 1 pistil.

Abronia maritima   RED SAND VERBENA

DESCRIPTION: Succulent sand-dune plant, many branched and
trailing; stems often 3-1/2 feet long. (Mugu
Lagoon)

FLOWERS: Red-violet, in compact clusters
subtended by an involucre of bracts; 5-lobed
calyx tubular and flared at the end, each lobe
cleft; no petals; 5 stamens; 1 pistil.

NYCTAGINACEAE

LEAVES: Opposite, thick, oval, 3/4 to 2-1/4 inches long, on 3/4 inch long stems.

FLOWERING: February - October

Abronia umbellata Plate 330   **PINK SAND VERBENA**

DESCRIPTION: Perennial herb, prostrate with slender branches, 8 to 40 inches long. Minutely downy. Found on sand dunes in Coastal Strand community.

FLOWERS: In compact clusters subtended by an involucre of bracts, rose-colored, often white in the center; 5-lobed calyx tubular and flared at the end, each lobe cleft; no petals; 3 stamens;1 pistil.

LEAVES: Opposite, ovate to lance-oblong, not thickened, 1 to 2-3/4 inches long; often margined with rounded teeth. Stems usually as long or longer than blades.

FLOWERING: January - December

Mirabilis laevis Plate 329   **WISHBONE BUSH**

DESCRIPTION: Low bush, somewhat woody stemmed, many branches; stems mat over each other and ends turn up. Found in Coastal Sage Scrub and open spaces in Chaparral.

FLOWERS: In an involucre of green bracts; calyx of 5 sepals, each cleft, giving an appearance of 10, red-violet, 1/2 inch long and look like petals; no petals; 5 orange-colored stamens; 1 pistil.

LEAVES: Opposite, 1 inch long, ovate to heart-shaped.

FLOWERING: December - June

NYMPHALEACEAE

WATER LILY FAMILY

These perennial aquatics are found throughout the world. One species grows in the Santa Monica Mountains as an introduced plant.

Nuphar luteum
ssp. polysepalum

*YELLOW POND-LILY, WOKAS

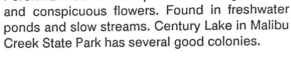

DESCRIPTION: Perennial freshwater aquatics with large leaves and conspicuous flowers. Found in freshwater ponds and slow streams. Century Lake in Malibu Creek State Park has several good colonies.

FLOWERS: Solitary, on stems rising several inches above the water, yellow, 4 to 6 inches across; 7-9 sepals; 12-18 narrow petals; many stamens with reddish anthers; pistils in a central column; 15-25 stigma-rays.

LEAVES: Deeply cordate and oval, pinnately veined, floating on the water, up to 1 foot long.

FLOWERING: April - September

OLEACEAE

OLIVE FAMILY

The Olive Family of 29 genera and 600 species includes ash, lilac, privet, olive, jasmine, and forsythia. In the Santa Monica Mountains only 2 species of ash are found. some Olive trees (*Olea europea*) are growing in Chaparral, and because of some reproduction are considered naturalized.

Recognition characteristics: Trees and shrubs, opposite leaves. Flowers usually have 2, 4, or not sepals; petals none, rarely 2-4; stamens 2, very rarely 4; 2-called superior ovary.

OLEACEAE

Fraxinus dipetala

CHAPARRAL FLOWERING ASH

DESCRIPTION: Deciduous tree or shrub, 6-20 feet high, small branches are more or less 4-angled. Grows on dry slopes and in canyons.

FLOWERS: In panicles on last year's twigs, can be staminate or pistillate or both, no sepals, 2 white petals 3/16 inch long; 2 stamens; 1 pistil; style obscurely lobed. Fruit is a single-seeded samara, 3/4 to 1-1/4 inch long, broadly winged to the base. Flowers appear in spring with the leaves.

LEAVES: Odd pinnate, 1-1/2 to 5 inches long; 3-7 leaflets, firm, ovate to obovate, noticeably serrate, each 3/4 to 4-1/2 inches long, on short petioles.

FLOWERING: March - April

Fraxinus velutina Plate 470

ARIZONA ASH

DESCRIPTION: Deciduous tree, 15-20 feet high, round branchlets. Grows on stream banks.

FLOWERS: Staminate and pistillate on separate plants; small green calyx; no petals; 2 stamens or 1 pistil; style conspicuously 2-lobed. Fruit is a single-seeded samara, 1 to 1-3/8 inches long, narrowly winged about halfway down the seed.

LEAVES: Odd pinnate, 4 to 9 inches long; 3-7 leaflets (usually 5), downy on the under surface; thickish lanceolate to obovate; each 3/4 to 3 inches long, entire to finely serrate; on short petioles.

FLOWERING: March - May

OLEACEAE

Olea europaea   *OLIVE

DESCRIPTION: Perennial, tree, up to 30 feet high, evergreen. Found in disturbed places and abandoned homesites. Once established will grow in Chaparral.

FLOWERS: About 1/8 inch diameter, white. Calyx lobed. Fruit is an olive, green turning black.

LEAVES: Opposite 4-ranked, narrow elliptical, 2-3/4 inches long 5/8 inch wide, dark green on top, light green below. Simple, entire, leathery, on a short stem.

FLOWERING: Early summer setting fruit that ripens in fall and winter, depending on watering cycle. No fruit will set in very dry years.

ONAGRACEAE

EVENING PRIMROSE FAMILY

The common name "Evening Primrose" is misleading; many of the plants bloom during the day and do not look like primroses, but they are a beautiful and interesting family.

Recognition characteristics: 4 sepals, 4 showy petals, 8 stamens, 4 united carpels form 1 pistil. An inferior ovary is so unusual that it is an important identifying feature. The ovary is narrow and so far below the flower that we might mistake it for a stem.

This family resembles the Mustards and Capers in some ways but can be distinguished from them: (1) The ovary is inferior instead of superior as in the Mustards and Capers, and (2) evening primroses have 8 stamens instead of the 6 displayed in the other two families. One species, *Ludwigia peploides* (Yellow Water-weed) is an exception to these characteristics. It is 5-merous.

The genus *Camissonia* can be distinguished from the genus *Oenothera* by the stigma. The *Camissonia* stigma is ball-shaped; the *Oenothera* stigma is 4-parted. Also *Camissonia* flowers open in the morning, *Oenothera* in the evening.

ONAGRACEAE

Camissonia bistorta   Plate 153

SUN-CUP

DESCRIPTION: Annual, prostrate stems often with a reddish tinge, 2 to 30 inches long. Found along the coast and inland in Coastal Strand, Coastal Sage Scrub, and open places in Chaparral.

FLOWERS: Axillary, about 1 inch across; 4 sepals bent downward when the flower opens; 4 yellow petals; 8 stamens; stigma capitate, elevated above the anthers. A brown spot at the base of each petal distinguishes sun-cup from others in the genus.

LEAVES: Basal rosette. Upper leaves alternate, lance-linear, 1 to 3 inches long. Leaves toward the upper end of stems are shorter, and wider.

FLOWERING: March - June

Camissonia boothii ssp. *decorticans*

SHREDDING PRIMROSE

DESCRIPTION: Annual, erect, with shiny, straw-colored stem that exfoliates. Found in loose soil and disturbed places. Eastern end of the mountains. Rare.

FLOWERS: In a compact spike becoming 1 foot long as the seeds form. Flowers 3/8 to 1/2 inch across; 4 sepals; 4 petals white; 8 stamens; stigma capitate. Seedpod 1 inch long.

LEAVES: Basal leaves oblanceolate, serrate, bright green spotted with red, 3/4 to 3 inches long. Upper leaves opposite, smaller and narrower.

FLOWERING: March - June

ONAGRACEAE

Camissonia californica Plate 152

**MUSTARD
EVENING PRIMROSE**

DESCRIPTION: Annual, erect, with short branches. Resembles some sparse-leaved mustard plants. Found on dry slopes in disturbed or burned areas in Grassland, Coastal Sage Scrub and Chaparral.

FLOWERS: Solitary, on a 3/4 inch stalk from leaf axils on upper part of plant; calyx fused, with 4 rounded points, splits and reflexes back in 2 sepals, each 1/8 inch long, when flower opens; 4 petals oval; about 1/2 inch in diameter, yellow or orange drying pink, with red markings near the base; stamens 4 long, 4 short, all free; 1 pistil with rounded stigma. Seed capsules needle-like, more than 1 inch long, reflex downward.

LEAVES: Basal leaves up to 6 inches long, narrowly lanceolate with an irregularly cleft margin, die back at flowering. Leaves on the stem are smaller, 1 to 2 inches long and 1/8 inch wide, irregularly toothed.

FLOWERING: March - May

Camissonia cheiranthifolia Plate 155
ssp. suffruticosa

**BEACH
EVENING PRIMROSE**

DESCRIPTION: Perennial herb, with several prostrate stems 1½ to 2 feet long, radiate from a central rosette; covered with gray, downy hairs. Found growing in sand near the ocean on both sides of Pacific Coast Highway in Point Mugu State Park.

FLOWERS: Single in leaf axils, about 3/4 inch across; 4 sepals; 4 petals, bright yellow; 8 stamens; stigma capitate.

ONAGRACEAE

LEAVES: Alternate, lower oblanceolate, thick, gray, 3/8 to 2-3/4 inches long; upper ovate and somewhat shorter.

FLOWERING: March - July

Camissonia micrantha Plate 154

SMALL
EVENING PRIMROSE

DESCRIPTION: Annual, usually several stemmed, prostrate, hairy, leafy, with outer layer of stem exfoliating, 2 to 20 inches long, gray. Found on dry disturbed soil in Coastal Sage Scrub and Chaparral. (Paramount Ranch) Fire-follower.

FLOWERS: Axillary, 1/4 inch across; 4 sepals; 4 petals yellow; 8 stamens; stigma capitate. Seedpods curved, 3/4 inch long, with an almost square cross-section.

LEAVES: Basal leaves in somewhat of a rosette, linear-lanceolate to oblong-lanceolate, 3/4 to 4 inches long, wavy margins, hairy. Upper leaves opposite and much smaller.

FLOWERING: February - June

FIELD NOTE: Several other species similar to this one are found in the Santa Monica Mountains.

Camisonia strigulosa

CONTORTED
EVENING PRIMROSE

DESCRIPTION: Annual, slender-stemmed, downy, 2 to 10 inches high, usually with a few basal branches. Found on dry slopes, loose soil, sandy places in Chaparral. Rare.

ONAGRACEAE

FLOWERS: Axillary, about 1/4 inch across; 4 sepals; 4 petals bright yellow; 8 stamens; stigma capitate. Seedpod cylindrical and snake-like, 1 to 1-1/2 inches long.

LEAVES: Linear to lance-linear, 1/16 inch wide or less, 1/4 to 1 inch long. Smaller leaves often in axils of lower leaves.

FLOWERING: April - June

Clarkia bottae   Plate 280   FAREWELL-TO-SPRING

DESCRIPTION: Annual, erect, stout, sparsely leaved, 1 to 3 feet high. Found in openings of many plant communities and on disturbed soil.

FLOWERS: On stems in leaf axils; 4 united sepals, unusually green, split on one side when flower opens; 4 petals, fan-shaped, pink-lavender, often flecked with red-purple; corolla center sometimes whitish; 8 stamens, 4 long, 4 short; 1 pistil with 4-part, head-like stigma. Buds pendent, flowers erect. Flower and seed capsule remain erect. Capsules 2 inches long.

LEAVES: Alternate, linear to lanceolate, 1 to 3 inches long and 1/4 to 3/4 inch wide; sparsely covered with short, downy hairs. Leaves dry up when plant goes to seed.

FLOWERING: April - June

Clarkia cylindrica   Plate 278   SPECKLED CLARKIA

DESCRIPTION: Annual, erect, branching, up to 1-1/2 feet tall. Found in open spots in Coastal Sage and Southern Oak Woodland.

ONAGRACEAE

FLOWERS: Singly at end of sparsely leaved stems; 4 sepals united and deflex to one side when flower opens; sepals to 3/4 inch long; 4 petals to 1-3/8 inches long, flecks of red-purple on purple to pinkish-lavender merging to a white center, a red-purple basal spot but no dark central splotch; 8 stamens, 4 outer with bluish anthers, inner 4 with yellow or bluish-gray anthers. Capsules are 1-2 inches long, 4-grooved, not hairy. Buds pendent, flowers erect.

LEAVES: Linear to lanceolate, to 2 inches long. 1/8 - 1/4 inch wide.

FLOWERING: April - July

Clarkia epilobioides Plate 49   **WILLOW-HERB CLARKIA**

DESCRIPTION: Annual, slender branching,18 inches high, sometimes taller; stem and leaves sparsely covered with short, downy hairs. Found in part shade in Coastal Sage Scrub, Chaparral and Southern Oak Woodlands.

FLOWERS: In leaf axils; 4 sepals to 3/16 inch long, united or in pairs when the pod opens; 4 petals obovate with a short narrow base, white with a pinish color with age, 3/8 inch long. Capsule about 1 inch long and 1/16 inch in diameter, somewhat 4-sided. Buds pendent, flowers erect.

LEAVES: Alternate, linear to narrowly lanceolate, about 1 inch long and 1/8 inch wide.

FLOWERING: March - May

ONAGRACEAE

Clarkia purpurea Plate 279   PURPLE CLARKIA

DESCRIPTION: Annual, erect to 1-1/2 feet with few branches. Found in open spot of many plant communities.

FLOWERS: Solitary in leaf axils and terminal stem; 4 sepals separate and deflex when flower opens; 4 petals to 5/8 inch long, pink to deep red, some with a wedge-shaped, dark purple spot; 8 stamens, 4 inner, 4 outer. Capsules conspicuously 8-ribbed. Buds, flowers and seedpods are erect.

LEAVES: Alternate, linear to lanceolate up to 2 inches long, less than 3/8 inch wide.

FLOWERING: April - July

Clarkia similis   CANYON CLARKIA

DESCRIPTION: Annual, erect, single stemmed or branched, 8 to 28 inches high. Found in shaded canyon slopes in Chaparral and Southern Oak Woodland. Rare.

FLOWERS: Solitary at branch ends; 4 sepals 3/8 inch long or less; 4 petals fan-shaped, white or pale pink flecked with red-purple in lower half, 1/4 to 1/2 inch long; 8 stamens in 2 series. Capsule 8-ribbed, not hairy; seeds brown. Buds pendent, flowers erect.

LEAVES: Alternate, linear to linear-lanceolate, 3/4 to 1-1/2 inches long, 1/8 to 5/16 inch wide.

FLOWERING: April - May

Clarkia unguiculata Plate 276   ELEGANT CLARKIA

DESCRIPTION: Annual, stout, erect, stem and leaves not hairy, grows in shade or sun, usually in fairly large numbers. Common.

ONAGRACEAE

FLOWERS: Solitary in leaf axils, showy; 4 sepals, spatulate, about 1/2 inch long; 4 petals lavender-pink to red-purple, 3/4 to 1 inch long, somewhat diamond-shaped, with narrow stemlike base about 1/2 petal length; 8 stamens outer 4 red orange, inner 4, much lighter; buds and calyx hairy. Seed capsules about 1 inch long, 8-ribbed, hairy, and on a short stem. Buds pendent, flowers erect.

LEAVES: Lanceolate to ovate up to 2-1/2 inches long, about 3 times longer than wide, and on short stems.

FLOWERING: April - June

Epilobium brachycarpum　　　FIELD WILLOW-HERB

DESCRIPTION: Annual, erect, branched above, 1 to 6-1/2 feet high; stem bark shreds in strips. Found on dry disturbed soil in Southern Oak Woodland.

FLOWERS: In a panicle, loosely spaced; 4 sepals; 4 petals deeply notched, pink to white; 8 stamens; 1 pistil. Seed capsule, 4-angled, about 1 inch long.

LEAVES: Alternate, linear to linear-lanceolate, 1 inch long, sometimes longer.

FLOWERING: June - September

Epilobium canum　Plate 263　　　CALIFORNIA FUCHSIA

DESCRIPTION: Perennial, woody at the base, much-branched, up to 2-1/2 feet high. Commonly found in dry areas, rocky slopes and cliffs.

ONAGRACEAE

FLOWERS: On short axillary stems; scarlet sepals and petals in tubular funnelform about 1 inch long with a basal bulge; sepals 4-parted; 4 petals 2-cleft; 8 stamens; 1 pistil; stamens and pistil exserted. Seedpod 4-sided, 3/4 inch long.

LEAVES: Lower opposite, upper alternate; green, woolly, lanceolate to narrow oblong, up to 1 inch long and 3/8 inch wide, smooth edged but sometimes finely toothed, stem hairy. Small flowering stems branch from main stems.

FLOWERING: July - November

Epilobium canum Plate 262
ssp. canum

HOARY FUCHSIA

DESCRIPTION: Perennial, woody at the base, much-branched, woolly, 1 to 2 feet high. Found in dry areas, rocky slopes and cliffs.

FLOWERS: On short axillary stems; scarlet sepals and petals in tubular funnelform about 1 inch long with a basal bulge; sepals 4-parted; 4 petals 2-cleft, 8 stamens; 1 pistil; stamens and pistil exserted. Seedpod is 4-sided, 3/4 inch long.

LEAVES: Lower often opposite and upper alternate; 3/8-1/2 inch long and 1/16 inch wide, filiform to linear-lanceolate, woolly, grayish-white, and not sticky; 1/2 to 2 inch side branches grow from the axils. Leaves opposite on side branches with several shorter leaves in the axils, appearing whorled.

FLOWERING: July - November

ONAGRACEAE

Epilobium ciliatum Plate 77
  ssp. ciliatum

WILLOW-HERB

DESCRIPTION: Perennial herb, erect, 3 feet high. Found in moist places. (Upper Zuma Canyon, Topanga Canyon, Lower Rustic Canyon, Santa Ynez Canyon)

FLOWERS: Solitary in leaf axils, about 5/16 inches across; 4 sepals; 4 petals deeply notched, white tinged with pink, aging red; 8 stamens, 4 long, 4 short. Slender seed capsule, reddish, 1-1/2 to 2-1/4 inches long. Seeds have a tuft of silky hairs on upper end.

LEAVES: Alternate, finely serrate, ovate to elliptice-lanceolate, 1-1/4 to 2-1/2 inches long. Upper leaves smaller and slightly woolly. Stem 1/8 to 3/16 inch.

FLOWERING: July - August

Epilobium pygmaeum

SMOOTH BOISDUVALIA

DESCRIPTION: Annual, usually erect but with some decumbent branches from the base, stems 4 to 12 inches long, leafy. Found in dry mud flats. No longer found in previously known locations in the Santa Monica area.

FLOWERS: Axillary, about 1/4 inch across; 4 sepals; 4 petals purple to white; 8 stamens; stigma 4-lobed.

LEAVES: Alternate, lance-ovate to oblong, finely saw-toothed, 3/8 to 5/8 inch long.

FLOWERING: May - June

438

ONAGRACEAE

Ludwigia peploides Plate 158
ssp. peploides   YELLOW WATER-WEED

DESCRIPTION: Perennial herb, reddish stems lying on the ground or floating. Rooting at the nodes. Found in wet places away from coast. (Century Lake and other places along Malibu Creek)

FLOWERS: Solitary in leaf-axils, 5 sepals, 5 yellow petals, 10 stamens, stigma capitate. Capsules about 1 inch long.

LEAVES: Alternate, oblong to oblong-spatulate, pinnately veined, 4 inches long on stems 1/8 to 1/4 inch long.

FLOWERING: May - October

Oenothera californica   CALIFORNIA
                                                 EVENING PRIMROSE

DESCRIPTION: Perennial herb, coarse-stemmed, usually branched, 4 to 20 inches high; branches prostrate or rise at an angle; stem bark exfoliating; hairs flattened against leaf or stem. Found in sandy soil along the Los Angeles River. Rare.

FLOWERS: One or more on 1 to 2 inch stems in leaf axils, white aging pink, open at sunset; 4 sepals 5/8 to 3/4 inch long; 4 petals, orbicular-obovate, about 1 inch long; 8 stamens; 4-lobed stigma. Seed capsules curved upward, round, 3/4 to 2 inches long. Buds pendent.

LEAVES: Lower oblanceolate to spatulate, 3/8 to 2-1/4 inches long; upper oblong to lanceolate; vary from undivided margins to wavy and toothed.

FLOWERING: April - June

ONAGRACEAE

Oenothera elata Plate 156
ssp. hirsutissima

**HOOKER'S
EVENING PRIMROSE**

DESCRIPTION: Perennial or biennial herb, branching, stout, usually red-stemmed, hairy, 3 to 7-1/2 feet high. Found on moist places in Coastal Sage Scrub, Chaparral, and Southern Oak Woodland. (Santa Ynez Canyon) Uncommon.

FLOWERS: In dense panicle 4 to 16 inches long, opens at sunset; 4 sepals, hairy, greenish, 3/4 to 1-3/4 inch long; 4 petals, yellow aging reddish, broadly obovate, 1 to 1-3/4 inches long, 8 stamens; 4-lobed stigma.

LEAVES: Lower oblanceolate to spatulate, 2 to 8 inches long; upper lanceolate; all with strongly wavy margin and hairy.

FLOWERING: June - September

ORCHIDACEAE

ORCHID FAMILY

The Orchid family is the largest family of flowering plants worldwide with 600-700 genera and 20,000 species. 2 genera, each represented by 1 species are native to the Santa Monica Mountains. One, the Stream Orchid, is found along moist stream banks. The other, the Rein Orchid, is found in Chaparral.

Epipactis gigantea Plate 386

STREAM ORCHID

DESCRIPTION: Perennial herb, alternate leaved, erect, 1 to 3 feet high. Found along moist stream banks. (Upper Zuma Creek, Cold Creek, Santa Ynez Creek, and others with some water all year)

FLOWERS: Solitary in leaf axils, 3 sepals, green; 3 petals, brownish; 1 fertile stamen; 3 united carpels combine with the stamens to form a complex column.

440

ORCHIDACEAE

LEAVES: Lower ovate, upper lanceolate; parallel veined, 2 to 6 inches long.

FLOWERING: March - June

Piperia unalascensis   **REIN ORCHID**

DESCRIPTION: Perennial, stiff stem 12 to 40 inches high. Found in Chaparral and Southern Oak Woodland. (Cold Creek) Rare.

FLOWERS: On a raceme 4 to 12 inches long, greenish; 3 sepals; 3 petals, 2 lateral alike, the third (lip) dissimilar.

LEAVES: Basal leaves alternate, 3 to 8 inches long, oblong lanceolate; lower stem leaves lanceolate, 4 to 6 inches long; upper leaves smaller.

FLOWERING: April - August

OROBANCHACEAE

BROOMRAPE FAMILY

Two species of the Broomrape family are native to the Santa Monicas, but very rare. Broomrapes are usually found at higher elevations than the Santa Monicas. The plants are parasitic on the roots of other plants, usually *Adenostoma, Artemisia, Eriogonum* and *Eriodictyon.*

Recognition characteristics: Flowers are scroph-like, 5 merous, in terminal racemes or spikes; plant grows in the root zone of its host.

OROBANCHACEAE

Orobanche bulbosa   Plate 387   CHAPARRAL BROOMRAPE

DESCRIPTION: Parasitic on roots of other plants, stout, fleshy, covered with a coarse waxy powder; 4 to 12 inches high. Found in Chaparral, usually with Chamise. (Topanga Canyon) Rare.

FLOWERS: In dense terminal pyramid (thyroid-paniculate), floral bracts; calyx 3/8 inch long; unequally cleft; corolla tube-like, 5-lobed, yellowish or brownish to purple or bluish.

LEAVES: Closely placed scales, 3/8 inch long, on the stem, not green but dark purplish-brown.

FLOWERING: April - July

Orobanche fasciculata   Plate 200   CLUSTERED BROOMRAPE

DESCRIPTION: Parasitic on roots of other plants, stout, fleshy, often with more than 1 stem, 2 to 8 inches high, covered with soft hairs throughout. Found in Chaparral and Coastal Sage Scrub. (Cornell Corners)

FLOWERS: Solitary, terminal on axillary stems 1 to 4 inches long; 5-lobed calyx bell-shaped; 5-lobed corolla tube-like, purplish-yellow or straw colored, about 1 inch long; 4 stamens.

LEAVES: Pointed scales, few, spaced along the stem, not green but purplish.

FLOWERING: April - July

OXALIDACEAE

950 species of oxalis plants are found throughout the world, mostly in tropic and subtropic climates. 4 species are found in the Santa Monica Mountains; one is native.

Our species are 5-merous, have trifoliate leaves, and an elastically explosive seed capsule.

Oxalis albicans Plate 146
  ssp. californica

OXALIS

DESCRIPTION: Perennial herb, several stems tufted on a stout woody taproot; stems 4 to 16 inches long, bearing leaves and flowers sparingly. Found in Coastal Sage Scrub and Chaparral.

FLOWERS: 1-3 on slender stems; 5 sepals, 5 petals yellow; 10 stamens; 5 pistils united at their bases, free above.

LEAVES: Trifoliolate, leaflets 5/16 to 5/8 inch wide, gray-green downy on both sides, margin fringed with hairs.

FLOWERING: March - May

Oxalis corniculata

*WEEDY OXALIS

DESCRIPTION: Perennial herb, several creeping stems, up to 1 foot long, rooting at the nodes. Found in lawns and gardens.

FLOWERS: On slender, 2 inch long stems, 1-3 each, 1/4 inch diameter; 5 sepals, 5 petals yellow; 10 stamens, 5 long, 5 short; 5 pistils united at their bases, free above.

LEAVES: Trifoliolate on 2- to 3-inch-long leaf stems; leaflets heart shaped, 5/8 inch across.

FLOWERING: March - November

OXALIDACEAE

Oxalis pes-caprae Plate 145   ***BERMUDA BUTTERCUP**

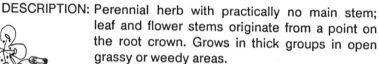

DESCRIPTION: Perennial herb with practically no main stem; leaf and flower stems originate from a point on the root crown. Grows in thick groups in open grassy or weedy areas.

FLOWERS: 5 sepals lanceolate, about 1/4 inch long; 5 petals deep yellow; 1/2 inch long; 10 stamens, 5 outer whorl short, 5 inner whorl long; 5 pistils united at their bases, free above. Individual flower stems are about 1/2 inch long — 3 to 10 originating at one point on the 8 to 12 inch supporting stalk. Since the flowers bloom in sequence, each stalk often seems to carry only one flower.

LEAVES: Palmately compound on 4 to 6 inch leaf stem; 3 leaflets, each heart-shaped and about 3/8 inch long.

FLOWERING: November - April

Oxalis rubra   ***ROSE OXALIS**

DESCRIPTION: Perennial herb, leafy with a woody root, 6 to 12 inches high. Grows as a garden escape. Native of South America.

FLOWERS: 6 to 12 on 1/2 to 1 inch stems attached to a 1/2 to 1 foot stalk; 5 sepals with orange spots near the tips; 5 petals each about 1/2 inch long, rose with darker veins; 10 stamens; 5 pistils united at their bases, free above.

LEAVES: Trifoliolate on 6 to 8 inch leaf stem; heart-shaped leaflets (5/8 to 3/4 inch wide), with dark spots and small conical bumps.

FLOWERING: May - July

PAEONIACEAE

PEONY FAMILY

One peony is native in our area. It blooms in late winter, surprising hikers who may be on a trail in Chaparral.

Paeonia californica Plate 384

CALIFORNIA PEONY

DESCRIPTION: Perennial herb to 1-1/2 feet tall, succulent, dark green; dormant in summer; begins to grow from its root system with the first fall rains, and dies back in late spring. Found in Chaparral.

FLOWERS: Solitary, globose, 1-1/2 inches wide, heavy-looking, bends over at end of a smooth, green stem; 5 sepals, sometimes 6, concave, greenish; 5 petals, dark maroon, partly hidden by sepals. Seedpods, usually 3, leathery, 1 inch long, light green, on flower stalk.

LEAVES: Alternate, palmately compound and divided; dark green above, light green below. Hollow stems grow in a clump from the roots.

FLOWERING: January - April

PAPAVERACEAE

POPPY FAMILY

Nine genera and 10 species of the Poppy family are represented in the Santa Monica Mountains. Worldwide, some 200 species are found mostly in subtropical and temperate zones of the northern hemis- phere, particularly in western North America.

Recognition characteristics: Deciduous sepals, generally crumpled petals, and many stamens.

PAPAVERACEAE

Argemone munita   Plate 61   PRICKLY POPPY

DESCRIPTION: Stout, branched, prickly stems 2 to 3 feet high; pale yellow sap. Found in dry sand and gravel. (Malibu Creek downstream from Malibu Lake Dam in Malibu Creek State Park, Medea Creek) Fire-follower.

FLOWERS: Solitary, white, showy, 2 to 5 inches in diameter; sepals densely spiny; 6 petals in 2 whorls of 3, crumpled; stamens 150 to 250. Seed capsule 1-1/2 to 2-1/4 inches long.

LEAVES: Deeply lobed, prickly, clasping at the base, 2 to 6 inches long.

FLOWERING: June - August

FIELD NOTE: The natural habitat appears to be the Simi Hills. Drainage into the Malibu Creek watershed could be responsible for the Malibu Creek colony.

Dendromecon rigida   Plate 148   BUSH POPPY

DESCRIPTION: Perennial shrub often 10 feet high, with slender erect branches. Found throughout the central and eastern part of the area in Chaparral as a pioneer plant. Rarely found in mature Chaparral.

FLOWERS: Solitary, terminal on short branchlets, showy; 2 sepals fall off when the petals open; 4 petals yellow; stamens many; 1 pistil, 2 stigmas. Seed capsule moderately curved; linear, 2 to 4 inches long.

LEAVES: Alternate, lanceolate to lance-oblong 1 to 4 inches long, leathery, on short stems.

FLOWERING: February - June

PAPAVERACEAE

Dicentra ochroleuca Plate 53 — BLEEDING HEART

DESCRIPTION: Perennial herb; 6 feet tall, with most of the leaves at the base of the plant. Several stems extend upright, each having a compound raceme of flowers at the end. Appears in Chaparral after a fire or in other disturbed areas. Found from Sepulveda Canyon westward. A fire-follower.

FLOWERS: In densely crowded clusters, cream color, 3/4 to 1 inch long; 2 sepals, about 3/16 inch long, fall off when the flower opens; 4 petals in 2 pairs, outer petals diverge at tips; purple spots on inner side near end of petals; 6 stamens in 2 sets of 3; 1 pistil closely surrounded by the stamens.

LEAVES: Alternate. Basal and on lower stems, 3-pinnate, deeply divided into many fine segments.

FLOWERING: May - July

FIELD NOTE: *Dicentra* is Greek for "twice-spurred," in reference to the flower shape.

Eschscholzia caespitosa Plate 246 — COLLARLESS CALIFORNIA POPPY

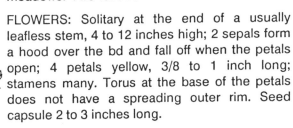

DESCRIPTION: Annual with several stems 4 to 12 inches high from a basal tuft of leaves; colorless sap. Found in Coastal Sage Scrub, sandy stream banks, and meadows. Fire-follower.

FLOWERS: Solitary at the end of a usually leafless stem, 4 to 12 inches high; 2 sepals form a hood over the bd and fall off when the petals open; 4 petals yellow, 3/8 to 1 inch long; stamens many. Torus at the base of the petals does not have a spreading outer rim. Seed capsule 2 to 3 inches long.

447

PAPAVERACEAE

LEAVES: Cleft into many narrow segments mostly 3/8 inch long or less.

FLOWERING: March - June

Eschscholzia californica Plate 245

CALIFORNIA POPPY

DESCRIPTION: Annual, sometimes perennial, branching stems 8 to 20 inches long. Colorless sap. Found in Coastal Sage Scrub, sandy stream banks, and meadows. Fire-follower.

FLOWERS: Solitary on 2 to 6 inch long stems branching from the main stem; 2 sepals form a hood over the bud and fall off when the petals open; 4 petals orange grading to yellow, up to 2 inches long; stamens many. Torus at the base of the petals has a spreading outer rim. Seed capsule 1-1/4 to 3-1/4 inches long.

LEAVES: Cleft into many narrow segments, the blades 3/4 to 2-1/4 inches long.

FLOWERING: February - September

FIELD NOTE: California Poppy is variable because people, organizations, and local governments tend to distribute seeds of the state flower at random.

Meconella denticulata

SMALL-FLOWERED MECONELLA

DESCRIPTION: Slender branching annual 4 to 10 inches high. Found on moist shady slopes in Chaparral and Coastal Sage Scrub.

FLOWERS: Solitary on 1-3/4 to 2-1/4 inch, thread-like stems; 3 sepals; 6 petals white, 1/8 inch long; 6 stamens. Seed capsule 1 to 1-3/8 inch long.

PAPAVERACEAE

LEAVES: Opposite; basal leaves 1 to 1-1/2 inches long, spatulate, with elongated winged stems; upper leaves spatulate to linear 3/8 to 1-1/4 inches long — no leaf stem.

FLOWERING: March - May

Papaver californicum Plate 247   FIRE POPPY

DESCRIPTION: Slender annual 1 to 2 feet high, milky sap. Found the first season after fires in Chaparral and Southern Oak Woodlands.

FLOWERS: Axillary on long slender stems; 2 sepals 3/8 inch long; 4 petals brick red with a basal greenish spot; stamens many; style slender, stigmas radiating disk-like. Seedpod club-shaped.

LEAVES: Pinnately divided into oblong to round segments. Segments toothed or lobed 1-1/4 to 3-1/2 inches long.

FLOWERING: April - May

Platystemon californicus Plate 59   CREAM CUPS

DESCRIPTION: Annual, branching from the base, hairy, somewhat reclining, 4 to 12 inches high. Found in Grassland, Chaparral, and Southern Oak Woodland. (South end of the Reagan Meadow near the Cage Canyon Trail, Malibu Creek State Park)

FLOWERS: Solitary on leafless, hairy stems 4 to 8 inches long; 3 sepals; 6 petals cream-colored, to 5/8 inch long; stamens many, with flattened filaments.

449

PAPAVERACEAE

LEAVES: Mostly on the lower part of the plant, lance-linear, 3/4 to 2 inches long, no stems.

FLOWERING: March - May

FIELD NOTE: *Platystemon* in Latin means broad stamens.

Romneya coulteri Plate 60   ***MATILIJA POPPY**

DESCRIPTION: Shrubby perennial with heavy branching stems, 3 to 8 feet high, colorless sap. Grows in colonies of many plants. Found in Chaparral and Coastal Sage Scrub. (In Malibu Creek State Park along the Cistern Trail and near the Visitors' Center, also on the trail between Rock Pool and Century Lake) It is believed that these colonies were introduced years ago, probably from rootstock taken from the Cuyama area in Santa Barbara County.

FLOWERS: At ends of somewhat leafy stems, showy; 3 sepals; 6 petals large, white, crumpled, each 2-1/4 to 4 inches long; stamens yellow, numerous. Buds 1 inch long.

LEAVES: Pinnately divided into 3-5 main segments in turn sparingly dentate to cleft. Leaves 2 to 8 inches long.

FLOWERING: May - July

Stylomecon heterophylla Plate 248   **WIND POPPY**

DESCRIPTION: Annual, simple — sometimes branching, 1 to 2 feet high, yellow sap. Found in Chaparral, Grassland and Southern Oak Woodland, especially after a fire.

FLOWERS: Axillary on 2 to 4 inch stems; 2 sepals; 4 petals orange-red with dark brown spot at base, 3/8 to 3/4 inch long; stamens many; style slender, short, with a head-like stigma.

450

PAPAVERACEAE

LEAVES: Alternate, pinnatifid, 3/4 to 4-1/2 inches long including stems.

FLOWERING: April - May

FIELD NOTE: *Stylomecon,* "style" and "poppy," draw attention to the style which is the diagnostic feature of the genus.

PLANTAGINACEAE

PLANTAIN FAMILY

One genus and 3 species grow in the Santa Monica Mountains. Plantains are widespread here as well as worldwide. 3 genera and 270 species are known.

Recognition characteristics: Plantains are 4-merous, have a basal rosette of parallel veined leaves. The flower stems are leafless.

Plantago erecta Plate 407   **CALIFORNIA PLANTAIN**

DESCRIPTION: Annual, shaggy haired with 1 or more leafless flower stems rising 2 to 10 inches from a basal rosette. Found in Coastal Sage Scrub, Grassland, and Chaparral.

FLOWERS: Many clustered in cylindrical spikes 1/4 to 1 inch long on 2 to 10 inch stems. 4 fused sepals; 4 fused petals, spreading; 4 stamens; 4 fused carpels forming 1 pistil. Each brownish-green flower about 1/8 inch long.

LEAVES: Basal, filiform to linear-lanceolate, 1¼ to 4-1/2 inches long.

FLOWERING: March - May

PLANTAGINACEAE

Plantago lanceolata Plate 103　　　　　　　　***ENGLISH PLANTAIN**

DESCRIPTION: Perennial herb with short, shaggy hairs; flower spikes about 4 times higher than leaf rosette. Found in lawns and other damp disturbed soil. Introduced from Europe.

FLOWERS: Many clustered on cylindrical 3/4 to 3 inch long spikes on 8 to 32 inch high stems; 4 fused sepals; 4 fused petals, spreading; 4 exserted stamens; 2 fused carpels forming 1 pistil.

LEAVES: Basal, lanceolate to lance-oblong, parallel veined, 2 to 8 inches long, in a rosette.

FLOWERING: April - August

Plantago major Plate 410　　　　　　　　***COMMON PLANTAIN**

DESCRIPTION: Perennial herb with several leafless flower stems 4 to 16 inches high, from a basal leaf rosette. Found in damp disturbed places.

FLOWERS: Many clustered on a dense, long spike, stem 4 to 16 nches long including the spike. 4 fused sepals, 4 fused petals, 4 stamens, 2 fused carpels forming 1 pistil. Each flower about 1/16 inch long.

LEAVES: Basal, thick, broadly elliptic to ovate, with conspicuous converging veins at base and apex, 2 to 8 inches long.

FLOWERING: April - September

PLATANACEAE

SYCAMORE FAMILY

Ten species of Sycamore are indigenous to temperate and sub-tropical climates of the northern hemisphere. The western sycamore is the only species found in the Santa Monicas, but others are available commercially.

Platanus racemosa   Plates 463, 465   **WESTERN SYCAMORE**

DESCRIPTION: Deciduous tree, 30 to 75 feet high, typically with huge, wide, spreading branches from a large trunk that may be leaning or even almost horizontal. Has thin exfoliating bark which exposes greenish and whitish areas, giving the trunk a mottled appearance. Found in stream bottoms in all parts of the mountains.

FLOWERS: In strings of pendulous, spherical heads, pistillate and staminate on same tree; pistillate in heads about 1 inch in diameter; staminate flowers in heads about 3/8 inch in diameter.

LEAVES: Alternate, deciduous, palmately 5-lobed, 6 to 10 inches and more broad. Woolly on both sides when young. Stipules are leafy, often 1 inch long, and sometimes completely encircle a young twig.

FLOWERING: February - April

PLUMBAGINACEAE

LEADWORT FAMILY

About 19 genera and 775 species are widely distributed about the world. Locally, we have 1 genus and 2 species, commonly called Marsh-rosemary. The Leadwort family is characteristically perennial, 5-merous, and grows in coastal marshes.

PLUMBAGINACEAE

Limonium californicum

**WESTERN
MARSH-ROSEMARY**

DESCRIPTION: Perennial with a reddish woody base, 8 to 16 inches high. Found in Coastal Salt Marsh and Coastal Strand.

FLOWERS: Small, pale violet, on a stem 8 to 16 inches high that branches from half way up the main stem. One-sided spikes of flowers 3/8 to 1-1/4 inches long are densely placed at branch terminals. Calyx 5-cleft, petals 5, stamens 5, pistils 5.

LEAVES: Basal, oblong to oblong-obovate, 2 to 8 inches long. No leaves on flower stems.

FLOWERING: July - December

Limonium perezii

*MARSH-ROSEMARY

DESCRIPTION: Perennial with a woody base, 16 to 24 inches high. Found near the ocean. Native of the Canary Islands.

FLOWERS: On a branching stem 16 to 24 inches high; calyx 5-cleft, purplish blue; petals 5, pale yellow; stamens 5, pistils 5.

LEAVES: Basal, rhombic-ovate to deltoid, 3 to 6 inches long on long stems.

FLOWERING: March - September

POACEAE

GRASS FAMILY

600 genera and 10,000 species of grasses are found world-wide in practically all habitats. The family incudes oats, wheat, rice, bamboo, corn, sorghum and sugar cane, as well as lawn grass, crabgrass, foxtail, and many more.

POACEAE

The extent of grasses in the Santa Monica Mountains is beyond the scope of this book. We have included some pictures but have omitted detailed descriptions. Bob Muns, in his booklet *Santa Monica Mountains Flora — a Check List*, has listed 47 genera and 99 species of the grass family, then left space to add additional species. This list combined with a general text on the flora of California or the Pacific Coast would give a solid base for study of the grass family.

Recognition characteristics: Herbs with linear leaves, alternate on the stem in 2 ranks, sheathed. Stem is round and hollow. Flowers are small, enclosed in 2 bracts, and in spikelets.

POLEMONIACEAE

PHLOX FAMILY

Primarily a North American family and most prominent in the western United States, the Phlox family is represented by 18 genera and 320 species. In the Santa Monica Mountains we can find 7 genera and 13 species.

Recognition characteristics: 5-merous flowers, 3 carpels fused to form a compound pistil, calyx of 5 united sepals, and corolla of 5 united petals.

Allophyllum glutinosum Plate 364   **STINKY GILIA**

DESCRIPTION: Annual, 1 or more stout stems from the base, each 4 to 24 inches long, hairy, sticky, and with an unpleasant odor. Found on shaded slopes in Coastal Sage Scrub and Chaparral throughout.

FLOWERS: 2 to 8 on stems 1/4 to 3/4 inch long; calyx 5-cleft 1/4 inch long; 5 petals fused, pale to medium violet blue, spreading widely, vaguely 2-lipped, 5 stamens exserted; a compound pistil exserted.

LEAVES: Alternate, hairy; basal leaves pinnately lobed with narrow irregular segments; upper less narrowly lobed. Leaves alternate, hairy.

FLOWERING: April - June

455

POLEMONIACEAE

Eriastrum densifolium PERENNIAL WOOL STAR

DESCRIPTION Perennial, erect, slender stems branching from a woody base, 8 to 24 inches high. Found in sandy soil in Coastal Strand and Coastal Sage Scrub.

FLOWERS: In head-like, cobwebby clusters on top of slender stems; bracts 3-5-lobed; calyx deeply 5-cleft; 5-lobed corolla trumpet-like, 5/8 to 3/4 inch long, blue, tube and throat yellow or white; 5 stamens well exserted; 3 carpels fused to form 1 pistil, exserted.

LEAVES: Alternate, irregularly pinnatifid with linear teeth.

FLOWERING: May - July

Eriastrum sapphirinum Plate 366 SAPPHIRE WOOL STAR

DESCRIPTION: Annual, erect, loosely branched, few leaved, 4 to 12 inches high. Found in Chaparral. Most common of this genus in the range.

FLOWERS: In clusters on top of slender stems; bracts slender; calyx 5-lobed; corolla a slender white or yellow, 1/2 inch long tube expanding to a flat, sapphire purple, 5-petaled flower; 5 stamens conspicuously exserted displaying large, white anthers.

LEAVES: Alternate, linear to 3-lobed, to 1-1/2 inches long.

FLOWERING: May - August

Gilia angelensis Plate 76 ANGEL'S GILIA

DESCRIPTION: Annual, erect, 5 to 24 inches high, slender. Found in Coastal Sage Scrub and Chaparral.

456

POLEMNIACEAE

FLOWERS: In 1-5 heads on slender, 3/8 to 2-inch long stems; 5-lobed calyx woolly; 5-lobed corolla bell-shaped, 1/4 inch long, blue-violet to white, the tube yellow, 5 sepals.

LEAVES: Lower pinnately divided into fine segments, 3/4 to 2 inches long. Upper leaves reduced and linear.

FLOWERING: March - May

Gilia australis   **SPLENDID GILIA**

DESCRIPTION: Annual, branched, with a basal rosette, 4 to 12 inches high. Found in Coastal Sage Scrub and Chaparral. Fire-follower. Uncommon.

FLOWERS: In cymes in 2's on unequal stems 3/16 to 1 inch long; calyx 5-notched; corolla funnelform, 5-lobed, whitish or pale violet, 3/16 to 3/8 inch long.

LEAVES: In a basal rosette, covered with shaggy hairs, 1-2-3-pinnate, 3/4 to 2-3/4 inches long; upper much reduced, bract-like, entire.

FLOWERING: March - June

Gilia capitata   Plate 73   **GLOBE GILIA**
ssp. abrotanifolia

DESCRIPTION: Annual, tall, slender, upper third branched, 8 to 32 inches high. Found on dry slopes in Coastal Sage Scrub and haparral. Evident after a fire.

FLOWERS: In a dense, many-flowered terminal head, on a 1-1/2 to 10 inch stem. Each head contains 50-100 flowrs, sometimes sparingly woolly hair, corolla 5-lobed, 1/4 inch long, white to light blue-violet; stamens 5; 3 united carpel form 1 pistil.

457

POLEMONIACEAE

LEAVES: Basal and lower stem leaves bipinnately cleft, 1-1/2 to 4 inches long. Upper leaves simple pinnate, 3-5 short segments.

FLOWERING: April - July

Leptodactylon californicum Plate 306   PRICKLY PHLOX

DESCRIPTION: Perennial shrub, widely branching, 2-3 feet tall, completely covered with bunches of prickly needle-like leaves; woolly hairs cover stems. Found in Chaparral and Coastal Sage Scrub throughout.

FLOWERS: In clusters on the outer edge of the plant; calyx of 3 needle-like green sepals-connected half-way up with a translucent membrane; sepals 3/8 inch long; corolla tube 1/2 inch long, then flares out into 5 separate oblanceolate petals; rose-pink; flower diameter 1 inch; 5 stamens attached to the corolla; 1 compound pistil.

LEAVES: Small, needle-like, light green needles, 5/16 inch long, thickly set in alternate bunches on all stems. Prickly.

FLOWERING: January - May

Linanthus dianthiflorus Plate 307   GROUND-PINK

DESCRIPTION: Annual, 2 to 5 inches high. Found in Grasslands, Coastal Sage Scrub, and Chaparral. (Udell Creek at Reagan Ranch Meadow in Malibu Creek State Park, Nicholas Flat, Leo Carrillo Trail, ridge west of Malibu Springs)

POLEMONIACEAE

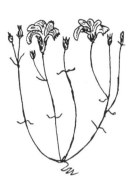

FLOWERS: Solitary or a few in a leafy cluster; calyx 5-cleft, about 1/2 inch long; corolla funnelform, pink, lilac or white, petals 3/8 to 1 inch long, outer edge fringed, dark basal spots, yellow throat; stamens 5.

LEAVES: Opposite, thread-like, 3/8 to 3/4 inch long.

FLOWERING: February - April

Linanthus liniflorus Plate 74   **FLAX-FLOWERED LINANTHUS**

DESCRIPTION: Annual, erect, 4 to 20 inches high, branching stems usually in pairs. Found in Coastal Sage Scrub, Chaparral, and Southern Oak Woodland.

FLOWERS: Solitary on slender stems 3/8 to 1 inch long; calyx 5-lobed; corolla short-funnelform, 3/8 to 1-1/4 inch long, the tube hidden by the calyx, usually white or with pink; stamens 5.

LEAVES: Cleft into linear segments, 3/8 to 1-1/4 inch long.

FLOWERING: April - July

Linanthus parviflorus Plate 308   **LINANTHUS**

DESCRIPTION: Annual, meadow plant, dainty, with few branches, 8-12 inches tall. Found usually in communities with more of the same species in Southern Oak Woodland, Grassland and Chaparral.

FLOWERS: In an umbel densely tufted, 6 or 7, dainty, about 1/4 inch long, cream-colored, occasionally pink, on slender 3/4 inch stems; 5 sepals; 5 petals; 5 stamens topped with prominent orange anthers; 1 pistil splitting into 3 stigmas which extend beyond the petals.

459

POLEMONIACEAE

LEAVES: Opposite but appear whorled; each leaf palmately lobed into 5-9 needle-like segments about 1/2 inch long; "whorls" about 3 inches apart.

FLOWERING: March - May

Navarretia hamata   **HOOKED NAVARRETIA**

DESCRIPTION: Annual, erect, usually freely branched from the base, 1-1/4 to 5 inches high. Found in Coastal Sage Scrub and Chaparral.

FLOWERS: In small heads subtended by broad pinnate bracts; calyx with 5 unequal lobes; corolla funnelform, light purple tube, dark purple throat and lobes; 5 stamens unequal, anthers exserted.

LEAVES: Clasping at the base, each leaf with 2-3 linear lobes on each side, terminal lobe usually 3-forked.

FLOWERING: April - June

Navarretia pubescens   Plate 362   **DOWNY NAVARRETIA**

DESCRIPTION: Annual, erect, branched from base or above, 3½ to 16 inches high. Found on dry slopes in Chaparral and Southern Oak Woodland. (Monte Nido, Conejo Grade, Malibu Creek State Park) Rare.

FLOWERS: In heads subtended by leaf-like bracts; without stems; calyx with 5 unequal lobes, hairy, ribbed on the back; corolla funnelform, 5-lobed, blue with violet or purple veins, tube and throat sometimes white, 3/8 to 1/2 inch long; 5 stamens unequal.

POLEMONIACEAE

LEAVES: 1-2 pinnate into linear segments. Leaves 3/4 to 2-1/4 inches long.

FLOWERING: May - June

FIELD NOTE: The Downy Navarretia population in the Santa Monica Mountains is a significant disjunction.

Phlox gracilis   **SLENDER PHLOX**

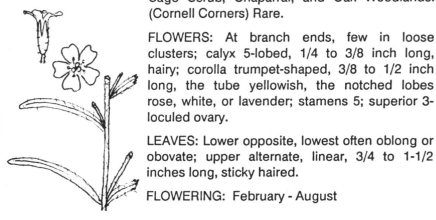

DESCRIPTION: Annual, erect stems, branching above, 4 to 8 inches high. Found in moist Grasslands, Coastal Sage Scrub, Chaparral, and Oak Woodlands. (Cornell Corners) Rare.

FLOWERS: At branch ends, few in loose clusters; calyx 5-lobed, 1/4 to 3/8 inch long, hairy; corolla trumpet-shaped, 3/8 to 1/2 inch long, the tube yellowish, the notched lobes rose, white, or lavender; stamens 5; superior 3-loculed ovary.

LEAVES: Lower opposite, lowest often oblong or obovate; upper alternate, linear, 3/4 to 1-1/2 inches long, sticky haired.

FLOWERING: February - August

POLYGALACEAE
MILKWORT FAMILY

The Milkwort family is almost worldwide with about 800 species. Only 1 species is native to the Santa Monica Mountains. This is a bush usually growing with other bushes making it somewhat obscure. At first glance, the blossom appears pea-like and requires close observation to make identification.

POLYGALACEAE

Polygala cornuta Plate 301
var. Fishiae

MILKWORT

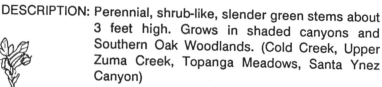

DESCRIPTION: Perennial, shrub-like, slender green stems about 3 feet high. Grows in shaded canyons and Southern Oak Woodlands. (Cold Creek, Upper Zuma Creek, Topanga Meadows, Santa Ynez Canyon)

FLOWERS: Solitary, red-purple, about 3/8 inch long, on 1/4 inch stem; 5 sepals, the inner two enlarged and petaloid; 3 petals attached at their bases, 2 narrow wings at sides and keel above; 8 stamens. Additional inconspicuous, self-pollinating blossoms low on plant remain as buds and open only when seeds are ripe. It is possible to confuse the flower with the pea family.

LEAVES: Alternate, simple, thin, not hairy, elliptic-oval about 1-1/4 inch long and 3/8 inch wide, on a short stem.

FLOWERING: May - July

FIELD NOTE: Milkwort reaches its northern limit in the Santa Monica Mountains.

POLYGONACEAE

BUCKWHEAT FAMILY

Worldwide, the Buckwheat family (Knotweed family) is composed of 40 genera and 800 species). 6 genera and 27 species are found in the Santa Monica Mountains. Members of this family locally are found at the seashore and inland, on the driest slopes, and in water. Mostly herbs, sometimes shrubs, both annual and perennial.

Recognition characteristics: Swollen nodes partially covered with a tubal nodal sheath formed by fusion at 2 stipules, alternating leaves (except genus *Pterostegia*, which has opposite leaves), and the absence of petals. The floral pattern of the Buckwheat family is in 2 configurations. Some genera have a cyclic floral pattern (flower parts whorled).

462

POLYGONACEAE

The flowers have 6 sepals in two whorls of three and no petals. Because the sepals are often colorful and can be mistaken for sepals and petals, it is possible to confuse with the Lily family. The other configuration is acyclic (flower parts spiralled). The flowers have 5 sepals and no petals. The 8 species of the genus *Polygonum* have this characteristic; most of the others are cyclic.

Polygonaceae: "Many knees" from the swollen nodes.

Chorizanthe staticoides   Plate 315   TURKISH RUGGING

DESCRIPTION: Reddish stems fork in repeated pairs, 4 to 12 inches high. Found in dry sandy places in Coastal Sage Scrub and Chaparral. (Upper Solstice Canyon, Upper Zuma Canyon, along Mulholland Highway east of Las Virgenes Road) Common.

FLOWERS: Solitary in the forks, several at ends of branches, subtended in a whorl of bracts; inflorescence somewhat flat-topped; 6-toothed calyx with 3 long and 3 short, rose colored, hairy, 3/16 inch long; no petals; 9 stamens.

LEAVES: Basal, spatulate-oblanceolate, 3/4 to 2-1/4 inches long on stems. Woolly below, slightly downy above. Bracts above are needle-like.

FLOWERING: April - July

Emex spinosa   *DEVIL'S THORN

DESCRIPTION: Annual. Branches lying on the ground or ascending, 12 to 32 inches high. Found in cultivated areas.

FLOWERS: At leaf axils subtended in a whorl of bracts; pistillate on thread-like stems, calyx urn-shaped, 6-lobed in 2 whorls; no petals; 3 styles. Staminate with no stems, calyx 5-6-lobed.

POLYGONACEAE

LEAVES: Alternate, oblong-ovate to somewhat triangular, 2 to 4-1/2 inches long, on stems. Thin, dry stipules.

FLOWERING: July - November

Eriogonum cinereum   Plate 32, 418   **ASHYLEAF BUCKWHEAT**

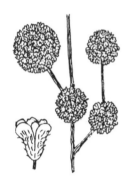

DESCRIPTION: Straggly shrub, freely branched, 1-1/2 to 4 feet high, white woolly. Found on beaches and bluffs near the coast in Coastal Strand and on slopes and ridges inland in Coastal Sage Scrub. (Mullholland Highway in Malibu Creek State Park) Common.

FLOWERS: Involucres at nodes and at branch terminals subtending heads of flowers 3/8 to 1/2 inch across, on long crooked stems; calyx 6-toothed, whitish to pinkish, hairy, 1/16 inch long, no petals.

LEAVES: Alternate, sometimes fascicled, ovate, 5/8 to 1 inch long, densely white woolly beneath and ash colored above. Margins wavy.

FLOWERING: June - December

FIELD NOTE: *Eriogonum* from the Greek means "woolly joint or angle," a reference to the hairy joints of some of the plants.

Eriogonum cithariforme   **CITHARA BUCKWHEAT**
  var. agnium

DESCRIPTION: Annual, branching from the base. Found in Chaparral. (Cold Creek)

FLOWERS: Involucres sessile and usually solitary at nodes subtending heads of flowers; calyx 6-lobed in 2 whorls, white tinged with rose; no petals.

464

POLYGONACEAE

LEAVES: Basal, oblanceolate to oblong, 3/8 to 1-1/4 inch long, wavy margin.

FLOWERING: May - August

FIELD NOTE: The Cithara Buckwheat population in the Santa Monica Mountains is a significant disjunction.

Eriogonum crocatum Plate 237   **CONEJO BUCKWHEAT**

DESCRIPTION: Perennial shrub, loosely branched, old leaves persistent. Found in Coastal Sage Scrub. (Conejo Grade) Rare.

FLOWERS: Involucres at terminal of 4 to 8 inch long stems, subtend flowers, forming dense cymes 1-1/4 to 3 inches across; calyx 6-lobed in 2 whorls, sulphur-yellow, 1/4 inch long; no petals.

LEAVES: Broadly ovate, 5/8 to 1-1/2 inches long, white woolly, alternate along the stems.

FLOWERING: April - July

Eriogonum elongatum Plate 319   **WAND BUCKWHEAT**

DESCRIPTION: Perennial herb, loosely branched at the base, white woolly, 2 to 4 feet high. Leafy below, bare above. Found in Coastal Sage Scrub and Chaparral.

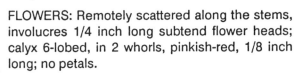

FLOWERS: Remotely scattered along the stems, involucres 1/4 inch long subtend flower heads; calyx 6-lobed, in 2 whorls, pinkish-red, 1/8 inch long; no petals.

LEAVES: Lance-oblong to narrowly ovate, wavy margin, white woolly below, almost hairless above, 1-1/4 to 2 inches long.

FLOWERING: August - November

POLYGONACEAE

FIELD NOTE: *Elongatum* in Latin refers to the "lengthened" stems.

Eriogonum fasciculatum Plates 31, 417

CALIFORNIA
BUCKWHEAT

DESCRIPTION: Perennial, low spreading shrub, branches 2 to 4 feet long, leafy. Found in Coastal Sage Scrub and openings in Chaparral. Common.

FLOWERS: Involucres at end of 1-1/4 to 4 inch long leafless stems, subtend the flowers, usually in heads about 1 inch in diameter; calyx 6-lobed, white or pinkish, 1/8 inch long, no petals.

LEAVES: Many fascicled, linear-oblong, 1/4 to 5/8 inch long, green above, white-woolly beneath, rolled backward from the center.

FLOWERING: May - November

Eriogonum gracile

SLENDER BUCKWHEAT

DESCRIPTION: Annual 3 foot tall plant grows on open slopes in inland areas. Often found in Chaparral bordering an intermittent streambed. Tends to colonize in a small area.

FLOWERS: Numerous, small, clustered in involucres distributed along elongated branches; 6 petal-like sepals, paper thin, white and/or pink (on same flower head) with a green vein; no petals; 9 stamens; 3 styles. Ovary superior. We need a 10x magnifying glass to look at the flowers.

LEAVES: Broadly-oblong, mostly basal on 2 inch long stems. Entire plant is slightly woolly. Leaves are usually gone by fall when the plants flower.

FLOWERING: August - November

POLYGONACEAE

Eriogonum parvifolium Plate 30   SEA-CLIFF BUCKWHEAT

DESCRIPTION: Perennial shrub, low spreading, loose, slender leafy branches 1 to 3 feet long. Found on dunes and bluffs along the beach in Coastal Strand and Coastal Sage Scrub.

FLOWERS: Involucres at the end of 3/4 to 2 inch stems subtend compound heads 3/8 to 3/4 inch in diameter; calyx 6-lobed, white or tinged rose; no petals.

LEAVES: Fascicled, round-ovate to lance-oblong, green above, densely white-woolly below, thick, 1/4 to 5/8 inch long.

FLOWERING: June - December

Eriogonum wrightii ssp. membranaceum   WRIGHTS' BUCKWHEAT

DESCRIPTION: Perennial, branched shrub 8 to 16 inches high and up to 2 feet across. Found in dry rocky places in Chaparral. Uncommon.

FLOWERS: Involucres about 1/8 inch long, on spikes, subtend several flowers; calyx 6-lobed, white to pink, 1/8 inch long; no petals.

LEAVES: Narrowly oblanceolate, densely white woolly under, greenish above, 1/8 to 1/4 inch long, sometimes 3/8 inch, edges roll inward toward the upper side. Leaf stem dilated to a brownish sheath clasping the plant stem.

FLOWERING: August - October

Lastarriaea coriacea   SPINE-FLOWER

DESCRIPTION: Slender-stemmed 2 to 10 inches high. Hairy. Found on Sandy slopes near the coast. (South of Point Dume) Rare.

467

POLYGONACEAE

FLOWERS: Solitary in axils, without bracts subtending the calyx. Calyx 5-6 lobed, leathery, no petals; 3 stamens.

LEAVES: Basal, linear, whorled, 3/4 to 1 inch long, between 1/32 and 1/16 inch wide; upper become whorled green bracts about 1/4 inch long.

FLOWERING: April - June

Mucronea californica Plate 394   **CALIFORNIA CHORIZANTHE**

DESCRIPTION: Annual, erect, fork in pairs near the base, 3 to 10 inches high, hairy. Found in dry sandy places in Grasslands and Coastal Sage Scrub. (Inland near Point Dume)

FLOWERS: 2 or 3 subtended by bracts; calyx tubular and flared, spine-tipped lobes, white, hairy, no petals.

LEAVES: Basal, spatulate to obovate, short stem, 3/8 to 1-1/4 inch long. Bract deeply 3-lobed, clasping the base, 1/4 to 3/8 inch long, hairy at nodes, spine-tipped.

FLOWERING: April - June

Polygonum amphibium Plate 318   **WATER**
   var. emersum   **SMARTWEED**

DESCRIPTION: Stems rising from perennial rhizomes, erect, 1 to 4 feet high, sometimes 6 feet. Found in ponds and swamps. (Nicholas Flat pond)

FLOWERS: In spikes 1-1/4 to 6 inches long; calyx 5-lobed, about 1/8 inch long, rose colored; no petals.

LEAVES: Lance-ovate to lanceolate, 2 to 8 inches long, short-stemmed.

FLOWERING: June - October

POLYGONACEAE

Polygonum arenastrum   *COMMON KNOTWEED

DESCRIPTION: Annual, dense prostrate mats up to 5 feet across. Found in disturbed soil at low elevations. Common.

FLOWERS: Borne in leaf axils; calyx 5-lobed, divided about 1/2 its length, greenish-white or pink. Seed with 2 sides convex, 1 concave.

LEAVES: Elliptical to 3/4 inch long; branch-leaves almost as long as stem-leaves.

FLOWERING: February - October

Polygonum argyrocoleon   *PERSIAN KNOTWEED

DESCRIPTION: Annual, erect, pale green stems. Found on south side of the mountains in fields and orchards. Native of Iran.

FLOWERS: Several in clusters at nodes of upper stems, subtended by bract-like leaves, giving appearance of a raceme; calyx 6-lobed, 1/16 inch long; no petals; 6 stamens. Seed is 3-angled, smooth, and shiny.

LEAVES: Linear, 3/8 to 1/14 inches long, upper leaves greatly reduced.

FLOWERING: June - September

Polygonum hydropiperoides   WATERPEPPER

DESCRIPTION: Perennial herb, 1 to 3 feet high, branching; stipule sheaths at nodes fringed with bristles. Found in swamps and at edges of ponds. (Bed of Los Angeles River)

FLOWERS: In slender racemes, 3/4 to 2-3/4 inches long, branching to form terminal panicles; calyx 5-lobed, white to rose, 1/16 inch long; stamens 8.

POLYGONACEAE

LEAVES: Linear-lanceolate to oblong-lanceolate, 2 to 6 inches long.

FLOWERING: June - October

Polygonum lapathifolium   **WILLOW WEED**

DESCRIPTION: Annual, stems simple or branched, usually swollen at nodes, can grow to 9 feet. Found in swamps and at edges of ponds.

FLOWERS: In slender spikes 3/8 to 2-1/4 inches long, often bent over; calyx 5-lobed, white, pink or purplish, slightly over 1/16 inch long.

LEAVES: Lanceolate, 2 to 8 inches long.

FLOWERING: July - October

Polygonum punctatum Plate 317   **WATER SMARTWEED**

DESCRIPTION: Perennial herb, stems root near the base then ascend obliquely, 1 to 3-1/2 feet high, simple or branched. Found in moist low places in the northwest edge of the mountains.

FLOWERS: In racemes 5/8 to 2-1/4 inches long, forming a panicle, loose at lower part, more compact at terminal; calyx prominently gland-dotted, 5-lobed, greenish, 1/16 inch long; no petals; 8 stamens.

LEAVES: Lanceolate to lance-elliptic, 2 to 6 inches long, short stemmed; sheathing stipules fringed with hairs on the margin.

FLOWERING: July - October

POLYGONACEAE

Pterostegia drymarioides   **THREAD STEM**

DESCRIPTION: Annual, slender stems, repeatedly forking in pairs, downy, prostrate, 4 to 16 inches long. Found in openings in shady areas.

FLOWERS: Subtended by 2-lobed leafy bracts; calyx 6-lobed, reddish, 1/32 inch long.

LEAVES: Opposite, fan-shaped to broadly elliptical, often deeply notched, 3/16 to 3/4 inch long.

FLOWERING: March - July

Rumex acetosella   ***SHEEP SORREL**

DESCRIPTION: Perennial herb, slender-stemmed 8 to 16 inches high. Found in cultivated ground and gardens. Common.

FLOWERS: In panicles, both terminal and axillary, turning red in age; staminate and pistillate flowers on different plants; calyx, 6-lobed, green, 1/32 inch long; no petals; 6 stamens exserted.

LEAVES: Narrow arrowhead-shaped, 1 to 3 inches long, with long stems.

FLOWERING: March - August

Rumex crispus   Plate 389   ***CURLY DOCK**

DESCRIPTION: Perennial herb, smooth-stemmed with a taproot, grows to 4 feet tall. Found in open fields and in Southern Oak Woodlands. Common.

FLOWERS: Many in upward branching panicles on long, slender stems; 6 sepals in 2 rows of 3, outer sepals about 1/16 inch long; 6 stamens; 3 styles.

471

POLYGONACEAE

LEAVES: Oblong-lanceolate, 1 foot long on long stems; leaf margin markedly wavy.

FLOWERING: March - June

Rumex hymenosepalus   Plate 390   **WILD RHUBARB**

DESCRIPTION: Perennial herb, smooth-stemmed, with tuberous roots, grows to 2 feet high in sandy soil. This desert plant is rare in the Santa Monicas. (Medea Creek near Cornell Corners)

FLOWERS: Compact panicle to 1 foot long on a sturdy stem; staminate and pistillate separate, but on same plant; 6 sepals in 2 rows of 3; 6 stamens, 6 styles.

LEAVES: Oblong-elliptic leaves, light green, fleshy, with wavy margin; on stout, reddish leaf stems set in 1 inch sheaths. The main vein is white-green merging to reddish at the base.

FLOWERING: January - May

FIELD NOTE: *Hymenosepalus* in Latin means "having membranous sepals."

Rumex maritimus   **GOLDEN DOCK**

DESCRIPTION: Annual, downy, yellow-green, 4 to 24 inches high. Found in wet places along streams. (Los Angeles River, Calleguas Creek) Rare.

FLOWERS: On leafy compound racemes, in densely crowded whorls; calyx 6-lobed, in 2 whorls of 3; no petals; 6 stamens.

LEAVES: Lanceolate, 1-1/4 to 10 inches long, lower leaves with a wavy margin.

FLOWERING: May - September

POLYGONACEAE

Rumex salicifolius   **WILLOW DOCK**

DESCRIPTION: Perennial herb, prostrate stems or rising at an angle, 1 to 3 feet high. Found in wet places along intermittent streams. Common.

FLOWERS: On a short panicle densely crowded; calyx 6-lobed, in 2 whorls of 3; no petals; 6 stamens.

LEAVES: Linear-lanceolate to oblong-lanceolate, 2-1/4 to 5 inches long, flat, bright green.

FLOWERING: May - September

PORTULACACEAE

PURSLANE FAMILY

Six genera and 8 species of the Purslane family are found locally, all native except *Portulaca oleracea* (Purslane). 19 genera and 580 species are known worldwide. Usually succulent.

Botanists differ in the floral interpretation of this family. Recent work shows that the 2 sepals are actually bracts and that the petals are petaloid sepals. Our descriptions in this book adopt the traditional and convenient contention that the flowers have 2 sepals (in some flowers free, in others fused), normally 5 petals (*Lewisia* has many), 4 or more stamens, and usually 2 to 5 styles.

Calandrinia breweri Plate 334   **BREWER'S RED MAIDS**

DESCRIPTION: Annual, trailing branches 4 to 16 inches long. Found in Chaparral after a fire and on disturbed soil. (South of Reagan Meadow, Malibu Creek State Park)

FLOWERS: Few, in leafy-bracted racemes; 2 sepals each 1/4 inch long, membrane margined toward base; 5 petals rose-red, 3/16 inch long. Seed capsules about 1/2 inch long.

PORTULACACEAE

LEAVES: Ovate-lanceolate or spatulate, basal 3/4 to 3 inches long, reduced higher on the stem.

FLOWERING: March - June

Calandrinia ciliata Plate 333

RED MAIDS

DESCRIPTION: Annual with several stems, light green, hairless, spreading from base, up to 16 inches tall. Usually found in Grasslands and the edge of Southern Oak Woodlands.

FLOWERS: In a leafy raceme of the main stalk, on 1-1/2 inch stems; 2 sepals; 5 petals rose-red; many stamens; 1 pistil; 3 style-branches.

LEAVES: Alternate, narrowly oblanceolate with an acute point, 3/4 to 3 inches long and about 1-1/2 inches apart along the stem.

FLOWERING: February - May

Calandrinia maritima

SEASIDE RED MAIDS

DESCRIPTION: Annual, branching from the base, spreading, 2 to 12 inches high, leaves mostly on lower part of stems. Found on sand on sea bluffs, and Coastal Sage Scrub.

FLOWERS: In terminal loose cymes; 2 sepals dark-veined; 5 petals, rose-red, 3/16 inch long.

LEAVES: Basal, spatulate-obovate, fleshy, 3/4 to 2 inches long. Reduced farther up the stems.

FLOWERING: March - May

PORTULACACEAE

Calyptridium monandrum Plate 304   **SAND CRESS**

DESCRIPTION: Annual, spreading from base, often prostrate, 2 to 6 inches long. Found in open places and sand, Coastal Sage Scrub and Chaparral.

FLOWERS: Few in a terminal panicle in short spikes, on one side of stem, and coiled in bud stage; 2 sepals, 3 petals white; 1 stamen.

LEAVES: Mostly basal rosette, linear-spatulate, 3/4 to 2-1/4 inches long. Stem leaves scattered and reduced.

FLOWERING: March - June

Claytonia exigua Plate 80   **COMMON MONTIA**

DESCRIPTION: Annual, dense, succulent, tufted 3/4 to 2-1/4 inches high. Leaves as high as the stems or higher. Found on grassy or gravelly slopes. (Seminole Hot Springs; Lake Eleanor) Rare.

FLOWERS: In racemes 3/4 inch long, 3-6 flowered; 2 sepals; 5 petals white or pinkish, 1/8-inch long.

LEAVES: Numerous basal, narrowly linear to linear-spatulate to 2-1/4 inches long. Stem leaves 2, opposite, linear to lance-ovate, 3/8 to 3/4 inch long.

FLOWERING: February - May

FIELD NOTE: The Common Montia population in the Santa Monica Mountains is a significant disjunction.

PORTULACACEAE

Claytonia perfoliata Plate 48   **MINER'S LETTUCE**

DESCRIPTION: Annual, succulent, green, branching from base, 4 to 12 inches high. Found in shady places throughout. Coastal Sage Scrub, Chaparral, and Oak Woodland. Common.

FLOWERS: In an elongated raceme above the orbicular leaf; sepals, rounded; 5 petals, 1/8 to 3/16 inch long.

LEAVES: Rhombid-ovate to elliptic-obovate, on a stem 2 to 8 inches long. Upper leaves 2, opposite, united around the stem, obliquely orbicular disk 3/8 to 3-1/4 inch broad.

FLOWERING: February - April

Lewisia rediviva Plate 282   **BITTER ROOT**

DESCRIPTION: Perennial herb, short branched stem 3/8 to 1 inch long, on a fleshy root. Found in gravelly slopes and rocky areas. (Rocky ridge near Ventura-Los Angeles County border)

FLOWERS: One at terminal of each stem, awl-shaped, membranous bracts whorled below the flower on the stem; 4-5 sepals, petaloid, rose-colored or white, 1/2 to 1 inch long; many petals, rose or white, 3/4 to 1 inch long.

LEAVES: Basal only, fleshy, linear, 3/4 to 2 inches long.

FLOWERING: March - June

FIELD NOTE: The Bitter Root population in the Santa Monica Mountains is a significant disjunction.

PORTULACACEAE

Portulaca oleracea   *PURSLANE

DESCRIPTION: Annual, prostrate, succulent, branching stems often form a mat up to 20 inches in diameter. Flower closes at night and on cloudy days. Found in gardens and as an escape throughout. Common.

FLOWERS: Without stems, about 1/4 inch across; 2 sepals; 5 petals notched at the end, yellow.

LEAVES: Alternate, obovate, 3/16 to 1 inch long, fleshy, clustered at ends of branches.

FLOWERING: May - September

POTAMOGETONACEAE

PONDWEED FAMILY

Two genera and 100 species of these perennial aquatic herbs inhabit freshwater sites throughout the world. 2 species of genus are found in the Santa Monica Mountains.

Recognition characteristics: Shallow freshwater, submerged plants growing from perennial rhizomes, leaves submerged or floating. Small flowers on spikes; 4 sepals, no petals, 4 stamens and 4 pistils.

Potamogeton crispus   *CURLED-LEAF PONDWEED

DESCRIPTION: Perennial aquatic herb with leaf blades attached directly at nodes of stem. Found in ponds and streams, sometimes forming mats. (Malibu Creek State Park, in Malibu Creek)

FLOWERS: On spikes 3/8 to 3/4 inch long from leaf axils; 4 sepals; no petals, 4 stamens; 4 pistils.

POTAMOGETONACEAE

LEAVES: Alternate, narrowly oblong, submerged in water; edges irregularly curled, finely toothed, with prominent midrib and 2 or more veins, 1-1/4 to 4 inches long, sessile. Stipules free of the rest of the leaf.

FLOWERING: July - September

FIELD NOTE: *Potamogeton* (Greek, *potamos*, a river, and *geiton*, a neighbor)

Potamogeton pectinatus   FENNEL-LEAF PONDWEED

DESCRIPTION: Perennial aquatic herb, stringlike branches and leaves, 1 to 6 feet long. Found in lakes and year-round ponds in the western part of the mountains. Common.

FLOWERS: Small, on thread-like spikes, in whorls; 4 sepals; no petals; 4 stamens; 4 pistils.

LEAVES: Alternate, hair-like tapering to a point, submerged in water, 1 to 6 inches long.

FLOWERING: May - July

FIELD NOTE: Wild ducks dive and feed on the submerged tubers.

Ruppia cirrhosa   DITCH-GRASS

DESCRIPTION: Aquatic herb, branching, submerged, with stems 2 to 3-1/2 feet long. Found in brackish water of lagoons. Common.

FLOWERS: several on short stems commonly attached at end of 12 inch long, or less, spiralling stem; calyx and corolla absent; 2 stamens; 4 or more pistils.

LEAVES: Alternate, thread-like, 3/4 to 4 inches long.

FLOWERING: March - August

PRIMULACEAE

PRIMROSE FAMILY

A family of herbal plants having simple, undivided leaves and perfect, regular flowers. Not to be confused with the Evening Primrose family.

Recognition characteristics: Calyx of 5 persistent sepals, corolla of 5 petals, 5 stamens ((*Samolus parvaflorus* has a second series of 5 sterile filaments or staminodia), and 5 united carpels form 1 pistil.

Anagallis arvensis   Plate 255   *SCARLET PIMPERNEL

DESCRIPTION: Annual, branched, low spreading, not hairy, 4 to 10 inches high. Stems are 4-sided. Found in many plant communities. Common.

FLOWERS: Solitary on axillary stems; 5 sepals narrow lanceolate; 5 petals oval, salmon colored; 5 stamens; 1 pistil. Scarlet stamen, pistils and lower edge of the petals; anthers bright yellow.

LEAVES: Opposite, ovate to oval, 1/4 to 3/4 inch long, clasping mainstem.

FLOWERING: March - July

FIELD NOTE: A blue flowered colony grows along upper Sycamore stream on volcanic rock.

Dodecatheon clevelandii   Plate 272   SHOOTING STAR

DESCRIPTION: This exquisite, 12 to 15 inch tall perennial herb looks like a bird in flight. Green rosettes appear in December, and the delicate blossoms in January and February. Found in grassy areas of Chaparral and Coastal Sage communities. (Rocky outcroppings on Boney Mountain are special)

FLOWERS: Several on slender stems, from umbels; 5 petals united at the base, pink on a long, leafless stem; 5 stamens. Superior ovary. Buds erect, flowers nodding.

479

PRIMULACEAE

LEAVES: In a rosette, spatulate, 3 inches long. No other leaves except 2 at the base of the umbel.

FLOWERING: January - April

FIELD NOTE: This perennial comes in two sub-species with minor color differences. The western end of the mountains is the southern limit for 1 subspecies, the eastern end of the mountains is the northern limit for the other subspecies.

Samolus parviflorus   WATER PIMPERNEL

DESCRIPTION: Perennial herb, erect solitary stem, sometimes branching above, 6 to 15 inches high. Found in moist places in Coastal Sage Scrub and Chaparral.

FLOWERS: In loose racemes on slender stems spread apart, small, white; calyx 5-cleft; corolla 5-lobed; 5 stamens and 5 staminodes.

LEAVES: In a basal rosette, obovate to round, 1 to 2 inches long, on short stems. Stem leaves alternate and shorter.

FLOWERING: June - August

RANUNCULACEAE
BUTTERCUP FAMILY

A large family of more than 35 genera and 2000 species, most of which grow in the cooler areas of the northern hemisphere. The Santa Monica Mountains is home to 4 genera and 9 species; all are native to the area.

Recognition characteristics: Herbs with compound leaves with sheaths at leaf bases; flowers with many stamens and many pistils; sepals and petals often not differentiated — all looking somewhat alike.

RANUNCULACEAE

Clematis lasiantha Plates 33, 453   **VIRGIN'S BOWER**

DESCRIPTION: Perennial, climbing, woody, with hairy stems. Flowers are showy but not clustered as with *Clematis ligusticifolia*. Found in Chaparral in Canyons.

FLOWERS: 1-3 on long axillary stems. 4 white sepals, about 1 inch long, wider than *Clematis ligusticifolia*; no petals; many stamens. Seeds tailed, forming a powder-puff-like ball.

LEAVES: Opposite, compound leaves with 3-5 leaflets, each cleft.

FLOWERING: March - June

Clematis ligusticifolia Plate 34   **WESTERN VIRGIN'S BOWER**

DESCRIPTION: Woody vine, 30 feet long, climbs into trees and shrubs, usually covering them. In bloom, flowers cover the plant and later become masses of tan-colored feathery seeds. Grows in Chaparral at edge of Southern Oak Woodlands.

FLOWERS: Many in clusters, white, 1/2 inch diameter; sepals white, 3/8 inch long, hairy on both sides; no petals; many stamens.

LEAVES: Opposite, compound, with 5 or 7 leaflets.

FLOWERING: April - August

Delphinium cardinale Plate 261   **SCARLET LARKSPUR**

DESCRIPTION: Perennial herb, 6 feet tall, erect, becomes noticeable in May when the scarlet blooms arrive. Prominent in Chaparral and Coastal Sage Scrub on dry ridges and slopes.

RANUNCULACEAE

FLOWERS: In open racemes on stems about 1-1/2 inches long; 5 sepals, one a spur, all scarlet; 4 petals, lower 2 scarlet and upper 2 yellow.

LEAVES: Basal divided into 5 twisted, linear, primary divisions, sometimes 8 inches wide; die back when flowers appear. Leaves higher on stem alternate, deeply 5-7- lobed; divided in linear segments. Veins slightly hairy.

FLOWERING: May - July

Delphinium parryi Plate 359
ssp. parryi

BLUE LARKSPUR

DESCRIPTION: Perennial herb, erect, usually branched, minutely downy, 1 to 2 feet high or more. Root is a cluster of woody branches. Found in grassy fields and open places in Coastal Sage Scrub, Chaparral and Southern Oak Woodlands.

FLOWERS: In racemes, on stems 5/8 to 1-1/4 inches long; 5 purple-blue sepals, one an almost straight spur; 4 petals, the upper 2 whitish, rounded and woolly tufted. Seedpod minutely downy.

LEAVES: 3-5-parted, then further divided into linear segments; minutely downy, 3/4 to 3 inches wide, on stems about 4 inches long. The lower leaves wither early. The leaf divisions at flowering time are usually less than 3/16 inch wide.

FLOWERING: June - July

RANUNCULACEAE

FIELD NOTE: 2 subspecies of *Delphinium parryi* are found in the Santa Monica Mountains; *ssp. blochmanae* is rare, blooms in April and May and is locally only known in an area near Long Grade Canyon. It differs from the description above by having indigo to violet sepals, white upper petals and lavender lower petals. This subspecies reaches its southern coastal limit in a disjunct Santa Monica Mountain population.

Delphinium patens Plate 358   BLUE LARKSPUR

DESCRIPTION: Perennial herb, not hairy, erect, slender stemmed, branching, 8 to 16 inches high, from tuberous root. Found in the borders of Chaparral and Southern Oak Woodlands.

FLOWERS: On an open raceme; 5 dark blue sepals, one a stout spur. 4 petals, the upper 2 white or cream, with blue lines, the lower 2 whitish with blue lines, with some hairs. Seedpod not downy.

LEAVES: Few, mostly near base, 1-1/2 to 3-1/2 inches wide, 3-parted with center part 3-cleft, lateral parts 2-cleft. Lower leaf stems 2 to 6 inches long. Leaf division at flowering time is 3/8 to 3/4 inch wide.

FLOWERING: March - Nov.

Ranunculus californicus Plate 231   CALIFORNIA
     var. californicas   BUTTERCUP

DESCRIPTION: Perennial herb, erect, growing 1 to 2-1/2 feet high, branching toward the top, hairy. Found in moist soils in semi-shade, in Grasslands and Southern Oak Woodland.

RANUNCULACEAE

FLOWERS: Solitary, about 1 inch in diameter, on 2 to 10 inch long stems; sepals, greenish-yellow, turned downward on stem; 9-15 yellow petals, radiating; 30-60 stamens.

LEAVES: Basal, 3/4 to 2-1/2 inches broad, 3-parted, each lobe somewhat wedge-shaped and lobed, hairy.

FLOWERING: February - May

Ranunculus cymbalaria   DESERT BUTTERCUP
var. saximontanus

DESCRIPTION: Perennial herb, usually hairless, rooting at nodes, 1 foot tall or less. Found in marshy meadows or mud in many plant communities.

FLOWERS: An elongated head on a 2 to 12 inch stem; sepals greenish-yellow; 5-12 petals, yellow 3/16-5/16 inch long, radiating; 20-35 stamens. Seed head is cone-like.

LEAVES: Basal, somewhat heart-shaped to ovate, 3/8 to 1-1/2 inches long and almost as broad; edges have shallow, rounded teeth; shiny green. Leaf stem is 3/4 to 2 inches long.

FLOWERING: June - August

Ranunculus hebecarpus   HAIRY-FRUITED BUTTERCUP

DESCRIPTION: Annual slender, somewhat erect, woolly, branching, 4 to 12 inches tall. Grows in shaded places.

FLOWERS: On axillary stems, minute, pale yellow flowers; 5 sepals, yellow; no petals or 1 or 2; stamens 10 or more. 4-10 seeds with hooked bristles.

RANUNCULACEAE

LEAVES: Basal round or kidney-shaped, 3-parted, each division notched or lobed, about 3/4 inch across, hairy, on stems 1-1/4 to 3-3/4 inches long. Leaves higher on stem divided into 3 narrowly oblong-ovate segments.

FLOWERING: March - May

Thalictrum fendleri Plates 187, 320   **MEADOW RUE**
  var. polycarpum

DESCRIPTION: Perennial herb, robust 2 to 6 feet high. Found in moist shaded areas along streambeds in Chaparral and Southern Oak Woodlands. Common.

FLOWERS: In panicles; pistillate and staminate flowers on separate plants; sepals greenish, petal-like; no petals; many stamens.

LEAVES: Compound with 3 leaflets in each segment. Leaflets mostly rounded, 5/8 to 1 inch long, 3-lobed, toothed. Sheath-like base.

FLOWERING: March - June

RESEDACEAE

MIGNONETTE FAMILY

Many of the 70 species of plants in this family come from the Mediterranian area. Our 1 representative is native to the Santa Monica Mountains.

Oligomeris linifolia   **OLIGOMERIS**

DESCRIPTION: Annual, erect, branching, hairless, 4 to 12 inches high. Found in alkaline soil. Has not been reported locally for many years.

FLOWERS: In terminal spikes 3/4 to 4 inches long, dense flowers about 1/16 inch long, subtended by bracts; 4 sepals, 2 petals, whitish stamens. Capsules 4-toothed.

485

RESEDACEAE

LEAVES: Alternate, narrowly linear, 3/8 to 1 inch long, often fascicled.

FLOWERING: February - July

RHAMMACEAE
BUCKTHORN FAMILY

This family of 58 genera and 900 species is represented in our area by 6 species of Ceanothus and 3 species of Rhamnus. Worldwide, the Buckthorn family includes trees, shrubs, vines, and sometimes herbaceous plants, but in the Santa Monica Mountains, all of the species are shrubs or small trees.

Recognition characteristics: The flowers are radial, usually 5 sepals, 5 petals, 5 stamens, 3 united carpels forming 1 pistil and a superior ovary. The stamens are opposite the petals.

Ceanothus crassifolius Plate 93   HOARY-LEAVED CEANOTHUS

DESCRIPTION: Shrub, open branched, 6 to 10 foot tall, small-leaved, stout grayish branches, evergreen leaves. Found on dry slopes in Chaparral, usually at the higher elevations such as the Boney Mountain area, but significant pockets are found at lower elevations as in the arroyo 1/2 mile east of the Diamond X Ranch at 800 ft. Not known east of Topanga Canyon.

FLOWERS: White, in showy clusters, on 3/8 inch stems; 5 sepals, petal-like, 5 petals narrower than sepals, very narrow at base; 5 stamens; 3-lobed style. Seed capsule 3-lobed, with stout erect horns, 5/16 inch across, becomes prominent before petals drop.

LEAVES: Opposite (although some may be missing), thick, leathery, broadly elliptic to round, with small points; olive-green above, woolly-white below, 5/8 to 1-1/4 inch long. Light green veins prominent from below. Four prominent globular stipules at each node along branchlets. Leaf stems 1/8 to 1/4 inch long.

FLOWERING: January - April

Ceanothus cuneatus Plate 96   **BUCK-BRUSH**

DESCRIPTION: An erect, rigid, 10 foot tall evergreen shrub. Found on dry sunny slopes in Chaparral, usually inland on the valley side of the mountains, almost never on the southern slopes of the mountains. (Ridges on the north side of Saddle Peak)

FLOWERS: White, in umbels; 5 sepals, 5 petals, 5 stamens, 3 united carpels forming 1 pistil. 3-lobed seed capsule with erect horns 3/16 inch across.

LEAVES: Opposite, wedge-shaped with narrow part near stem (cuneate); finely woolly on underside, gray-green above; 1/4 to 1/2 inch long, flat, and firm. Thick corky stipules at the base of leaf stems.

FLOWERING: February - April

Ceanothus leucodermis Plate 94   **WHITE THORN**

DESCRIPTION: Evergreen shrub, 6 to 12 feet high, widely diverging branches and short, spiny branchlets, pale green, smooth bark. Found in Chaparral. (Northeast of Saddle Peak at the 2000 foot level, on the northwest slope of Boney Mountain at 2400 feet, and northeast of Peak 2793) Rare.

RHAMNACEAE

FLOWERS: In 1-1/4 to 3 inch long clusters, white to blue. 5 merous.

LEAVES: Alternate, elliptical-oblong to ovate, with a white bloom on both sides; 3/8 to 1 inch long on short stems. Thin stipules at leaf stem base drop early. 3 distinct veins from base of leaf.

FLOWERING: April - June

Ceanothus megacarpus Plates 95, 439

BIG-POD
CEANOTHUS

DESCRIPTION: Evergreen shrub, compact, 12 feet tall with grayish-brown, fluted trunk. Found throughout the Chaparral, often in pure stands. Common except on the higher elevations of Boney Mountain.

FLOWERS: In small clusters, white, 5 merous. Seedpods 3/8 to 1/2 inch wide, barely lobed, laterally horned with low crests.

LEAVES: Mostly alternate, spatulate to obovate, often notched at the apex, 3/8 to 3/4 inch long; dull green and pebbly on top, fine grayish-white hairs on underside; firm, on short stems with 2 thick, corky stipules at base. Leaf has 1 main vein.

FLOWERING: January - April

FIELD NOTE: Most Chaparral shrubs root-crown sprout after a fire; this one does not. Every year, usually in July, the seedpods virtually explode and eject dull olive, 3/16 inch, hard seeds by the millions. This event can be heard and felt by anyone in the Chaparral. Many years later and only after a fire, some of the seeds will sprout and help rebuild a burned-over Chaparral.

RHAMNACEAE

Ceanothus oliganthus Plate 339 **HAIRY-LEAVED CEANOTHUS**

DESCRIPTION: Shrub, 9 feet tall with a tree-like trunk; young branches hairy, not spiny, often reddish tinted. Found in Chaparral, usually on north facing slopes of higher peaks. Sometimes found at lower elevations in shade. Hybridizes with *c. spinosus* and *c. leucodermis.*

FLOWERS: In loose panicles 5/8 to 2 inches long; deep blue or purplish; 5 merous. Fruit of 3 rounded apical segments without horns.

LEAVES: Alternate, evergreen, 3-veined, ovate, 5/8 to 1-1/2 inches long, dark green on top, lighter and downy underneath, saw-toothed. Leaf-like stipules drop early.

FLOWERING: March - April

Ceanothus spinosus Plates 340, 438 **GREENBARK CEANOTHUS**

DESCRIPTION: Tree-like shrub 18 feet tall, prominent, smooth green bark; main branches flexible, upward curving; ultimate branchlets short, stiff, spiny, stick out. Found in Chaparral.

FLOWERS: In compound clusters 1-1/2 to 10 inches long on somewhat leafy stems; pale blue to nearly white; 5 merous. Fruit of three rounded apical segments without horns.

LEAVES: Alternate, evergreen, elliptic to oblong 1/2 to 1-1/2 inches long with notched apex; mostly 1 veined except some larger leaves with 3 veins from base; bright green above, slightly lighter below; some stiff hairs on underside midrib. Leaf-like stipules drop early.

FLOWERING: February - May

FIELD NOTE: Hybridizes with *c. oliganthus.*

RHAMNACEAE

Rhamnus californica Plates 405, 428   **COFFEEBERRY**

DESCRIPTION: Large shrub to 15 feet high, evergreen. Found on dry slopes in Chaparral, nearly always in the pure shade of trees such as Coast Live Oaks, and more frequently near streams than higher on the slopes. Common.

FLOWERS: In axillary clusters, greenish; staminate and pistillate separate but on same shrub; 5-merous. Fruit black or red when ripe, 3/8 inch in diameter.

LEAVES: Alternate, lanceolate to oblong, woolly underneath, 1-1/4 to 2-3/4 inches long.

FLOWERING: May - June

Rhamnus crocea Plate 404   **REDBERRY**

DESCRIPTION: Evergreen shrub branching, 3 to 6 feet tall, with spiny branchlets. Grows in Coastal Sage Scrub and open Chaparral, and commonly found in western end of the range, diminishing in number toward the eastern end. (Point Mugu State Park)

FLOWERS: In axillary clusters; staminate and pistillate separate but on same shrub; 4 sepals (rarely 5); 4 petals; 4-5 stamens or 1 pistil. Fruit a 2-seeded, 1/4 inch, red berry.

LEAVES: Alternate, evergreen, often clustered, elliptic, less than 5/8 inch long, hard leathery, shiny, sometimes slightly downy.

FLOWERING: January - April

RHAMNACEAE

Rhamnus ilicifolia Plates 406, 429
[R. crocea ssp. ilicifolia]

**HOLLYLEAF
REDBERRY**

DESCRIPTION: Shrub, to 12 feet, sometimes tree-like, some times branching from the base. Found in Chaparral.

FLOWERS: In axillary clusters. Staminate and pistillate separate but on the same shrub; 4 sepals (rarely 5); 4 petals; 4-5 stamens or 1 pistil. Fruit a red berry, slightly larger than *R. crocea*.

LEAVES: Alternate, oval to roundish, without hairs or slightly downy on the underside, 3/4 to 2 inches long, spine-tipped, serrated.

FLOWERING: January - June

ROSACEAE

ROSE FAMILY

Trees, shrubs, vines, or herbs. Flowers are usually bisexual. 5 fused sepals, usually 5 petals but sometimes none (as with *Alchemilla* and *Cerococarpus*). 5, 10 or more stamens, 1 or 5 or many pistils. Leaves are alternate.

Adenostoma fasciculatum Plate 91

**CHAMISE,
GREASEWOOD**

DESCRIPTION: Important Chaparral shrub, 3 to 8 feet tall, with basal burl, red-brown bark, needle-like leaves. Root-crown-sprouts after a fire and also germinates from seed, making it an important fire recovery plant.

FLOWERS: On main branch terminals, crowded, small, white, about 3/16 inch in diameter, on short branches; 5-lobed calyx, 5 petals, 10 stamens, 1 pistil.

491

ROSACEAE

LEAVES: Linear, 3/16 to 3/8 inch long, resinous, evergreen, clustered on short, lateral shoots along every branch.

FLOWERING: April - June

Adenostoma sparsifolium Plate 92   **RED SHANK**

DESCRIPTION: Tree-like, 6 to 18 feet high, with shredding, red-brown bark, a more open appearance than *A fasciculatum*. Found throughout at higher elevations. (Boney Mountain, Saddle Peak) and occasionally at lower inland locations (Cold Creek). The north slope of Boney Mountain supports some pure stands.

FLOWERS: In loose open panicles about 3 to 4 inches long, white, persisting as rust-colored bracts, sepals and seeds well into fall.

LEAVES: Thread-like, 1/4 to 5/8 inch long, alternate leaves. Less dense than *A. fasci culatum.*

FLOWERING: July - August

FIELD NOTE: Pure stands of Red Shank are rare, the other known major places in the south are outside the Santa Monica Mountains (south Laguna Mountains of San Diego County, Western Cayuma Valley north of Santa Barbara, and in northern Baja).

Aphanes occidentalis   **LADY'S MANTLE**

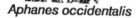

DESCRIPTION: Annual, branching, hairy, delicate, 1 to 4 inches high. Found on grassy areas in Southern Oak Woodlands.

492

ROSACEAE

FLOWERS: Urn-shaped, hairy, about 1/16 inch long; 5 sepals, no petals, 1 stamen, 1 or 2 pistils. Seedpod not hairy.

LEAVES: Alternate, deeply 3-parted, the divisions again 3-5-cleft.

FLOWERING: March - June

Cercocarpus betuloides   Plates 397, 441

MOUNTAIN MAHOGANY

DESCRIPTION: Shrub or small tree, often to 20 feet, stiff spreading branches, gray bark. Found throughout on dry slopes in Chaparral. Common.

FLOWERS: 2 or 3 in a cluster on short stems, woolly, 1/4 inch wide, whitish; 5 sepals, no petals, many stamens, 1 pistil. Seed with 2 to 3 inch-long spiral, silky plume.

LEAVES: Alternate, more or less broadly elliptical, narrowing at stem end, 1/3 to 1 inch long, saw-toothed edges from middle to tip, dark green and hairless on top, lighter and downy below; evergreen, leathery.

FLOWERING: March - May

Chamaebatia australis   Plate 82

SOUTHERN MOUNTAIN MISERY

DESCRIPTION: Shrub 2 to 7 feet tall, evergreen, strong resinous odor, downy, sticky, with dark bark. Found on dry ridges in a few inland locations. (Rocky Oaks) Rare.

FLOWERS: Clustered in convex panicles; floral tube well-shaped, 1/8 inch long; 5 sepals hairy; 5 petals white, 3/16 inch long; stamens many.

ROSACEAE

LEAVES: Alternate, elliptical in outline, 2-3-pinnate, 1-1/2 to 3 inches long.

FLOWERING: April - May

FIELD NOTE: This plant is disjunct from its normal range of San Diego County and Baja.

Heteromeles arbutifolia Plates 89, 427   TOYON

DESCRIPTION: Tree, to 30 feet, freely branching, often with several trunks coming from ground level; bears red berries into the winter.

FLOWERS: White, about 5/16 inch across, in large terminal compound panicles; 5-cleft calyx, 5 petals, 10 stamens in pairs, 2 or 3 pistils. Fruit a red, berry-like, ovoid pome.

LEAVES: Oblong, 4 to 5 inches long, sharply toothed, tough, leathery; dark green above and lighter below, lightly downy underneath - sometimes.

FLOWERING: June - July

FIELD NOTE: Yellow-berried plants can be found but are rare. These have been given a varietal name by some botanists: *H. a. var. cerina.* (Decker Road north of Decker School Road)

Holodiscus discolor Plate 90   CREAM BUSH,
                                                   OCEAN SPRAY

DESCRIPTION: Can be a shrub or an 18 foot tree; gray bark, brown to red on older trees. May be found in protected canyons, occasionally on Chaparral ridges. (Upper Carlisle Canyon, Santa Ynez Canyon) Rare.

494

ROSACEAE

FLOWERS: 1/4 inch wide, white, in a dense compound panicle; 5 sepals; 5 petals; many stamens, about 20 with 3 opposite each petal and 1 opposite each sepal; 5 pistils.

LEAVES: Alternate, deeply toothed, broadly ovate, 2 to 3-1/2 inches long.

FLOWERING: May - August

FIELD NOTE: New growth from the base of the shrub is very straight and is often called "Arrowwood."

Potentilla anserina Plate 183   SILVERWEED
  ssp. pacifica

DESCRIPTION: Plant, low, prostrate stems root at nodes to produce new plants. Found in wet places on Coastal Strand or lagoons.

FLOWERS: Solitary on 4-inch stem, 1 inch across, yellow; 5 sepals, 5 petals, 20-25 stamens, many pistils.

LEAVES: Basal, pinnate, 8 to 20 inches long with 7-31 leaflets oppositely arranged. Leaflets obovate, saw-toothed, 1 to 2-1/4 inches long, green above, downy beneath.

FLOWERING: April - August

Potentilla glandulosa Plate 184   STICKY CINQUEFOIL
  ssp. glandulosa

DESCRIPTION: Perennial from a woody base, erect stems, often reddish, 1 to 2 feet; leafy, branching above, long and soft hairs, sticky. Found in open areas in many plant communities.

495

ROSACEAE

FLOWERS: Many in terminal clusters, pale creamy white to yellow; floral tube hairy, about 1/4 inch broad; 5 hairy sepals; 5 petals; 25 stamens; many pistils.

LEAVES: Basal leaves pinnately compound up to 15 inches long; 5-9 leaflets, obovate, 3/8 to 1½ inches long, saw-toothed; dark green on top, lighter below. Upper leaves reduced.

FLOWERING: May - July

Prunus ilicifolia Plates 130, 430
ssp. ilicifolia   **HOLLYLEAF CHERRY**

DESCRIPTION: Evergreen tree, sometimes 24 feet tall, dense. An important Chaparral plant as well as Southern Oak Woodland.

FLOWERS: Small, white, in a 2-inch raceme; 5 sepals; 5 petals. Fruit a red berry with large seed.

LEAVES: Leather-like, ovate or round, 1 to 2 inches long, margin coarsely spine-toothed and irregularly curled.

FLOWERING: April - May

Rosa californica Plates 316, 424
                          WILD ROSE

DESCRIPTION: Bush, 3 to 9 feet tall, branching, usually in a mass like a briar patch, armed with flattened thorns. Found in moist places in several plant communities.

FLOWERS: 1 to many in a panicle, 1 to 2 inches in diameter, rose-pink; 5 sepals, 5 petals, many stamens. Fruit a red, ovoid, 5/8 inch long rose hip.

ROSACEAE

LEAVES: Each with 5, sometimes 7, leaflets, oval, 3/8 to 1-3/8 inches long, saw-toothed, downy above, hairy below.

FLOWERING: May - August, variable

Rubus discolor   ***HIMALAYA-BERRY**

DESCRIPTION: Shrub, sprawling, vine-like, to 9 feet tall, introduced. Grows in damp places. Blooms later than does *R. ursinus.*

FLOWERS: White, about 1 inch across, in a branching terminal. Staminate and pistillate separate but on same plant; 5 sepals broad, about 1/4 inch long, reflex back on stem; 5 petals, broad, white but sometimes pinkish; many stamens, or many pistils. Fruit a roundish, edible blackberry.

LEAVES: 5-foliate, each leaflet 4 to 5 inches long, coarsely saw-toothed; evergreen.

FLOWERING: May - August

Rubus ursinus Plates 78, 443   **CALIFORNIA BLACKBERRY**

DESCRIPTION: Native shrub with running stems that build a mound-like structure. Grows in fields, canyons, and stream banks. Blooms earlier than *R. procerus.*

FLOWERS: In cluster of few toward tip of lateral branches; staminate and pistillate separate but on same plant; 5 sepals; 5 petals; many stamens or many pistils. Staminate petals narrow, about 5/8 inch long; pistillate petals smaller. Fruit an oblong, edible blackberry, about 3/4 inch long.

497

ROSACEAE

LEAVES: 3-foliate, pinnate, leaflets 2 to 5 inches long, ovate-pointed, saw-toothed or shallowly lobed. Prickly stems.

FLOWERING: March - May

Sanguisorba minor   *BURNET

DESCRIPTION: Perennial herb, branching, leafy, 4 to 20 inches high. Once an escape from cultivation, now occurs naturally.

FLOWERS: Staminate low on bush, upper ones pistillate or bisexual; 4 sepals, oval, purple-tinged; no petals; stamens purple-tinged; 2 pistils.

LEAVES: Pinnate, 7 to 21 leaflets.

FLOWERING: April - July

RUBIACEAE

MADDER FAMILY

The Madder family is important to the rest of the world with 500 genera and 6-7000 species. Many trees, shrubs, and herbs are included. Coffee, quinine, gardenia and many other ornamentals are commercially important. In the Santa Monica Mountains, 2 genera and 6 species do not adequately represent the family.

Recognition   characteristics: Leaves opposite or whorled, usually simple and with a smooth edge. Flowers are 4 or 5 merous, inferior ovary. Plant has stipules (usually leaf-like). The *Rubaceae* family is sometimes confused with the *Caprifoliaceae* family which usually has no stipules.

RUBIACEAE

Galium andrewsii   PHLOX-LEAVED BEDSTRAW

DESCRIPTION: Perennial herb with matted, prickly tufts, 1-1/4 to 4-1/2 inches high, grayish-green, stems 4-angled, pungent. Found in Southern Oak Woodland, north slopes, west end of mountains, higher elevations.

FLOWERS: Pistillate solitary, axillary on short stems; staminate few in terminal cymes; calyx obsolete; corolla 4-lobed, 1/8 inch wide, greenish white; 4 stamens or 2 styles; inferior ovary. Berries black, not hairy.

LEAVES: Opposite, but appear whorled in 4's because the 2 stipules are leaf-like and not obviously different from the leaves. Awl-shaped, bright green or silvery, to 3/8 inch long.

FLOWERING: April - June

Galium angustifolium Plate 29   NARROW-LEAVED
ssp. angustifolium   BEDSTRAW

DESCRIPTION: Perennial, shrubby, erect, stiff branches, 1 to 3-1/2 feet high; young stems 4-angled. Found in Coastal Sage Scrub and Chaparral.

FLOWERS: Usually pistillate and staminate on separate plants, sometimes on same; calyx obsolete; 4-lobed corolla greenish-white, 1/16 inch wide; 4 stamens or 2 styles, inferior ovary. Fruit covered with white bristles.

LEAVES: Opposite, but appear 4-whorled because of 2 leaf-like stipules not obviously different from leaves; linear, 3/16 to 3/4 inch long, with hair on margins. Leaves on branchlets smaller than on main stems.

FLOWERING: March - September

499

RUBIACEAE

Galium aparine Plate 28   *ANNUAL BEDSTRAW

DESCRIPTION: Annual, weak, 4-angled stemmed, clambering over other plants, 1 to 2 feet long, often in dense masses. Found in half shade, Grassland, Southern Oak Woodland.

FLOWERS: Few, solitary to 5 in cymes on long lateral branches: calyx obsolete, 4-lobed corolla, whitish; 4 stamens; 2 styles. Fruit covered with hooked hairs.

LEAVES: 6-8 opposite, but appear whorled because of leaf-like stipules not obviously different from leaves; spatulate or linear-oblanceolate, 5/8 to 2-3/4 inches long, surface somewhat rough from small bristly hairs.

FLOWERING: March - August

Galium cliftonsmithii   SHRUBBY BEDSTRAW

DESCRIPTION: Perennial herb, stems 4-angled, branching, 1 to 2 feet high. Found in Southern Oak Woodland.

FLOWERS: Few on short lateral branches, staminate and pistillate on separate plants; no calyx; corollas flattened; 4 petals, greenish or pale yellow; 4 stamens or 2 pistils. Inferior ovary. Fruit fleshy, not hairy.

LEAVES: In 4's ovate or elliptical, 1/4 to 5/8 inch long, shiny, pungent, ending in a sharp hair.

FLOWERING: May - July

Galium nuttallii   CLIMBING BEDSTRAW

DESCRIPTION: Perennial herb, slender climbing branches 8 to 80 inches long. Found in Coastal Sage Scrub and Chaparral.

500

RUBIACEAE

FLOWERS: Many staminate and pistillate on separate plants; staminate in few-flowered cymes on leafy branches; pistillate solitary from leaf-axils; calyx obsolete; 4-lobed corolla greenish yellow, 1/8 inch across. Fruit fleshy, not hairy, becomes black with age.

LEAVES: Opposite, but appear whorled because of 2 leaf-like stipules not obviously different from leaves; linear or lanceolate to narrowly ovate, 1/8 to 5/16 inch long, dark green, hairy on both sides.

FLOWERING: March - September

Sherardia arvensis   *FIELD MADDER

DESCRIPTION: Annual, slender, 4-angled stems, 3 to 8 inches long, branched from the base, lying on the ground and rooting at nodes. Stout hairs. Found in fields and lawns.

FLOWERS: Solitary in upper axils, 2 or 3 in each head; subtended by deeply divided involucres set on slender stems, calyx of 6 teeth; 4-lobed corolla trumpet-shaped, pink or lavender; 4 stamens; style 2-cleft; 1 pistil. Fruit dry, paired.

LEAVES: 5 or 6 in each whorl, the lower obovate, the upper linear or lanceolate, up to 1/2 inch long.

FLOWERING: January - July

501

SALICACEAE

All 6 of the trees found here are indicators of the Riparian Woodland plant community. All are catkin-bearing but not uniquely so.

Recognition characteristics: Staminate and pistillate flowers are on separate trees and shrubs; staminate flowers have no sepals or petals, 2 or more stamens, no pistils; pistillate flowers have no sepals, petals or stamens. 2 fused pistils. Both types of flowers are in catkins. Leaves are alternate.

Populus balsamifera   BLACK COTTONWOOD
  ssp. trichocarpa

DESCRIPTION: Largest of the poplars, grows to well over 100 feet high and 2 to 3 feet in diameter. Thick, deeply furrowed bark is distinctive on larger trees. Found along stream bottoms in sandy soil near year-round moisture.

FLOWERS: In catkins, without petals (apetalous); staminate and pistillate on separate trees. Ripe seed capsules split, releasing minute airborne seeds covered with white, cotton-like hair.

LEAVES: Alternate, ovate, dark green above, silvery beneath, on round petioles. Netted veins distinctly visible underneath.

FLOWERING: February - April

Populus fremontii Plate 467   FREMONT COTTONWOOD
  ssp. fremontii

DESCRIPTION: Smaller than Black Cottonwood but still sometimes 75 feet tall or more, with a broad open crown. Can tolerate more exposure and warmer temperatures than can Black Cottonwood. Found along streams near year-round moisture.

SALICACEAE

FLOWERS: In catkins without petals; staminate and pistillate on separate trees.

LEAVES: Delta-shaped, 2 to 4 inches wide, almost as long, bright green both sides, irregularly saw-toothed. Flattened leaf stems distinctly different from the round stems of Black Cottonwood.

FLOWERING: March

FIELD NOTE: Named *populus* (Latin for "people") because the many moving leaves on the tree resemble the populace. John C. Fremont (from which comes *fremontii*) led several expeditions to California. During his second expedition in 1843-44, plants were collected and a Botanical Appendix was a part of the published report. Although he is well-known for leading an army against the Mexican government in 1846-47 and for signing the treaty at Campo de Cahuenga that brought California into the United States, among botanists he is remembered by plants named in his honor.

Salix exigua   SANDBAR WILLOW

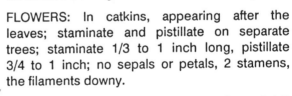

DESCRIPTION: Shrub 6 to 15 feet high. Found along streams on sandbars along the west end of the range.

FLOWERS: In catkins, appearing after the leaves; staminate and pistillate on separate trees; staminate 1/3 to 1 inch long, pistillate 3/4 to 1 inch; no sepals or petals, 2 stamens, the filaments downy.

LEAVES: Linear to lance-linear, 1-1/2 to 3-1/2 inches long and 3/8 inch wide, edges smooth or minutely saw-toothed, downy underneath.

FLOWERING: October - April

SALICACEAE

Salix laevigata   **BLACK WILLOW**

DESCRIPTION: Tree to 45 feet high, with a distinct trunk. Found along streams.

FLOWERS: Staminate and pistillate on separate trees; catkins 1-1/4 to 4 inches long; no sepals or petals; 4-6 stamens.

LEAVES: Lanceolate, finely saw-toothed, light green on both sides, 4-1/2 inches long, 1-1/4 inches wide.

FLOWERING: March - May

Salix lasiolepis   Plate 460   **ARROYO WILLOW**

DESCRIPTION: Small tree, branching, 10 to 18 feet tall. Grows along summer-dry arroyos and streams.

FLOWERS: Staminate and pistillate on separate trees; catkins appear before leaves; no sepals or petals; 2 stamens, not hairy.

LEAVES: Oblanceolate, 4 inches long and 3/4 inch wide, dark green above, a whitish bloom beneath.

FLOWERING: January - March

FIELD NOTE: *Salix*, from the Latin, means "to leap or spring," a characteristic of its fast growth.

SAURURACEAE

LIZARD-TAIL FAMILY

The Lizard-tail family is very small — 5 genera and 7 species worldwide. The genus *Anemopsis* has only 1 species, and this species is native of southwestern United States and northern Mexico.

504

SAURURACEAE

Anemopsis californica Plate 119   YERBA MANSA

DESCRIPTION: Perennial herb, in colonies, with many hollow stems, hairy, and leaves reaching to 2 feet high. Grows in wet places, sometimes alkaline. (Point Mugu Lagoon, 8 miles west of L.A. County line; Malibu Lagoon; spring near Calabasas)

FLOWERS: Many subtended by bracts, white and about 1/4 inch long, on cone-shaped spikes 3/8 to 1-1/2 inches long, subtended by a whorl of about 6 petal-like bracts, white aging to red, to 1-1/4 inch long; no sepals or petals; 5-8 stamens; 2 or 3 stigmas.

LEAVES: Clasping, mostly at lower part of stems, broadly ovate, about 5 inches long, some smaller leaves usually in axil. Basal leaves elliptic-oblong, 1-1/2 to 7 inches long on long stems.

FLOWERING: March - September

SAXIFRAGACEAE
SAXIFRAGE FAMILY

Most of the 30 genera and 580 species of this family are native to the temperate and cooler regions of the northern hemisphere. The 3 genera and 4 species found locally are native.

We expect difficulty in separating *Rosaceae,* and *Crassulaceae* by the characteristics because the differences are somewhat complex and not easily distinguished.

Recognition characteristics: Alternate basal leaves without stipules; 5 merous flowers; the 2 ovules sit in a cup-like structure from the edge of which arise the sepals, petals, and stamens.

SAXIFRAGACEAE

Boykinia occidentalis Plate 43   **COAST BOYKINIA**

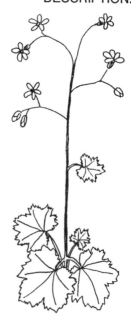

DESCRIPTION: Perennial herb, erect slender stems, 8 to 24 inches high, brown-hairy. Found growing near streams, often on rock. (Topanga Canyon, Santa Ynez Canyon) Rare.

FLOWERS: Many in a panicle, minutely downy; floral cup purplish, hairy, 5 sepals pointed, not hairy; 5 petals, white, pinkish with age, about 1/8 inch long, spreading and conspicuous; 5 stamens; 2 styles.

LEAVES: Basal tuft and alternate; lower leaves cordate, 5-7-lobed with bristled teeth; leaf stems 2 to 6 inches long; upper leaves smaller; stipules brownish, bristle-like.

FLOWERING: May - July

FIELD NOTE: Coast Boykinia reaches its southern coastal limits in disjunct Santa Monica Mountain populations.

Boykinia rotundifolia   **ROUND-LEAVED BOYKINIA**

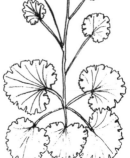

DESCRIPTION: Perennial herb, stout, with soft, shaggy hairs, 1 to 3 feet high. Found near streams, often on rock. (Blue Gorge, Upper Sycamore Canyon at the Waterfall)

FLOWERS: In a panicle, 3/4 to 6 inches long, minutely downy; floral cup slightly woolly, striate; 5 sepals 3/16 inch long; 5 petals white, about 1/16 inch long, barely exceeding the calyx; 5 stamens; 2 styles.

LEAVES: Basal tuft and alternate; round-cordate, shallowly round-lobed, scalloped, 2 to 4-1/2 inches wide. Stipules not evident.

FLOWERING: June - July

SAXIFRAGACEAE

Lithophragma affine   Plate 44   **WOODLAND STAR**

DESCRIPTION: Perennial herb, hairy, 8 to 20 inches high, open with few leaves. Found in Southern Oak Woodlands and Riparian Woodlands. Common.

FLOWERS: 5-9 scattered along upper stem, on stems slightly more than 1/16 inch long; floral cup cone-shaped and inflated; 5 sepals; 5 petals, white, each 3-lobed, 3/16 to 3/8 inch long; 5 stamens; 3 styles.

LEAVES: Basal palmately 3-lobed, each lobe divided into sharp pointed lobules. Upper leaves 1-3-lobed, alternate.

FLOWERING: February - June

Saxifraga californica   Plate 46   **CALIFORNIA SAXIFRAGE**

DESCRIPTION: Perennial herb, 4 to 12 inches high; leaves and flowering stem grow from a short woody base. Found in shade in Coastal Sage Scrub, Chaparral, and Southern Oak Woodland.

FLOWERS: On leafless stems 4 to 12 inches high, loosely branched above; floral cup shallow; 5 sepals 1/16 inch long, bent back with age, often purplish; 5 petals white, obovate to broadly elliptic, about 3/16 inch long; 10 stamens.

LEAVES: Basal, ovate to oblong-elliptic, saw-toothed, about 2-1/4 inches long.

FLOWERING: February - June

SCROPHULARIACEAE

FIGWORT FAMILY

This important family is well represented worldwide with 200 genera and 3000 species. About 40 genera are native to the United States with 11 genera and 32 species found in the Santa Monicas. Two species are non-native here. Foxglove furnishes cardiac glyco-cides for the medical community, and many other plants are used ornamentally.

Recognition characteristics: Calyx 5 united sepals; 5 united petals, bilaterally symmetrical; 4 stamens (*Verbascum* is an exception with 5 stamens), 2 long, 2 short, or sometimes with an added infertile staminode; 2 united superior ovaries.

Antirrhinum coulterianum Plate 102   **WHITE SNAPDRAGON**

DESCRIPTION: Erect, annual, usually non-branching, 3 or 4 feet tall; main stem not hairy except along the raceme during flowering.

FLOWERS: In dense raceme more or less on one side of stem; single bract, hairy, lance-linear, 1/8 inch long at base of each stem; calyx 5 unequal segments 1/8 to 3/16 inch long, hairy; corolla white to lavender, 1/2 inch long; lower part 3-lobed, with sac-like pouch, upper part 2 winged and much smaller, slightly hairy. Blooming begins at lower end of raceme and progresses to the terminal, so lower seeds mature before tip flowers blossom.

LEAVES: Lower can be opposite, upper alternate; lower lance-ovate to ovate about 1 inch long, folded in at the center vein, and arching downward. Little or no stem.

FLOWERING: April - July

508

SCROPHULARIACEAE

Antirrhinum kelloggii Plate 377   TWINING SNAPDRAGON

DESCRIPTION: Annual, slightly woolly at the base and nowhere else, 1 to 3-1/2 feet high, upper stem vine-like and supported by flower stems entwined in nearby bushes. Found in Chaparral on dry slopes, especially after a burn. (Liberty Canyon, and Reagan Ranch, Malibu Creek State Park)

FLOWERS: Solitary in axils of narrow leafy bracts, on long, slender, arching stems 2 to 4-1/2 inches long; calyx 5-cleft, 1/4 inch long; corolla 2-lipped, 1/2 inch long, blue with pale violet; 4 stamens, 2 long and 2 short.

LEAVES: Lower leaves ovate, crowded, 3/4 inch long or less on short stems. Upper leaves narrower and longer, not crowded, no stem.

FLOWERING: March - May

Antirrhinum multiflorum Plate 310   ROSE SNAPDRAGON

DESCRIPTION: Perennial herb, stout, sticky, leafy, hairy, 3 to 5 feet high. Found in Chaparral on dry slopes in disturbed areas. (Upper Zuma Canyon; along Mulholland Highway east of Las Virgenes Road) Often a second year fire-follower.

FLOWERS: In a raceme 2 to 20 inches long, all on one side, stems about 1/4 inch long; calyx 5-cleft, uneven, upper about 1/2 inch long, lower about 1/4 inch; corolla 2-lipped, rose-red with white or cream on lower lip, sticky, hairy, about 3/4 inch long.

LEAVES: Lanceolate, 3/8 to 2-1/4 inches long, without stems, progressing up the stem into leafy bracts.

FLOWERING: May - July

SCROPHULARIACEAE

Antirrhinum nuttallianum   Plate 311   VIOLET SNAPDRAGON

DESCRIPTION: Annual, erect, leafy, woolly, sticky, 4 to 40 inches high with twining horizontal branchlets. Found in dry disturbed places in Chaparral and Coastal Sage Scrub.

FLOWERS: In a loose raceme, leafy bracted, on stems 1/4 to 3/4 inch long; calyx 5-cleft, uneven, length about 1/8 to 3/16 inch long — longer segment uppermost; corolla 2-lipped, violet, 1/2 inch long, sticky and woolly.

LEAVES: Ovate, 3/4 to 1-1/2 inches long near base, upper leaves smaller.

FLOWERING: March - July

Castilleja affinis   Plate 265   COAST PAINTBRUSH

DESCRIPTION: Perennial, small shrub with a semi-woody base. Single stem or sometimes branched, purplish. About 18 inches tall. Grows in Coastal Sage Scrub and Chaparral.

FLOWERS: Hairy, bracts with 2-3 pairs of long narrow lobes, scarlet at the tips. Calyx about 1 inch long, cleft about half way on 2 sides, 4 rounded lobes, scarlet at the tips. Corolla to 1-3/8 inches long, the helmet-like upper lip about 2/3 as long. Thin red or yellowish margins. Lower lip about 1/16 inch long and dark green to brownish.

LEAVES: Rough to the touch because of hairs. Lanceolate, up to 4 inches long, usually undivided but sometimes with 1-3 pairs of slender lobes. Alternate.

FLOWERING: February - May

SCROPHULARIACEAE

FIELD NOTE: The plants are usually found close to shrubs because of their partial parasitic nature on the roots of other plants. Paintbrush has the ability to provide its own food when host plants aren't available.

Castilleja densiflora   OWL'S-CLOVER

DESCRIPTION: Annual, erect, slender, branching above, 4 to 14 inches high, minutely downy. Found on Grasslands and Coastal Sage Scrub.

FLOWERS: In a spike, dense, subtended by bracts usually 3-lobed and purple-tipped, finely downy, 3/8 to 3/4 inch long; calyx deeply 4-cleft, downy, 3/8 to 1 inch long; corolla 2-lipped, 3/8 to 1 inch long, purplish, often yellowish with 3 prominent purple spots on the lower lip; 4 stamens.

LEAVES: Alternate, linear or linear-lanceolate, 3/4 to 3 inches long, upper leaves with a pair of lateral lobes.

FLOWERING: March - May

Castilleja exserta Plate 283   PURPLE OWL'S-CLOVER

DESCRIPTION: Annual, erect, sometimes branching, 4 to 16 inches high, hairy. Found on Grasslands, Coastal Sage Scrub and Chaparral. Common.

FLOWERS: In a spike, dense, subtended by bracts palmately 5-7-lobed and greenish at the base, greenish-purple in the middle, and rose-purple at the tips, 3/8 to 3/4 inch long; calyx 4-lobed, color of bracts; corolla 2-lipped, 1/2 to 1-1/4 inches long, crimson or purplish, often with white or yellow at tip with purple dots on lower lip; upper lip hooked at tip; 4 stamens.

511

SCROPHULARIACEAE

LEAVES: Alternate, deeply pinnately cleft into thread-like divisions, 3/8 to 3/4 inch long.

FLOWERING: March - May

Castilleja foliosa Plate 266   **WOOLLY PAINT BRUSH**

DESCRIPTION: Perennial, small shrub to 2 feet tall, woolly white with small branching hairs on stems and leaves. Grows in dry, open places.

FLOWERS: Bracts with 1-2 pair of lobes, scarlet at the tips; calyx scarlet at tip, more or less yellow in the middle, 3/4 inch long, cleft about 2/5 its length, 4-lobes; corolla 7/8 inch long, upper lip helmet-like, about 1/2 as long; thin, reddish margins; lower lip about 1/16 inch long, dark green.

LEAVES: Linear, alternate, woolly, to 1 inch long. Usually undivided or upper leaves 3-lobed.

FLOWERING: February - April

Castilleja martinii Plate 265   **INDIAN PAINTBRUSH**

DESCRIPTION: Perennial, several stems from woody root-crown, branching, to 2-1/2 feet tall. Stems covered with unbranched straight hairs, some sticky.

FLOWERS: Bracts 2-cleft, scarlet tipped; calyx to 3/4 inch long, 4-lobed with red yellow green and brown zones. Corolla erect, sharp pointed and well exserted.

LEAVES: Lanceolate, wavy margins, to 2 inches long, usually entire but occasionally upper leaves have a pair of lobes; green to gray-green.

FLOWERING: March - May

SCROPHULARIACEAE

Castilleja stenantha Plate 264

ANNUAL PAINTBRUSH,
CALIFORNIA THREADTORCH

DESCRIPTION: Annual, slender, unbranching, grows to 4 feet tall. Usually found in moist places.

FLOWERS: Bracts slender and tapering to a point, red-tipped; calyx green, 1 inch long, 4-cleft into narrow lobes; corolla 1 to 1-1/2 inches long, upper lip dull, reddish-yellow on back, lightly fuzzy, lower lip yellow, small.

LEAVES: Linear-lanceolate, entire, to 3 inches long.

FLOWERING: May - June

Collinsia heterophylla Plate 312

CHINESE HOUSES

DESCRIPTION: Annual, simple stem or an occasional branch, 8 to 20 inches high. Found in Southern Oak Woodlands, Grasslands, Coastal Sage Scrub, and Chaparral, usually in part shade. Common.

FLOWERS: In whorls of 2-7 flowers on short stems or none; bracts 3/16 to 3/4 inch long; calyx 5-cleft, green to red-purple, about 1/4 inch long; 2-lipped corolla, lower 3-lobed, about 3/4 inch long, rose-purple or violet, upper lip 2-lobed and lighter, occasionally all white; 4 stamens.

LEAVES: Opposite, lanceolate to lance-oblong. 3/8 to 3-3/4 inches long.

FLOWERING: March - June

FIELD NOTE: The circular arrangement of flowers in crowded tiers suggests successively flaring roof-lines of Chinese structures.

SCROPHULARIACEAE

Collinsia parryi   BLUE-EYED MARY

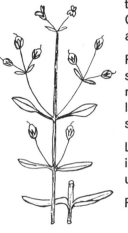

DESCRIPTION: Annual, simple stem or an occasional branch, 1 to 2 feet high, minutely woolly. Found in Chaparral, particularly burned or disturbed areas. Rare.

FLOWERS: 1-2 with leafy bracts subtending, on stems 3/8 to 1-1/2 inches long; calyx 5-cleft, minutely downy, about 1/4 inch long; corolla 2-lipped, violet-blue, about 3/8 inch long; 4 stamens.

LEAVES: Opposite, lanceolate, 5/8 to 1-1/2 inches long. Lower leaf stems to 3/4 inch long, upper almost without stems.

FLOWERING: March - May

Cordylanthus rigidus Plate 100   BIRD'S BEAK
ssp. setigerus

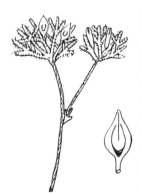

DESCRIPTION: Annual, branching, sparsely leaved, hairy, 1 to 3-1/2 feet high. Found on dry slopes in open places in Coastal Sage Scrub. Chaparral, and Southern Oak Woodland. Common.

FLOWERS: In head-like clusters of about 10 flowers, at stem nodes and terminals, subtended by leafy bracts. Calyx of 2 green sepals about 5/8 inch long; corolla 2-lipped, bird-beak shaped, white with purplish markings, about 5/8 inch long; 4 stamens; and 1 pistil. Superior ovary. Seed capsule 3/8 inch long.

LEAVES: Alternate, 3/8 to 1-1/4 inches long with 3 filiform lobes widened toward tip.

FLOWERING: May - August

SCROPHULARIACEAE

Cordylanthus maritimus   SALT-MARSH BIRD'S BEAK

DESCRIPTION: Annual, branching, often lying on the ground, woolly, 8 to 16 inches long. Found in Salt Marshes. (Mugu Lagoon)

FLOWERS: Subtended by oblong bracts with short, sharp teeth near apex usually; calyx 3/4 inch long, with very small, sharp, terminal teeth; corolla hidden by calyx, small, sharp, terminal teeth, 2-lipped, the upper with purplish, thin margins; 4 stamens.

LEAVES: Alternate, lance-oblong, green with a whitish bloom.

FLOWERING: May - September

Keckiella cordifolia Plate 258   HEART-LEAVED PENSTEMON

DESCRIPTION: Perennial plant, vine-like, slender stems ten feet or more long climb over shrubs. Found in canyons and on hillsides in semi-shade, including Coastal Sage and Chaparral plant communities.

FLOWERS: Scarlet, 2-lipped tube, with 2-lobed upper and 3-lobed lower; 5 sepals green, pointed, covering 1/4 inch or more of tube base; 5 stamens, 4 with anthers, one conspicuous, broadened and with hairs on one side resembling a toothbrush; 1 pistil. Seed capsule splits into 4 sections.

LEAVES: Opposite, oval, sometimes pointed, and with age, heart-shaped, 1/2 to 1-1/2 inches long, small serrations on the tip half.

FLOWERING: March - August and sometimes later.

SCROPHULARIACEAE

Linaria canadensis Plate 372   BLUE TOADFLAX
var. texana

DESCRIPTION: Annual, sometimes biennial, slender, sparsely leaved stem, 1 to 2-1/2 feet high, short spreading branches at base. Found on dry slopes, often in burned areas. (Mandeville Canyon, Point dume, Santa Ynez Canyon) Rare.

FLOWERS: In racemes, spaced apart, on stems 1/8 to 3/8 inch long; calyx 5-parted, minutely woolly, 1/8 inch long; corolla, 2-lipped, blue-violet, 1/4 to 1/2 inch long, with a curved spur 3/16 to 3/8 inch long; 4 stamens.

LEAVES: Narrow linear without stems, 1/4 to 1 inch long. Basal leaves wider than upper.

FLOWERING: March - May

Linaria pinifolia   *GARDEN TOADFLAX

DESCRIPTION: Annual, to 3 feet high, with short, horizontal, basal branches. Found in Chaparral. (Decker Road) Rare.

FLOWERS: Calyx 5-cleft; corolla, 2-lipped, purple with some yellow, about 5/8 inch long with a straight spur.

LEAVES: Linear, 3/4 to 1-1/2 inches long, elliptic on basal branches.

FLOWERING: April - May

Mimulus aurantiacus Plate 256   BUSH MONKEY FLOWER
                                           STICKY MONKEY FLOWER

DESCRIPTION: Perennial shrub, much-branched, leafy, sticky, 1 to 4 feet high. Found on dry slopes in Chaparral, Coastal Sage Scrub, and Southern Oak Woodland.

SCROPHULARIACEAE

FLOWERS: In leaf axils, on 1/4 inch stems, usually in pairs; calyx 5-cleft, densely hairy and sticky, 1 to 1-1/2 inches long, upper lobes 3/8 inch long, lower about 3/16 inch long; corolla, orange-yellow, 2 inches long; 4 stamens; 2 stigmas.

LEAVES: Opposite, lanceolate to oblong, light green, sticky, not hairy, finely toothed, no stems, up to 3 inches long.

FLOWERING: March - July

NOTE: [*M. longiflorus var. rutilus*] is found a few miles north of the Santa Monica Mountains in the Santa Susana Mountains. Integrating or hybridizing forms bearing flowers from yellow to velvet red can be found.

FIELD NOTE: Touch the bifid stigma with a dry grass stem and watch it close. This closing action has a function: a bee upon entering the plant will brush pollen on the stigma; the stigma closes and is pollinated. Upon backing out, the bee does not deposit the plant's own pollen, thereby insuring cross pollination.

Mimulus brevipes Plate 141   **YELLOW MONKEY FLOWER**

DESCRIPTION: Annual, woolly erect, 4 to 32 inches high. Found on dry exposed places in Chaparral and Coastal Sage Scrub, usually inland. Common.

FLOWERS: On stems from leaf axils, showy with a wide-open throat; 5-cleft calyx woolly, 3/4 to 1 inch long, ridges green, intervening spaces light, upper lobes longer than lower; corolla 2-lipped, yellow, 3/4 to 2 inches long; 4 stamens; 2 stigmas.

517

SCROPHULARIACEAE

LEAVES: Lower leaves alternate, on slender stems 2 to 3 inches long; upper leaves opposite, spaced apart, linear to lanceolate, 3/4 to 2-1/4 inches long, short term or none.

FLOWERING: April - June

Mimulus cardinalis Plate 257 **SCARLET MONKEY FLOWER**

DESCRIPTION: Perennial herb, light green, softly hairy to 2-1/2 feet high, likes moisture. Found on the banks of many year-round streams. Not common.

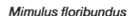

FLOWERS: Solitary, orange-red, some yellow, on long stem; 2-lipped corolla, irregular, 1-1/2 to 2 inches long; 5 petals connected.

LEAVES: Opposite, clasping, longer than wide, sharply toothed.

FLOWERING: April - October

Mimulus floribundus **SLIMY MONKEY FLOWER**

DESCRIPTION: Annual, shaggy haired, sticky, much-branched 4 to 20 inches long. Found near moisture. Rare.

FLOWERS: In leaf axils on stems 3/4 to 1 inch long; calyx 5-cleft, keeled, 1/4 to 3/8 inch long; corolla, 5-lobed, unequal, yellow, 1/4 to 5/8 inch long.

LEAVES: Opposite, ovate to lance-ovate, saw-toothed, scattered, somewhat palmately veined, 5/8 to 1-1/2 inches long. Stems none to 3/4 inch.

FLOWERING: April - August

518

SCROPHULARIACEAE

Mimulus guttatus Plate 142   **CREEK MONKEY FLOWER**

DESCRIPTION: Perennial herb, rooting at the nodes, stems more or less hollow, 16 to 40 inches high. Found in wet places. Common.

FLOWERS: In a raceme, in leaf axils, on stems 3/4 to 2-1/4 inches long; calyx 5-cleft, bell-shaped; corolla 2-lipped, yellow, spotted red, 5/8 to 1-1/2 inches long; 4 stamens; 2 stigmas.

LEAVES: Opposite, oval, 3/8 to 3 inches long, upper leaves without stems, lower long-stemmed.

FLOWERING: March - August

Mimulus pilosus Plate 140   **DOWNY MONKEY FLOWER**

DESCRIPTION: Annual, branching, 4 to 16 inches high. Found on gravelly bars and stream banks. (Upper Solstice Canyon) Uncommon.

FLOWERS: In leaf axils throughout the plant, on 3/8 to 5/8 inch long stems; calyx 5-cleft, unequal lobes, hairy, bell-shaped, 1/4 inch long; corolla 5-lobed (obscurely 2-lipped), yellow with maroon spots on the lower lip, 5/16 inch long; 4 stamens.

LEAVES: Opposite, lanceolate to oblong, without stems, 3/8 to 1-1/4 inches long.

FLOWERING: April - September

Pedicularis densiflora Plate 267   **INDIAN WARRIOR**

DESCRIPTION: Perennial, erect, 6 to 15 inches high. Found in isolated colonies in shade of shrubs in Chaparral.

SCROPHULARIACEAE

FLOWERS: In a dense spike-like raceme; calyx 5-toothed, deep red, 3/8 to 1/2 inch long; corolla 2-lipped, arched, deep purple-red, about 1 inch long; 4 stamens; 1 pistil. Superior ovary.

LEAVES: In a basal rosette and alternate on the stem, 2 to 6 inches long on short stems, 2-pinnate into many dentate narrow lobes.

FLOWERING: January - May

Penstemon centranthifolius Plate 260   **SCARLET BUGLER**

DESCRIPTION: Perennial herb, erect, not hairy, white bloom, 1 to 4 feet high. Found in dry areas in Coastal Sage Scrub and Chaparral.

FLOWERS: Axillary in opposite pairs; calyx cup-shaped, 5-lobed, 1/8 to 1/4 inch long; corolla tubular, 5-lobed, scarlet, 1 to 1-1/2 inches long, 3/16 inch wide; 4 stamens and 1 staminode.

LEAVES: Opposite, lower spatulate, smooth edged, 1-1/4 to 3 inches long on short stems; upper lanceolate, ear-like base, clasping.

FLOWERING: April - July

Penstemon heterophyllus Plate 376   **FOOTHILL PENSTEMON**
var. australis

DESCRIPTION: Perennial shrub, woody base, minutely downy, in clumps 1 to 2 feet high. Found on dry hillsides in Chaparral and Southern Oak Woodland. (Upper Solstice Canyon)

FLOWERS: In racemes, paired, in upper leaf bracts; calyx 5-parted; corolla tubular, 2-lipped, the upper 2-lobed, the lower 3-cleft, rose-violet with blue or lilac lobes; 4 stamens and 1 staminode.

SCROPHULARIACEAE

LEAVES: Opposite, linear, 1 to 1-3/8 inches long, 1/8 inch wide in fascicles.

FLOWERING: April - June

FIELD NOTE: *Penstemon* comes from the Greek for "fifth stamen" and refers to a staminode, the sterile filament in the lower throat of the flower. Penstemons have 4 stamens, and the staminode is an identifying feature.

Penstemon x parishii   **HYBRID SCARLET BUGLER**

DESCRIPTION: Perennial herb, stems few to several, 1 to 4 feet high, without hairs, whitened with a bloom. Hybrid between *P. spectabilis* and *P. centranthifolius*. Found where both parent plants grow. (Southeast of Calabasas)

FLOWERS: In racemes, paired in upper leaf bracts; calyx 5-parted; corolla tubular, red-purple, throat gradually enlarged to 1/4 to 3/8 inch wide, 2-lipped, upper 2-lobed, lower 3-cleft; 4 stamens and 1 staminode.

LEAVES: Opposite, basal spatulate, 1-1/4 to 2-3/4 inches long; upper lanceolate, clasping, shallowly serrate.

FLOWERING: April - July

Penstemon spectabilis Plate 375   **NOTABLE PENSTEMON,**
var. subviscosis   **SHOWY PENSTEMON**

DESCRIPTION: Perennial herb, several stems from the base, erect, not hairy, green or with a white bloom. Found in Coastal Sage Scrub and Chaparral.

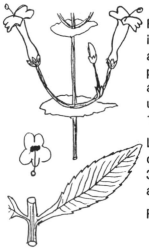

SCROPHULARIACEAE

FLOWERS: In long compound racemes, paired in upper leaf bracts; calyx deeply 5-parted about 1/4 inch high; corolla tubular, lavender-purple, whitish inside, 1 to 1-1/4 inches long, abruptly expanded at the throat, 2-lipped, the upper 2-lobed, the lower 3-cleft; 4 stamens and 1 staminode. Stem and calyx minutely downy.

LEAVES: Opposite, lower broadly lanceolate to ovate, coarsely toothed, 3/4 to 4 inches long, 3/4 to 2 inches broad; upper in pairs united about the stem.

FLOWERING: April - June

Scrophularia californica   Plate 385   COAST FIGWORT

DESCRIPTION: Perennial herb, open, minutely woolly, a few hairs, coarse stems 5-1/2 to 6 feet high, stems 4-angled. Found in moist soil in shade in Southern Oak Woodlands and Riparian Woodlands. Most often along streams on the south side of the mountains.

FLOWERS: In loose cymes; calyx 5-lobed, 1/8 inch long; corolla 2-lipped, 2-lobed upper protrudes, 3-lobed lower with center lobe deflexed, 5/16 to 1/2 inch long, red-brown to maroon; 4 stamens and 1 staminode.

LEAVES: Opposite, triangular-ovate to ovate, dentate, 1-1/4 to 4 inches long, 3/4 to 3 inches wide, on 5/8 to 2 inch long stem.

FLOWERING: February - July

SCROPHULARIACEAE

Verbascum blattaria Plate 144   ***MOTH MULLEIN**

DESCRIPTION: Perennial, erect, hairy, sticky, 1-1/2 to 4 feet high. Found in moist places. (Santa Maria Creek) Rare.

FLOWERS: In racemes on stems 3/8 to 5/8 inch long; calyx 5-parted, 1/4 inch long; corolla wheel-shaped, 5 yellow petals, 1 to 1-1/4 inch across; 5 stamens with shaggy hairs.

LEAVES: Alternate, lanceolate, elliptic to ovate, lower with margin of rounded teeth, 3/4 to 4-1/2 inches long, no leaf stem.

FLOWERING: June - September

FIELD NOTE: The flowers bloom in an unusual sequence. Buds several inches apart along the stem come into bloom simultaneously. Several buds are in each cluster, so the two series of blossoms appear to chase each other up the stalk.

Veronica anagallis-aquatica Plate 365   ***SPEEDWELL**

DESCRIPTION: Perennial herb, succulent, not hairy, erect, 1-1/2 to 3-1/2 feet high. Found in and along streams. Common.

FLOWERS: Many, in axillary racemes; 4 sepals; corolla 4-lobed, upper lobe wider than lower, pale lavender with violet lines; 2 stamens; 1 pistil.

LEAVES: Opposite, oblong-lanceolate, toothed, 3/8 to 4 inches long. Lower on short stems, upper sessile.

FLOWERING: May - September

SCROPHULARIACEAE

Veronica persica Plate 363   *PERSIAN SPEEDWELL

DESCRIPTION: Annual, several low-spreading stems, 4 to 16 inches long, covered with downy hairs. Found in disturbed places in shade. (Old Cabin site, Upper Sycamore Canyon)

FLOWERS: Axillary on slender 1 inch stems; 4 sepals, hairy, elliptic; corolla 4-lobed, 1/4 to 3/8 inch wide, blue, veined; 2 stamens; 1 pistil.

LEAVES: Lower opposite, upper alternate, round to ovate, scallopped or saw-toothed edges, 1/4 to 3/4 inch long, 3 or 5 veins radiating from the base.

FLOWERING: February - May

SELAGINELLACEAE

SPIKE MOSS FAMILY

700 Spike Moss species live throughout the world, mostly in the tropics, but some in temperate regions. They spore produce and usually are low, moss-like plants. *Selaginella biglovii*, the only local species, is 2 to 8 inches high. Found on dry rocky slopes.

Selaginella biglovii Plate 481   SPIKE MOSS

DESCRIPTION: Perennial plant, moss-like, turfy mat, rooting only at the base, repeatedly branched, 2 to 8 inches high. Found on dry, sunny rock faces and rocky soil.

FLOWERS: None. Reproduction is by spores; cone-like strobili erect at tips of short, lateral branches.

SELAGINELLACEAE

LEAVES: Scale-like, rigidly appressed-imbricate, 1/16 to 1/8 inch long, spirally arranged, looks like 4 longitudinal rows.

FLOWERING: None.

FIELD NOTE: Pour some water on a dried plant and watch it earn its name "Resurrection Plant."

SIMAROUBACEAE

QUASSIA FAMILY

Trees and shrubs, estimated at 32 genera and 200 species throughout the world. One genus and species is found in the Santa Monica Mountains and it is an escape from residential plantings.

Ailanthus altissima   ***TREE OF HEAVEN**

DESCRIPTION: Tree 15 to 60 feet high.

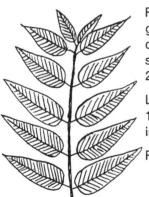

FLOWERS: In panicles; calyx 5-cleft; 5 petals greenish; staminate flowers with 10 stamens; ovary in pistillate flowers 2 to 5 cleft. Seeds spirally twisted, single-winged samara, 1-1/4 to 2 inches long.

LEAVES: Odd-pinnate, 1 to 2 feet long, with 11 to 25 leaflets, lanceolate to oblong, 3 to 7 inches long.

FLOWERING: June

SOLANACEAE

NIGHTSHADE FAMILY

Eighty-five genera and 2300 species of this important family grow throughout the world. The Santa Monicas are home to 7 genera and 14 species, some non-native. Medicinal plants, ornamentals, food plants (potatoes, tomatoes), and poisonous ones all belong to this important family.

Recognition characteristics: Alternate leaves, regular flowers, 5-merous with 5 stamens. Fruit is a berry or capsule. Some similarities with the *Scrophulariaceae* family can cause confusion. Exceptions occur, but most *Scrophulariaceae* flowers are bilaterally similar rather than regular and have 4 stamens.

Datura stramonium   *JIMSON-WEED

DESCRIPTION: Annual, erect, few-branched, 1 to 5 feet high. Found in disturbed soil.

FLOWERS: Solitary in leaf axils, showy; calyx 5-toothed with sheath 1-1/2 to 1-3/4 inches long, teeth 3/16 to 3/8 inch long and unequal; corolla white, 2-1/4 to 3 inches long, flared 1-1/4 to 2 inches across, 5-toothed, the teeth about 1/4 inch long. Capsule erect, ovoid, to 2 inches long, often with spines.

LEAVES: Alternate, ovate to elliptic 2 to 8 inches long, on stems half as long, 6 to 8 lobes, wavy margin.

FLOWERING: June - September

FIELD NOTE: In 1676, Nathaniel Bacon led a revolt of Virginia colonists against the government, Governor Berkeley's troops defending the capital at Jamestown ate a meal including Datura stramonium leaves. The men became sick and hallucinated so were unable to defend the town. Governor Berkeley ran away and Bacon burned Jamestown. We now refer to Datura as Jimson-Weed, a contraction of "Jamestown."

Datura wrightii Plates 58, 422   DATURA, TOLGUACHA

DESCRIPTION: Perennial herb, erect, widely branched, 1-1/2 to 3 feet tall, minutely grayish-pubescent. Found in dry open places in sandy, gravelly, or clay soil in Coastal Sage Scrub and Grassland. Common.

FLOWERS: Solitary in leaf axils, showy; calyx 5-toothed, 2-3/4 inches long; corolla funnelform, flaring 4 to 8 inches across, bearing 5 tendril-like teeth about 3/8 inch long; 5 stamens; 1 pistil; capsule, globose, 1-1/2 inches in diameter, densely prickly.

LEAVES: Alternate, ovate, unequally formed, 1-1/2 to 5 inches long, slightly wavy margin.

FLOWERING: April - October

Lycium californicum   CALIFORNIA DESERT THORN
                CALIFORNIA BOXTHORN

DESCRIPTION: Shrub 3 to 6 feet high, intricately branched, dense, spine tipped branches. Found in Coastal Sage Scrub near the coast on dry slopes.

FLOWERS: In leaf axils on short stems; calyx 2-4 toothed, 1/8 inch long; corolla white with purple, about 1/8 inch long, 5-lobed, each about 1/8 inch long, wheel-shaped to reflexed back; 4 stamens.

LEAVES: Fleshy, cylindrical, 1/8 to 3/8 inches long, short stems or none.

FLOWERING: March - July

SOLANACEAE

Lycopersicon esculentum   ***TOMATO**

DESCRIPTION: Annual, hairy, sticky, with a distinctive aroma, many branches, sprawling, 3 to 6 feet long. Found as an escape from gardens. Needs water.

FLOWERS: 1-5 on a short raceme, nodding; calyx 5-toothed; corolla 5-toothed, yellow; 5 stamens. Fruit of cultivated tomatoes usually revert to a 1 inch round red berry.

LEAVES: Alternate, 4 to 12 inches long, pinnately divided with toothed or lobed segments.

FLOWERING: March - October

Nicotiana bigelovii   **INDIAN TOBACCO**

DESCRIPTION: Annual, hairy, sticky, odorous, 16 to 48 inches high. Found in burned and disturbed areas of Chaparral and Coastal Sage Scrub. (Liberty Canyon, Griffith Park, Malibu Creek, north of Lake Sherwood) Rare.

FLOWERS: In racemes; calyx 5-cleft about half the length, hairy, 5/8 to 3/4 inch long, teeth unequal; corolla white, 1-1/2 to 2-3/4 inches long, trumpet-shaped, 5-lobed, 1-1/4 to 2 inches across.

LEAVES: Alternate, lanceolate to ovate-oblong, 2 to 8 inches long. Short stems lower, no stems upper.

FLOWERING: May - June

Nicotiana glauca Plate 147   ***TREE TOBACCO**

DESCRIPTION: Perennial shrub or small tree 6 to 24 feet high, erect, loose, open, not hairy. Found throughout, prefers disturbed areas, sandy stream banks, and roadsides. Common.

SOLANACEAE

FLOWERS: In panicles; calyx 5-cleft, 3/8 inch long, unequally toothed; corolla 5-lobed, tubular, narrowly flared, greenish-yellow 1-1/4 to 1-1/2 inches long.

LEAVES: Alternate, ovate, 1-1/4 to 3-1/4 inches or more long, on long stems.

FLOWERING: April - September

FIELD NOTE: Tree Tobacco was introduced from South America in the late 1800's and has since spread throughout the Santa Monica Mountains by claiming any territory "improved" by progress. We find this poisonous plant on most of the bulldozed firebreaks, roads, trails, and unoccupied building sites.

Petunia parviflora   **WILD PETUNIA**

DESCRIPTION: Annual, diffusely branched, minutely downy, prostrate, 4 to 16 inches long. Found in Riparian Woodlands on sandy soil and in dried creek beds. (Malibu Lake)

FLOWERS: Calyx 5-cleft into linear lobes, 1/8 inch long; corolla funnelform, purplish with white tube, 1/4 inch long, 5-lobed; 5 stamens.

LEAVES: Somewhat opposite, oblong-linear to spatulate, 3/16 to 1/2 inch long.

FLOWERING: April - August

Salpichroa origanifolia   ***LILY-OF-THE-VALLEY VINE**

DESCRIPTION: Perennial from a woody rootstock, several viney branches. 1-1/2 to 5 feet long, sparsely white haired. Found in fields and orchards.

FLOWERS: Solitary in leaf axils; calyx 5-toothed, 1/8 inch long; corolla urn-shaped, 1/4 inch long, white, 5-lobed; 5 stamens, anthers exserted. Yellowish berry, 3/8 to 1/2 inch long.

SOLANACEAE

LEAVES: Broadly elliptic to ovate, 3/8 to 1-1/4 inches long, stems 1/2 to 2/3 leaf length.

FLOWERING: May - October

Solanum americanum   *LITTLE WHITE NIGHTSHADE

DESCRIPTION: Annual, spreading, 1 to 2 feet high, mature stems sparsely woolly. Found in damp areas.

FLOWERS: In clusters on slender stems; calyx deeply 5-cleft, 1/8 inch long; corolla deeply 5-cleft, white or slightly purple, 1/4 inch across, 5 stamens; anthers prominent. Berry shiny black, 1/4 inch in diameter.

LEAVES: Ovate to elliptic, sparingly-toothed, wavy, or smooth-margined, 1-1/2 to 4 inches long, stems 1/2 to 2/3 as long as blade.

FLOWERING: April - November

Solanum douglasii Plates 27, 420   WHITE NIGHTSHADE

DESCRIPTION: Perennial, branching, minutely woolly, 3 to 6 feet high. Found in Coastal Sage Scrub, Chaparral, Coastal Strand and Southern Oak Woodlands. Prefers shade. Common.

FLOWERS: On long stems; calyx deeply 5-cleft, 1/8 inch long; corolla white with greenish basal spots, lobed, 3/8 to 3/4 inch across; 5 stamens, short; anthers yellow, prominent. Berry black 1/4 to 3/8 inch in diameter.

LEAVES: Ovate, sparingly-toothed, wavy, 3/4 to 4 inches long; stems 3/8 to 1 inch long.

FLOWERING: January - December

530

SOLANACEAE

Solanum elaeagnifolium

*SILVERLEAF NETTLE
WHITE HORSE-NETTLE

DESCRIPTION: Perennial, stem and foliage covered with grayish-white fine hairs, up to 3 feet high. Found in disturbed soils near habitations. (Stokes Canyon, Hope Ranch)

FLOWERS: In a cyme; stem and calyx with yellow spines 1/8 inch long; calyx 5-pointed, to 3/8 inch long; corolla 5-lobed, violet or blue, 3/4 to 1-1/4 inches in diameter; 5 stamens; anthers yellow, prominent, to 3/8 inch long. Berry yellow or brownish, about 1/2 inch in diameter.

LEAVES: Simple, lance-oblong to lance-linear, 1-1/4 to 3-1/2 inches long.

FLOWERING: May - September

Solanum rostratum   ***BUFFALO BERRY**

DESCRIPTION: Annual, stem covered with awl-shaped, yellowish prickles, 1-1/2 to 3 feet high, covered with star-shaped, soft hairs. Found in disturbed areas.

FLOWERS: Calyx 5-lobed, covered with prickles; corolla 5-lobed, yellow, 3/4 to 1 inch across; 5 stamens; 2 types of anthers.

LEAVES: 1-2 pinnatifid 2 to 4 inches long.

FLOWERING: May - September

Solanum sarrachoidcs   ***HAIRY NIGHTSHADE**

DESCRIPTION: Annual, branching, 4 to 20 inches long, shaggy haired, sticky. Found in cultivated fields.

SOLANACEAE

FLOWERS: About 5 in clusters on hairy stems; calyx deeply 5-cleft, 1/8 inch long; corolla deeply 5-cleft, white, 3/16 inch across; 5 stamens; anthers prominent. Berry yellowish, 1/4 inch in diameter.

LEAVES: Ovate, 1 to 2-1/2 inches long, sparsely toothed, wavy or smooth-margined.

FLOWERING: May - October

Solanum Xanti Plates 361, 421   **PURPLE NIGHTSHADE**

DESCRIPTION: Perennial, woody stemmed, 1-1/2 to 3 feet high, stems covered with soft, short hairs. Found in Chaparral and Southern Oak Woodland. Common.

FLOWERS: 6 to 8 cymes; calyx 5-lobed, 1/4 inch long; corolla shallowly 5-lobed, dark lavender to deep violet, with 2 green dots at the base of each segment; 5 stamens, anthers prominent. Berry greenish, 5/16 inch in diameter.

LEAVES: Ovate, usually smooth margined, sometimes wavy, 3/4 to 1-1/2 inches long.

FLOWERING: February - July

TROPAEOLACEAE

*NASTURTIUM FAMILY

Two genera and 92 species are native of the western hemisphere from Mexico to South America, none in the United States. One species is found in the Santa Monicas as an escape from flower gardens.

Recognition characteristics: Alternate leaves, flowers solitary, axillary, bilaterally symmetrical, 5 sepals, 5 petals, 8 stamens, 3 stigmas.

TROPAEOLACEAE

Tropaeolum majus   *NASTURTIUM

DESCRIPTION: Annual succulent, prostrate, vine-like, not hairy. Found as an escape on seacliffs, along roads and near houses.

FLOWERS: Solitary, on long stems from leaf axils, showy; 5 sepals, one with a spur; 5 petals 1-1/4 to 2-1/2 inches wide; 8 stamens unequal.

LEAVES: Nearly circular, stem attached to lower surface rather than margin, 1-1/2 to 6 inches wide, about 9-nerved.

FLOWERING: January - December

TYPHACEAE

CATTAIL FAMILY

The cattail family of 1 genus and 15 species is widespread throughout the United States. 2 species are native to the Santa Monicas. Cattails are perennial herbs of fresh water marshland. Leaves are basal, linear and erect.

Recognition characteristics: Flowers are borne in a tightly compacted spike, the staminate flowers above, the pistillate flowers below. The calyx is reduced to a series of slender jointed threads or bristles, there are no petals. Staminate flowers have 2-5 stamens; pistillate flowers have a stem below the ovary.

Typha domingensis   NARROW-LEAVED CATTAIL

DESCRIPTION: Perennial marshland and water plants, narrow leaves, 6 to 9 feet tall. Found at the edges of ponds, in marshes, and in year-round streams.

FLOWERS: In a tightly compacted, tandem, spike pistillate below, light cinnamon brown, 6 to 10 inches long; 5/8 to 7/8 inch thick; staminate above tapering, narrower and about as long as pistillate; golden-yellow pollen. The interval between the two is about 3/4 inch.

TYPHACEAE

LEAVES: Parallel veined, 6 to 9 feet high, 1/4 to 1/2 inch wide. 6-9 leaves per plant.

FLOWERING: June - July

Typha latifolia Plate 388   BROAD-LEAVED CATTAIL

DESCRIPTION: Perennial marshland and water plants, narrow leaves, 3 to 7-1/2 feet tall. Found at the edge of ponds, in marshes, and in year round streams.

FLOWERS: In tightly compacted spike; pistillate low on spike, dark green-brown to red-brown, 4 to 7 inches long and 3/4 to 1-1/4 inches thick; staminate above, where spike tapers, narrower and about as long; orange-yellow pollen; no interval between the two.

LEAVES: Parallel veined, narrow leaves, 3 to 7-1/2 feet high, 3/8 to 5/8 inch wide. 12-16 leaves per plant.

FLOWERING: June - July

URTICACEAE

NETTLE FAMILY

Forty-five genera and 550 species worldwide with 4 genera and 5 species in the Santa Monica Mountains. This family grows in both temperate and tropical regions.

Recognition characteristics: Stinging hairs are diagnostic when present, simple leaves on stems. Flowers are unisexual, the staminate flowers with 4-5 sepals, no petals, 4-5 stamens; pistillate flowers with 4-5 sepals, occasionally none, no petals, 1 pistil.

URTICACEAE

Hesperocnide tenella Plate 396   ANNUAL STINGING NETTLE

DESCRIPTION: Annual, slender stemmed, 8 to 20 inches high, stinging hairs. Found on shady slopes of Coastal Sage Scrub and Chaparral.

FLOWERS: Staminate and pistillate mixed in clustered heads in leaf axils; staminate calyx 4-parted, lobes equal; pistillate calyx tube constricted at the apex; no petals.

LEAVES: Opposite with minute stipules, ovate, edges scalloped, 3/16 to 1 inch long. Slender stems almost as long as the leaf blades.

FLOWERING: April - June

Parietaria hespera   PELLITORY

DESCRIPTION: Annual, loosely branched, slender, trailing on the ground, not rooting, soft hairs, 4 to 10 inches long, without stinging hairs. Found on moist shady slopes in Southern Oak Woodland and Chaparral.

FLOWERS: Few in clusters in leaf axils, subtended by 1/8 inch long leafy bracts; 4 sepals 1/32 inch long; no petals.

LEAVES: Alternate without stipules, ovate to lance-ovate, 3-veined, 3/16 to 3/8 inch long on short stems.

FLOWERING: April - May

Soleirolia soleirolii   *BABY TEARS

DESCRIPTION: Perennial herb, creeping, rooting at the nodes, 1 to 4 inches high, with soft, not stinging hairs. Found in moist shady places as an escape. (Franklin Canyon Reservoir)

535

URTICACEAE

FLOWERS: Solitary in leaf axils; staminate calyx 4-parted, no petals, 4 stamens; pistillate calyx tubular contracted at the apex, no petals.

LEAVES: Alternate, round, less than 1/4 inch long.

FLOWERING: May - October

Urtica dioica　Plate 395　　　　　　　　　　　STINGING NETTLE
　ssp. holosericea

DESCRIPTION: Perennial herb, densely hairy, stout, 3 to 8 feet high, bristly and densely woolly, stinging hairs. Found in damp shady places, usually near streams. Common.

FLOWERS: Clustered on paired racemes in axils; staminate clusters loose, nearly as long as the leaves; pistillate clusters denser and shorter; pistillate calyx deeply 4-parted of uneven lengths, no petals.

LEAVES: Opposite, lanceolate to narrow-ovate, coarsely saw-toothed, woolly, 2 to 5 inches long, on stems 3/8 to 1-3/4 inches long, stipules 3/16 to 3/8 inch long.

FLOWERING: July - September

Urtica urens　　　　　　　　　　　　　　*DWARF NETTLE

DESCRIPTION: Annual, erect, 1/2 to 1-1/2 feet high, branching from the base — sometimes simple, leafy, stinging hairs. Found in Chaparral and Riparian Woodlands. Common.

FLOWERS: In clusters on axillary stems usually shorter than the leaf stems; pistillate and staminate in same cluster; pistillate calyx deeply 4-parted, 2 long and 2 short, hairy margins; no petals.

536

URTICACEAE

LEAVES: Opposite, 3-5 veined, deeply saw-toothed, 5/8 to 1-1/4 inches long, stems 3/8 to 3/4 inch long, leafy stipules.

FLOWERING: January - April

VALERIANCEAE

VALERIAN FAMILY

Two species, each of a different genus, represent this family in the Santa Monica Mountains. Worldwide 13 genera and 400 species are found, mostly north temperate or Andean.

Recognition characteristics: Flowers in cymose panicles, rudimentary or no calyx, a corolla of 5 united petals (ours are spurred), 1-4 stamens, 1 functional pistil. Leaves are opposite or in basal rosette.

Centranthus ruber   *RED VALERIAN

DESCRIPTION: Perennial herb, without hairs, 1 to 3 feet high. Found in moist areas as an escape from cultivation.

FLOWERS: Many in a terminal compound raceme, crowded, red to pink or white; calyx rudimentary; corolla 5-lobed, bilaterally symmetrical, slender tube 3/8 inch long, slender prominent spur; 1 stamen exserted.

LEAVES: Opposite, ovate to lance-ovate, 1-1/4 to 4 inches long, usually with smooth margins, short stem or none.

FLOWERING: April - August

VALERIANCEAE

Plectritis ciliosa   LONG-SPURRED PLECTRITIC
ssp. insignis

DESCRIPTION: Annual, slender, erect, unbranched stem, 4 to 16 inches high. Found on grassy slopes in partial shade and Southern Oak Woodlands. (Latigo Canyon. Upper Malibu Creek. Not known in the eastern part of the Santa Monicas)

FLOWERS: In a head at terminal of stem; calyx obsolete; corolla 2-lipped 5-lobed, deep pink with a pair of deep red dots at base of middle lobe, 1/8 inch long with long slender spur; 3 stamens.

LEAVES: Obovate to narrow-oblong, 1/2 to 1-1/2 inches long, upper without stem.

FLOWERING: March - May

VERBENACEAE

VERVAIN FAMILY

The Vervain family is mainly from tropical and subtropical areas. Of the 75 genera and 3000 species, only 2 genera and 4 species are native to the Santa Monica Mountains.

Recognition characteristics: Calyx 5-lobed, except *Lippia* has 2-4-lobed calyx; a 5-lobed bilaterally symmetrical corolla, 2 long and 2 short stamens, 1 style. Leaves are opposite.

This family can be mistaken for *Boraginaceae* which has alternate leaves and a 4-lobed ovary. *Lamiaceae* has a 4-lobed ovary and 1 style. Some *Verbenaceae* have 4-sided stems, leading to the possibility of confusion with *Lamiaceae*.

Phyla lanceolata   FROG FRUIT

DESCRIPTION: Perennial herb, stems prostrate, rooting at lower nodes, 10 to 16 inches long, covered with small, stiff hairs. Found in wet soil. (Lake Sherwood)

538

VERBENACEAE

FLOWERS: In dense spikes 3/8 to 5/8 inch long, on long stems from leaf axils; calyx small, 2-lobed; corolla cylindrical, 2-lipped, pale blue to lavender, about 1/8 inch long. Nutlets 2.

LEAVES: Opposite or whorled, lanceolate to ovate, 3/4 to 1-1/2 inches long, saw-toothed.

FLOWERING: May - September

Phyla nodiflora   *GARDEN LIPPIA

DESCRIPTION: Perennial herb, matted, light gray and covered with small stiff hairs. Found on moist soil.

FLOWERS: In ovoid spikes 3/16 to 5/16 inch long, on stems 5/8 to 1-1/4 inches long, from leaf axils; calyx small, 2-lobed; corolla rose to white, about 3/16 inch long. Nutlets 2.

LEAVES: Opposite or whorled, narrow-oblanceolate to narrow-obovate, smooth-margined to saw-toothed, 3/8 to 3/4 inch long, on short stem.

FLOWERING: May - October

Verbena lasiostachys Plate 360   **COMMON VERVAIN**

DESCRIPTION: Perennial herb, branching, more or less sprawling on the ground with tips rising, 1 to 3 feet long, shaggy hairs. Found in many plant communities on both dry and damp soil. Common.

FLOWERS: In terminal spikes, 2 to 8 inches long; calyx 5-toothed 3/32 inch long, hairy; corolla, 2-lipped, 5-lobed, purple, about 3/32 inch long. Nutlets 4.

LEAVES: Opposite, oblong to oblong-ovate, incised and coarsely saw-toothed, often 3-5-cleft, hairy on both surfaces, 4 to 6 inches long.

FLOWERING: April - September

VERBENACEAE

Verbena lasiostachys
var. scabrida

ROBUST VERVAIN

DESCRIPTION: Perennial herb, erect, 1 or more stems rising from the base, branching above, herbage bright green, less hairy than *V. lasiostachys*. Found in moist places in several plant communities. (Point Dume, Lake Sherwood)

FLOWERS: In dense terminal spikes, 1-1/4 to 4 inches long; calyx 5-toothed, 1/8 inch long, hairy; corolla, 2-lipped, 5-lobed, hairy. Nutlets 4.

LEAVES: Opposite, ovate to oblong-ovate, irregularly and coarsely saw-toothed. Lower usually 3-cleft or 3-lobed.

FLOWERING: May - October

VIOLACEAE

VIOLET FAMILY

The world has 850 species of plants belonging to the violet family, only 1 of which is native locally, and it is shy.

Recognition characteristics: 5 sepals, 5 petals, 5 stamens, and 3 united carpels forming 1 pistil. The flower is zygomorphic — a Greek word meaning "yoke-shaped."

Viola pedunculata   Plate 143

CALIFORNIA GOLDEN VIOLET
JOHNNY-JUMP-UP

DESCRIPTION: Several slender stems rise from a thick perennial rootstock. Branching, sprawling, downy, 4 to 14 inches long. Usually grows in a colony with other violets in shaded grassy slopes. (Reagan Meadow in Malibu Creek State Park)

FLOWERS: Solitary, 1 to 1-1/2 inches across on 6 inch long stems, bright yellow with a dark brown center; 5 sepals, 5 petals, 5 stamens, 1 pistil.

VIOLACEAE

LEAVES: Bright green, deltoid-ovate, coarsely toothed, 1/2 to 1-1/2 inch long leaves, minutely downy or not at all, stems about 2 inches long.

FLOWERING: February - April

VISCACEAE
MISTLETOE FAMILY

The Mistletoe family consists of 450 species, 2 of which are native to the Santa Monica Mountains. These are parasitic shrubs on tree branches, each parasite selective of its host. Flowers are small; the fruit is a round whitish berry. Leaves typically are opposite and leathery.

Phoradendron tomentosum   Plate 88   SYCAMORE MISTLETOE
ssp. macrophyllum

DESCRIPTION: Perennial parasitic plant, short, green. Found on sycamore trees, sometimes on cottonwoods, willow, ash and walnut. Velvety to nearly hairless. Stems to 5 feet long.

FLOWERS: Jointed spikes 5/8 to 1-1/4 inches long, from leaf-axils; pistillate joints with about 12 flowers, the staminate about 20. Staminate and pistillate on separate plants. Berry is white, tinged with pink, about 3/16 inch in diameter.

LEAVES: Opposite, elliptic-obovate to oblanceolate, thick, fleshy, 3/8 to 2 inches long, yellow-green.

FLOWERING: December - March

FIELD NOTE: *Phorodendron*, from the Greek, means "thief tree" because it draws much of its nourishment from the tree, conspicuously so in the winter when the sycamore has lost its leaves and the evergreen mistletoe is very evident.

VISCACEAE

Phoradendron villosum Plate 86
ssp. villosum

OAK MISTLETOE

DESCRIPTION: Perennial parasitic plant, stout greens, covered with soft shaggy hairs. Found on oak trees, rarely on bay-laurel and manzanita.

FLOWERS: Jointed spikes, often clustered, 3/8 to 5/8 inch long, grow from leaf axils; pistillate joints 6-flowered, the staminate 12-flowered. Staminate and pistillate flowers in separate plants. Berry is pinkish white about 3/16 inch in diameter.

LEAVES: Opposite, oblanceolate to obovate, thick, 1-1/4 to 1-1/2 inches long, dark green, hairy.

VITACEAE

GRAPE FAMILY

About 700 species of the Grape family are found throughout the world, only 1 of which is native to our mountains. Some introduced species have escaped and become established, but are not described here.

Vitis girdiana Plate 411

GRAPE

DESCRIPTION: A long-stemmed woody, climbing vine. Found near streams or canyon bottoms. (Griffith Park and Malibu Creek Canyon)

FLOWERS: In clusters on stems opposite the leaves, small, greenish. Berries black, about 1/4 inch in diameter.

LEAVES: Alternate, simple, palmately veined, round to heart-shaped, obscurely lobed to deeply 3-lobed, green on top, light gray underneath.

FLOWERING: May - June

542

ZANNICHELLIACEAE

GRASS-WRACK FAMILY

Zannichellia palustris is the sole representative of the family in our local mountains. It is found in pools and slow moving streams.

ZOSTERACEAE

EELGRASS FAMILY

The two species of "Surf Grass" along our coast are found from the low intertidal zone to 20 feet deep. *Phyllospadix torreyi* is common in sandy protected areas; *P. scouleri* prefers the rocks of heavy surf.

ZYGOPHYLLACEAE

CALTROP FAMILY

This tropical and subtropical family consists of 30 genera and 250 species, only 1 of which is found in the Santa Monica Mountains.

Recognition characteristics: 5-merous, superior ovary, 5 united carpels form 1 pistil. Opposite pinnately compound leaves, persistent stipules.

Tribulus terrestris   ***PUNCTURE VINE**

DESCRIPTION: Annual, branching, trailing on the ground, 8 to 40 inches long, woolly. Found in disturbed areas and along roads. Common.

FLOWERS: Solitary on axillary stems. 5 sepals; 5 petals, yellow, 1/8 inch long; 10 stamens. Seedpod is spined.

LEAVES: Opposite, pinnate; leaflets in 4 to 7 pairs, oblong or elliptic, 3/16 to 1/2 inch long.

FLOWERING: April - October

543

Plant Geography

by TIMOTHY THOMAS

The botanical heritage of California includes the oldest, tallest, and most massive known plants on the earth's surface. California is also known for its high percentage of plants that occur nowhere else, those with highly restricted distributions, known as endemics. These plants are the products of adaptations to an environment that occurs along on an active crustal boundary creating new habitats. Summer drought or mediterranean climate, diverse geologic substrate and an active migrational history, corresponding to the dramatic shifts in the global climate of the Pleistocene (ice age) have all contributed to the creation of California plant diversity.

Areas with a variety of plant habitats, such as the Santa Monica Mountains, have a high potential for species of restricted (endemic) distributions. The west end of the Santa Monica Mountains has the greatest topographic variety and is indeed the location for six endemic plants. Nine species and subspecies of the genus Dudleya or live forever have been found in the Santa Monica Mountains; three are endemic. The Conejo Buckwheat is known only from the Conejo Grade, and one station near Westlake. The Santa Susana Mountains tarweed occurs in the Simi Hills just north of the Santa Monica Mountains, and several populations have been found in the Santa Monica Mountains. The *Lyon's Pentachaeta* now seems to be restricted to the Santa Monica Mountains, its original distribution included the Palos Verdes Peninsula and the isthmus of Catalina but has not been seen since the 1930's.

The study of plants in the Santa Monica Mountains by botanists began at least by the end of the 1800's. We are familiar with the names of a few of those early botanists for their names have been preserved as botanical names of flowers, such as: *Astragalus Brauntonii, Corethrogyne filaginifolia ssp. piersonii.* Through the efforts of those early botanists, we now know of over a dozen species of plants that historically occurred in these mountains. Some of those species are designated in the *Flora of the Santa Monica Mountains* as rare, because they either have become very uncommon or haven't been located for many years in this region, most likely due to habitat loss.

Species distributions are not continuous, even common species are limited to certain habitats. The uncommon species habitat requirements could then be expected to have a highly restricted distribution. Several plants that are considered rare in the Santa Monica Mountains are approaching the limits to their range of tolerances and occur at very few sites, although they might be common elsewhere within their distribution. One of the factors that make the Santa Monica Mountains unique and ecologically diverse is the occurrence of a number of species at the extreme limits of their distributions. The topographic variability and proximity to the climatic modifier of the coast are major factors that have provided refugia for plant species for hundreds of thousands of years. During the past two million years (the ice age) there have been major migrational patterns of plants as a result of the fluctuating climatic environments resulting from the expanding and retreating ice caps. Limits of distributions occur in the Santa Monica Mountains that show floristic affinities with four major regions: Northern, Southern, Deserts and the Channel Islands. Major disjunctions or species whose distributions are discontinuous from their major population centers also contribute to the unique floristic composition of the Santa Monica Mountains.

SPECIES WITH NORTHERN AFFINITIES REACHING THEIR SOUTHERN LIMIT IN THE SANTA MONICA MOUNTAINS. During the last full glacial episode, climatic belts were depressed southward providing habitat in the Santa Monica Mountains for the Coastal Redwood and other northern coastal species. A recently discovered population in the Santa Monica Mountains of the Montana state flower, bitter-root (*Lewisia rediviva ssp. rediviva*), represents a 190 mile disjunction south of its nearest known population. Other species having their southern mainland limit in the Santa Monica Mountains include:

Quercus lobata	*Calochortus venustus*
Coreopsis gigantea	*Festuca eastwoodae*
Delphinium parryi ssp. blochmanae	*Clarkia cylindrica*

SPECIES WITH SOUTHERN AFFINITIES REACHING THEIR NORTHERN LIMIT IN THE SANTA MONICA MOUNTAINS. A population of Southern Mountain Misery (*Chamaebatis australis*) has recently been located in the Santa Monica Mountains, representing a disjunction of 111 miles north of its previously known northern location (San Diego Co.) Other species reaching their northern limit includes:

545

Centaurium venustum　　　　　　Oenothera californica
Lasthenia coronaria　　　　　　　Polygala cornuta ssp. fishiae
Phacelia minor

SPECIES WITH DESERT AFFINITIES REACHING A COASTAL STATION IN THE SANTA MONICA MOUNTAINS. The ice age ended approximately 10,000 years ago and was followed by an extreme warming, drying trend that reached much hotter and dryer conditions than at present. It probably was during this high temperature period, known as the xerothermic, that desert species moved coastward. Some of the species include:

Juniperus californica　　　　　Isomeris arborea
Haplopappus linearifolius　　　Stanleya pinnata
Opuntia basilaris

SPECIES WITH AFFINITIES TO THE CHANNEL ISLANDS. Sea level lowered approximately 300 feet during the ice age as the ice caps expanded. This caused the islands to expand in size, the four northern Channel Islands (Anacapa, Santa Cruz, Santa Rosa, and San Miguel) became one large island and the four southern islands each became larger. At the same time the shoreline along the Santa Monica Mountains moved south creating a narrow ocean gap between them and the northern island complex, reducing a dispersal barrier for some species. The Santa Monica Mountains, being a coastal mountain range, have a modified climate as compared with more continental ranges, providing ecological conditions favorable to species occurring on the Channel Islands. A list of some of these species include:

Cercocarpus betuloides ssp. blanchae　　Lepichinia fragrans
Pentachaeta lyonii　　　　　　　　　　　Coreopsis gigantea

SPECIES WITH THEIR CENTERS OF DISTRIBUTION IN THE SANTA MONICA MOUNTAINS. A few of the most common plants found in these mountains find their optimal growth conditions here. The limits of their distribution approximate equal distances north and south of these mountains. Two common examples are:

Ceanothus megacarpus
Salvia leucophylla

PLANT CONSERVATIONS

The biologic significance of the Santa Monica Mountains lies in its ecologic diversity. Each element eliminated through habitat degradation harms the plant species diversity and the organism dependent upon those plants, as well as reducing the resiliency of those ecosystems to deal with catastrophic events. Species that occur with extremely limited distributions such as the six endemic plants in the Santa Monica Mountains are the most sensitive, in terms of continued existence, to habitat alteration. We would be deceiving ourselves if we considered ourselves successful at saving a rare species without saving its habitat. Habitat Technological advancements and the needs of an expanding human population have created a species extinction at an accelerated rate. This rate is predicted to result in an extinction of approximately one sixth of the world organisms, a larger number than occurred during the last major biological extinction event, 65 million years ago (*Cretaceous*). In the Foreward of the International Union for Conservation of Nature and Natural Resources and World Wildlife Fund's Plant Conservation Programme 1984-85, Peter Raven (one of the authors of the *Flora of the Santa Monica Mountains* and the director of the Missouri Botanical Garden) counselled us: "What ought to frighten us now is that a major portion of this extinction is likely to occur during the lives of those who are reading these words. The estimate just presented suggests the loss of at least two plant species per day over the next half century. . . only a redoubled effort to study, name, and understand the plants of the world will provide a sound basis for improving the situation, and for saving as many as possible of these plants while this is still possible."

Index

551

552

553

559

560

centimeters   inches

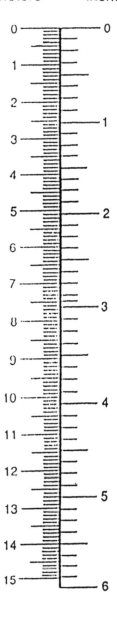

NOTES

NOTES

NOTES

NOTES

NOTES

NOTES

NOTES

NOTES